D0196167

Understanding International Conflicts

An Introduction to Theory and History

Sixth Edition

Joseph S. Nye, Jr.
Harvard University

PEARSON
Longman

New York San Francisco Boston
London Toronto Sydney Tokyo Singapore Madrid
Mexico City Munich Paris Cape Town Hong Kong Montreal

Vice President and Publisher: Priscilla McGeehon
Editor in Chief: Eric Stano
Senior Marketing Manager: Elizabeth Fogarty
Production Manager: Savoula Amanatidis
Text Design and Project Coordination: Elm Street Publishing Services, Inc.
Cover Designer/Manager: John Callahan
Cover Photo: Courtesy of Getty Images, Inc.
Photo Researcher: Jody Potter
Senior Manufacturing Buyer: Al Dorsey
Printer and Binder: R.R. Donnelley and Sons Company—Crawfordsville
Cover Printer: Phoenix Color Corporation

Library of Congress Cataloging-in-Publication Data

Nye, Joseph S.
Understanding international conflicts : an introduction to theory
and history / Joseph S. Nye, Jr.—6th ed.
    p. cm.—(Longman classics in political science)
  Includes bibliographical references and index.
  ISBN 0-321-39395-3
  1. International relations. 2. War (International law) 3. World
politics-20th century. 4. World politics—21st century. I. Title. II. Series.

JZ1305.N94 2007
327.109'04—dc22
                                                      2006008702

Please visit our website at http://www.ablongman.com

ISBN 0-321-39395-3

1 2 3 4 5 6 7 8 9 10—DOC—09 08 07 06

For MHN, as always, and our grandchildren

Contents

CHAPTER 5   THE COLD WAR   **115**

CHAPTER 6   INTERVENTION, INSTITUTIONS, AND REGIONAL
AND ETHNIC CONFLICTS   **157**

Foreword

Professor Nye is a man of many talents. He has written with clarity, elegance, and erudition about topics that are also great interests of mine: international and regional organization, the interplay between interdependence and traditional interstate competition, the political and ethical role of nuclear weapons, American foreign policy during and after the Cold War, the limits and possibilities of international governance, etc. He gracefully acknowledges having been my student, and we have taught together the Harvard course on conflict that served as a basis for this book. But I have learned at least as much from him as he thinks he has learned from me—not only because of his expertise in international economic affairs, but also because he has brought to his understanding of world politics a precious practical experience as a high official in the Carter and Clinton administrations. And he has brought to his study of international conflicts a thoughtful serenity worthy of one of those great American leaders of the end of the eighteenth century and the beginning of the nineteenth—a serenity made of a talent for rising high above the daily events; of a curiosity for, and knowledge of, political philosophy that helps him ask questions of permanent importance and put events in perspective; of a gift for understanding how theory can nourish the study of history, and how the latter leads inevitably to philosophical and ethical conclusions. These are the skills of such authors as Tocqueville, Max Weber, and Raymond Aron. Particularly valuable in these days of methodological battles are his understanding of the limits of generalization and of the many ways of interpreting events. His sense of reality never amounts—even in the study of those cold monsters, the states—to a cynical rejection of ethics, and in the study of power it is not surprising that he attaches great importance to what he has called *soft power*: not the power to coerce, bully, browbeat, and bribe, but the power to attract, to persuade, to influence through wisdom, example, and attentiveness. These are qualities whose importance in world affairs is often undervalued, and which are more necessary than ever in American foreign policy.

A discriminating and penetrating intelligence has alerted him to the important innovations, which were introduced in the twentieth century into strategic and economic affairs, and yet safeguarded him from faddish enthusiasms and fashionable slogans. He is a man of deep values and generous beliefs, but also of great discernment, detachment, and determination. All these virtues are present in this book. It is, in my opinion, the best textbook available to intelligent students of world politics. It blends perfectly history, political philosophy, political theory, and analysis. It explains events instead of drowning the reader in excessive detail. It does what any good social scientist ought to do: *explain* (i.e., show the causes), *interpret* (give us the meaning), *evaluate* both politically and morally. It distinguishes the world of inter-state conflict from that of "complex interdependence," the term crafted by Nye and by his friend and mine, Robert Keohane. It shows the tensions between the need to fight terrorism, to prevent the proliferation of nuclear weapons, and to support democracy against tyrannies, and the need to preserve the norms of international law and international legitimacy. It shows both the originality and the limits of globalization and of the information revolution. Above all, it is a wise book—wise because of Nye's ability to see the many sides of an issue and the many arguments an event can provoke; wise because of his almost distinctive distrust of excesses (in the case of U.S. foreign policy, both those of "declinism," which prospered—and he warned against—a dozen years ago, and those of unilateralism, the *hubris* of today, which his latest books eloquently denounce.) It is also wise because of the impeccable mix of humanity, common sense, prudence, and integrity that characterizes a personality so richly successful in writing, in teaching, in reflecting on the variety of human experiences, and in acting as an imaginative, farsighted, and dynamic academic entrepreneur. I admire his balance and his gifts, and I like him as a fine and good man whose friendship I deeply appreciate.

STANLEY HOFFMANN
Buttenwieser University Professor
Harvard University

Preface

This text grows out of the course on international conflicts in the modern world that I taught as part of the Harvard core curriculum for more than a decade. It is also informed by five years of experience as a policy maker at the assistant secretary level in three national security bureaucracies in Washington—the State Department, the Pentagon, and the National Intelligence Council. Its aim is to introduce students to the complexities of international politics by giving them a good grounding in the traditional realist theory before turning to liberal and constructivist approaches that became more prominent after the Cold War. I try to present difficult concepts in clear language with historical examples so students will gain a practical understanding of the basic vocabulary of international politics.

Twice in the first half of the twentieth century, the great powers engaged in devastating world wars that cost nearly 50 million lives. The second half of the century was wracked by a cold war, regional wars, and the threat of nuclear weapons. Why did those conflicts happen? Could they happen again in the twenty-first century? Or will rising economic and ecological interdependence, the growth of transnational and international institutions, and the spread of democratic values bring about a new world order? How will globalization and the information revolution influence international politics in this new century? No good teacher can honestly answer such questions with certainty, but we can provide our students with conceptual tools that will help them shape their own answers as the future unfolds. That is the purpose of this book.

This is not a complete textbook with all the concepts or history a student will need. Instead, it is an example of how to think about the complex and confusing domain of international politics. It should be read not for a complete factual account, but for the way it approaches the interplay of theory and history. Neither theory nor history alone is sufficient. Historians who believe that understanding comes from simply recounting the facts fail to make explicit the hidden principles by which they select some facts rather than others. Equally mistaken are political scientists who become so isolated and entangled in a maze of abstract theory that they mistake their mental constructs for reality. Only by going back and forth between history and theory can we avoid such mistakes. This text is an example of such a dialogue between theory and history. When combined with the suggested reading and the study questions, it can provide the central thread for an introductory course or for individual readers to teach themselves the equivalent of such a course. Alternatively, it can be used as a supplementary text in a course as an example of one approach to the subject. Issues of ethics are discussed throughout the text, but particularly in Chapters 1, 5, and 6.

The sixth edition of this book, the third as part of the "Longman Classics in Political Science" series, has been updated with new materials on constructivist theory and soft power (Chapters 1, 3, and elsewhere); new material on the Cold War (Chapter 5); Middle East conflicts, including the Iraq War (Chapters 6 and 9); international institutions, including the United Nations (Chapters 6 and 7), the impact of globalization and the information revolution (Chapters 7 and 8); transnational threats to global security, such as terrorism and the proliferation of nuclear technology (Chapters 8 and 9); power and interdependence in international political economy, including conflicts over energy (Chapters 7 and 8); and intervention and American power (Chapters 6 and 9). The text has been revised and updated throughout to reflect more recent developments on the international scene such as the wars in Afghanistan and Iraq, the rise of China as a world power, and the growing roles of nongovernmental organizations, transnational corporations, terrorist networks, and other nonstate actors in international affairs. In addition, each chapter's suggested readings have been updated with new editions and more current texts for reference. Finally, the glossary and chronologies have been brought up to date.

Over the years I sometimes taught this course with junior colleagues Stephan Haggard, Yuen Khong, Michael Mandelbaum, and M. J. Peterson. I have learned from all of them, and, I am sure, unconsciously stolen a number of their ideas. The same is true of Stanley Hoffmann, who has taught me since graduate days and has been a constant source of inspiration. I am grateful to him and to Robert Keohane, who has provided so many ideas as well as friendship. David Dressler, Charles Maier, and Ernest May helped by commenting on the manuscript. Others who reviewed the manuscript and offered constructive comments include June Teufel Dreyer, University of Miami; Kathie Stromile Golden, University of Colorado—Colorado Springs; J. Douglas Nelson, Anderson University; George Shambaugh, Georgetown University; Edward S. Minalkanin, Southwest Texas State University; Michael Barnett, University of Wisconsin—Madison; Kelechi Kalu, University of North Colorado; Howard Lehman, University of Utah; Dan Reiter, Emory University; Peter D. Feaver, Duke University; Richard A. Melanson, Brown University; John Williams, East Carolina University; Clifford Griffin, North Carolina State University; Christopher Housenick, Pennsylvania State University; Nathan Jensen, Washington University—St. Louis; Elizabeth Larus, University of Mary Washington; and Theodore Vastal, Oklahoma State University. I want also to thank my head course assistants: Vin Auger, Peter Feaver, Meryl Kessler, Sean Lyn-Jones, Pam Metz, John Owen, Gideon Rose, and Gordon Silverstein. Veronica McClure was a wonderful colleague in transcribing and correcting my prose. Richard Wood, Dan Philpott, Zachary Karabell, Carl Nagin, Neal Rosendorf, Alex Scacco, and Matt Kohut helped on earlier editions. Sean Misko provided excellent assistance and wise judgment in helping to prepare this edition. I am fortunate to have had their help. Over the years I have also learned greatly from my students. To all, I am deeply grateful.

JOSEPH S. NYE, JR.

Is There an Enduring Logic of Conflict in World Politics?

Marble relief commemorating Athenians who died in the Peloponnesian War

The world is shrinking. The *Mayflower* took three months to cross the Atlantic. In 1924, Charles Lindbergh's flight took 33 hours. Fifty years later, the Concorde did it in three hours. Ballistic missiles can do it in 30 minutes. At the beginning of the twenty-first century, a transatlantic flight costs one-third of what it did in 1950, and a call from New York to London costs only a small percentage of what it did at midcentury. Global Internet communications are nearly instantaneous and transmission costs are negligible. An environmentalist in Asia or a human rights activist in Africa today has a power of communication once enjoyed only by large organizations such as governments or transnational corporations. On a more somber note, nuclear weapons have added a new dimension to war that one writer calls "double death," meaning that not only could individuals die, but under some circumstances the whole human species could be threatened. And as the September 2001 terrorist attacks on New York and Washington illustrated, technology is putting into the hands of nonstate actors destructive powers that once were reserved solely to governments. As the effects of distance shrink, conditions in remote poor countries such as Afghanistan suddenly become highly relevant to America and Europe.

Yet some other things about international politics have remained the same over the ages. Thucydides's account of Sparta and Athens fighting the Peloponnesian War 2,500 years ago reveals eerie resemblances to the Arab-Israeli conflict after 1947. The world at the beginning of the twenty-first century is a strange cocktail of continuity and change. Some aspects of international politics have not changed since Thucydides. There is a certain logic of hostility, a dilemma about security that goes with interstate politics. Alliances, balances of power, and choices in policy between war and compromise have remained similar over the millennia.

On the other hand, Thucydides never had to worry about nuclear weapons, HIV/AIDS, or global warming. The task for international relations students is to build on the past but not be trapped by it, to understand the continuities as well as the changes. We must learn the traditional theories and then adapt them to current circumstances. The early chapters of this book will provide you with a historical and theoretical context in which to place the phenomena of the information revolution, globalization, interdependence, and transnational actors that are discussed in the later chapters. I found in my experience in government that I could ignore neither the age-old nor the brand-new dimensions of world politics.

International politics would be transformed if separate states were abolished, but world government is not around the corner. And while nonstate actors such as transnational corporations, nongovernmental organizations, and terrorist groups present new challenges to governments, they do not replace states. The peoples who live in the nearly 200 states on this globe want their independence, separate cultures, and different languages. In fact, rather than vanishing, nationalism and the demand for separate states have increased. Rather than fewer states, this new century will probably see more. World government would not automatically solve the problem of war. Most wars today are civil or ethnic wars. Between the end of the Cold War in 1989 and the end of the twentieth century, 111 armed conflicts occurred in 74 locations around the world. Seven were interstate wars and nine were intrastate wars with foreign intervention.[1] In fact, the bloodiest wars of the nineteenth century were not among the quarreling states of Europe but the Taiping rebellion in China and the American Civil War. We will continue to live in a world of rival communities and separate states for quite some time, and it is important to understand what that means for our prospects.

WHAT IS INTERNATIONAL POLITICS?

The world has not always been divided into a system of separate states. Over the centuries there have been three basic forms of world politics. In a *world imperial system*, one government controls most of the world with which it has contact. The greatest example in the Western world was the Roman Empire. Spain in the sixteenth century and France in the late seventeenth century tried to gain similar supremacy, but they failed. In the nineteenth century, the British Empire spanned the globe, but even the British had to share the world with other strong states. Ancient world empires—the Sumerian, the Persian, the Chinese—were actually regional empires. They thought they ruled the world, but they were protected from conflict with other empires by lack of communication. Their fights with barbarians on the peripheries of the empire were not the same as wars among roughly equal states.

A second basic form of international politics is a *feudal system*, in which human loyalties and political obligations are not fixed primarily by territorial boundaries. Feudalism was common in Europe after the collapse of the Roman Empire. An individual had obligations to a local lord, but might also owe duties to some distant noble or bishop as well as to the pope in Rome. Political obligations were determined to a large extent by what happened to one's superiors. If a ruler married, an area and its people might find their obligations rearranged as part of a wedding dowry. Townspeople born French might suddenly find themselves made Flemish or even English. Cities and leagues of cities sometimes had a special semiindependent status. The crazy quilt of wars that accompanied the feudal situation were not what we think of as modern territorial wars. They could occur within as well as across territories and were related to these crosscutting, nonterritorial loyalties and conflicts.

A third form of world politics is an *anarchic system of states*, composed of states that are relatively cohesive but with no higher government above them. Examples include the city-states of ancient Greece or Machiavelli's fifteenth-century Italy. Another example of an anarchic state system is the dynastic territorial state whose coherence comes from control by a ruling family. Examples can be found in India or China in the fifth century B.C. Large territorial dynasties reemerged in Europe about 1500, and other forms of international polities such as city-states or loose leagues of territories began to vanish. In 1648, the Peace of Westphalia ended Europe's Thirty Years' War, sometimes called the last of the great wars of religion and the first of the wars of modern states. In retrospect, that treaty enshrined the sovereign territorial state as the dominant form of international organization.

Thus today when we speak of international politics, we usually mean this territorial state system, and we define *international politics* as politics in the absence of a common sovereign, politics among entities with no ruler above them. International politics is a self-help system. Thomas Hobbes, the seventeenth-century English philosopher, called such anarchic systems a "state of nature." For some, the words *state of nature* may conjure up images of a herd of cows grazing peacefully on a farm, but that is not what Hobbes meant. Think of a Texas town without a sheriff in the days of the Old West, or Lebanon after its government broke down in the 1970s, or Somalia in the 1990s. Hobbes's state of nature is not benign; it is a war of all against all because there is no higher ruler to enforce order. As Hobbes famously declared, life in such a world tends to be nasty, brutish, and short.

The result is that legal, political, and social differences exist between domestic and international politics. Domestic law is generally obeyed and if not, the police and courts enforce sanctions against lawbreakers. International law, on the other hand, rests on competing legal systems, and there is no common enforcement; no international police to enforce International law.

Force plays a different role in domestic and international politics. In a well-ordered domestic political system, the government has a monopoly on the legitimate use of force. In international politics, no one has a monopoly on the use of force. Because international politics is the realm of self-help, and some states are stronger than others, there is always a danger that they may resort to force. When force cannot be ruled out, the result is mistrust and suspicion.

Domestic and international politics also differ in their underlying sense of community. In a well-ordered domestic society, a widespread sense of community gives rise to common loyalties, standards of justice, and views of what is legitimate authority. In international politics, divided peoples do not share the same loyalties. Any sense of global community is weak. People often disagree about what seems just and legitimate. The result is a great gap between two basic political values: order and justice. In such a world, most people place national concerns before international justice. Law and ethics play a role in international politics, but in the absence of a sense of community norms, they are not as binding as they are in domestic politics.

Of the three basic systems—*world imperial, feudal,* and *anarchic system of states*—some people speculate that the twenty-first century may see the gradual evolution of a new feudalism, or less plausibly, an American world empire. We will look at those questions in the final chapter.

Two Views of Anarchic Politics

International politics is anarchic in the sense that there is no higher government. But even political philosophy offers two different views of how harsh a state of nature need be. Hobbes, who wrote in a seventeenth-century England wracked by civil war, emphasized insecurity, force, and survival. He described humanity as being in a constant state of war. A half century later, John Locke, writing in a more stable England, argued that although a state of nature lacked a common sovereign, people could develop ties and make contracts, and therefore anarchy was less threatening. Those two views of a state of nature are the philosophical precursors of two current views of international politics, one more pessimistic and one more optimistic: the *realist* and *liberal* approaches to international politics.

Realism has been the dominant tradition in thinking about international politics. For the realist, the central problem of international politics is war and the use of force, and the central actors are states. Among modern Americans, realism is exemplified by the writings and policies of President Richard Nixon and his secretary of state, Henry Kissinger. The realist starts from the assumption of the anarchic system of states. Kissinger and Nixon, for example, sought to maximize the power of the United States and to minimize the ability of other states to jeopardize U.S. security. According to the realist, the beginning and the end of international politics is the individual state in interaction with other states.

The other tradition, *liberalism,* can be traced back in Western political philosophy to Baron de Montesquieu and Immanuel Kant in eighteenth-century France and Germany, respectively, and such nineteenth-century British philosophers as Jeremy Bentham and John Stuart Mill. A modern American example can be found in the writings and policies of political scientist and President Woodrow Wilson.

Liberals see a global society that functions alongside the states and sets part of the context for states. Trade crosses borders, people have contacts with each other (such as students studying in foreign countries), and international institutions such as the United Nations create a context in which the realist view of pure anarchy is insufficient. Liberals complain that realists portray states as hard billiard balls careening off one another in the attempt to balance power, but that is not enough because people do have contacts across borders and because there is an international society. Realists, claim liberals, overstate the difference between domestic and international politics. Because the realist picture of anarchy as a Hobbesian "state of war" focuses only on extreme situations, in the liberals' view it misses the growth of economic interdependence and the evolution of a transnational global society.

Realists respond by quoting Hobbes: "Just as stormy weather does not mean perpetual rain, so a state of war does not mean constant war."[2] Just as Londoners carry umbrellas on sunny April days, the prospect of war in an anarchic system makes states keep armies even in times of peace. Realists point to previous liberal predictions that went awry. For example, in 1910 the president of Stanford University said future war was no longer possible because the nations could not afford it. Books proclaimed war to be obsolete; civilization had gone beyond war. Economic interdependence, ties

---

1910: THE "UNSEEN VAMPIRE" OF WAR

If there were no other reason for making an end of war, the financial ruin it involves must sooner or later bring the civilized nations of the world to their senses. As President David Starr Jordan of Leland Stanford University said at Tufts College, "Future war is impossible because the nations cannot afford it." In Europe, he says, the war debt is $26 billion, "all owed to the unseen vampire, and which the nations will never pay and which taxes poor people $95 million a year." The burdens of militarism in time of peace are exhausting the strength of the leading nations, already overloaded with debts. The certain result of a great war would be overwhelming bankruptcy.

—*The New York World* [3]

between labor unions and intellectuals, and the flow of capital all made war impossible. Of course, these predictions failed catastrophically in 1914, and the realists were vindicated.

Neither history nor the argument stopped in 1914. The 1970s saw a resurgence of liberal claims that rising economic and social interdependence was changing the nature of international politics. In the 1980s, Richard Rosecrance, a California professor, wrote that states can increase their power in two ways, either aggressively by territorial conquest or peacefully through trade. He used the experience of Japan as an example: In the 1930s, Japan tried territorial conquest and suffered the disaster of World War II. But since then, Japan has used trade and investment to become the second largest economy in the world (measured by official exchange rates), and a significant power in East Asia. Japan succeeded without a major military force. Thus Rosecrance and modern liberals argue that the nature of international politics is changing.

Some new liberals look even further to the future and believe that dramatic growth in ecological interdependence will so blur the differences between domestic and international politics that humanity will evolve toward a world without borders. For example, everyone will be affected without regard to boundaries if the depletion of ozone in the upper atmosphere causes skin cancer. If carbon dioxide accumulation warms the climate and causes the polar ice caps to melt, rising seas will affect all coastal states. Some problems such as AIDS and drugs cross borders with such ease that we may be on our way to a different world. Professor Richard Falk of Princeton argues that these transnational problems and values will alter the state-centric orientation of the international system that has dominated for the last 400 years. Transnational forces are undoing the Peace of Westphalia, and humanity is evolving toward a new form of international politics.

In 1990, realists replied, "Tell that to Saddam Hussein!" Iraq showed that force and war are ever-present dangers when it invaded its small neighbor Kuwait. Liberals responded by arguing that politics in the Middle East is the exception. Over time, they say, the world is moving beyond the anarchy of the sovereign state system. These divergent views on the nature of international politics and how it is changing will not soon be reconciled. Realists stress continuity; liberals stress change. Both claim the high ground of realism with a small r. Liberals tend to see realists as cynics whose fascination with the past blinds them to change. Realists, in turn, call the liberals utopian dreamers and label their thought "globaloney."

Who's right? Both are right and both are wrong. A clear-cut answer might be nice, but it would also be less accurate and less interesting. The mix of continuity and change that characterizes today's world makes it impossible to arrive at one simple synthetic explanation.

Because it involves changeable human behaviors, international politics will never be like physics: it has no strong determinist theory. What is more, realism and liberalism are not the only approaches. For much of the past century *Marxism*, with its predictions of class conflict and warfare caused by problems among capitalist states, was a credible alternative for many people. Even before the 1991 collapse of the Soviet Union, however, the failure of Marxist theory to account for peace among major capitalist states and warfare among some communist states left it lagging in the explanatory competition. In the 1960s and 1970s, *dependency theory* was popular. It predicted that the wealthy countries in the "center" of the global marketplace would control and hold back poorer countries on the "periphery." While dependency theory helped illuminate some structural causes of economic inequality, it lost credibility when it could not explain why, in the 1980s and 1990s, peripheral countries in East Asia such as South Korea, Singapore, and Malaysia grew more rapidly than "central" countries such as the United States and Europe. This loss of credibility was underlined when Fernando Henrique Cardoso, an academic leader among dependency theorists in the 1970s, turned to liberal policies of increasing dependence on global markets after he was elected president of Brazil in the 1990s.

In the 1980s, analysts on both sides of the realist-liberal divide attempted to devise more deductive theories similar to those of microeconomics. "Neorealists" such as Kenneth Waltz and "neoliberals" such as Robert Keohane developed structural models of states as rational actors constrained by the international system. Neorealists and neoliberals increased the simplicity and elegance of theory, but they did so at the cost of discarding much of the rich complexity of classical realist and liberal theories. "By the end of the 1980s, the theoretical contest that might have been was reduced to relatively narrow disagreements within one state-centric rationalist model of international relations."[4]

More recently, a diverse group of theorists labeled *constructivists* has argued that realism and liberalism fail to adequately explain long-term change in world politics. Constructivists emphasize the importance of ideas and culture in shaping both the reality and the discourse of international politics. They stress the ultimate subjectivity of interests and their links to changing identities. There are many types of constructivists, but they all tend to agree that the two major theories are far from being true pictures of the world, and that we need not just explanations of how things are, but explanations of how they become what they are. Constructivists have focused on important questions about identities, norms, culture, national interests, and international governance.[5] They believe that leaders and other people are motivated not only by material interests, but also by their sense of identity, morality, and what a society or culture considers appropriate. And such norms change over time.

Neorealists and neoliberals take for granted how the goals that states sought changed over time. Constructivists draw on different fields and disciplines to examine the processes by which leaders, peoples, and cultures alter their preferences, shape their identities, and learn new behavior. For example, both slavery in the nineteenth century and racial apartheid in South Africa were once accepted by most states, but later were widely opposed. Constructivists ask, why the change? What role did ideas play? Will the practice of war go the same way someday? What about the concept of the sovereign nation-state? The world is full of political entities such as tribes, nations, and nongovernmental organizations. Only in recent centuries has the sovereign state been a dominant concept. Constructivists suggest that concepts such as nation and sovereignty that give meaning to our lives as well as to our theories are socially constructed, not just "out there" as permanent reality. Feminist constructivists add that the language and imageries of war as a central instrument of world politics have been heavily influenced by gender.

Constructivism is an approach rather than a theory, but it provides both a useful critique and an important supplement to the main theories of realism and liberalism. Though sometimes loosely formulated and lacking in predictive power, constructivist approaches remind us of what the two main theories often miss. As we shall see in the next chapter, it is important to look beyond the instrumental rationality of pursuing current goals and to ask how changing identities and interests can sometimes lead to subtle shifts in states' policies, and sometimes to profound changes in international affairs. Constructivists help us understand how preferences are formed and knowledge is generated prior to the exercise of instrumental rationality. In that sense, constructivist thought complements rather than opposes the two main theories. We will illustrate the questions of understanding long-term change in the next chapter and return to it in the final chapter.

When I was working in Washington and helping formulate American foreign policies as an assistant secretary in the State Department and the Pentagon, I found myself borrowing elements from all three types of thinking: realism, liberalism, and constructivism. I found all of them helpful, though in different ways and in different circumstances. Sometimes practical men and women wonder why we should bother with theories at all. The answer is that theories are the road maps that allow us to make sense of unfamiliar terrain. We are lost without them. Even when we think we are just using common sense, there is usually an implicit theory guiding our actions. We simply do not know or have forgotten what it is. If we are more conscious of the theories that are guiding us, we are better able to understand their strengths and weaknesses and when best to apply them. As the British economist John Maynard Keynes once put it, practical men who consider themselves above theory are usually listening to some dead scribbler from the past whose name they have long forgotten.[6]

Building Blocks

Actors, goals, and *instruments* are three concepts that are basic to theorizing about international politics, but each is changing. In the traditional realist view of international politics, the only significant "actors" are the states, and only the big states really matter. But this is changing. The number of states has grown enormously in the last half century: In 1945 there were about 50 states in the world; by the beginning of the twenty-first century, there were four times that many with more to come. More important than the number of states is the rise of *nonstate actors.* Today large multinational corporations straddle international borders and sometimes command more economic resources than many nation-states do (Table 1.1). At least 12 transnational corporations have annual sales that are larger than the gross domestic product (GDP) of more than half the states in the world.[7] The sales of companies such as Shell, IBM, and Wal-Mart are larger than the GDP of countries such as Hungary, Ecuador, and Senegal. While these multinational corporations lack some types of power such as military force, they are very relevant to a country's

TABLE 1.1   Select Sales of Multinational
            Corporations, 2004 (in US $)

Wal-Mart Stores	$288 billion
Royal Dutch Shell (U.K./Netherlands)	269 billion
General Motors (U.S.)	194 billion
DaimlerChrysler (Germany/U.S.)	177 billion
Toyota (Japan)	173 billion
General Electric (U.S.)	153 billion
Total (France)	153 billion
IBM (U.S.)	96 billion
Siemens (Germany)	92 billion
Nestlé (Switzerland)	70 billion
Sony (Japan)	67 billion

Source: "The Fortune Global 500," *Fortune.*

economic goals. In terms of the economy, IBM is more important to Belgium than is Burundi, a former Belgian colony.

A picture of the Middle East without the warring states and the outside powers would be downright silly, but it would also be woefully inadequate if it did not include a variety of nonstate actors. Multinational oil companies such as Shell, British Petroleum, and Exxon Mobil are one type of nonstate actors, but there are others. There are large intergovernmental institutions such as the United Nations, and smaller ones such as the Arab League and the Organization of Petroleum Exporting Countries (OPEC). There are nongovernmental organizations (NGOs), including the Red Cross and Amnesty International. There are also a variety of transnational ethnic groups, such as the Kurds who live in Turkey, Syria, Iran, and Iraq, and the Armenians scattered throughout the Middle East and the Caucasus. Terrorist groups, drug cartels, and mafia organizations transcend national borders and often divide their resources among several states. International religious movements, particularly political Islam in the Middle East and North Africa, add a further dimension to the range of possible nonstate actors.

The question is not whether state or nonstate groups are more important— usually the states are—but how new complex coalitions affect the politics of a region in a way that the traditional realist views fail to disclose. States are the major actors in current international politics, but they do not have the stage to themselves.

What about *goals?* Traditionally the dominant goal of states in an anarchic system is military security. Countries today obviously care about their military security, but they often care as much or more about their economic wealth (Table 1.2), about social issues such as stopping drug traffic or the spread of AIDS, or about ecological changes. Moreover, as threats change, the definition of security changes; military security is not the only goal that states pursue. Looking at the relationship between the United States and Canada, where the prospects of war are exceedingly slim, a Canadian diplomat once said his fear was not that the United States would march

TABLE 1.2   Estimated GDP of Select Countries, 2002
(in US $ in Purchasing Power Parity)

United States	$11.8 trillion
China	7.3 trillion
Japan	3.8 trillion
India	3.3 trillion
Germany	2.4 trillion
Brazil	1.5 trillion
Russia	1.4 trillion
Indonesia	828 billion
South Africa	491 billion
Argentina	484 billion
Saudi Arabia	310 billion
Vietnam	227 billion
Guatemala	60 billion
Iraq	54 billion
Albania	17 billion
Jamaica	11 billion
Eritrea	4 billion

Source: CIA World Factbook, 2005.

into Canada and capture Toronto again as it did in 1813, but that Toronto would be programmed out of relevance by a computer in Texas—a rather different dilemma from the traditional one of states in an anarchic system. Economic strength has not replaced military security (as Kuwait discovered when Iraq invaded in August 1990), but the agenda of international politics has become more complex as states pursue a wider range of goals. Humanitarian and human rights issues have become more important, and some analysts refer to individual human security rather than the security of states.

Along with the goals, the *instruments* of international politics are also changing. The realist view is that military force is the only instrument that really matters. Describing the world before 1914, the British historian A. J. P. Taylor defined a great power as one able to prevail in war. States obviously use military force today, but the past half century has seen changes in its role. Many states, particularly large ones, find it more costly to use military force to achieve their goals than was true in earlier times. As Professor Stanley Hoffmann of Harvard University has put it, the link between military strength and positive achievement has been loosened.

What are the reasons? One is that the ultimate means of military force, nuclear weapons, are hopelessly muscle-bound. Although they have numbered more than 50,000, nuclear weapons have not been used in war since 1945. The disproportion between the vast devastation nuclear weapons can inflict and any reasonable political goals has made leaders understandably loath to employ them. So the ultimate form of military force is for all practical purposes too costly for national leaders to use in war.

Even conventional force has become more costly when it is used to rule nation-alistic populations. In the nineteenth century, European countries conquered other parts of the globe by fielding a handful of soldiers armed with modern weapons and then administered their colonial possessions with relatively modest garrisons. But in an age of socially mobilized populations, it is difficult to rule an occupied country whose people feel strongly about their national identity. Americans found this out in Vietnam in the 1960s and 1970s; the Soviets discovered it in Afghanistan in the 1980s. Vietnam and Afghanistan had not become more powerful than the nuclear superpowers, but trying to rule those nationalistically aware populations was too expensive for either the United States or the Soviet Union. Foreign rule is very costly in an age of nationalism.

A third change in the role of force relates to internal constraints. Over time there has been a growing ethic of antimilitarism, particularly in democracies. Such views do not prevent the use of force, but they make it a politically risky choice for leaders, particularly when its use is large or prolonged. It is sometimes said that democracies will not accept casualties, but that is too simple. The United States, for example, expected some 10,000 casualties when it planned to enter the Gulf War in 1990, but it was loath to accept casualties in Somalia or Kosovo, where its national interests were less deeply involved. And if the use of force is seen as unjust or illegit-imate in the eyes of other nations, this can make it costly for political leaders in democratic polities. Force is not obsolete, and terrorist nonstate actors are less con-strained than states by moral concerns, but force is more costly and more difficult for most states to use than in the past.

Finally, a number of issues simply do not lend themselves to forceful solutions. Take, for example, economic relations between the United States and Japan. In 1853, Commodore Perry sailed into a Japanese port and threatened bombardment unless Japan opened its ports to trade. This would not be a very useful or politically acceptable way to solve current U.S.-Japan trade disputes. Thus while force remains a critical instrument in international politics, it is not the only instru-ment. The use of economic interdependence, communication, international insti-tutions, and transnational actors sometimes plays a larger role than force. Military force is not obsolete as an instrument—witness the fighting in Afghanistan, where the Taliban government had sheltered the terrorist network that carried out the September 2001 attacks on the United States, or the American and British use of force to overthrow Saddam Hussein in 2003. But it was easier to win the war than to win the peace in Iraq, and military force alone is not sufficient to protect against terrorism. While military force remains the ultimate instrument in international politics, changes in its cost and effectiveness make today's international politics more complex.

The basic game of security goes on. Some political scientists argue that the bal-ance of power is usually determined by a leading, or hegemonic state—such as Spain in the sixteenth century, France under Louis XIV, Britain in most of the nine-teenth century, and the United States in most of the twentieth century. Eventually the top country will be challenged, and this challenge will lead to the kind of vast conflagrations we call hegemonic, or world, wars. After world wars, a new treaty sets the new framework of order: the Treaty of Utrecht in 1713, the Congress of Vienna in 1815, the United Nations system after 1945. If nothing basic has changed in international politics since the struggle for supremacy between Athens and Sparta, will a new challenge lead to another world war, or is the cycle of hegemonic war over? Will a rising China challenge the United States? Has nuclear technology made world war too devastating? Has economic interdependence made it too costly? Will nonstate actors such as terrorists force governments to cooperate? Has global society made war socially and morally unthinkable? We have to hope so, because the next hegemonic war could be the last. But first, it is important to understand the case for continuity.

THE PELOPONNESIAN WAR

Thucydides is the father of realism, the theory most people use when thinking about international politics even when they do not know they are using a theory. Theories are the indispensable tools we use to organize facts. Many of today's leaders and editorial writers use realist theories even if they have not heard of Thucydides. A member of the Athenian elite who lived during Athens's greatest age, he participated in some of the events described in his *History of the Peloponnesian War*. Robert Gilpin, a realist, asserted, "In honesty, one must inquire whether or not twentieth-century students of international relations know anything that Thucydides and his fifth-century B.C. compatriots did not know about the behavior of states." He then answered his own query: "Ultimately international politics can still be characterized as it was by Thucydides."[8] Gilpin's proposition is debatable, but to debate it, we must know Thucydides's argument. And what better introduction to realist theory is there than one of history's great stories? However, like many great stories, it has its limits. One of the things we learn from the Peloponnesian War is how to avoid too simplistic a reading of history.

A Short Version of a Long Story

Early in the fifth century, Athens and Sparta (Figure 1.1) were allies that had cooperated to defeat the Persian Empire (480 B.C.). Sparta was a conservative land-oriented state that turned inward after the victory over Persia; Athens was a commercial and sea-oriented state that turned outward. In the middle of the century, Athens had 50 years of growth that led to the development of an Athenian empire. Athens formed the Delian League, an alliance of states around the Aegean Sea, for mutual protection against the Persians. Sparta, in turn, organized its neighbors on the Peloponnesian peninsula into a defensive alliance. States that had joined Athens freely for protection against the Persians soon had to pay taxes to the Athenians. Because of the growing strength of Athens and the resistance of some to its growing empire, a war broke out in 461 B.C., about 20 years after the Greek defeat of the Persians. By 445 B.C., the first Peloponnesian War ended and was followed by a treaty that promised peace for 30 years. Thus Greece enjoyed a period of stable peace before the second, more significant, Peloponnesian War.

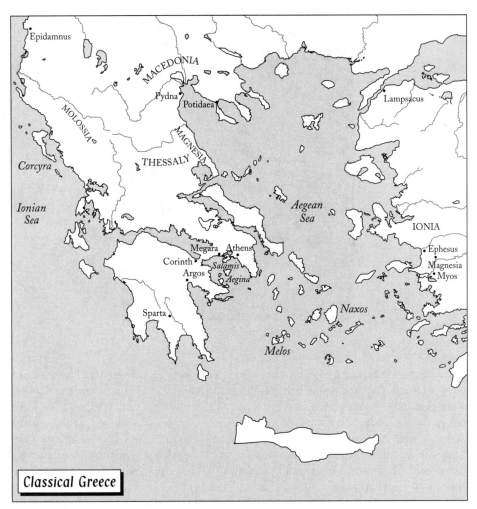

FIGURE 1.1   Classical Greece

In 434 B.C., a civil war broke out in the small peripheral city-state of Epidamnus. Like a pebble that begins an avalanche, this event triggered a series of reactions that led ultimately to the Peloponnesian War. Large conflicts are often precipitated by relatively insignificant crises in out-of-the-way places, as we shall see when we discuss World War I.

In Epidamnus, the democrats fought with oligarchs over how the country would be ruled. The democrats appealed to the city-state of Corcyra, which had helped establish Epidamnus, but were turned down. They then turned to another city-state, Corinth, and the Corinthians decided to help. This angered the Corcyraeans, who sent a fleet to recapture Epidamnus, their former colony. In the process, the Corcyraeans defeated the Corinthian fleet. Corinth was outraged and declared war on Corcyra. Corcyra, fearing the attack from Corinth, turned to Athens for help. Both Corcyra and Corinth sent representatives to Athens.

Bust of Thucydides

The Athenians, after listening to both sides, were in a dilemma. They did not want to break the truce that had lasted for a decade, but if the Corinthians (who were close to the Peloponnesians) conquered Corcyra and took control of its large navy, the balance of power among the Greek states would be tipped against Athens. The Athenians felt they could not risk letting the Corcyraean navy fall into the hands of the Corinthians, so they decided to become "a little bit involved." They launched a small endeavor to scare the Corinthians, sending ten ships with instructions not to fight unless attacked. But deterrence failed; Corinth attacked, and when the Corcyraeans began to lose the battle, the Athenian ships were drawn into the fray more than intended. The Athenian involvement infuriated Corinth, which in turn worried the Athenians. In particular, Athens worried that Corinth would stir up problems in Potidaea, which, although an Athenian ally, had historic ties to Corinth. Sparta promised to help Corinth if Athens attacked Potidaea. When a revolt did occur in Potidaea, Athens sent forces to put it down.

At that point there was a great debate in Sparta. The Athenians appealed to the Spartans to stay neutral. The Corinthians urged the Spartans to go to war and warned them against failing to check the rising power of Athens. Megara, another important city, agreed with Corinth because contrary to the treaty, the Athenians had banned Megara's trade. Sparta was torn. The Spartans voted in favor of war because they were afraid that if Athenian power was not checked, Athens might control the whole of Greece. Sparta went to war to maintain the balance of power among the Greek city-states.

Athens rejected Sparta's ultimatum, and war broke out in 431 B.C. The Athenian mood was one of imperial greatness, with pride and patriotism about their city and their social system, and optimism that they would prevail in the war. The early phase of the war came to a stalemate. A truce was declared after ten years (421 B.C.), but the truce was fragile and war broke out again. In 413 B.C., Athens undertook a very risky venture. It sent two fleets and infantry to conquer Sicily, the great island off the south of Italy, which had a number of Greek colonies allied to Sparta. The result was a terrible defeat for the Athenians. At the same time Sparta received additional money from the Persians, who were only too happy to see Athens trounced. After the defeat in Sicily, Athens was internally divided. In 411 B.C. the oligarchs overthrew the democrats, and 400 oligarchs attempted to rule Athens. These events were not the end, but Athens never really recovered. An Athenian naval victory in 410 B.C. was followed five years later by a Spartan naval victory, and by 404 B.C. Athens was compelled to sue for peace. Sparta demanded that Athens pull down the long walls that protected it from attack by land-based powers. Athens's power was broken.

Causes and Theories

This is a dramatic and powerful story. What caused the war? Thucydides is very clear. After recounting the various events in Epidamnus, Corcyra, and so forth, he said that those were not the real causes. What made the war inevitable was the growth of Athenian power and the fear this caused in Sparta.

Did Athens have a choice? With better foresight, could Athens have avoided this disaster? Pericles, the Athenian leader in the early days of the war, had an interesting answer for his fellow citizens. "It is right and proper for you to support the imperial dignity of Athens. Your empire is now like a tyranny: it may have been wrong to take it, but it is certainly dangerous to let it go."[9] In other words, Pericles told Athenians that they had no choice. Perhaps they should not be where they were, but once they had an empire, there was not much they could do about it without even larger risks. Thus Pericles favored war. But there were other voices in Athens, such as those of the Athenian delegates to the debate in Sparta in 432 B.C. who said to the Spartans, "Think, too, of the great part that is played by the unpredictable in war: think of it now before you are actually committed to war. The longer a war lasts, the more things tend to depend on accidents."[10] That turned out to be good advice; why didn't the Athenians heed their own counsel? Perhaps the Athenians were carried away by emotional patriotism or anger that clouded their reason. But there is a more interesting possibility: perhaps the Athenians acted rationally but were caught in a security dilemma.

Security dilemmas are related to the essential characteristic of international politics: *anarchic organization*, the absence of a higher government. Under anarchy, independent action taken by one state to increase its security may make all states more insecure. If one state builds its strength to make sure that another cannot threaten it, the other, seeing the first getting stronger, may build its strength to protect itself against the first. The result is that the independent efforts of each to build its own strength and security makes both more insecure. It is an ironic result, yet neither has acted irrationally. Neither has acted from anger or pride, but from fear caused by the threat perceived in the growth of the other. After all, building defenses is a rational response to a perceived threat. States could cooperate to avoid this security dilemma; that is, they could agree that neither should build up its defenses and all would be better off. If it seems obvious that states should cooperate, why don't they?

An answer can be found in the game called the Prisoner's Dilemma. (Security dilemmas are a specific type of Prisoner's Dilemma.) The Prisoner's Dilemma scenario goes like this: Imagine that somewhere the police arrest two men who have small amounts of drugs in their possession, which would probably result in one-year jail sentences. The police have good reason to believe these two are really drug dealers, but they do not have enough evidence for a conviction. As dealers, the two could easily get 25-year jail sentences. The police know that the testimony of one against the other would be sufficient to convict the other to a full sentence. The police offer to let each man off if he will testify that the other is a drug dealer. They tell them that if both testify, both will receive 10-year sentences. The police figure this way these dealers will be out of commission for 10 years; otherwise they are both in jail for only a year and soon will be out selling drugs again.

The suspects are put in separate cells and are not allowed to communicate with each other. Each prisoner has the same dilemma: He can secure his own freedom by squealing on the other, sending him to jail for 25 years, and go free himself, or he can stay silent and spend a year in jail. But if each prisoner squeals, they both get 10 years in jail. Each prisoner thinks, "I'm better off if I squeal. If he stays quiet and if I don't talk, I'll spend a year in jail. What if the other guy does talk? If I squeal too, I get 10 years, but if I'm quiet, I'll spend 25 years in jail and he'll be free; I'll be a sucker. If I help him by staying quiet, how can I be sure that he won't squeal on me?"

That is the basic structural dilemma of independent rational action. The best outcome for the individual is to cheat on the other and get to go free. The second best outcome is for both to stay silent and spend a year in jail. A worse outcome is for both to squeal and spend 10 years behind bars. Worst of all is to be played for a sucker by staying quiet while the other talks and consequently spend 25 years in jail. If each person does what is best for himself, they both wind up with a bad outcome. Choosing the best outcome, freedom, is the expression of a rational preference, but if both independently seek their own best outcome, they both get a bad result. Cooperation is difficult in the absence of communication. If the two could talk to each other, they might agree to make a deal to stay silent and both spend one year in jail.

But even if communication were possible, there is another problem: trust and credibility. Continuing with the metaphor in the Prisoner's Dilemma, each suspect could say to himself, "We are both drug dealers. I have seen the way the other acts. How do I know that after we've made this deal, he won't say, 'Great! I've convinced him to stay quiet. Now I can get my best outcome, without risk of getting imprisoned.'" Similarly, in international politics the absence of communication and trust encourages states to provide for their own security, even though doing so may reduce all states to mutual insecurity. In other words, one state could say to another,

"Don't build up your armaments and I will not build up my armaments, and we will both live happily ever after," but the second state may wonder whether it can afford to trust the first state.

The Athenian position in 432 B.C. looks very much like the Prisoner's Dilemma. In the middle of the century, the Athenians and Spartans agreed they were both better off to have a truce. Even after the events in Epidamnus and the dispute between Corcyra and Corinth, the Athenians were reluctant to break the truce. The Corcyraeans finally convinced the Athenians with the following argument: "There are three considerable naval powers in Hellas: Athens, Corcyra, and Corinth. If Corinth gets control of us first, and you allow our navy to be united with hers, you will have to fight against the combined fleets of Corcyra and the Peloponnese. But if you receive us into your alliance, you will enter upon the war with our ships as well as your own."[11]

Should Athens have cooperated with the Peloponnesians by keeping the treaty and turning Corcyra down? If they did, what would have happened if the Peloponnesians had cheated and captured the Corcyraean fleet? Then the naval balance would have been two to one against Athens. Should Athens have trusted the Peloponnesians to keep their promises? The Athenians decided to break the treaty, the equivalent of squealing on the other prisoner. Thucydides explains why: "The general belief was that whatever happened, war with the Peloponnese was bound to come."[12] If so, Athens could not risk letting the strong navy of Corcyra pass into the hands of Corinth.

Inevitability and the Shadow of the Future

Ironically, the belief that war was inevitable played a major role in causing it. Athens felt that if the war was going to come, it was better to have two-to-one naval superiority rather than one-to-two naval inferiority. The belief that war was imminent and inevitable was critical to the decision. Why should that be so? Look again at the Prisoner's Dilemma. At first glance, it is best for each prisoner to cheat and let the other fellow be a sucker, but because each knows the situation, they also know that if they can trust each other, both should go for second best and cooperate by keeping silent. Cooperation is difficult to develop when playing the game only once. Playing a game time after time, people can learn to cooperate, but if it is a onetime game, whoever cheats can get the reward and whoever trusts is a sucker. Political scientist Robert Axelrod played the Prisoner's Dilemma on a computer with different strategies. He found that after many games, on average the best results were obtained with a strategy he calls *tit for tat*—"I will do to you what you did to me." If on the first move you cheat, I should cheat. If you cheat again, I should cheat again. If you cooperate, I should cooperate. If you cooperate again, I cooperate again. Eventually, players find that the total benefit from the game is higher by learning to cooperate. But Axelrod warns that tit for tat is a good strategy only when you have a chance to continue the game for a long period, when there is a "long shadow of the future." When you know you are going to be playing with the same people for a long time, you can learn to cooperate.

That is why the belief that war is inevitable is so corrosive in international politics. When you believe war is inevitable, you are very close to the last move. When you get to the last move (which may involve your survival—in other words, whether you will ever play in this game again), then you may worry about whether you can still trust your opponent. If you suspect your opponent will cheat, it is better to rely on yourself and take the risk of defecting rather than cooperating. That is what the Athenians did. Faced with the belief that war would occur, they decided they could not afford to trust the Corinthians or the Spartans. It was better to have the Corcyraean navy on their side than against them when it looked like the last move in the game and inevitable war.

Was the Peloponnesian War really inevitable? Thucydides had a pessimistic view of human nature; he stated, "My work is not a piece of writing designed to meet the taste of an immediate public, but was done to last forever."[13] His history shows human nature caught in the situation of the Prisoner's Dilemma then and for all time. Thucydides, like all historians, had to emphasize certain things and not others. Thucydides concluded that the cause of the war was the growth of the power of Athens and the fear it caused in Sparta. But the Yale classicist Donald Kagan argues that Athenian power was in fact *not* growing: before the war broke out in 431 B.C. the balance of power had begun to stabilize. And though, says Kagan, the Spartans worried about the rise of Athenian power, he contends they had an even greater fear of a slave revolt. Both Athens and Sparta were slave states and both feared that going to war might provide an opportunity for the slaves to revolt. The difference was that the slaves, or Helots, in Sparta were 90 percent of the population, far greater than Athens's slave percentage, and the Spartans had recently experienced a Helot revolt in 464 B.C.

Thus the immediate or precipitating causes of the war, according to Kagan, were more important than Thucydides's theory of inevitability admits. Corinth, for example, thought Athens would not fight; it misjudged the Athenian response, partly because it was so angry at Corcyra. Pericles overreacted; he made mistakes in giving an ultimatum to Potidaea and in punishing Megara by cutting off its trade. Those policy mistakes made the Spartans think that war might be worth the risk after all. Kagan argues that Athenian growth caused the first Peloponnesian War but that the Thirty-Year Truce doused that flame. So to start the second Peloponnesian War, "the spark of the Epidamnian trouble needed to land on one of the rare bits of flammable stuff that had not been thoroughly drenched. Thereafter it needed to be continually and vigorously fanned by the Corinthians, soon assisted by the Megarians, Potidaeans, Aeginetans, and the Spartan War Party. Even then the spark might have been extinguished had not the Athenians provided some additional fuel at the crucial moment."[14] In other words, the war was not caused by impersonal forces but by bad decisions in difficult circumstances.

It is perhaps impudent to question Thucydides, the father figure of historians, but very little is ever truly inevitable in history. Human behavior is voluntary, although there are always external constraints. Karl Marx observed that men make history, but not in conditions of their own choosing. The ancient Greeks made flawed choices because they were caught in the situation well described by Thucydides and by the

Prisoner's Dilemma. The security dilemma made war highly probable, but *highly probable* is not the same as *inevitable*. The 30-year unlimited war that devastated Athens was not inevitable. Human decisions mattered. Accidents and personalities make a difference even if they work within limits set by the larger structure, the situation of insecurity that resembles the Prisoner's Dilemma.

What modern lessons can we learn from this ancient history? We need to be aware of both the continuities and the changes. Some structural features of international politics predispose events in one direction rather than another. That is why it is necessary to understand security dilemmas and the Prisoner's Dilemma. On the other hand, such situations do not prove that war is inevitable. There are degrees of freedom, and human decisions can sometimes prevent the worst outcomes. Cooperation does occur in international affairs, even though the general structure of anarchy tends to discourage it.

It is also necessary to beware of patently shallow historical analogies. During the Cold War, it was often popular to say that because the United States was a democracy and a sea-based power while the Soviet Union was a land-based power and had slave labor camps, America was Athens and the Soviet Union was Sparta locked into replaying a great historical conflict. But such shallow analogies ignored the fact that ancient Athens was a slave-holding state, wracked with internal turmoil, and that democrats were not always in control. Moreover, unlike in the Cold War, Sparta won.

Another lesson is to be aware of the selectivity of historians. No one can tell the whole story of anything. Imagine trying to tell everything that happened in the last hour, much less the entire story of your life or a whole war. Too many things happened. A second-by-second account in which everything was replicated would take as long to tell as it took for the events to happen in the first place. Thus historians always abstract. To write history, even the history of the last hour or the last day, we must simplify. We must select. What we select is obviously affected by the values, inclinations, and theories in our minds, whether explicit or inchoate.

Historians are affected by their contemporary concerns. Thucydides was concerned about how Athenians were learning the lessons of the war, blaming Pericles and the democrats for miscalculating. He therefore stressed those aspects of the situation we have described as the Prisoner's Dilemma. Yet while these aspects of the war were important, they are not the whole story. Thucydides did not write much about Athenian relations with Persia, or the decree that cut off Megara's trade, or about Athens's raising the amount of tribute that others in the Delian League had to pay. Thucydides's history was not deliberately misleading or biased, but it is an example of how each age tends to rewrite history because the questions brought to the vast panoply of facts tend to change over time.

The need to select does not mean that everything is relative or that history is bunk. Such a conclusion is unwarranted. Good historians and social scientists do their best to ask questions honestly, objectively bringing facts to bear on their topic. But they and their students should be aware that what is selected is by necessity only part of the story. Always ask what questions the writer was asking as well as whether he or she carefully and objectively ascertained the facts. Beware of biases. Choice is a very important part of history and of writing history. The cure to misunderstanding history is to read more, not less.

THE RISE OF CHINA

Ever since Thucydides's explanation of the Peloponnesian War, historians have known that the rise of a new power has been attended by uncertainty and anxieties. Often, though not always, violent conflict has followed. The rise in the economic and military power of China, the world's most populous country, will be a central question for Asia and for American foreign policy at the beginning of a new century. Explaining why democratic Athens decided to break a treaty that led to war, Thucydides pointed to the power of expectations of inevitable conflict. "The general belief was that whatever happened, war with the Peloponnese was bound to come," he wrote. Belief in the inevitability of conflict with China could have similar self-fulfilling effects.

—*The Economist, June 27, 1998* [15]

ETHICAL QUESTIONS AND INTERNATIONAL POLITICS

Given the nature of the security dilemma, some realists believe that moral concerns play no role in international conflicts. However, ethics do play a role in international relations, although not the same role as in domestic politics. Moral arguments have been used since the days of Thucydides. When Corcyra went to Athens to plead for help against Corinth, it used the language of ethics: "First of all, you will not be helping aggressors, but people who are the victims of aggression. Secondly, you will win our undying gratitude."[16] Substitute *Bosnia* for *Corcyra* and *Serbia* for *Corinth*, and those words could be uttered in modern times.

Moral arguments move and constrain people. In that sense morality is a powerful reality. However, moral arguments can also be used rhetorically as propaganda to disguise less elevated motives, and those with more power are often able to ignore moral considerations. During the Peloponnesian War, the Athenians sailed to the island of Melos to suppress a revolt. In 416 B.C., the Athenian spokesmen told the Melians that they could fight and die or they could surrender. When the Melians protested that they were fighting for their freedom, the Athenians responded that "the strong do what they have the power to do and the weak accept what they have to accept."[17] In essence, the Athenians stated that in a realist world, morality has little place. Might makes right. When Iraq invades Kuwait, or the United States invades Grenada or Panama, or the Indonesians suppress a revolt in East Timor, they all to some degree employ similar logic. But, in the modern world, it is increasingly less acceptable to state one's motives as plainly as Thucydides suggests the Athenians did in Melos. Does this mean that morality has come to occupy a more prominent place in international relations, or simply that states have become more adept at propaganda? Has international politics changed dramatically, with states more attuned to ethical concerns, or is there a clear continuity between the actions of the Athenians 2,500 years ago and the actions of Iraq or Serbia in the late twentieth century?

Moral arguments are not all the same. Some are more compelling than others. We ask whether they are logical and consistent. For instance, when the activist

Phyllis Schlafly argued that nuclear weapons are a good thing because God gave them to the free world, we should wonder why God also gave them to Stalin's Soviet Union and Mao's China. Moral arguments are not all equal.

The basic touchstone for moral arguments is impartiality—the view that all interests are judged by the same criteria. Your interests deserve the same attention as mine. Within this framework of impartiality, however, there are two different traditions in Western political culture about how to judge moral arguments. One descends from Immanuel Kant, the eighteenth-century German philosopher, the other from British utilitarians of the early nineteenth century such as Jeremy Bentham. As an illustration of the two approaches, imagine walking into a poor village and finding that a military officer is about to shoot three people lined up against the wall. You ask, "Why are you shooting these peasants? They look quite harmless." The officer says, "Last night somebody in this village shot one of my men. I know somebody in this village is guilty, so I am going to shoot these three to set an example." You say, "You can't do that! You're going to kill an innocent person. If only one shot was fired, then at least two of these people are innocent, perhaps all three. You just can't do that." The officer takes a rifle from one of his men and hands it to you saying, "You shoot one of them for me and I'll let the other two go. You can save two lives if you will shoot one of them. I'm going to teach you that in civil war you can't have these holier-than-thou attitudes." What are you going to do?

You could try to mow down all the troops in a Rambo-like move, but the officer has a soldier aiming his gun at you. So your choice is to kill one innocent person in order to save two or to drop the gun and have clean hands. The Kantian tradition that you do things only when they are right would require that you refuse to perpetrate the evil deed. The utilitarian tradition might suggest that if you can save two lives, you should do it. If you choose the Kantian solution, imagine the numbers were increased. Suppose there were 100 people against the wall. Or imagine you could save a city full of people from a terrorist's bomb. Should you refuse to save a million people in order to keep your hands and conscience clean? At some point, consequences matter. Moral arguments can be judged in three ways: by the motives or intentions involved, by the means used, and by their consequences or net effects. Although these dimensions are not always easily reconciled, good moral argument tries to take all three into account.

Limits on Ethics in International Relations

Ethics plays less of a role in international politics than in domestic politics for four reasons. One is the weak international consensus on values. There are cultural and religious differences over the justice of some acts. Second, states are not like individuals. States are abstractions, and although their leaders are individuals, statesmen are judged differently than when they act as individuals. For instance, when picking a roommate, most people want a person who believes "thou shalt not kill." But the same people might vote against a presidential candidate who said, "Under no circumstances will I ever take an action that will lead to a death." A president is entrusted by citizens to protect their interests, and under some circumstances this may require the use of force. Presidents who saved their own souls but failed to protect their people would not be good trustees.

In private morality, sacrifice may be the highest proof of a moral action, but should leaders sacrifice their whole people? During the Peloponnesian War, the Athenians told the leaders of the island of Melos that if they resisted, Athens would kill everyone. The Melian leaders resisted and their people were slaughtered. Should they have come to terms? In 1962, should President Kennedy have run a risk of nuclear war to force the Soviets to remove missiles from Cuba when the United States had similar missiles in Turkey? Different people may answer these questions differently. The point is when individuals act as leaders of states, their actions are judged somewhat differently.

A third reason ethics plays a lesser role in international politics is the complexity of causation. It is hard enough to know the consequences of actions in domestic affairs, but international relations has another layer of complexity: the interaction of states. That extra dimension makes it harder to accurately predict consequences. A famous example is the 1933 debate among students at the Oxford Union, the debating society of Oxford University. Mindful of the 20 million people killed in World War I, the majority of students voted for a resolution that they would never again fight for king and country. But someone else was listening: Adolf Hitler. He concluded that democracies were soft and that he could press them as hard as he wanted because they would not fight back. In the end, he pressed too far and the result was World War II, a consequence not desired or expected by those students who voted never to fight for king and country. Many later did, and many died.

A more trivial example is the "hamburger argument" of the early 1970s when people were worried about shortages of food in the world. A number of students in American colleges said, "When we go to the dining hall, refuse to eat meat because a pound of beef equals eight pounds of grain that could be used to feed poor people around the world." Many students stopped eating hamburger and felt good about themselves, but they did not help starving people in Africa or Bangladesh one bit. Why not? The grain freed up by not eating hamburgers in America did not reach the starving people in Bangladesh because those starving had no money to buy the grain. The grain was simply a surplus on the American market, which meant American prices went down and farmers produced less. To help peasants in Bangladesh required getting money to them so they could buy some of the excess grain. By launching a campaign against eating hamburger and failing to look at the complexity of the causal chain that would relate their well-intended act to its consequences, the students failed.

Finally, there is the argument that the institutions of international society are particularly weak and that the disjunction between order and justice is greater in international than in domestic politics. Order and justice are both important. In a domestic polity, we tend to take order for granted. In fact, sometimes protesters purposefully disrupt order for the sake of promoting their view of justice. But if there is total disorder, it is very hard to have any justice; witness the bombing, kidnapping, and killing by all sides in Lebanon in the 1980s or in Somalia in the 1990s. Some degree of order is a prior condition for justice. In international politics, the absence of a common legislature, central executive, or strong judiciary makes it much harder to preserve the order that precedes justice.

Three Views of the Role of Morality

At least three different views of ethics exist in international relations: those of the *skeptics*, the *state moralists*, and the *cosmopolitans*. Although there is no logical connection, people who are realists in their descriptive analysis of world politics often tend to be either skeptics or state moralists in their evaluative approach, whereas those who emphasize a liberal analysis tend toward either the state moralist or cosmopolitan moral viewpoints.

Skeptics. The *skeptic* says that moral categories have no *meaning* in international relations because no institutions exist to provide order. In addition, there is no sense of community, and therefore no moral rights and duties. For the skeptics, the classic statement about ethics in international politics was the Athenians' response to the Melians' plea for mercy: "The strong do what they have the power to do and the weak accept what they have to accept." Might makes right. And that, for the skeptics, is all there is to say.

Philosophers often say that *ought* (moral obligation) implies *can* (the capacity to do something). Morality requires choice. If something is impossible, we cannot have an obligation to do it. If international relations are simply the realm of "kill or be killed," then presumably there is no choice, and that would justify the skeptics' position. But international politics consists of more than mere survival. If choices exist in international relations, pretending choices do not exist is merely a disguised form of choice. To think only in terms of narrow national interests is simply smuggling in values without admitting it. The French diplomat who once told me, "What is moral is whatever is good for France," was ducking hard choices about why only French interests should be considered. The leader who says, "I had no choice," often did have a choice, albeit not a pleasant one. If there is some degree of order and of community in international relations—if it is not constantly "kill or be killed"—then there is room for choices. Anarchy means without government, but it does not necessarily mean chaos or total disorder. There are rudimentary practices and institutions that provide enough order to allow some important choices: balance of power, international law, and international organizations. Each is critical to understanding why the skeptical argument is not sufficient.

Thomas Hobbes argued that to escape from "the state of nature" in which anyone might kill anyone else, individuals give up their freedom to a leviathan, or government, for protection because life in the state of nature is nasty, brutish, and short. Why then don't governments form a superleviathan? Why isn't there a world government? The reason, Hobbes said, is that insecurity is not so great at the international level as at the individual level. Governments provide some degree of protection against the brutality of the biggest individuals taking whatever they want, and the balance of power among states provides some degree of order. Even though states are in a hostile posture of potential war, "they still uphold the daily industry of their subjects." The international state of nature does not create the day-to-day misery that would accompany a state of nature among individuals. In other words, Hobbes believed that the existence of states in a balance of power alleviates the condition of international anarchy enough to allow some degree of order.

Liberals point further to the existence of international law and customs. Even if rudimentary, such rules put a burden of proof on those who break them. Consider the Persian Gulf crisis in 1990. Saddam Hussein claimed that he annexed Kuwait to recover a province stolen from Iraq in colonial times. But because international law forbids crossing borders for such reasons, an overwhelming majority of states viewed his action as a violation of the UN charter. The 12 resolutions passed by the UN Security Council showed clearly that Saddam's view of the situation ran against international norms. Law and norms did not stop Saddam from invading Kuwait, but they did make it more difficult for him to recruit support, and they contributed to the creation of the coalition that expelled him from Kuwait.

International institutions, even if rudimentary, also provide a degree of order by facilitating and encouraging communication and some degree of reciprocity in bargaining. Given this situation of nearly constant communication, international politics is not always, as the skeptics claim, "kill or be killed." The energies and attention of leaders are not focused on security and survival all the time. Cooperation (as well as conflict) occurs in large areas of economic, social, and military interaction. And even though cultural differences exist about the notion of justice, moral arguments take place in international politics and principles are enshrined in international law.

Even in the extreme circumstances of war, law and morality may sometimes play a role. The *just war doctrine,* which originated in the early Christian church and became secularized after the seventeenth century, prohibits the killing of innocent civilians. The prohibition on killing innocents starts from the premise "thou shalt not kill." But if that is a basic moral premise, how is any killing ever justified? Absolute pacifists say that no one should kill anyone else for any reason. Usually this is asserted on Kantian grounds, but some pacifists add a consequentialist argument that "violence only begets more violence." Sometimes, however, the failure to respond to violence can also beget more violence. For example, it is unlikely that Osama bin Laden would have left the United States alone if President Bush had turned the other cheek after September 11.

In contrast to pacifism, the just war tradition combines a concern for the intentions, means, and consequences of actions. It argues that if someone is about to kill you and you refuse to act in self-defense, the result is that evil will prevail. By refusing to defend themselves, the good die. If one is in imminent peril of being killed, it can be moral to kill in self-defense. But we must distinguish between those who can be killed and those who cannot be killed. For example, if a soldier rushes at me with a rifle, I can kill him in self-defense, but the minute the soldier drops the rifle, puts up his hands, and says, "I surrender," he is a prisoner of war and I have no right to take his life. In fact, this is enshrined in international law, and also in the U.S. military code. An American soldier who shoots an enemy soldier after he surrenders can be tried for murder in an American court. Some American officers in the Vietnam War were sent to prison for violating such laws. The prohibition against intentionally killing people who pose no harm also helps explain why terrorism is wrong. Some skeptics argue that "one man's terrorist is just another man's freedom fighter." However, under just war doctrine, you can fight for freedom, but you cannot target innocent civilians. Though they are often violated, some norms exist even under the harshest international circumstances. The rudimentary sense of justice enshrined in an imperfectly obeyed international law belies the skeptics' argument that no choices exist in a situation of war.

We can therefore reject complete skepticism because some room exists for morality in international politics. Morality is about choice, and meaningful choice varies with the conditions of survival. The greater the threats to survival, the less room for moral choice. At the start of the Peloponnesian War, the Athenians argued, "Those who really deserve praise are the people who, while human enough to enjoy power, nevertheless pay more attention to justice than they are compelled to do by their situation."[18] Unfortunately, the Athenians lost sight of that wisdom later in their war, but it reminds us that situations with absolutely no choice are rare and that national security and degrees of threat are often ambiguous. Skeptics avoid hard moral choices by pretending to the contrary. To sum up in an aphorism: Humans may not live wholly by the word, but neither do they live solely by the sword.

Many writers and leaders who are realists in their descriptive analysis are also skeptics in their views about values in world politics. But not all realists are complete skeptics. Some recognize that moral obligations exist, but say that order has to come first. Peace is a moral priority, even if it is an unjust peace. The disorder of war makes justice difficult, especially in the nuclear age. The best way to preserve order is to preserve a balance of power among states. Moral crusades disrupt balances of power. For example, if the United States becomes too concerned about spreading democracy or human rights throughout the world, it may create disorder that will actually do more damage than good in the long run.

The realists have a valid argument, up to a point. International order is important, but it is a matter of degrees, and there are trade-offs between justice and order. How much order is necessary before we start worrying about justice? For example, after the 1990 Soviet crackdown in the Baltic republics in which a number of people were killed, some Americans urged a break in relations with the Soviet Union. In their view, Americans should express their values of democracy and human rights in foreign policy, even if that meant instability and the end of arms control talks. Others argued that while concerns for peace and for human rights were important, it was more important to control nuclear weapons and negotiate an arms reduction treaty. In the end, the American government went ahead with the arms negotiations, but linked the provision of economic aid to respect for human rights. Over and over in international politics, the question is not absolute order versus justice, but how to trade off choices in particular situations. The realists have a valid point of view, but they overstate it when they argue that it has to be all order before any justice.

State Moralists. State moralists argue that international politics rests on a society of states with certain rules, although those rules are not always perfectly obeyed. The most important rule is state sovereignty, which prohibits states from intervening across borders into each others' jurisdiction. The political scientist Michael Walzer, for example, argues that national boundaries have a moral significance because states represent the pooled rights of individuals who have come together for a common life. Thus respect for the sovereignty and territorial integrity of states is related to respect for individuals. Others argue more simply that respect for sovereignty is the best way to preserve order. "Good fences make good neighbors," in the words of the poet Robert Frost.

In practice, these rules of state behavior are frequently violated. In the last few decades, Vietnam invaded Cambodia, China invaded Vietnam, Tanzania invaded Uganda, Israel invaded Lebanon, the Soviet Union invaded Afghanistan, the United States invaded Grenada and Panama, Iraq invaded Iran and Kuwait, the United States and Britain invaded Iraq, and NATO bombed Serbia because of its mistreatment of ethnic Albanians in the province of Kosovo—to name just a few examples. Determining when it is appropriate to respect another state's sovereignty is a long-standing challenge. In 1979, Americans condemned the Soviet invasion of Afghanistan in strong moral terms. The Soviets responded by pointing to the Dominican Republic, where in 1965 the United States sent 25,000 troops to prevent the formation of a communist government. The intention behind the American intervention in the Dominican Republic, preventing a hostile regime from coming to power in the Caribbean, and the intention of the Soviet intervention in Afghanistan, preventing the formation of a hostile government on their border, were quite similar.

To find differences, we have to look further than intentions. In terms of the means used, very few people were killed by the U.S. intervention in the Dominican Republic, and the Americans soon withdrew. In the Afghan case, many people were killed, and the Soviet forces remained for nearly a decade. In the 1990s, some critics compared the Iraqi invasion of Kuwait with the American invasion of Panama. In December 1989, the United States sent troops to overthrow the

---

INTERVENTION

Imagine the following scene in Afghanistan in December 1979:

An Afghan communist leader came to power promoting a platform of greater independence from the Soviet Union. This worried Soviet leaders because an independent regime on their border might foment trouble throughout Central Asia (including Soviet Central Asia) and would create a dangerous precedent of a small communist neighbor escaping the Soviet Empire. Imagine the Russian general in charge of the Soviet invasion force confronting the renegade Afghan leader, whom he is about to kill, explaining why he is doing these things against the international rules of sovereignty and nonintervention. "So far as right and wrong are concerned, China and others think there is no difference between the two and if we fail to attack you, it is because we are afraid. So by conquering you, we shall increase not only the size but the security of our empire. We rule the Central Asian landmass and you are a border state, and weaker than the others. It is therefore particularly important that you should not escape."

Those words are Thucydides's Melian dialogue with the word *China* added and *Central Asia* substituted for *sea* and *border state* for *islands*. Intervention is not a new problem!

Panamanian dictator Manuel Noriega, and in August 1990, Iraq sent troops into Kuwait to overthrow the emir. Both the United States and Iraq violated the rule of nonintervention. But again there were differences in means and consequences. In Panama, the Americans put into office a government that had been duly elected but that Noriega had not permitted to take office. The Americans did not try to annex Panama. In Kuwait, the Iraqi government tried to annex the country and caused much bloodshed in the process. Such considerations do not mean that the Panama case was all right or all wrong, but as we will see in Chapter 6, problems often arise when applying simple rules of nonintervention and sovereignty.

Cosmopolitans. Cosmopolitans such as the political theorist Charles Beitz see international politics not just as a society of states, but as a society of individuals. When we speak about justice, say the cosmopolitans, we should speak about justice for individuals. They argue that realists focus too much on issues of war and peace. If realists focused on issues of distributive justice—that is, who gets what—cosmopolitans contend that realists would notice the interdependence of the global economy. Constant economic intervention across borders can sometimes have life-or-death effects. For example, it is a life-and-death matter if you are a peasant in the Philippines and your child dies of a curable disease because the local boy who went to medical school is now working in the United States for a much higher salary.

Cosmopolitans argue that national boundaries have no moral standing; they simply defend an inequality that should be abolished if we think in terms of distributive justice. Realists (who include both moral skeptics and some state moralists) reply that the danger in the cosmopolitans' approach is that it may lead to enormous disorder. Taken literally, efforts at radical redistribution of resources are likely to lead to violent conflict because people do not give up their wealth easily. A more limited cosmopolitan argument rests on the fact that people often have multiple loyalties—to families, friends, neighborhoods, and nations; perhaps to some transnational religious groups; and to the concept of common humanity. Most people are moved by pictures of starving Sudanese children or Kosovar refugees, for some common community exists beyond the national level, albeit a weaker one. We are all humans.

Cosmopolitans remind us of the distributive dimensions to international relations in which morality matters as much in peace as in war. Policies can be designed to assist basic human needs and basic human rights without destroying order. And in cases of gross abuse of human rights, cosmopolitan views have been written into international laws such as the international convention against genocide. As a result, policy makers are more conscious of moral concerns. For example, President Clinton has said that one of his worst mistakes was not to have done more to stop genocide in Rwanda in 1994, and the United States and other countries have supported African peacekeeping troops in efforts to suppress genocidal violence in the Sudanese province of Darfur.

Of the approaches to international morality, the skeptic makes a valid point about order being necessary for justice but misses the trade-offs between order and justice.

The state moralist who sees a society of states with rules against intervention illustrates an institutional approach to order but does not provide enough answers regarding when some interventions may be justified. Finally, the cosmopolitan who focuses on a society of individuals has a profound insight about common humanity but runs the risk of fomenting enormous disorder by pursuing massive redistributive policies. Most people develop a hybrid position; labels are less important than the central point that trade-offs exist among these approaches.

Because of the differences between domestic and international politics, morality is harder to apply in international politics. But just because there is a plurality of principles, it does not follow there are no principles at all. How far should we go in applying morality to international politics? The answer is to be careful, for when moral judgments determine everything, morality can lead to a sense of outrage, and outrage can lead to heightened risk. Prudence can be a virtue, particularly when the alternative is disastrous unintended consequences. After all, there are no moral questions among the incinerated. But we cannot honestly ignore morality in international politics. Each person must study events and make his or her own decisions about judgments and trade-offs. The enduring logic of international conflict does not remove the responsibility for moral choices, although it does require an understanding of the special setting that makes those choices difficult.

While the specific moral and security dilemmas of the Peloponnesian War are unique, many of the issues recur over history. As we trace the evolution of international relations, we will see again and again the tension between realism and liberalism, between skeptics and cosmopolitans, between an anarchic system of states and international organizations. We will revisit the Prisoner's Dilemma and continue to grapple with the ethical conundrums of war. We will see how different actors on the world stage have approached the crises of their time and how their goals and instruments vary. As mentioned at the outset, certain variables that characterize international politics today simply did not exist in Thucydides's day: no nuclear weapons, no United Nations, no Internet, no transnational corporations, no cartels. The study of international conflict is an inexact science combining history and theory. In weaving our way through theories and examples, we try to keep in mind both what has changed and what has remained constant so we may better understand our past and our present and better navigate the unknown shoals of the future.

Chronology: Peloponnesian Wars

490 B.C.	First Persian War
480 B.C.	Second Persian War
478 B.C.	Spartans abdicate leadership
476 B.C.	Formation of Delian League and Athenian Empire
464 B.C.	Helot revolt in Sparta
461 B.C.	Outbreak of first Peloponnesian War
445 B.C.	Thirty-Year Truce
445–434 B.C.	Ten years of peace

434 B.C.	Epidamnus and Corcyra conflicts
433 B.C.	Athens intervenes in Potidaea
432 B.C.	Spartan Assembly debates war
431 B.C.	Outbreak of second Peloponnesian War
430 B.C.	Pericles's Funeral Oration
416 B.C.	Melian dialogue
413 B.C.	Athens's defeat in Sicily
411 B.C.	Oligarchs revolt in Athens
404 B.C.	Athens defeated, forced to pull down walls

STUDY QUESTIONS

1. What role should ethical considerations play in the conduct of international relations? What role *do* they play? Can we speak meaningfully about moral duties to other nations or their populations? What are America's moral obligations in Iraq?

2. Is there a difference between moral obligations in the realms of domestic politics and international politics? On the basis of the Melian dialogue, did the Athenians act ethically? Did the Melian elders?

3. What is *realism*? How does it differ from the liberal view of world politics?

4. What does Thucydides pinpoint as the main causes of the Peloponnesian War? Which were immediate? Which were underlying?

5. What sort of theory of international relations is implicit in Thucydides's account of the war?

6. Was the Peloponnesian War inevitable? If so, why and when? If not, how and when might it have been prevented?

NOTES

1. Peter Wallensteen and Margareta Sollenberg, "Armed Conflict, 1989–2000," report no. 60, in Margareta Sollenberg ed., *States in Armed Conflict 2000* (Uppsala, Sweden: Uppsala University, Department of Peace and Conflict Research, 2001), p. 10.

2. Thomas Hobbes, *Leviathan*, ed. C. B. MacPherson (London: Penguin, 1981), p. 186.

3. *The New York World*, "From Our Dec. 13 Pages, 75 Years Ago," *International Herald Tribune*, December 13, 1985.

4. Miles Kahler, "Inventing International Relations: International Relations Theory After 1945," in Michael W. Doyle and G. John Ikenberry, eds., *New Thinking in International Relations Theory* (Boulder, CO: Westview, 1977), p. 38.

5. Emanuel Adler, "Constructivism in International Relations: Sources, Contributions, Debates and Future Directions," in Walter Carlsnaes, Thomas Risse, and Beth Simmons, eds., *Handbook of International Relations* (Thousand Oaks, CA: Sage, 2003).

6. John Maynard Keynes, *The General Theory of Employment, Interest and Money* (London: Macmillan, 1936), p. 383.

7. Sales and GNP are different measures, and this somewhat exaggerates the role of corporations. Nonetheless the comparison is interesting.

8. Robert Gilpin, *War and Change in World Politics* (Cambridge: Cambridge University Press, 1981), pp. 227–228.

9. Thucydides, *History of the Peloponnesian War*, trans. Rex Warner, ed. M. K. Finley (London: Penguin, 1972), p. 161.

10. Ibid., pp. 82–83.

11. Ibid., p. 57.

12. Ibid., p. 62.

13. Ibid., p. 48.

14. Donald Kagan, *The Outbreak of the Peloponnesian War* (Ithaca, NY: Cornell University Press, 1969), p. 354. For an alternative interpretation of the realities of Athenian expansion, see G. E. M. de Ste. Croix, *The Origins of the Peloponnesian War* (Ithaca, NY: Cornell University Press, 1972), pp. 60, 201–203.

15. Joseph S. Nye, Jr., "As China Rises, Must Others Bow?" *The Economist*, June 27, 1998, p. 23.

16. Thucydides, *History of the Peloponnesian War*, p. 55.

17. Ibid., p. 402.

18. Ibid., p. 80.

SELECTED READINGS

1. Morgenthau, Hans, *Politics Among Nations* (New York: Knopf, 1989), chap. 1.

2. Waltz, Kenneth, *Man, the State, and War* (New York: Columbia University Press, 1959), pp. 1–15.

3. Moravscik, Andrew, "Taking Preferences Seriously: A Liberal Theory of International Politics," *International Organization* 51:4 (Autumn 1997), pp. 513–553.

4. Ba, Alice, and Matthew J. Hoffmann, "Making and Remaking the World for IR 101: A Resource for Teaching Social Constructivism in Introductory Classes," *International Studies Perspectives* 4:1 (February 2003), pp. 15–33.

5. Thucydides, *History of the Peloponnesian War*, trans. Rex Warner, ed. M. K. Finley (London: Penguin, 1972), pp. 35–87, 400–408.

6. Kagan, Donald, *The Outbreak of the Peloponnesian War* (Ithaca, NY: Cornell University Press, 1969), pp. 31–56, 345–356.

FURTHER READINGS

Axelrod, Robert M., *The Evolution of Cooperation* (New York: Basic, 1984).

Bagby, Laurie, "The Use and Abuse of Thucydides," *International Organization* 48:1 (Winter 1994), pp. 131–153.

Baldwin, David, *Neorealism and Neoliberalism: The Contemporary Debate* (New York: Columbia University Press, 1993).

Beitz, Charles R., *Political Theory and International Politics* (Princeton, NJ: Princeton University Press, 1979).

Betts, Richard, "Should Strategic Studies Survive?" *World Politics* 50:1 (October 1997), pp. 7–54.

Brown, Michael, et al., *Theories of War and Peace* (Cambridge, MA: MIT Press, 1998).

Bull, Hedley, *The Anarchical Society: A Study of Order in World Politics* (New York: Columbia University Press, 1977).

Caporaso, James A., ed., "Dependence and Dependency in the Global System," special issue, *International Organization* 32:1 (Winter 1978).

Dessler, David, "Constructivism Within a Positivist Social Science," *Review of International Studies* 25 (1999).

Doyle, Michael W., Ways of War and Peace (New York: Norton, 1997).

Doyle, Michael W., and G. John Ikenberry, eds., *New Thinking in International Relations Theory* (Boulder, CO: Westview, 1997).

Elshtain, Jean Bethke, Women and War, 2nd ed., (Chicago: University of Chicago Press, 1994).

Finnemore, Martha, and Kathryn Sikkink, "Taking Stock: The Constructivist Research Program in International Relations and World Politics," *Annual Review of Political Science* 4 (June 2001), pp. 391–416.

Gaddis, John Lewis, *The Landscape of History: How Historians Map the Past* (New York: Oxford University Press, 2002).

Gilpin, Robert, *War and Change in World Politics* (Cambridge: Cambridge University Press, 1981).

Goldstein, Joshua S., War and Gender (Cambridge: Cambridge University Press, 2001).

Hinsley, F. H., Power and the Pursuit of Peace (London: Cambridge University Press, 1967).

Hoffmann, Stanley, *Duties Beyond Borders: On the Limits and Possibilities of Ethical International Politics* (Syracuse, NY: Syracuse University Press, 1981).

Jervis, Robert, "Realism, Game Theory, and Cooperation," *World Politics* 40:3 (April 1988), pp. 317–349.

Katzenstein, Peter J., ed., The Culture of National Security (New York: Columbia University Press, 1996).

Katzenstein, Peter J., Robert Keohane, and Stephen Krasner, "International Organization and the Study of World Politics," International Organization 52:4 (Fall 1998).

Keohane, Robert O., ed., Neo-Realism and Its Critics (New York: Columbia University Press, 1986).

Kissinger, Henry, Diplomacy (New York: Simon & Schuster, 1994).

Lapid, Yosef, and Friedrich Kratochwil, eds., *The Return of Culture and Identity in International Relations Theory* (Boulder, CO: Lynne Rienner, 1996).

Levy, Jack S., War in the Modern Great Power System, 1495–1975 (Lexington: University Press of Kentucky, 1983).

Mercer, Jonathan, "Anarchy and Identity," International Organization 49:2 (Spring 1995), pp. 229–252.

Oneal, John, and Bruce Russett, "The Classical Liberals Were Right: Democracy, Interdependence, and Conflict, 1950–1985," International Studies Quarterly 41 (1997), pp. 267–293.

Rawls, John, *The Law of Peoples* (Cambridge, MA: Harvard University Press, 1999).

Rosecrance, Richard N., The Rise of the Trading State: Commerce and Conquest in the Modern World (New York: Basic, 1986).

Rosenau, James N., Turbulence in World Politics: A Theory of Change and Continuity (Princeton, NJ: Princeton University Press, 1990).

Ruggie, John G., "What Makes the World Hang Together: Neo-Utilitarianism and the Social Constructivist Challenge," *International Organization* 52:4 (1998), pp. 855–885.

Spruyt, Hendrik, *The Sovereign State and Its Competitors* (Princeton, NJ: Princeton University Press, 1994).

Ticknor, Ann J., *Gender in International Relations* (New York: Columbia University Press, 1992).

Van Evera, Stephen, *The Causes of War* (Ithaca, NY: Cornell University Press, 1999).

Waever, Ole, "The Sociology of a Not-So-International Discipline: American and European Developments in International Relations," *International Organization* 52:4 (1998), pp. 687–727.

Waltz, Kenneth N., *Theory of International Politics* (Reading, MA: Addison-Wesley, 1979).

Walzer, Michael, *Just and Unjust Wars* (New York: Basic, 1977), pts. 1 and 2.

Welch, David A., "Why IR Theorists Should Stop Reading Thucydides," *Review of International Studies* (July 2003), pp. 301–319.

Wendt, Alexander, "Anarchy Is What States Make of It: The Social Construction of Power Politics," *International Organization* 46:2 (Spring 1992), pp. 391–427.

Zacher, Mark, "The Territorial Integrity Norm," *International Organization* 55:2 (2001).

Origins of the Great Twentieth-Century Conflicts

Otto von Bismarck

INTERNATIONAL SYSTEMS AND LEVELS OF CAUSATION

War is often explained in terms of international systems, but what is an "international system"? According to the dictionary, a *system* is a set of interrelated units. Many domestic political systems are easy to identify because of clear institutional referents: the presidency, Congress, Parliament, and so forth. International political systems are less centralized and less tangible. Without the United Nations, an international system would still exist. The international system consists not only of states. The international political system is the *pattern of relationships* among the states.

Do not be misled, however, by the institutional concreteness of domestic political systems. They also include intangible aspects such as public attitudes, the role of the press, or some of the unwritten conventions of constitutions. The important point about any system, however, is that the whole pattern is greater than the sum of the parts, that is, the building blocks we defined in Chapter 1 as actors, instruments, and goals. Systems can create consequences not intended by any of their constituent actors. For example, think of the market system in economics. Every business firm in a perfect market tries to maximize its profits, but the market system produces competition that reduces profits to the break-even point, thereby benefiting the consumer. The businessperson does not set out to benefit the consumer, but individual firms' pattern of behavior in a perfect market leads to that effect. In other words, the system produces the consequences, which may be quite different from the intention of the actors in the system.

The international political system can similarly lead to effects the actors did not originally intend. For example, in 1917 when the Bolsheviks came to power in Russia, they regarded the whole system of interstate diplomacy that had preceded World War I as bourgeois nonsense. They intended to sweep away the interstate system and hoped that revolutions would unite all the workers of the world and abolish borders. Transnational proletarian solidarity would replace the interstate system. Indeed, when Leon Trotsky took charge of the Russian Foreign Ministry, he said his intent was to issue some revolutionary proclamations to the peoples of the world and then "close up the joint." But the Bolsheviks found that their actions were soon affected by the nature of the interstate system. In 1922, the new communist state signed the Treaty of Rapallo with Germany. It was an alliance of the outcasts, the countries that were not accepted in the post–World War I diplomatic world. And in 1939, Josef Stalin entered a pact with his ideological archenemy, Adolf Hitler, in order to turn Hitler westward. Soviet behavior, despite Trotsky's initial proclamations and illusions, soon became similar to that of other actors in the international system.

The distribution of power among states in an international system helps us make predictions about certain aspects of states' behavior. The tradition of *geopolitics* holds that location and proximity will tell a great deal about how states will behave. Because neighbors have more contact and points of potential friction, it is not surprising that half of the military conflicts between 1816 and 1992 began between neighbors.[1] A state that feels threatened by its neighbor is likely to act in accord with the old adage that "the enemy of my enemy is my friend." This pattern has always been found in anarchic systems. For example, three centuries before Christ's birth, the Indian writer Kautilya pointed out that the states of the Indian subcontinent tended to ally with distant states to protect themselves against their neighbors, thus producing a checkerboard pattern of alliances. Machiavelli noted the same behavior among the city-states in fifteenth-century Italy. In the early 1960s, as West African states emerged from colonial rule, there was a great deal of talk about African solidarity, but the new states soon began to produce a checkerboard pattern of alliances similar to what Kautilya described in ancient India. Ghana, Guinea, and Mali were ideologically radical while Senegal, Ivory Coast, and Nigeria were relatively conservative, but they were also balancing against the strength of their neighbors. Another example was the pattern that developed in East Asia after the Vietnam War. If the Soviet Union were colored black, China would be red, Vietnam black, and Cambodia red. A perfect checkerboard pattern developed. Ironically, the United States entered the Vietnam War because policy makers believed in a domino theory, according to which one state would fall to communism, leading another state to fall, and so forth. With more foresight, the United States should have realized that the game in East Asia was more like checkers than dominoes, and the United States might have stayed out. The checkerboard pattern based on "the enemy of my enemy is my friend" is an old tradition of geopolitics that helps us make useful predictions in an anarchic situation.

Levels of Analysis

Systems are not the only way of explaining what happens in international politics. In *Man, the State, and War*, Kenneth Waltz distinguishes three levels of causation for war, which he calls "images": the *individual,* the *state,* and the *international system*.

Explanations at the level of the individual are rarely sufficient because the very nature of international politics implies *states* rather than individuals. Too much emphasis on an individual's intentions may blind us to the unintended consequences of individual acts caused by the larger systems in which individuals operate. Taking the African example, if we focused primarily on the sincerity of African leaders' intentions for pan-African unity, such as that of the first president of Tanzania, Julius K. Nyerere, we would miss the importance of the effect of the anarchic structure on those new African states.

This is not to say that individuals never matter. Quite the contrary. Pericles made a difference in the Peloponnesian War. In 1991, Iraq's Saddam Hussein was a critical factor in the Gulf War, as was George W. Bush with the 2003 Iraq War. In the 1962 Cuban missile crisis, John F. Kennedy and Nikita Khrushchev faced the possibility of nuclear war and the ultimate decision was in their hands. But why they found themselves in that incredible position cannot be explained at the level of individuals. Something in the structure of the situation brought them to that point. Similarly, knowing something about the personality of Kaiser Wilhelm II or Hitler is necessary to an understanding of the causes of World War I and World War II, but it is not a sufficient explanation. As we see later, it made a difference that Kaiser Wilhelm fired his chancellor, Otto von Bismarck, in 1890, but that does not mean World War I was brought about primarily by Kaiser Wilhelm.

Another version of Waltz's first image looks for explanations not in the particularities of individuals, but in their common characteristics, the "human nature"

SYSTEMS AND WAR

After the last war, the international system developed two rigid camps. This bipolarity led to a loss of flexibility and heightened insecurity. One of the new alliances developed around an authoritarian land-based power, the other around a democratic power with an expansive commerce and culture that held naval supremacy. Each side feared that the other would achieve a decisive advantage in the conflict that both expected. Ironically, it was civil conflict in a small, weak state threatening a marginal change in the alliances that heightened the sense of threat in both alliances and actually triggered the war.

   Which war does this describe: the Peloponnesian War, World War I, or the Cold War?

---

common to all individuals. For example, we could take a Calvinist view of international politics and assign the ultimate cause of war to the evil that lies within each of us. That would explain war as the result of an imperfection in human nature. But such an explanation does not tell us why some evil leaders go to war and others do not, or why some good leaders go to war and others do not. Explanation at the level of human nature cannot give the answer. Such a theory *overpredicts*, meaning that while it accounts for some things, it also accounts for too much. By not discriminating, it is not explaining. The hands of a stopped clock tell the correct time twice a day, but most of the time they mislead us.

   Overpredicting also plagues some efforts to explain international politics at the second level of analysis, the nature of the state or society. There is a similar question—if certain types of societies cause war, then why do some "bad" societies or "bad" states not go to war? And why do some good societies or good states go to war? Insert your favorite description for "good" and "bad"—"democratic," "communist," "capitalist," or whatever. For example, after World War I there was a great deal of enthusiasm for the belief that the victory of the democracies would mean less chance of war. But clearly democracies can go to war, and often do. After all, Athens was a democracy. Marxist theorists argued that war would be abolished when all states were communist, but obviously there have been military clashes among communist countries—witness China versus the Soviet Union or Vietnam versus Cambodia. Thus the nature of the society, democratic or capitalist or communist, is not a sufficient predictor of how likely it is to go to war.

   One proposition (which we discuss later) suggests that if *all* countries were democratic, there would be less war. In fact, cases in which liberal democracies have fought against other liberal democracies are difficult to find, although democracies have fought against authoritarian states in many situations. The cause of this empirical finding and whether it will continue to hold in the future is not clear, but it suggests something interesting to investigate at this second level of analysis.

   Interesting explanations often involve an interplay between the second (the state or society) and third (the international system) levels of analysis. But which is more important, the system or the nature of the states in the system? A system-level analysis is explanation from the outside in—looking at the way the overall system constrains state action. The second level is explanation from the inside out— explaining outcomes by what is happening inside the states.

Because we often need information about both levels of analysis, where should we start? A good rule of thumb is to start with the simplest approach, for if a simple explanation is adequate, it is preferable. This is called *the rule of parsimony* or *Occam's razor*, after the fourteenth-century philosopher William of Occam, who argued that good explanations shave away unnecessary detail. *Parsimony*—the ability to explain a lot with a little—is only one of the criteria by which we judge the adequacy of theories. We are also interested in the *range* of a theory (how much behavior it covers) and its *explanatory* fit (how many loose ends or anomalies it accounts for). Nonetheless, parsimony suggests a place to start. Because systemic explanations tend to be the simplest, they provide a good starting point. If they prove to be inadequate, then we can look at the units of the system and add complexity until a reasonable fit is obtained.

Systems: Structure and Process

How simple or complicated should a systemic explanation be? Some neorealists, such as Kenneth Waltz, argue for extreme parsimony and focus only on structure. Liberals and constructivists argue that Waltz's concept of system is so spare it explains very little. We can understand this dispute by distinguishing between two aspects of systems: structure and process. The *structure* of a system refers to its distribution of power, and the *process* refers to patterns and types of interaction among its units. Structure and process obviously affect each other, and may vary with the length of the period we examine, but structure is more basic and changes more slowly than process.

Economists characterize the structure of markets by the concentration of sellers' power. A monopoly has one big seller, a duopoly two big sellers, and an oligopoly several big sellers; in a perfect market selling power is widely dispersed. Similarly, political scientists describe as *unipolar* the structure of an international system with one preponderant power. In *bipolar* systems, two major centers of power, either two large countries or two tightly knit alliance systems, dominate politics. *Multipolar* structures have three or more centers of power, and where there is a large number of roughly equal countries, we speak of a dispersed distribution of power.

To return to the earlier economic example, the firms that tried to maximize profits in a perfect market found themselves benefiting the consumer, but that result depended on the structure of the market system. If the market were a monopoly or oligopoly, the result would be quite different. The large firm could increase profits by restricting production in order to raise prices. Thus when the structure of the system is known, economists are better able to predict behavior and who will benefit.

Similarly, political analysts look at the structure of the international system to predict behavior of states and their propensity toward war. Unipolar systems tend to erode as states try to preserve their independence by balancing against the preponderant power—often referred to as the *hegemon*—or a rising state eventually challenges the leader. In multipolar or dispersed-power systems, states form alliances to balance power, but alliances are flexible. Wars may occur, but they will be relatively limited in scope. In bipolar systems, alliances become more rigid, which in turn contributes to the probability of a large conflict, perhaps even a global war. Some analysts say that "bipolar systems either erode or explode." This happened in the Peloponnesian War when Athens and Sparta tightened their grips on their respective alliances. It was also true before 1914, when the multipolar European balance of power gradually consolidated into two strong alliance systems that lost their flexibility. But predictions about war based on multipolarity versus bipolarity encountered a major anomaly after 1945. During the Cold War the world was bipolar with two big players, the United States and its allies and the Soviet Union and its allies, yet no overall central war occurred for more than four decades before the system eroded with the decline of the Soviet Union. Some people say nuclear weapons made the prospect of global war too awful. Thus the structure of the international system offers a rough explanation, but this does not explain enough all by itself.

We learn more if we look beyond a system's structure and examine its process, the regular pattern of interactions among the states. The distinction between structure and process at any given time can be illustrated by the metaphor of a poker game. The *structure* of a poker game is in the distribution of power, that is, how many chips the players have and how many high cards they are dealt. The *process* is how the game is played and the types of interactions among the players. (How are the rules created and understood? Are the players good bluffers? Do they obey the rules? If players cheat, are they likely to get caught?) For example, allowing the players in Prisoner's Dilemma games to communicate with one another alters the nature of the game. So, too, when states communicate with one another and reach mutually beneficial agreements or create well-understood norms and institutions, they add to the repertoire of state strategies and can thus alter political outcomes. The process of an international system is determined by three elements: (1) its structure (bipolar structures tend to produce less flexible processes), (2) the cultural and institutional context that surrounds the structure and determines the incentives and capabilities states have for cooperation, and (3) whether the states are revolutionary or moderate in their goals and instruments.

Revolutionary and Moderate Goals and Instruments

How do state goals affect international processes? As constructivist theories point out, most systems exist in a cultural context that involves some basic rules or practices that define appropriate behavior. States can challenge those rules and practices or they can accept them. An international system may have either a stable or revolutionary process, depending on the identity and goals of the major states. In the eighteenth century, for example, the basic rule of the game was the legitimacy of the monarchical state—the divine right of rulers—and maintaining a balance of power among these monarchies. The 1713 Treaty of Utrecht referred explicitly to the importance of the balance of power. There were many small wars, but few large ones disrupted the system. Consider Frederick the Great of Prussia and the way he treated his neighbor, Maria Theresa (1717–1780) of Austria. In 1740, Frederick decided he wanted Silesia, a province belonging to Maria Theresa. Frederick had no great revolutionary cause, only a simple goal of aggrandizement. He did not try to incite a popular revolution against Maria Theresa by appealing to the people in Silesia to overthrow the German-speaking autocrats of Vienna. After all, Frederick was a German-speaking autocrat in Berlin. He took Silesia because he wanted it and was careful not to do anything else that would damage Austria or the basic principle of monarchical legitimacy.

Compare that to the French Revolution (1789–1799) half a century later, when the prevailing view in France was that all monarchs should be sent to the gallows or the guillotine and that power should emanate from the people. Napoleon spread this revolutionary idea of popular sovereignty throughout Europe, and the Napoleonic Wars (1799–1815) posed an enormous challenge to both the rules of the game and the balance of power. The moderate process and stable balance of the system in the middle of the century changed to a revolutionary process and unstable balance at the end of the century. We refer to changes like the French Revolution as *exogenous* to a structural theory because they cannot be explained inside the theory. This is an example of how a realist structural theory can be supplemented by constructivist work.

In addition to changing their goals, states can also change their means. The process of a system is also affected by the nature of the instruments that states use. Different means can have stabilizing or destabilizing effects. Some instruments change because of technology. For example, the development of new weapons such as the machine gun made World War I a particularly bloody encounter. Means can also change because of new social organization. In the eighteenth century, Frederick the Great (1740–1786) not only had limited goals, he was also limited by his means. He had a mercenary army with limited loyalties and poor logistics. Eighteenth-century armies generally campaigned in the summer, when food was readily available or when the treasury had accumulated enough gold to pay soldiers who were often from the fringes of society. When the food or the gold ran out, the soldiers deserted. The French Revolution changed the social organization of war to what the French called the *levée en masse*, or what we call the draft. As constructivists point out, soldiers' sense of identity changed as people came to understand themselves as citizens rallied to the concept of a motherland, and there was a feeling that all should participate. War was no longer a matter between a few thousand mercenaries who campaigned far away; war now involved everyone. This large-scale involvement and mass support overwhelmed the old mercenary infantries. The change in the means available to states also helped change the process of the eighteenth-century international system.

Statesmen regularly judged the European balance to be satisfactory or unsatisfactory on the basis of factors that had little or nothing directly to do with power and its distribution—e.g., the rank and status a state enjoyed, its honor and prestige, whether it was considered worthy of alliance, whether it was allowed a voice in international questions, etc. It helps explain how crises could and did arise when the balance of power was not affected or threatened, but the balance of satisfactions was. It shows how devices other than power-political ones—international laws, Concert practices, alliances used as devices for restraining one's ally—were more common and more useful in promoting and preserving the European equilibrium than power-political ones such as rival alliances or blocking coalitions.

—*Paul Schroeder, "The Nineteenth Century System"*[2]

The Structure and Process of the Nineteenth-Century System

These distinctions help us understand the nineteenth-century origins of the great twentieth-century conflicts. By the rule of parsimony, we should first seek a simple structural explanation such as neorealists offer to explain what happened over the course of the nineteenth century.

At the beginning of the century Napoleon tried to create French hegemony over Europe, but he failed. His efforts united the other countries in a coalition that eventually defeated France. Had he succeeded, he would have changed the system to a unipolar structure. But after Napoleon's defeat in 1815 the Congress of Vienna restored the old multipolar order, with five major powers balancing each other: Britain, Russia, France, Prussia, and Austria. Revolutionary France changed the process of the system for 20 years and threatened to change its structure, but in the end, France failed to make the structure of the European interstate system unipolar.

For realists who emphasize structure, the big change came with the unification of Germany in 1870. The nineteenth-century system remained multipolar, but there was a major change in the distribution of power in central Europe. Before that, Germany consisted of 37 states and had been an arena of international politics in which others intervened. After 1870, Germany became a united actor. Furthermore, it was located right in the center of Europe, which had tremendous geopolitical consequences. From a structural perspective, a united Germany was potentially either too strong or too weak. If Germany was strong enough to defend itself against both Russia and France at the same time, it was also strong enough to defeat either the Russians or the French alone. And if Germany was not strong enough to defeat Russia and France simultaneously, it might look weak enough to invite the Russians and the French to join together to invade it.

But the newly unified German state in the center of Europe did not produce instability because of its brilliant first chancellor, Otto von Bismarck. From 1870 to

1890, Bismarck was such an agile diplomat that he allayed the sense of threat on the part of his neighbors, thus delaying the effects of this major structural change on the system's political process. But Bismarck's successors were not so adept. From 1890 on, the alliance systems of Europe grew more rigid, with one alliance centered on Germany and another on Russia and France. The bipolarity of alliances gradually grew more and more rigid and finally exploded in 1914.

This structural explanation of nineteenth-century change has a strong core of truth, but is not an adequate explanation by itself. It does not account for the role of an individual such as Bismarck, and it does not tell us why the other European states allowed Germany to unify in the first place. Why didn't Germany's neighbors try to prevent the unification? If Britain and France could see this challenger arising, why didn't they stop it at the time? Perceptions and domestic politics must be invoked to answer those questions. The structural explanation says little about why the bipolarity of alliances took 30 years to develop, and does not allow for the possibly crucial role of individual leadership. If the kaiser had not fired Bismarck in 1890, or if Bismarck's successors had kept his treasured alliance with Russia (which appealed to shared ideological interests in monarchical autocracy), perhaps the evolving bipolarity could have been avoided. If Bismarck's successors had not challenged Britain by launching a naval arms race, perhaps Britain's role in the conflict could have been avoided. Although the structural explanation of changes in the nineteenth-century system has much to offer, it is too narrowly deterministic. It removes the role of human choice and makes World War I look inevitable in 1870. It provides a start, but it does not tell us enough.

As constructivists remind us, we also need to take into account the changes in European culture and ideas that influenced the process, or patterns of relations, in the nineteenth-century system. There we find a change in states' goals and instruments that altered the incentives for cooperation. The ideology of democratization and nationalism grew stronger over the course of the nineteenth century and had a major effect on states' goals. The state and the ruler were no longer the same. Louis XIV's (1638–1715) famous saying, *"L'état c'est moi"* ("I am the state") no longer held. In the eighteenth century, Frederick behaved in Prussia much as he wanted. He was not constrained by elected ministers or parliamentarians. Democratization added broader domestic influences to the complexity of international politics. Napoleon carried the new ideas across Europe, challenging and fomenting nationalism in other countries. The Napoleonic Wars may have failed to change the *structure* of European politics, but they certainly caused profound changes in the *process*. The Austrian Prince Metternich (1773–1858) and his counterparts succeeded in restoring the old order at the Congress of Vienna in 1815, but beneath a surface of stability were the volcanic forces of nationalism and democracy that erupted in the revolutions of 1848.

As the century progressed, both peoples and leaders began to see themselves differently. The nationalist challenge to the legitimacy of dynastic rulers led to some strange alliances that defied the classical balance of power. For example, in 1866, France failed to support Austria when it was attacked by Prussia, a long-term error from the structural point of view. France was opposed to Austrian repression of nationalism in the part of Italy that Austria occupied. Bismarck played on the nationalistic views of other German states in unifying Germany under Prussian leadership, but nationalism became a restraint on what could be done later. When Bismarck took Alsace-Lorraine from France in the war of 1870, he created nationalist resentment in France that prevented France and Germany from becoming potential alliance partners in the future. As constructivist approaches point out, the new ideologies changed states' goals and made the process of international politics less moderate over the course of the nineteenth century.

There were also changes in the means. The application of new industrial technology to military purposes produced massive yet inflexible instruments of war. Railway mobilization schedules, the ability to get large numbers of troops in one place at one time, began to play a key role in war by the middle of the century. Near the end, machine guns and trenches made a mockery of the idea of short, sharp, limited wars that Bismarck used so successfully in the 1860s. Both structure and process help explain the changes in the nineteenth-century international system in Europe and the origins of World War I. We started with neorealist structure because it is simpler, but found that it provided only a partial explanation. Constructivist attention to process reminds us not to be blind to social change.

A Modern Sequel

The so-called German problem from the nineteenth century reemerged in debates when East and West Germany were reunified in 1990. At first, Foreign Minister Eduard Shevardnadze of the Soviet Union argued that the reunification of Germany would profoundly destabilize the balance of power in Europe. Leaders once again asked, "How many German-speaking states are consistent with stability in Europe?" Over time, that question has had different answers. As we have seen, the Congress of Vienna in 1815 included 37 German-speaking states. Bismarck felt there should be two, not one. He did not want the Austrians included in his new German empire because he feared they would dilute Prussian control of the new state. Hitler had a different answer: one, which would be the center of a world empire, thus leading to World War II. In 1945, the victorious Allies eventually decided on three: East, West, and Austria. And there is always the quip attributed to a Frenchman at the end of World War II: When asked how many Germanys there should be, he replied, "I love Germany so much that the more, the better."

The decline of Soviet power in Eastern Europe in the late 1980s ended the bipolar structure of postwar politics and made possible Germany's reunification. But reunification created new anxieties about the union of 80 million people with Europe's largest economy located in the heart of the continent. Would Germans search for a new role? Would they again cast about, turn eastward, and then westward? Would they be drawn into the countries to their east where German influence had always been strong? John Mearsheimer, a University of Chicago political scientist, said the answer was "back to the future." He relied on structural realist analysis to reach pessimistic conclusions that the future will be like the past because the structure of the situation is similar to the past.

The Berlin Wall coming down, 1989

But things have changed in three ways. At the structural level, the United States is involved in Europe and the United States is nearly four times the size of the reunified Germany. Structuralists worry that the Americans will not stay involved. With the Cold War over, at some point the Americans may turn isolationist and go home. But there are important nonstructural changes as well. The process of international politics in Europe has been transformed by the development of new institutions. The European Union unites Germany and other European states in a way they were never tied together before. A third change is not at the system level, but at the domestic level. Germany's domestic politics represent a half century of democracy, and changes in popular values have transformed a warfare state into a welfare state. The Germany that caused trouble in the heart of Europe in 1870, 1914, and 1939 was not democratic. Which of these approaches, structural or process or domestic, will best predict the future of Europe? We should pay attention to all three, but thus far predictions based on process and domestic change seemed to have fared best.

Domestic Politics and Foreign Policy

Neorealism, which rests very heavily on the systemic level of analysis, says that states act similarly because of the international system. A state's position in the system makes it act in a certain way, and states with similar positions act similarly.

Large states act in one way and small states in another. But this is not enough. Because a parsimonious system level of analysis is often inadequate, we must look at what happens inside the units in the system. States are not black boxes. Domestic politics matters. After all, the Peloponnesian War began with a domestic conflict between the oligarchs and the democrats in Epidamnus. The domestic politics of Germany and the Austro-Hungarian Empire played significant roles in the onset of World War I. To understand the end of the Cold War, we must look inside the Soviet Union at the failure of its centrally planned economy. It is easy to find examples in which domestic politics mattered, but can we generalize about them? After we have said that domestic politics is important, is there anything else to say?

Two major theories, Marxism and liberalism, rest heavily on the second level of analysis and the proposition that states will act similarly if they have similar domestic societies. To predict foreign policy, these theories look at the internal organization of the state. Marxists argue that the source of war is capitalism. In Lenin's view, monopoly capital requires war: "Inter-imperialist alliances are inevitably nothing more than a truce in the periods between wars."3 War can be explained by the nature of capitalist society. As we will see later, Marxism did not do a very good job of explaining the onset of World War I. Moreover, it does not fit the experience of the second half of the twentieth century. Communist states, such as the Soviet Union, China, and Vietnam, were involved in military clashes with each other, while the major capitalist states in Europe, North America, and Japan maintained peaceful relations. The arguments that capitalism causes war do not stand up in historical experience.

Classical liberalism, the philosophy that dominated much of British and American thought in the nineteenth century, came to the opposite conclusion: Capitalist states tend to be peaceful because war is bad for business. One strand of classical liberalism was represented by free traders such as Richard Cobden (1804–1865), who led the successful fight to repeal England's Corn Laws, protectionist measures that had regulated Britain's international grain trade for 500 years. Like others of the Manchester School of British economists, he believed that it was better to trade and to prosper than to go to war. If we are interested in getting richer and improving the welfare of citizens, asserted Cobden, then peace is best. In 1840 he expressed the classical view, saying "We can keep the world from actual war, and I trust that the world will do that through trade."4

The liberal view was very powerful on the eve of World War I. A number of books, including a classic by Norman Angell, *The Great Illusion* (1910), said that war had become too expensive. To illustrate the optimism of classical liberalism on the eve of World War I, we can look at the philanthropists of that era. Andrew Carnegie, the steel magnate, established the Carnegie Endowment for International Peace in 1910. Carnegie worried about what would happen to the money he had given to this foundation after lasting peace broke out, so he put a provision in his will to cover this possibility. Edward Ginn, a Boston publisher, did not want Carnegie to get all the credit for the forthcoming permanent peace, so he set up the World Peace Foundation devoted to the same cause. Ginn also worried about what to do with the rest of the money after peace was firmly established, so he designated it for low-cost housing for young working women.

This liberal outlook was severely discredited by World War I. Even though bankers and aristocrats had frequent contact across borders, and labor also had transnational contacts, none of this helped stop the European states from going to war with each other. Statistical analysis has found no strong correlation between states' involvement in war and whether they are capitalist or democratic. The classical Marxist and liberal views are opposites in their view of the relationship between war and capitalism, but they are similar in locating the causes of war in domestic politics, and especially in the nature of the economic system.

Liberalism Revived

The two world wars and the failure of collective security in the interwar period discredited liberal theories. Most writing about international politics in the United States after World War II was strongly realist in flavor. However, as transnational economic interdependence increased, the late 1960s and 1970s saw a revival of interest in liberal theories. There are three strands of this liberal thinking: economic, social, and political. The political strand has two parts, one relating to institutions and the other to democracy.

The economic strand focuses heavily on trade. Liberals argue that trade is important, not because it prevents states from going to war, but because it may lead states to define their interests in a way that makes war less important to them. Trade offers states a way to transform their position through economic growth rather than through military conquest. Richard Rosecrance points to the example of Japan. In the 1930s, Japan thought the only way to gain access to markets was to create a "Greater East Asia Co-Prosperity Sphere," which in turn required conquering its neighbors and requiring them to trade. Already in 1939, Eugene Staley, a Chicago economist, argued that part of Japan's behavior in the 1930s could be explained by economic protectionism at the time. Staley believed that when economic walls are erected along political boundaries, possession of territory is made to coincide with economic opportunity. A better solution for avoiding war is to pursue economic growth in an open trading system without military conquest. In contrast to the 1930s, Japan today has successfully transformed its position in the world through trade. Japan's share of the world product went from about 5 percent in 1960 to about 12 percent today, making it the second largest national economy in the world (measured by official exchange rates).

Realists reply that Japan was able to accomplish this amazing economic growth because somebody else was providing for its security. Specifically, Japan relied on the United States for security against its large nuclear neighbors, the Soviet Union and China. Some realists predicted that, with the Soviet Union gone, the United States would withdraw its security presence in East Asia and raise barriers against Japanese trade. Japan would remilitarize, and eventually there would be conflict between Japan and the United States as predicted by theories of hegemonic transition.

On the other hand, liberals replied that modern Japan is a very different domestic society from the Japan of the 1930s. It is nonmilitarist, partly because of economic opportunities. The most attractive career opportunities in Japan are in business, not in the military. Liberals argue that the realists are not paying enough attention to domestic politics and the way that Japan has changed as a result of economic opportunities. Whatever the outcome, the liberal economic argument says trade may not prevent war, but it does lead to changes in how states see their opportunities, which in turn may lead to a social structure that is less inclined to war.

The second form of liberalism is social. It argues that person-to-person contacts reduce conflict by promoting understanding. Such transnational contacts occur at many levels, including through students, businesspeople, and tourists. Such contacts make others seem less foreign and less hateful. That, in turn, leads to a lower likelihood of conflict. The evidence for this view is mixed. After all, bankers, aristocrats, and labor union officials had broad contacts in 1914, but that did not stop them from killing one another once they put on khaki uniforms. Obviously, the idea that social contact breeds understanding and prevents war is far too simple. Nonetheless, it may make a modest contribution to understanding. Western Europe today is very different from 1914. There are constant contacts across international borders in Europe, and textbook editors try to treat other nationalities fairly. The images of the other peoples of Europe are very different from the images of 1914. Public-opinion polls show that a sense of European identity coexists with a sense of national identity. Transnational society affects what people in a democracy want from their foreign policy. It is worth noting how France responded to the reunification of Germany in 1990. A residue of uncertainty and anxiety remained among the foreign policy experts, but public-opinion polls showed that most French people welcomed German unification. Such attitudes were a sharp contrast to those of August 1914.

The third form of liberalism emphasizes the role of institutions; this strand is often labeled "neoliberalism." Why do international institutions matter? According to the Princeton political scientist Robert O. Keohane, they provide information and a framework that shapes expectations. They allow people to believe there is not going to be a conflict. They lengthen the shadow of the future and reduce the acuteness of the security dilemma. Institutions reduce the effect of the

A MODERN LIBERAL VIEW

What is interesting and different about the world since 1945 is that a peaceful trading strategy is enjoying much more efficacy than ever before. Through mechanisms of industrial-technological development and international trade, nations can transform their positions in international politics, and they can do so while other states also benefit from the enhanced trade and growth that economic cooperation makes possible.

—*Richard Rosecrance, The Rise of the Trading State*[5]

anarchy that the realists assume. Hobbes saw international politics as a state of war. He was careful to say that a state of war does not mean constant fighting, but a propensity to war, just as cloudy weather means a likelihood of rain. In the same sense, a state of peace means a propensity toward peace, and that people can develop peaceful expectations when anarchy is limited and stabilized by international institutions.

Institutions stabilize expectations in four ways. First, they provide a sense of continuity; for example, most Western Europeans expect the European Union to last. It is likely to be there tomorrow. At the end of the Cold War, many Eastern European governments agreed and made plans to join the European Union. That affected their behavior even before they eventually joined in 2004. Second, institutions provide an opportunity for reciprocity. If the French get a little bit more today, the Italians might get a little more tomorrow. There is less need to worry about each transaction because over time it will likely balance out. Third, institutions provide a flow of information. Who is doing what? Are the Italians actually obeying the rules passed by the European Union? Is the flow of trade roughly equal? The institutions of the union provide information on how it is all working out. Finally, institutions provide ways to resolve conflicts. In the European Union, bargaining goes on within the Council of Ministers and in the European Commission, and there is also a European court of justice. Thus institutions create a climate in which expectations of stable peace develop.

Classical liberals expect "peace breaking out all over"; today's liberals look for *islands* of peace where institutions and stable expectations have developed. The political scientist Karl Deutsch called such areas "pluralistic security communities" in which war between countries became so unthinkable that stable expectations of peace developed. Institutions helped reinforce such expectations. The Scandinavian countries, for example, once fought each other bitterly, and the United States fought Britain, Canada, and Mexico. Today such actions are unthinkable. The advanced industrial countries seem to have a propensity for peace, and institutions such as the European Union, the North American Free Trade Agreement (NAFTA), and the Organization of American States create a culture in which peace is expected and provide forums for negotiation. Expectations of stability can provide a way to escape the Prisoner's Dilemma situations that realists assume. They lengthen and strengthen the shadow of the future.

Some realists expect the security dilemma to reemerge in Europe despite the liberal institutions of the European Union (EU). After the high hopes that greeted European integration in 1992, some opposition arose to further unity, particularly in disputes over the single European currency, the euro, which came into use in 2002. Countries such as Great Britain feared that ceding further power to the government of the European Union would jeopardize the autonomy and prosperity of the individual nations. Efforts in 2003 and 2004 to develop a new European constitution proved difficult, and in 2005 voters in France and the Netherlands refused to ratify it. At the same time, Britain and others worried that if they opted out of the European Union entirely, countries such as Germany, France, and Italy that opted in would gain a competitive edge. Despite such obstacles to further integration, the former communist countries of central Europe were attracted to join. While the European Union was not becoming a superstate, its institutions helped transform relations between European states.

Liberal Democracy and War

Liberals argue that realists pay insufficient attention to the fourth strand of liberalism: democratic values. Germany today is a different country than the Germany of 1870, 1914, or 1939. It has experienced a half century of democracy, with parties and governments changing peacefully. Public-opinion polls show that the German people do not seek an expansive international role. Thus liberals are skeptical of realist predictions that fail to account for the effects of democracy.

Is there a relationship between domestic democracy and a state's propensity to go to war? The issue is disputed. At a conference sponsored by the Institute of Peace in Washington in 1990, two former officials of the Reagan administration gave diametrically opposed views. Carl Gershman, president of the National Endowment for Democracy, argued, "It should be self-evident that a society organized democratically will behave more peacefully in its foreign relations." Eugene Rostow, former director of the Arms Control and Disarmament Agency, replied, "The notion that liberal democratic states do not go to war is the latest in a long series of myths which idealistic people have sought to save them from war."[6]

Absolute rulers can easily commit their states to war, as did Frederick the Great when he wanted Silesia in 1740 or Saddam Hussein when he invaded Kuwait in 1990. As Immanuel Kant and other classical liberals pointed out, in a democracy the people can vote against war. But the fact that a country is democratic does not mean its people will always vote against war. As we have seen statistically, democracies seem to be involved in wars as often as other countries. Democratic electorates have often voted for war. In ancient Greece, Pericles roused the people of Athens to go to war; in 1898, the American electorate dragged a reluctant President McKinley into the Spanish-American War. In 2003, opinion polls and a congressional vote supported President Bush's calls for war against Iraq, though public opinion later soured as the conflict dragged on.

Michael Doyle, a political scientist at Columbia, has pointed to a more limited proposition that can be derived from Kant and classical liberalism; namely, the idea that liberal democracies do not fight *other liberal democracies*. The fact that two democratic states do not fight each other is a correlation, and some correlations involve spurious causation. Fires and the presence of fire engines are highly correlated, but we do not suspect fire engines of causing fires. One possible source of spurious causation is that democratic countries tend to be rich countries, rich countries tend to be involved with trade, and according to trade liberalism, they are not likely to fight each other. But that dismissal does not fit with the fact that rich countries have often fought each other—witness the two world wars. Liberals suggest that the cause behind the correlation is a question of legitimacy. Maybe people in democracies think it is wrong to fight other democracies because there is something wrong

DEMOCRACY AND PEACE

A coalition for democracy—it's good for America. Democracies, after all, are more likely to be stable, less likely to wage war. They strengthen civil society. They can provide people with the economic opportunities to build their own homes, not to flee their borders. Our efforts to help build democracies will make us all more secure, more prosperous, and more successful as we try to make this era of terrific change our friend and not our enemy.

—*President William J. Clinton, Remarks to the 49th Session*
of the UN General Assembly, September 26, 1994

The survival of liberty in our land increasingly depends on the success of liberty in other lands. The best hope for peace in our world is the expansion of freedom in all the world. America's vital interests and our deepest beliefs are now one. . . . So it is the policy of the United States to seek and support the growth of democratic movements and institutions in every nation and culture, with the ultimate goal of ending tyranny in our world.

—*President George W. Bush, Second Inaugural Address,*
Washington, D.C., January 20, 2005

with solving disputes through killing when the other people have the right of consent. In addition, constitutional checks and balances on making war may work better when there is widespread public debate about the legitimacy of a battle. It is harder to rouse democratic peoples when there is no authoritarian demon like Hitler or Saddam Hussein.

Although these liberal theories need exploration via detailed case studies to look at what actually happened in particular instances, they do have promise. If the number of democracies in the world grows, there might be less propensity for war, at least among the democracies. But a word of caution is in order. It may be less true in the early stages of transition to democracy. Some of the new democracies may be plebiscitary democracies without a liberal domestic process of free press, checks on executive power, and regular elections. The warring governments of Croatia, Serbia, and Bosnia were elected, though they were far from liberal democracies. The same was true of Ecuador and Peru, which fought a border skirmish in 1995. The character of a democracy, therefore, appears to matter. The theorized relation is between liberal democracies, not all democracies.

Defining National Interests

Whatever their form of government, "states act in their national interest." That statement is normally true, but it does not tell us much unless we know how the states define their national interests. Realists say that states have little choice in defining their national interest because of the international system. They must define their interest in terms of balance of power or they will not survive, just as a company in a perfect market that wants to be altruistic rather than maximize profits will not survive. So for the realists, a state's position in the international system determines its national interests and predicts its foreign policies.

Liberals and constructivists argue that national interests are defined by much more than the state's position in the international system, and they have a richer account of how state preferences and national interests are formed. The definition of the national interests depends in large part on the type of domestic society and culture a state has. For example, a domestic society that values economic welfare and places heavy emphasis on trade, or that views wars against other democracies as illegitimate, defines its national interests very differently from a despotic state that is similarly positioned in the international system. Liberals argue that this is particularly true if the international system is moderate, that is, if it is not purely anarchic. If institutions and channels of communication provide stable expectations of continuing peace, the Prisoner's Dilemma may be escaped.

Because these nonpower incentives can help shape how states define their interests, it is important to know how closely a particular situation approximates the abstract concept of anarchy. If an international situation is totally anarchic, if you may be killed by your neighbor tomorrow, then limited opportunities exist for democracy or trade preferences to influence foreign policy. Survival comes first. But if the system only partially approximates anarchy because of institutions and stable expectations of peace, then some of these other factors related to domestic society and culture are likely to play a larger role. Realist predictions are more likely to be accurate in the Middle East, for example, and liberal predictions in Western Europe. Knowing the context helps us gauge the likely predictive value of different theories.

Variations in Foreign Policies

Even states in similar situations sometimes define their interests and strategies differently—witness Bismarck's, the Kaiser's, and Hitler's solutions to Germany's security dilemma. When systemic differences fail to explain different foreign policies, we tend to look at domestic causes. Some of these are idiosyncratic to each of the 200-odd states in the world, but some can be captured by generalizations.

A variety of factors in domestic affairs sometimes make states act similarly. We have looked at trade and democracy, but there are others. For example, is there a revolution? Revolutionary leaders often view their predecessors' foreign policies and even the whole international system as illegitimate. Revolutions often create instability in the entire region because revolutionary leaders frequently seek to export their ideology while neighboring states seek to contain it, as happened with France and its neighbors in the 1790s, with Russia after 1917, and with Iran and Iraq in 1980. Sometimes the revolutionary state invades its neighbors; sometimes it is invaded. Another low-level generalization is that poorly integrated countries, such as Germany or Austria before 1914, are more likely to project internal problems outward. German leaders diverted attention away from social democracy at home to expansion abroad. However, this tendency to find external scapegoats does not always hold true; some countries with poor internal integration, like Myanmar (Burma) today, turn inward.

Other regularities are sought in the behavior of bureaucracies. Because bureaucracies have standard operating procedures and do not change quickly, some analysts believe foreign policy can be predicted by looking at the inertia of foreign policy and military bureaucracies. We will look at this in relation to the Cuban Missile Crisis in Chapter 5. Certainly the German military bureaucracy resisted changes in its military plans in 1914. But bureaucratic predictions can mislead. After its defeat by mobile, irregular guerrilla forces in Vietnam, the American military adopted a strategy of high mobility during the Gulf War and won. Bureaucracies may not change quickly, but they can change.

Scholars in the subfield of international political economy have sought parsimonious ways to explain foreign policies by linking the world economy to domestic interests. For example, the different ways that open trade affects labor, landowners, and capital might influence policy in predictable ways, as we shall see in the case of Germany in the next chapter. Moreover, political coalitions at home can shift as a result of changing international opportunities and pressures.

Many variations in foreign policy behavior yield only low-level generalizations. They are at best hypotheses to test rather than perfect predictions. Domestic politics matter, and liberal theories help, but in different ways and at different times and different places.

COUNTERFACTUALS

In 1990, President Václav Havel of Czechoslovakia spoke before the U.S. Congress. Six months earlier he had been a political prisoner. "As a playwright," Havel said, "I'm used to the fantastic. I dream up all sorts of implausible things and put them in my plays. So this jolting experience of going from prison to standing before you today, I can adjust to this. But pity the poor political scientists who are trying to deal with what's probable."[7] Few people, including Soviets and Eastern Europeans, predicted the collapse of the Soviet Empire in Eastern Europe in 1989. Humans sometimes make surprising choices, and human history is full of uncertainties. How can we sort out the importance of different causes and different levels of analysis?

International politics is not like a laboratory science. Controlled experiments do not exist because it is impossible to hold other things constant while looking at the one thing that changes. Aristotle said one should be as precise in any science as the subject matter allows. Do not try to be too precise if the precision will be spurious. International politics involves so many variables, so many changes occurring at the same time that events are overdetermined—there are too many causes. But as analysts, we still want to sort out causes to get some idea of which ones are stronger than others. As you will see when we look at World War I in the next chapter, one of the useful tools we can use is mental experiments called counterfactuals.

Counterfactuals are *contrary-to-fact conditionals*, but it is simpler to think of them as thought experiments to define causal claims. Because there is no actual, physical laboratory for international politics, we imagine situations in which one thing changes while other things are held constant and then construct a picture of how the world would look. Actually, like speaking prose, we use counterfactuals every day. Many students might say, "If I had not eaten so much dinner, I could concentrate better on this reading." A few might use fancier counterfactuals: "If I hadn't skipped dinner at the student union, I wouldn't have met her, and my life would be much simpler today."

Though often without admitting it, historians use a more elaborate version of the same procedure to weigh causes. For example, imagine that the Kaiser had not fired Bismarck in 1890. Would that have made World War I less likely? Would Bismarck's policies have continued to lower the sense of threat that other countries felt from Germany and thus curbed the growing rigidity of the two alliance systems? In this instance, the use of a counterfactual examines how important a particular personality was in comparison to structural factors. Here is another counterfactual related to World War I: Suppose Franz Ferdinand's driver in Sarajevo had turned left instead of right at the crucial intersection and the Austrian archduke had not been assassinated; would the war have started? This counterfactual illuminates the role of the accidental. How important was the assassination? Given the overall tensions inherent in the alliance structure, might some other spark have ignited the flame had this one not occurred? Or to take a more recent example that illuminates the role of individuals in foreign policy, what if Albert Gore had been elected instead of George W. Bush in the closely contested presidential race of 2000? Some political observers speculate that after the Al Qaeda attacks on September 11, 2001, either man would have responded by using force against the Taliban government that had given haven to the terrorists, but that Gore might not have decided to invade Iraq, where the connection to the September 11 attacks was not established.

Contrary-to-fact conditional statements provide a way to explore whether a cause is significant, but there are also pitfalls in such "iffy history." Poorly handled counterfactuals may mislead by destroying the meaning of history. The fact is that once something has happened, other things are not equal. Time is a crucial dimension. We say that historical events are "path dependent"; that is, once events start down a certain path, all possible futures are not equally probable. Some events are more likely than others. We can use four criteria to test whether our counterfactual thought experiments are good or useful: plausibility, proximity, theory, and facts.

Plausibility

A useful counterfactual has to be within the reasonable array of options. This is sometimes called *cotenability*. It must be plausible to imagine two conditions existing at the same time. Suppose someone said that if Napoleon had had stealth bombers, he could have won the Battle of Waterloo (1815). She may say that such a counterfactual is designed to test the importance of military technology, but it makes little sense to imagine twentieth-century technology in a nineteenth-century setting. The two are not cotenable. Although it might be good for laughs, it is not a fruitful use of counterfactual thinking because of the anachronism involved. In real life, there never was a possibility of such a conjunction.

Proximity in Time

Each major event exists in a long chain of causation, and most events have multiple causes. The further back in time we go, the more causes that must be held constant. The closer in time the questioned event is to the subject event (did A cause B?), the more likely the answer is yes. Consider Pascal's (1623–1662) famous counterfactual statement that if Cleopatra's nose had been shorter, she would have been less attractive to Marc Antony, and the history of the Roman Empire would have been different. If the history of the Roman Empire had been different, the history of Western European civilization would have been different. Thus the length of Cleopatra's nose was one of the causes of World War I. In some trivial sense, that may be true, but millions of events and causes channeled down to August 1914. The contribution of Cleopatra's nose to the cause of World War I is so small and remote that the counterfactual is more amusing than interesting when we try to ascertain why the war broke out. Proximity in time means that the closeness of two events in the chain of causation allows us better to control other causes and thereby obtain a truer weighing of factors.

Relation to Theory

Good counterfactual reasoning should rely on an existing body of theory that represents a distillation of what we think we know about things that have happened before. We should ask whether a counterfactual is plausible considering what we know about all the cases that have given rise to these theories. Theories provide coherence and organization to our thoughts about the myriad of causes and help us to avoid random guessing. For example, there is no theory behind the counterfactual that if Napoleon had had stealth aircraft he would have won the Battle of Waterloo. The very randomness of the example helps explain why it is amusing, but also limits what we can learn from the mental exercise.

But suppose we were considering the causes of the Cold War and asked, what if the United States had been a socialist country in 1945, would there have been a Cold War? Or suppose the Soviet Union had come out of World War II with a capitalist government; would there have been a Cold War? These counterfactual questions explore the theory that the Cold War was caused primarily by ideology. An alternative hypothesis is that the bipolar international structure caused the Cold War. Given the distribution of power after World War II, we could expect some sort of tension even if the United States had been socialist. And the counterfactual reasoning can be bolstered by observing that countries with a similar communist ideology have fought each other. The counterfactual allows us to assess theories of balance of power versus theories of ideological causation. In general, counterfactuals related to theory are more interesting and useful because the mental exercise ties into a broader body of knowledge.

Facts

It is not enough to imagine fruitful hypotheses. They must be carefully examined in relation to the known facts. Counterfactuals require accurate facts and careful history. In examining the plausibility of a mental experiment, we must ask whether what is held constant is faithful to what actually happened. We must be wary of piling one counterfactual on top of another in the same thought experiment. Such multiple counterfactuals are confusing because too many things are being changed at once, and we are unable to judge the accuracy of the exercise by a careful examination of its real historical parts.

In summary, we frequently use counterfactuals in our everyday lives. They are especially useful in international politics because there is no laboratory setting such as in physical science. But we need to be careful in constructing counterfactuals, for some are better constructed and thus more fruitful than others. Counterfactuals help us relate history to theory and make better judgments as we try to understand a world with no controlled experiments.

Some historians are purists who say counterfactuals that ask what might have been are not real history. Real history is what actually happened. Imagining what might have happened is not important. But such purists miss the point that we try to understand not just what happened, but *why* it happened. To do that, we need to know what else *might* have happened, and that brings us back to counterfactuals. So while some historians interpret history as simply the writing down of what happened, many historians believe that good counterfactual analysis is essential to good historical analysis. The purists help warn us against poorly disciplined counterfactuals such as Napoleon's stealth bombers. But, as we see in the next chapter, there is a distinction between saying that some counterfactual analysis is trivial and saying that good counterfactual analysis is essential to clear thinking about causation.

CHRONOLOGIES: EUROPE

The Seventeenth Century

1618–1648	Thirty Years' War: conflict between Catholic and Protestant Europe; last of the great religious wars; Germany devastated
1643–1715	Louis XIV, king of France
1648	Peace of Westphalia; end of Thirty Years' War
1649–1660	English King Charles I beheaded; commonwealth under Oliver Cromwell
1652–1678	Series of Anglo-French and Anglo-Dutch wars for supremacy of the seas
1660	Stuart restoration in England; accession of Charles II
1682–1725	Peter the Great begins "Westernization" of Russia
1683	Turkish siege of Vienna repulsed
1685	Louis XIV revokes Edict of Nantes; persecution of French Protestants
1688–1689	Glorious Revolution in England
1688–1697	War of the League of Augsburg; general war against Louis XIV

The Eighteenth Century

1700–1721	Great Northern War: Russia, Poland, and Denmark oppose Swedish supremacy in the Baltic; Russia emerges as a European power
1701–1714	War of the Spanish Succession and the Treaty of Utrecht; results in permanent separation of French and Spanish thrones; further decline of French power
1707	Great Britain formed by union of England and Scotland
1740–1748	War of the Austrian Succession
1756–1763	Seven Years' War: Britain and France in colonial wars; France ejected from Canada and India; Britain emerges as world's major colonial power
1775–1783	War of the American Revolution
1789–1799	French Revolution
1799	Coup d'état by Napoleon Bonaparte in France
1799–1815	Napoleonic Wars make France preeminent power on European continent

The Nineteenth Century

1801	United Kingdom formed by union of Great Britain and Ireland
1804–1814	Napoleon I, emperor of France
1806	End of Holy Roman Empire; imperial title renounced by Francis II
1810	Kingdom of Holland incorporated in French Empire
1812	French invasion of Russia; destruction of Napoleon's army
1814–1815	Congress of Vienna: monarchies reestablished in Europe
1815	Battle of Waterloo: Napoleon escapes from Elba but is defeated by British and Prussian armies
1833–1871	Unification of Germany
1837–1901	Victoria, queen of England: period of great industrial expansion and prosperity
1848	Revolutions in France, Germany, Hungary, and Bohemia; publication of Karl Marx's *Communist Manifesto*
1848–1916	Franz Joseph, emperor of Austria; becomes ruler of the Austro-Hungarian Empire in 1867
1852–1870	Napoleon III, emperor of Second French Empire
1854–1856	Crimean War: Britain and France support Ottomans in war with Russia
1855–1881	Alexander II, czar of Russia
1859–1870	Italian political unification and cultural nationalism led by Garibaldi
1861	Emancipation of Russian serfs by Czar Alexander II
1862–1890	Otto von Bismarck, premier and chancellor of Germany, forges German Empire
1864–1905	Russian expansion in Poland, Balkans, and central Asia
1867	Austro-Hungarian Empire founded
1870–1871	Franco-Prussian War: German invasion of France; Third French Republic created
1870–1914	European imperialism at peak; industrial growth; rise of labor movements and Marxism

1871	Paris Commune: Paris, a revolutionary center, establishes own government and wars with national government
1878	Congress of Berlin: division of much of Ottoman Empire among Austria, Russia, and Britain
1881	Alexander II of Russia assassinated
1882	Triple Alliance of Germany, Austria-Hungary, and Italy; renewed in 1907
1899–1902	Boer War in South Africa

The First Decade of the Twentieth Century

1904	Dual Entente between Britain and France
1904–1905	Russo-Japanese War ends in Russian defeat; Japan emerges as world power
1907	Russia joins Britain and France in Triple Entente

STUDY QUESTIONS

1. What were the main goals of the Congress of Vienna? Did the Congress restore the antebellum European order or did it shape a new one?

2. What were the characteristics of the European system from 1815 to 1848? Did they differ from those of the eighteenth-century balance of power and from those of the late nineteenth-century international systems? What factors caused changes?

3. What was the effect of the rise of Germany on the European system? What was Bismarck's strategy in Europe? Was he concerned with maintaining the balance or overturning it?

4. Why do liberals think democracy can prevent war? What are the limits to their view?

5. What are Waltz's three images? How can they be combined?

6. What is the difference between the structure and process of an international system? Is constructivism useful for understanding how processes change?

7. What is counterfactual history? Can you use it to deal with current issues such as the causes of the war in Iraq?

NOTES

1. Paul R. Hensel, "Territory: Theory and Evidence on Geography and Conflict," in John A. Vazquez, ed., *What Do We Know About War?* (New York: Rowman & Littlefield, 2000), p. 62.

2. Paul Schroeder, "The Nineteenth Century System: Balance of Power or Political Equilibrium?" *Swords & Ploughshares* 4:1 (October 1989), p. 4.

3. V. I. Lenin, *Imperialism: The Highest Stage of Capitalism* (New York: International Publishers, 1977), p. 119.

4. Richard Cobden, quoted in Kenneth N. Waltz, *Man, the State, and War: A Theoretical Analysis* (New York: Columbia University Press, 1959), p. 104.

5. Richard Rosecrance, *The Rise of the Trading State: Commerce and Conquest in the Modern World* (New York: Basic, 1986), p. ix.

6. *U.S. Institute of Peace Journal* 3:2 (June 1990), pp. 6–7.

7. Václav Havel, "Address to U.S. Congress," *Congressional Record*, February 21, 1990, pp. S 1313–1315.

Selected Readings

1. Waltz, Kenneth, *Man, the State, and War: A Theoretical Analysis* (New York: Columbia University Press, 1959), pp. 1–15, 224–238.
2. Levy, Jack S., "Domestic Politics and War," in Robert I. Rotberg and Theodore K. Rabb, eds., *The Origin and Prevention of Major Wars* (Cambridge: Cambridge University Press, 1989), pp. 79–99.
3. Detwiler, Donald, *Germany: A Short History* (Carbondale, IL: Southern Illinois University Press, 1989), pp. 104–148.
4. Ritter, Harry, "Counterfactual Analysis," in *Dictionary of Concepts in History* (New York: Greenwood Press, 1986), pp. 70–73.
5. Doyle, Michael, "Kant, Liberal Legacies, and Foreign Affairs," *Philosophy and Public Affairs* 12:3 (Summer 1983), pp. 205–235.

Further Readings

Albrecht-Carrie, René, *A Diplomatic History of Europe Since the Congress of Vienna* (New York: Harper & Row, 1973).

Bartlett, C. J., *The Global Conflict: The International Rivalry of the Great Powers, 1880–1990* (London: Longman, 1994).

Blight, James G., and Janet M. Lang, *The Fog of War: Lessons from the Life of Robert S. McNamara* (Lanham, MD: Rowman & Littlefield, 2005).

Brown, Michael, and Sean Lynn-Jones, eds., *Debating the Democratic Peace* (Cambridge, MA: MIT Press, 1996).

Bueno de Mesquita, Bruce, and David Lalman, "Empirical Support for Systemic and Dyadic Explanations of International Conflict," *World Politics* 41:1 (October 1988), pp. 1–20.

Byman, Daniel and Kenneth Pollack, "Let Us Now Praise Great Men: Bringing the Statesman Back In," *International Security* 24:4 (Spring 2001), pp 107–146.

Craig, Gordon A., *Germany, 1866–1945* (New York: Oxford University Press, 1978).

Evangelista, Matthew, "Domestic Structure and International Change," in Michael Doyle and John Ikenberry, eds., *New Thinking in International Relations Theory* (Boulder, CO: Westview, 1997).

Fearon, James D., "Counterfactuals and Hypothesis Testing in Political Science," *World Politics* 43:2 (January 1991), pp. 169–195.

Goldstein, Judith, and Robert O. Keohane, *Ideas and Foreign Policy* (Ithaca, NY: Cornell University Press, 1993).

Hoffmann, Stanley, "Liberalism and International Affairs," in *Janus and Minerva: Essays in the Theory and Practice of International Politics* (Boulder, CO: Westview, 1987), pp. 394–417.

Hopf, Ted, "Polarity, the Offense-Defense Balance, and War," *American Political Science Review* 85:2 (June 1991), pp. 475–494.

Isaacson, Walter and Evan Thomas, *The Wise Men: Six Friends and the World They Made* (New York: Simon & Schuster, 1986)

Jervis, Robert, *Perception and Misperception in International Politics* (Princeton, NJ: Princeton University Press, 1976).

Kennedy, Paul M., *Strategy and Diplomacy, 1870–1945: Eight Studies* (London: Allen & Unwin, 1983).

Keohane, Robert O., *After Hegemony* (Princeton, NJ: Princeton Unversity Press, 1984).

Keohane, Robert O., and Joseph S. Nye, Jr., *Power and Interdependence: World Politics in Transition* (New York: HarperCollins, 1989).

Kissinger, Henry A., *A World Restored: Metternich, Castlereagh, and the Problems of Peace, 1812–22* (Boston: Houghton Mifflin, 1973).

Lipson, Charles, *Reliable Partners: How Democracies Have Made a Separate Peace* (Princeton, NJ: Princeton University Press, 2003).

Mansield, Edward, and Jack Snyder, *Electing to Fight: Why Emerging Democracies Go to War* (Cambridge, MA: MIT Press, 2005).

Mearsheimer, John, "Back to the Future," *International Security* 15:1 (Summer 1990), pp. 5–56.

Milner, Helen, *Interests, Institutions and Information* (Princeton, NJ: Princeton University Press, 1997).

Nye, Jr., Joseph S., "Neorealism and Neoliberalism," *World Politics* 40:2 (January 1988), pp. 235–251.

Owen, John M., "How Liberalism Produces Democratic Peace," *International Security* 19:2 (Fall 1994), pp. 87–125.

Rosato, Sebastian, "The Flawed Logic of Democratic Peace Theory," *American Political Science Review* 97:4 (November 2003), pp. 585–602.

Russett, Bruce, *Grasping the Democratic Peace: Principles for a Post–Cold War World* (Princeton, NJ: Princeton University Press, 1993).

Schroeder, Paul, "Historical Reality vs. Neorealist Theory," *International Security* 19:1 (Summer 1994), pp. 108–148.

Taylor, A. J. P., *The Struggle for Mastery in Europe, 1848–1918* (Oxford: Clarendon, 1971).

Vasquez, John A., ed., *What Do We Know About War?* (New York: Rowman & Littlefield, 2000).

Zakaria, Fareed, *The Future of Freedom: Illiberal Democracy at Home and Abroad* (New York: Norton, 2003).

Zelikow, Philip, and Condoleezza Rice, *Germany Unified and Europe Transformed: A Study in Statecraft* (Cambridge, MA: Harvard University Press, 1997).

Balance of Power
and World War I

World War I: The aftermath of battle

BALANCE OF POWER

World War I is often blamed on the *balance of power,* one of the most frequently used concepts in international politics and one of the most confusing. The term is loosely used to describe and justify all sorts of things. The eighteenth-century British philosopher David Hume described the balance of power as a constant rule of prudent politics, but the nineteenth-century British liberal Richard Cobden called it "a chimera—an undescribed, indescribable, incomprehensible nothing."[1]

something
or wished hoped
for

59

Woodrow Wilson, the American president during World War I, thought the balance of power was an evil principle because it encouraged statesmen to treat nations like cheeses to be cut up for political convenience regardless of the concerns of their peoples.

Wilson also disliked the balance of power because he believed it caused wars. Defenders of balance-of-power policies argue that they produce stability. However, peace and stability are not the same thing. Over the five centuries of the European state system, the great powers were involved in 119 wars. Peace was rare; during three-quarters of the time there was war involving at least one of the great powers. Ten of those wars were large general wars with many of the great powers involved— what we call hegemonic, or world wars. Thus if we ask whether the balance of power preserved peace very well over the five centuries of the modern state system, the answer is no.

That is not surprising because states balance power not to preserve peace, but to preserve their independence. The balance of power helps preserve the anarchic system of separate states. Not every state is preserved. For example, at the end of the eighteenth century, Poland was, indeed, cut up like a cheese, with Poland's neighbors—Austria, Prussia, and Russia—all helping themselves to a large slice. More recently, in 1939 Stalin and Hitler made a deal in which they carved up Poland again and gave the Baltic states to the Soviet Union. Thus Lithuania, Latvia, and Estonia spent half a century as Soviet republics until 1991. The balance of power has not preserved peace and has not always preserved the independence of each state, but it has preserved the anarchic state system.

POWER

To understand the balance, we have to start with power. Power, like love, is easier to experience than to define or measure. *Power* is the ability to achieve one's purposes or goals. More specifically, it is the ability to affect others to get the outcomes one wants. Robert Dahl, a Yale political scientist, defines *power* as the ability to get others to do what they otherwise would not do. But when we measure power in terms of the changed behavior of others, we have to know their preferences. Otherwise, we may be as mistaken about our power as the fox who thought he was hurting Br'er Rabbit when he threw him into the briar patch. Knowing in advance how other people or nations would behave in the absence of our efforts is often difficult.

The behavioral definition of power can be useful to analysts and historians who devote considerable time to reconstructing the past, but to practical politicians and leaders it may seem too ephemeral. Because the ability to influence others is usually associated with the possession of certain resources, political leaders commonly define power this way. These resources include population, territory, natural resources, economic size, military forces, and political stability, among others. The virtue of this definition is that it makes power appear more concrete, measurable, and predictable than the behavioral definition. Power in this sense means holding the high cards in the international poker game. A basic rule of poker is that if your opponent is showing cards that can beat anything you hold, fold your hand. If you know you will lose a war, don't start it.

Some wars, however, have been started by the eventual losers, which suggests that political leaders sometimes take risks or make mistakes. Japan in 1941 and Iraq in 1990 are examples. Often the opponent's cards are not all showing in the game of international politics. As in poker, bluffing and deception can make a big difference. Even without deception, mistakes can be made about which power resources are most relevant in particular situations. For example, France and Britain had more tanks than Hitler in 1940, but Hitler's tanks had greater maneuverability and his military utilized better military strategy.

Power conversion is a basic problem that arises when we think of power in terms of resources. Some countries are better than others at converting their resources into effective influence over other countries' behavior, just as some skilled card players win despite being dealt weak hands. *Power conversion* is the capacity to convert potential power, as measured by resources, to realized power, as measured by the changed behavior of others. To predict outcomes correctly, we need to know about a country's skill at power conversion as well as its possession of power resources.

Another problem is determining which resources provide the best basis for power in any particular context. *Power resources* always depend on the context. Tanks are not much good in swamps; uranium was not a power resource in the nineteenth century. In earlier periods, power resources were easier to judge. For example, in the agrarian economies of eighteenth-century Europe, population was a critical power resource because it provided a base for taxes and recruitment of infantry. In population, France dominated western Europe. Thus at the end of the Napoleonic Wars (1799–1815), Prussia presented its fellow victors at the Congress of Vienna (1815) with a precise plan for its own reconstruction in order to maintain the balance of power. Its plan listed the territories and populations it had lost since 1805 and the territories and populations it would need to regain equivalent numbers. In the prenationalist period, it was not significant that many of the people in those provinces did not speak German or feel themselves to be Prussian. However, within half a century, nationalist sentiments mattered very much.

Another change of context that occurred during the nineteenth century was the growing importance of industry and rail systems that made rapid mobilization possible. In the 1860s, Bismarck's Germany pioneered the use of railways to transport armies in Europe for quick victories. Although Russia had always had greater population resources than the rest of Europe, they were difficult to mobilize. The growth of the rail system in western Russia at the beginning of the twentieth century was one of the reasons the Germans feared rising Russian power in 1914. Further, the spread of rail systems on the Continent helped deprive Britain of the luxury of concentrating on naval power. There was no longer time, should it prove necessary, to insert an army to prevent another great power from dominating the Continent.

The application of industrial technology to warfare has long had a powerful impact. Advanced science and technology have been particularly critical power resources since the beginning of the nuclear age in 1945. But the power derived from nuclear weapons has proven to be so awesome and destructive that its actual application is muscle-bound. Nuclear war is simply far too costly. Indeed, there are many situations where any use of force may be inappropriate or too costly.

Even if the direct use of force were banned among a group of countries, military force would still play an important background role. For example, the American military role in deterring threats to allies, or of assuring access to a crucial resource such as oil in the Persian Gulf, means that the provision of protective force can be used in bargaining situations. Sometimes the linkage may be direct; more often, as we will see in Chapter 7, it is a factor not mentioned openly but present in the back of leaders' minds.

Coercing other states to change is a direct or commanding method of exercising power. Such *hard power* can rest on inducements ("carrots") or threats ("sticks"). But there is also a soft or indirect way to exercise power. A country may achieve its preferred outcomes in world politics because other countries want to emulate it or have agreed to a system that produces such effects. In this sense, it is just as important to set the agenda and attract others in world politics as it is to force others to change in particular situations. This aspect of power—that is, getting others to want what you want—is called attractive, or *soft power* behavior. Soft power can rest on such resources as the attraction of one's ideas or on the ability to set the political agenda in a way that shapes the preferences others express. Parents of teenagers know that if they have structured their children's beliefs and preferences, their power will be greater and will last longer than if they had relied only on active control. Similarly, political leaders and constructivist theorists have long understood the power that comes from setting the agenda and determining the framework of a debate. The ability to establish preferences tends to be associated with intangible power resources such as culture, ideology, and institutions.

Soft power is not automatically more effective or ethical than hard power. Twisting minds is not necessarily better than twisting arms. Moral judgments depend on the purposes for which power is used. The terrorist leader Osama bin Laden, for example, had soft power in the eyes of his followers who carried out the attacks in 2001. Nor is soft power associated with liberal rather than realist theory. Power is the ability to affect others to get the outcomes you want regardless of whether its sources are tangible. Soft power is often more difficult for governments to wield, slower to show results, and not effective in many cases. But analysts ignore it at their peril. For example, in 1762, when Frederick the Great of Prussia was about to be defeated by a coalition of France, Austria, and Russia, he was saved because the new Russian Czar Peter (1728–1762) idolized the Prussian monarch and pulled his troops out of the anti-Prussian coalition. In 1917, Great Britain had greater soft power than Germany in American opinion, and that affected the United States' entry on Britain's side in World War I. More recent examples would include Franklin Roosevelt's Four Freedoms attracting European support in World War II; young people behind the Iron Curtain listening to American music and news on Radio Free Europe during the Cold War; and the recent ability of the European Union to attract other countries.

TABLE 3.1   Leading States and Major Power Resources

Period	Leading State	Major Resources
Sixteenth century	Spain	Gold bullion, colonial trade, mercenary armies, dynastic ties
Seventeenth century	Netherlands	Trade, capital markets, navy
Eighteenth century	France	Population, rural industry, public administration, army, culture (soft power)
Nineteenth century	Britain	Industry, political cohesion, finance and credit, navy, liberal norms (soft power), island location (easy to defend)
Twentieth century	United States	Economic scale, scientific and technical leadership, location, military forces and alliances, universalistic culture and liberal international regimes (soft power)
Twenty-first century	United States	Technological leadership, military and economic scale, hub of transnational communications (soft power)

Hard and soft power are related, but they are not the same. Material success makes a culture and ideology attractive, and decreases in economic and military success lead to self-doubt and crises of identity. But soft power does not rest solely on hard power (Table 3.1). The soft power of the Vatican did not wane as the size of the Papal States diminished in the nineteenth century. Canada, Sweden, and the Netherlands today tend to have more influence than some other states with equivalent economic or military capability. The Soviet Union had considerable soft power in Europe after World War II but squandered it after its invasion of Hungary in 1956 and Czechoslovakia in 1968.

What resources are the most important sources of power today? A look at the five centuries of modern state systems shows that different power resources played critical roles in different periods. The sources of power are never static and they continue to change in today's world. Moreover, they vary in different parts of the world. Soft power is becoming more important in relations among the postindustrial societies in an information age in which the democratic peace prevails; hard power is often more important in industrializing and preindustrial parts of the world.

In an age of information-based economies and transnational interdependence, power is becoming less transferable, less tangible, and less coercive, as we shall see in more detail in Chapters 7 and 8. Traditional analysts would predict the outcome of conflict mainly on the basis of whose army wins. Today, in conflicts like the struggle against transnational terrorism, it is equally important whose story wins. Hard power is necessary against hardcore terrorists, but it is equally important to use soft power to win the hearts and minds of the moderate population that might otherwise be won over by the terrorists.

The transformation of power is not the same in all parts of the world. The twenty-first century will certainly see a greater role for informational and institutional power, but as the Gulf War demonstrated, hard military power remains an important instrument. Economic scale, both in markets and in natural resources, will also remain important. The service sector grows within modern economies, and the distinction between services and manufacturing continues to blur. Information will become more plentiful, and the critical resource will be organizational capacity for rapid and flexible response. Political cohesion will remain important, as well as the nurturing of a universalistic, exportable popular culture.

The difficulty of measuring changing power resources is a major problem for leaders trying to assess the balance of power. For analysts of international politics, additional confusion ensues when the same word is used for different things. We must try to separate and clarify the underlying concepts covered by the loose use of the same words. The term *balance of power* commonly refers to at least three different things.

Balances as Distributions of Power

Balance of power can mean, in the first sense, any distribution of power. Who has the power resources? Sometimes people use the term *balance of power* to refer to the status quo, the existing distribution of power. Thus in the 1980s, some Americans argued that if Nicaragua became a communist state, the balance of power would be changed. Such a use of the term is not very enlightening. If one little state changed sides, that might slightly alter the existing distribution of power, but it was a rather trivial change and did not tell us much about deeper changes occurring in world politics.

The term can also refer to a special (and rarer) set of situations in which power is distributed equally. This usage conjures up the image of a set of scales in balance or equilibrium. Some realists argue that stability occurs when there is an equal balance, but others argue that stability occurs when one side has a preponderance of power so the others dare not attack it. *Hegemonic stability theory* holds that imbalanced power produces peace. A strong dominant power ensures stability, but when that strong power begins to slip and a new challenger rises, war is more likely. Consider Thucydides's explanation of the Peloponnesian War: the rise of the power of Athens and the fear it created in Sparta fits this hegemonic transition theory. As we will see later in this chapter, so does World War I.

However, we must be cautious about such theories, for they tend to overpredict conflict. In the 1880s, the United States passed Great Britain as the largest economy in the world. In 1895, the United States and Britain disagreed over borders in South America, and it looked as if war might result. There was a rising challenger, an old hegemon, and a cause of conflict, but you do not read about the great British-American War of 1895 because it did not occur. As Sherlock Holmes pointed out, we can get important clues from dogs that do not bark. In this case, the absence of war leads us to look for other causes. Realists point to the rise of Germany as a more proximate threat to Britain. Liberals point to the increasingly democratic nature of the two English-speaking countries and to transnational cultural ties between the old leader and the new challenger. The best we can conclude about the balance of power in the first sense of the term is that changes in the unequal distribution of power among leading states may be a factor, but not the sole factor, in explaining war and instability.

Balance of Power as Policy

The second use of the term refers to balance of power as a policy of balancing. Balance of power predicts that states will act to prevent any one state from developing a pre- ponderance of power. This prediction has a long pedigree. Lord Palmerston, British foreign secretary in 1848, said that Britain had no eternal allies or perpetual enemies; Britain thought only of its interests. Sir Edward Grey, the British foreign minister in 1914, did not want to go to war, but eventually did because he feared Germany would gain preponderance in Europe by controlling the Continent. And in 1941, when Hitler invaded the Soviet Union, Prime Minister Winston Churchill said Britain should make an alliance with Stalin, against whom he had been fulminating just a few years before. Churchill said, "If Hitler invaded Hell, I would make at least a favorable reference to the Devil in the House of Commons."[2] These are good examples of balance of power as policy.

Predicting such behavior rests on two basic assumptions: (1) The structure of international politics is an anarchic system of states, and (2) states value their indepen- dence above all else. A balance-of-power policy does not necessarily assume that states act to maximize power. In fact, a state might choose a very different course of action if it wished to maximize power. It might choose to *bandwagon*, that is, join whoever seems stronger and share in the victor's gains. Bandwagoning is common in domestic politics in which politicians flock to an apparent winner. Balance of power, however, predicts that a state will join whoever seems *weaker* because states will act to keep any one state from developing a preponderance of power. Bandwagoning in international politics carries the risk of losing independence. In 1939 and 1940, the Italian dictator Mussolini joined Hitler's attack on France as a way to get some of the spoils, but Italy became more and more dependent on Germany. That is why a balance-of-power policy says, "Join the weaker side". Balance of power is a policy of helping the underdog because if you help the top dog, it may eventually turn around and eat you.

States can try to balance power unilaterally by developing armaments or by forming alliances with other countries whose power resources help balance the top dog. This is one of the more interesting and powerful predictions in international politics. The contemporary Middle East is a good example. As we see in Chapter 6, when Iran and Iraq went to war in the early 1980s, some observers thought all Arab states would support Saddam Hussein's Iraq, which represented the Ba'ath Party and Arab forces, against Ayatollah Khomeini's Iran, which represented Persian culture and the minority Shi'ite version of Islam. But Syria, despite having a secular leader from the Ba'ath Party, became an ally of Iran. Why? Because Syria was worried about the growing regional power of its neighbor Iraq. Syria chose to balance Iraqi power regardless of its ideological preferences. Efforts to use ideology to predict state behavior are often wrong, whereas counterintuitive predictions based on balancing power are often correct.

Of course, there are exceptions. Human behavior is not fully determined. Human beings have choices, and they do not always act as predicted. Certain situations predispose people toward a certain type of behavior, but we cannot always predict the details. If someone shouts "Fire!" in a crowded lecture hall, we could predict that students would run for the exits, but not *which* exits. If all choose one exit, the stampede may prevent many from getting out. Theories in international politics often have large exceptions. Even though balance of power in a policy sense is one of the strongest predictors in international politics, its record is far from perfect.

Why do countries sometimes eschew balance of power and join the stronger rather than the weaker side, or stand aloof, thus ignoring the risks to their independence? Some countries may see no alternatives or believe they cannot affect the balance. If so, a small country may decide it has to fall within the sphere of influence of a great power while hoping that neutrality will preserve some freedom of action. For example, after World War II Finland was defeated by the Soviet Union and was far from the center of Europe. The Finns felt neutrality was safer than trying to become part of the European balance of power. They were in the Soviet sphere of influence, and the best they could do was bargain away independence in foreign policy for a large degree of control over their domestic affairs.

Another reason that balance-of-power predictions are sometimes wrong has to do with perceptions of threat. For example, a mechanical accounting of the power resources of countries in 1917 would have predicted that the United States would join World War I on the side of Germany because Britain, France, and Russia had 30 percent of the industrial world's resources while Germany and Austria had only 19 percent. This did not happen, in part, because the Americans perceived the Germans as militarily stronger and the aggressor in the war and because the Germans underestimated America's military potential.

Perceptions of threat are often influenced by the *proximity* of the threat. A neighbor may be weak on some absolute global scale, but threatening in its region or local area. Consider Britain and the United States in the 1890s: Britain could have fought, but instead chose to appease the United States. It conceded to the United States on many issues, including the building of the Panama Canal, which allowed America to improve its naval position. One reason is that Britain was more worried about its neighbor Germany than it was about the distant Americans. The United States was larger than Germany, but proximity affected which threat loomed larger in British eyes. Proximity also helps explain the alliances after 1945. The United States was stronger than the Soviet Union, so why didn't Europe and Japan ally with the Soviet Union against the United States? The answer lies partly in the proximity of the threat. From the point of view of Europe and Japan, the Soviets were an immediate threat and the United States was far away. The Europeans and the Japanese called in the distant power to rebalance the situation in their immediate neighborhood. The fact that proximity often affects how threats are perceived qualifies any predictions based on simple mechanical toting up of power resources.

Another exception to balance-of-power predictions relates to the growing role of economic interdependence in world affairs. According to a balance-of-power policy, France should not wish to see Germany grow, but because of economic integration, German growth stimulates French growth. French politicians are more likely to be reelected when the French economy is growing. Therefore, a policy of trying to hold back German economic growth would be foolish because the French and German economies are so interdependent. In economic considerations, joint gains would often be lost by following too simple a balance-of-power policy.

Finally, ideology sometimes causes countries to join the top dog rather than the underdog. Even in Thucydides's day, democratic city-states were more likely to align with Athens and oligarchies with Sparta. Britain's appeasement of the United States in the 1890s, or the Europeans joining with the Americans in an alliance of democracies after 1945, owed something to the influence of ideology, as well as to the proximity of the threat. On the other hand, we must be careful about predicting too much from ideology, because it often leads to colossal mistakes. Many Europeans believed that Stalin and Hitler could not come together in 1939 because they were at opposite ends of the ideological spectrum; but balance-of-power considerations led them to an alliance against the countries in the middle of the ideological spectrum. Likewise, in the 1960s the United States mistakenly treated China, the Soviet Union, Vietnam, and Cambodia as similar because they were all communist. A policy based on balance of power would have predicted that those communist states would balance each other (as they eventually did), which would have been a less expensive way to pursue stability in East Asia.

Balance of Power as Multipolar Systems

The third way in which the term *balance of power* is used is to describe multipolar historical cases. Europe in the nineteenth century is sometimes held up as the model of a moderate multipolar balance-of-power system. Historians such as Edward Gulick use the term *classical balance of power* to refer to the European system of the eighteenth century. In this sense, a balance of power requires a number of countries that follow a set of rules of the game that are generally understood. Since this use of the term *balance of power* refers to historical systems, we look at the two dimensions of systems, *structure* and *process*, that were introduced in Chapter 2. It is true that the multipolar balance-of-power system in the nineteenth century produced the longest interval without world war in the modern state system—1815 to 1914—but we should not romanticize or oversimplify a complex story (Table 3.2).

The structure of the nineteenth-century European balance of power changed toward the end of the century. From 1815 to 1870 five major powers often shifted alliances to prevent any one from dominating the Continent. From 1870 to 1907

TABLE 3.2   Structural Changes in the Pre–World War I Balance of Power

1815–1870	Loose Multipolarity
1870–1907	Rise of Germany
1907–1914	Bipolarity of Alliances

there were six powers after the unification of Germany and Italy, but the growing strength of Germany eventually led to the problems that brought about the end of the system. Over the next seven years, the two alliance systems, the Triple Entente (Great Britain, France, and Russia) and the Triple Alliance (Germany, Austria-Hungary, and Italy) polarized into tight blocs whose loss of flexibility contributed to the onset of World War I.

[handwritten margin note: Multipolar, Too Blocs, To WAR]

In terms of process, the nineteenth-century balance-of-power system divides into five periods (Table 3.3). At the Congress of Vienna, the states of Europe brought France back into the fold and agreed on certain rules of the game to equalize the players. From 1815 to 1822 these rules formed the "Concert of Europe." The states concerted their actions, meeting frequently to deal with disputes and to maintain an equilibrium. They accepted certain interventions to keep governments in power domestically when their replacements might lead to a destabilizing reorientation of policy. This became more difficult with the rise of nationalism and democratic revolutions, but a truncated concert persisted from 1822 to 1854. This concert fell apart in midcentury when revolutions of liberal nationalism challenged the practices of providing territorial compensation or restoring governments to maintain equilibrium. Nationalism became too strong to allow such an easy cutting up of cheeses.

The third period in the nineteenth-century balance-of-power system, from 1854 to 1870, was far less moderate and was marked by five wars. One, the Crimean War, was a classic balance-of-power war in which France and Britain prevented Russia from pressing the declining Ottoman Empire. The other conflicts, however, were related to the unification of Italy and Germany. Political leaders abandoned old rules and began to use nationalism for their expedient purposes. Bismarck, for example, was not an ideological German nationalist. He was a deeply conservative man who wanted Germany united under the Prussian monarchy. But he was quite prepared to use nationalist appeals and wars to defeat Denmark, Austria, and France in bringing this about. He returned to a more conservative style once he had accomplished his goals.

The fourth period, 1870 to 1890, was the Bismarckian balance of power in which the new Prussian-led Germany played the key role. Bismarck played flexibly with a variety of alliance partners and tried to divert France overseas into imperialistic adventures and away from its lost province of Alsace-Lorraine. He limited German imperialism in order to keep the balancing act in Europe centered on Berlin.

TABLE 3.3   **Process of the Pre–World War I Balance of Power**

1815–1822	Concert of Europe
1822–1854	Loose Concert
1854–1870	Nationalism and the Unification of Germany and Italy
1870–1890	Bismarck's Revived Concert
1890–1914	The Loss of Flexibility

Bismarck's successors, however, were not as agile. From 1890 to 1914 there was a balance of power, but flexibility was gradually lost. Bismarck's successors did not renew his treaty with Russia; Germany became involved in overseas imperialism, challenged Britain's naval supremacy, and did not discourage Austrian confrontations with Russia over the Balkans. These policies exacerbated the fears of neighboring states that felt threatened by rising German power, further polarized the system, and led to World War I.

Alliances

Balance of power as a multipolar system is intimately related to the concept of alliances. *Alliances* are formal or informal arrangements that sovereign states enter into with each other in order to ensure their mutual security. They can be motivated by military concerns: two medium-sized states might decide they will be more secure against threats from a larger state by forming an alliance. Traditionally, military alliances have been one of the focal points of international politics.

States might also ally for nonmilitary reasons. As mentioned earlier, ideology often draws states together, though it can also cause conflicts. Economic concerns might be another reason for an alliance, particularly in those parts of the modern world where purely military concerns are receding.

Alliances collapse for as many reasons as they form, but in general states cease to ally when they come to see each other as irrelevant or as threats to their security. That might occur because the regime in one state changes. Before, the two states might have shared a common ideology; now they are opposed. Thus China and the United States were allies when the Nationalists were in power before 1949 and enemies after the Communists came to power in 1949. Of course, there may be other reasons for an alliance to end. One state may grow more powerful. It might view the other state as a rival, while the other state might view it as a threat and look for alliances elsewhere to balance that threat.

The hallmarks of Bismarck's alliance system were its flexibility and its complexity. The former made the resulting balance-of-power system stable because it allowed for occasional crises or conflicts without causing the whole edifice to crumble. Germany was at the center of the system, and Bismarck can be likened to an expert juggler who keeps several balls in the air. If one ball falls, the juggler can continue to keep the others aloft and even bend down to retrieve the errant one.

Yet complexity was also the system's weakness. When Bismarck was succeeded by less adroit leaders, the alliance system could not be maintained. Rather than channeling conflict away from Germany, as Bismarck did by encouraging France to expend its energies on colonial ventures in Africa, German decision makers in the years leading up to 1914 allowed alliances to lapse and tension to grow. Instead of renewing the German entente with Russia, the Kaiser let Russia float into an alliance with France and later Britain. What was once a fluid, multipolar alliance system gradually evolved into two alliance blocs, with dangerous consequences for European stability.

THE ORIGINS OF WORLD WAR I

World War I killed more than 15 million people. In one battle, the Somme, 1.3 million were killed and wounded. Compare that to 36,000 casualties when Bismarck defeated Austria in 1866. The United States lost about 55,000 troops in both Korea and Vietnam. World War I was a horrifying war of trenches, barbed wire, machine guns, and artillery that ground up a generation of Europe's youth. It not only destroyed people, it destroyed three European empires: the German, Austro-Hungarian, and Russian. Until World War I, the global balance of power was centered in Europe. After World War I, Europe still mattered, but the United States and Japan emerged as major players. World War I also ushered in the Russian Revolution in 1917 and the beginning of the ideological battles that racked the twentieth century.

How could such an event happen? Prince Bernhard von Bülow, the German chancellor from 1900 to 1909, met with his successor, Bethmann Hollweg, in the chancellor's palace in Berlin shortly after the war broke out. Here is how von Bülow described what he remembered:

> Bethmann stood in the center of the room; shall I ever forget his face, the look in his eyes? There is a picture by some celebrated English painter, which shows the wretched scapegoat with a look of ineffable anguish in its eyes, such pain as I now saw in Bethmann's. For an instant we neither of us spoke. At last I said to him, "Well, tell me, at least, how it all happened." He raised his long, thin arms to heaven and answered in a dull, exhausted voice: "Oh, if I only knew!" In many later polemics on war guilt I have often wished it had been possible to produce a snapshot of Bethmann Hollweg standing there at the moment he said those words. Such a photograph would have been the best proof that this wretched man had never wanted war.[3]

Generations of historians have examined the origins of World War I and tried to explain why war came. As we will see, it is impossible to isolate one cause, but it is possible to break the question down into distinct levels. At each of these levels, the balance of power—as *a multipolar system* and as the *policy* of separate states and individual leaders—is essential to an understanding of the war's outbreak. As the alliance system became less flexible, the balance of power became less multipolar and the likelihood of war increased.

Three Levels of Analysis

Parts of the answer lie at each of the three levels of analysis. Parsimony suggests we start with the simplest causes, see how much they explain, and go on to more complexity as needed. Thus we look first at the system-level explanations, both the structure and the process; then at the domestic societal level; and finally at the individuals. Then we use counterfactual thought experiments to see how the pieces fit together to explain World War I.

At the structural level, there were two key elements: the rise of German power and the increased rigidity in the alliance systems. The rise of German power was

Trench warfare during World War I

truly impressive. German heavy industry surpassed that of Great Britain in the 1890s, and the growth of German gross national product at the beginning of the century was twice that of Great Britain's. In the 1860s, Britain had 25 percent of the world's industrial production, but by 1913 its share had shrunk to 10 percent, and Germany's share had risen to 15 percent. Germany transformed some of its industrial strength into military capability, including a massive naval armaments program. A strategic aim of Germany's "Tirpitz Plan" of 1911 was to build the second largest navy in the world, thereby advancing itself as a world power. This expansion alarmed Britain's First Lord of the Admiralty, Winston Churchill (1874–1965). Britain began to fear becoming isolated and worried about how it would defend its far-flung empire. These fears were increased during the Boer War due to German sympathy for the Boers, the Dutch settlers in South Africa, against whom Britain was fighting at the end of the century.

In 1907, Sir Eyre Crowe, permanent secretary of the British Foreign Office, wrote a document famous in the history of British foreign policy, a long memorandum in which he tried to interpret German foreign policy. He concluded that although German policy was vague and confused, Britain clearly could not allow one country to dominate the continent of Europe. Crowe argued that the British response was nearly a law of nature.

Britain's response to Germany's rising power contributed to the second structural cause of the war: the increasing rigidity in the alliance systems in Europe. In 1904, parting from its geographically semiisolated position as a balancer off the coast of Europe, Britain moved toward an alliance with France. In 1907, the Anglo-French partnership broadened to include Russia (already allied with France) and became known as the Triple Entente. Germany, seeing itself encircled, tightened its relations with Austria-Hungary. As the alliances became more rigid, diplomatic flexibility was lost. The balance of power was no longer characterized by the shifting alignments that characterized the balance of power during Bismarck's day. Instead, the major powers wrapped themselves around two poles.

What about changes in the process? The structural shift to bipolarity affected the process by which the nineteenth-century balance-of-power system had worked. In addition, constructivists would point to three other reasons for the loss of moderation in the early twentieth-century balance of power. These included transnational ideas that were common to several countries. One was the rise of nationalism. In eastern Europe there was a movement calling for all Slavic-speaking peoples to come together. Pan-Slavism threatened both the Ottoman and Austro-Hungarian empires, which each had large Slavic populations. A nationalistic hatred of Slavs arose in Germany. German authors wrote about the inevitability of the Teutonic-Slavic battles and schoolbooks inflamed nationalist passions. Nationalism proved to be stronger than socialism when it came to bonding working classes together, and stronger than the capitalism that bound bankers together. Indeed, it proved stronger than family ties among the monarchs. Just before the war broke out, the Kaiser wrote to Russian Czar Nicholas II (1868–1918) and appealed to him to avoid war. He addressed his cousin as "Dear Nicky" and signed it "Yours, Willie." The Kaiser hoped that because war was impending over the assassination of a fellow royal family member, the Austrian Archduke Franz Ferdinand, the Czar would see things the same way he did. But by then nationalism had overcome any sense of aristocratic or monarchical solidarity, and that family telegram had no impact in preventing war.

A second cause for the loss of moderation in the early twentieth-century balance of power was a rise in complacency about peace. The great powers had not been involved in a war in Europe for 40 years. There had been crises—in Morocco in 1905–1906, in Bosnia in 1908, in Morocco again in 1911, and the Balkan wars in 1912—but they had all been manageable. However, the diplomatic compromises that resolved these conflicts caused frustration. Afterward, there was a tendency to ask, "Why should my side back down? Why didn't we make the other side give up more?" Additionally, there was growing acceptance of social Darwinism. Charles Darwin's ideas of survival of the fittest made good sense as a statistical construct about genetics of natural species over generations, but they were misapplied to human society and unique events. Darwin's ideas were used to justify the view that "the strong *should* prevail." And if the strong should prevail, why worry about peace? Long wars seemed unlikely, and many leaders believed short decisive wars won by the strong would be a welcome change.

A third contributing factor to the loss of flexibility in the early twentieth-century balance of power was German policy. As Eyre Crowe said, it was vague and confusing. There was a terrible clumsiness about the Kaiser's policy. The Germans were no different in having "world ambitions," but they managed to press them forward in a way that antagonized everybody at the same time—just the opposite of the way Bismarck played the system in the 1870s and 1880s. The Kaiser focused too much on hard power and neglected soft power. The Germans antagonized the British by starting a naval arms race (Figure 3.1). They antagonized the Russians over issues in Turkey and the Balkans, and they antagonized the French over a protectorate in Morocco. The Kaiser tried to shock Britain into a friendship, believing that if he scared Britain enough, it would realize how important Germany was and pursue improved relations. Instead, he scared the British first into the arms of the French, and then into the arms of the Russians. So by 1914, the Germans thought they had to break out of this encirclement and thereby deliberately accepted the risk of war. Thus the rise of nationalism, increased complacency, social Darwinism, and German policy all contributed to the loss of moderation in the process of the international system and helped contribute to the onset of World War I.

The second level of analysis allows us to examine what was happening in domestic society and politics prior to World War I. We can safely reject one explanation at that level: Russian revolutionary Vladimir Lenin's argument that the war was caused by the financial capitalists. In Lenin's view, World War I was simply the final stage of capitalist imperialism. But the war did not arise out of imperialist conflicts on the colonial peripheries as Lenin had expected. In 1898, Britain and France confronted each other at Fashoda in the Sudan as the British tried to complete a north-south line from South Africa to Egypt, while the French tried to create an east-west line of colonies in Africa. If war had occurred then, it might have fit Lenin's explanation. But, in fact, the war broke out 16 years later in Europe, and even then bankers and businessmen strongly resisted it. Bankers believed the war would be bad for business. Sir Edward Grey, the British foreign minister, thought he had to follow Eyre Crowe's advice and that Britain had to prevent Germany from gaining mastery of the European balance of power. But Grey also worried about getting the London bankers to go along with declaring war. We can therefore reject the

---

THE KAISER'S REACTION TO BRITAIN'S DECLARATION OF WAR

Edward VII [the Kaiser's uncle and King of England 1901–1910] in the grave is still stronger than I, who am alive! And to think there have been people who believed England could be won over or pacified with this or that petty measure!!! . . . Now this whole trickery must be ruthlessly exposed and the mask of Christian pacifism roughly and publicly torn from the face [of Britain], and the pharisaical sham peace put in the pillory!! And our consuls in Turkey and India, agents and so forth, must fire the whole Mohammedan world to fierce revolt against this hateful, lying, unprincipled nation of shopkeepers; for if we are to bleed to death, England will at least lose India.

—Kaiser Wilhelm II[4]

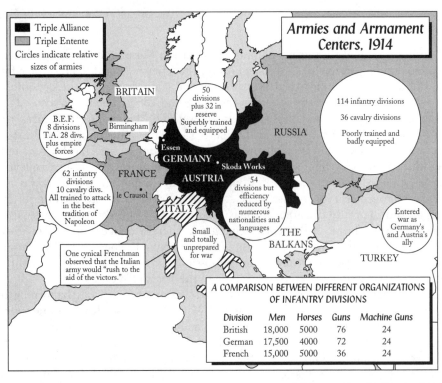

FIGURE 3.1 The European Balance of Military Power in 1914

Leninist explanation. But two other domestic causes need to be taken more seriously: the internal crisis of the declining Austro-Hungarian and Ottoman empires, and the domestic political situation in Germany.

Both Austria-Hungary and Ottoman Turkey were multinational empires and were therefore threatened by the rise of nationalism. In addition, the Ottoman government was very weak, very corrupt, and an easy target for nationalist groups in the Balkans that wanted to free themselves from centuries of Turkish rule. The Balkan wars of 1912 pushed the Turks out, but in the next year the Balkan states then fell to war among themselves when dividing the spoils. The conflicts whetted the appetite of some Balkan states to fight Austria: if the Turks could be pushed out, then why not the Austrians too?

Serbia took the lead among the Balkan states. Austria feared disintegration from this nationalistic pressure and worried about the loss of status that would result. In the end, Austria went to war against Serbia not because a Serb assassinated its Archduke, Franz Ferdinand (1863–1914), but because Austria wanted to weaken Serbia and prevent it from becoming a magnet for nationalism among the Balkan Slavs. General Conrad, the Austrian chief of staff in 1914, exposed his motives very clearly: "For this reason, and not as vengeance for the assassination, Austria-Hungary must draw the sword against Serbia. . . . The monarchy had been seized by the throat and had to choose between allowing itself to be strangled, and making a last effort to prevent its destruction."[5] Disintegration of an empire because of nationalism was the more profound cause of the war; the slain Franz Ferdinand was a pretext.

Another important domestic-level explanation of World War I lay in the domestic politics of Germany. German historian Fritz Fischer and his followers argue that Germany's social problems were a key cause of the war. According to Fischer, Germany's efforts toward world hegemony were an attempt by German elites to distract attention from the poor domestic integration of German society. He notes that Germany was ruled by a domestic coalition of landed aristocrats and some very large industrial capitalists, called the Coalition of Rye and Iron. This ruling coalition used expansionist policies to provide foreign adventures instead of domestic reform—circuses in place of bread. They viewed expansionism as an alternative to social democracy. Internal economic and social tensions are not sufficient to explain World War I, but they do help explain one source of the pressure that Germany put on the international system after 1890.

What about the first level of analysis, the role of individuals? What distinguished the leadership on the eve of World War I was its mediocrity. The Austro-Hungarian emperor, Franz Josef (1830–1926), was a tired old man who was putty in the hands of General Conrad and Count Berchtold, his duplicitous foreign minister. Ironically, Franz Ferdinand, the crown prince who was assassinated at Sarajevo, would have been a restraining force, for the potential heir had liberal political views. In Russia, Czar Nicholas II was an isolated autocrat who spent most of his time resisting change at home. He was served by incompetent foreign and defense ministers and was strongly influenced by his sickly and neurotic wife. Most important was Kaiser Wilhelm II (1859–1941), who had a great sense of inferiority. He was a blusterer,

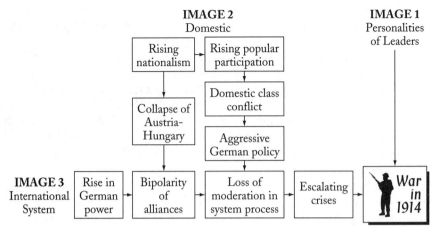

FIGURE 3.2   Causes of World War I

a weak man who was extremely emotional. He led Germany into a risky policy without any skill or consistency. To quote von Bülow:

> William II did not want war, if only because he did not trust his nerves not to give way under the strain of any really critical situation. The moment there was danger, his majesty would become uncomfortably conscious that he could never lead an army into battle. He was well aware that he was neurasthenic. His more menacing jingo speeches were intended to give the foreigner the impression that here was another Frederick the Great or Napoleon.[6]

Personality did make a difference. There was something about the leaders, the Kaiser in particular, that made them significant contributory causes of the war. The relationship among some of the systemic, societal, and individual causes are illustrated in Figure 3.2.

Was War Inevitable?

When several causes exist, each of which could be sufficient, we call a situation *overdetermined*. If World War I was overdetermined, does that mean it was inevitable? The answer is no, war was not inevitable until it actually broke out in August 1914. And even then it was not inevitable that four years of carnage had to follow.

Let us distinguish three types of causes in terms of their proximity in time to the event we are studying. The most remote are deep causes, then come intermediate causes, and those immediately before the event are precipitating causes. By analogy, ask how the lights came to be on in your room. The precipitating cause is that you flicked the switch, the intermediate cause is that someone wired the building, and the deep cause is that Thomas Edison discovered how to distribute electricity.

Another analogy is building a fire: The logs are the deep cause, the kindling and paper are the intermediate cause, and the actual striking of the match is the precipitating cause.

In World War I, the deep causes were changes in the structure of the balance of power and certain aspects of the domestic political systems. Especially important reasons were the rise of German strength, the development of a bipolar alliance system, the rise of nationalism and the resultant destruction of two declining empires, and German politics. The intermediate causes were German policy, the rise in complacency about peace, and the personal idiosyncrasies of the leaders. The precipitating cause was the assassination of Franz Ferdinand at Sarajevo by a Serbian terrorist.

Looking back, things always look inevitable. Indeed, we might say that if the assassination had not occurred, some other precipitating incident would have caused the war. Some say precipitating events are like buses—they come along every ten minutes. Thus the specific event at Sarajevo was not all that important; some incident would probably have occurred sooner or later. This type of argument can be tested by counterfactual history. We can ask, "What if?" and, "What might have been?" as we look carefully at the history of the period. What if there had been no assassination in Sarajevo? What if the Social Democrats had come to power in Germany? There is also the issue of probability. The deep and intermediate causes suggested a high probability of war, but a high probability is not the same as inevitability. Using the metaphor of the fire again, logs and kindling may sit for a long time and never be lit. Indeed, if it rains before somebody comes along with a match, they may not catch fire even when a Sarajevo occurs.

Suppose there had been no assassination in Sarajevo in 1914, and no crisis occurred until 1916; what might have happened? One possibility is that the growth in Russian strength might have deterred Germany from recklessly backing Austria. In 1914, General von Moltke and Foreign Secretary Jagow, two of the German leaders who were most influential in precipitating the war, believed that war with Russia was inevitable. They knew Germany would have a problem fighting a war on two fronts and would have to knock out one side before fighting the other. Russia, although larger, was technologically backward and had a poor transportation system, so it could be put off for the second strike. They reasoned that Germany ought first to rush westward to knock out the French. After victory in the west, Germany could turn east and take its time to defeat the Russians. Indeed, that was the Schlieffen Plan, the war plan of the German general staff, which called for a rapid sweep through Belgium (violating Belgian neutrality in the process) to knock out France quickly, and then to turn east.

But this strategy might have become obsolete by 1916 because Russia was using French money to build railroads. In the 1890s it would have taken the Russians two or three months before they could have transported all their troops to the German front, giving Germany ample time to fight France first. By 1910, that time had shrunk to 18 days, and the German planners knew they no longer had a large margin of safety. By 1916, the margin would have been gone and Germany might have had to drop its two-front strategy. Consequently, some German leaders thought that

Britain's King George V visits his cousin Kaiser Wilhelm II
at Potsdam for a wedding a little more than a year before
WWI's outbreak

a war in 1914 was better than a war later. They wanted to seize the crisis to wage and win a preventive war.

If no assassination and crisis had occurred in 1914, and the world had made it to 1916 without a war, it is possible the Germans might have felt deterred, unable to risk a two-front war. They might have been more careful before giving Austria a blank check, as they did in 1914. Or they might have dropped the Schlieffen Plan and concentrated on a war in the east only. Or they might have come to terms with Great Britain or changed their view that the offense had the advantage in warfare. In summary, in another two years, a variety of changes related to Russian strength might have prevented the war. Without war, German industrial strength would have continued to grow. Ironically, without war, the British historian A. J. P. Taylor has speculated, Germany might have won mastery over Europe. Germany might have become so strong that France and Britain would have been deterred.

We can also raise counterfactuals about what might have happened in Britain's internal affairs if two more years had passed without war. In *The Strange Death of Liberal England*, historian George Dangerfield tells of Britain's domestic turmoil. The

Liberal Party was committed to withdrawing British troops from Ireland while the Conservatives, particularly in Northern Ireland, were bitterly opposed. There was a prospect of mutiny in the British army. If the Ulster Revolt had developed, it is quite plausible that Britain would have been so internally preoccupied that it would not have been able to join the coalition with France and Russia. Certainly many historically significant changes could have occurred in two more years of peace.

What Kind of War?

Another set of counterfactuals raises questions about what *kind* of war would have occurred rather than *whether* a war would have occurred. It is true that Germany's policies frightened its neighbors and that Germany in turn was afraid of being encircled by the Triple Entente, so it is reasonable to assume war was more likely than not. But what kind of war? The war did not have to be what we now remember as World War I. Counterfactually, four other wars were possible.

One was a simple local war. Initially, the Kaiser expected a replay of the Bosnian crisis of 1908–1909 when the Germans backed the Austrians, and Austria was therefore able to make Russia stand down in the Balkans. On July 5, 1914, the Kaiser promised full support to Austria-Hungary. And with that, he went on vacation. When the Kaiser returned from his cruise, he found that the Austrians had filled in the blank check he left them by issuing an ultimatum to Serbia. When he realized that, the Kaiser made great efforts to keep the war from escalating, thus the Nicky-Willie telegrams referred to earlier. If his efforts had been successful, we might today recall not World War I, but merely a relatively minor Austrian-Serbian War of August 1914.

A second counterfactual possibility was a one-front war. When the Russians mobilized their troops, the Germans also mobilized. The Kaiser asked General von Moltke whether he could limit the preparations to just the eastern front. Von Moltke replied that it was impossible because any change in the timetables for assembling the troops and supplies would create a logistical nightmare. He told the Kaiser that if he tried to change the plans, he would have a disorganized mass instead of an army. However, after the war, General von Staab of the railway division of the German army admitted that it might have been possible, after all, to alter the mobilization schedules successfully. Had the Kaiser known that and insisted, there might have been a one-front war.

A third counterfactual is to imagine a two-front war without Britain: Germany and Austria versus France and Russia (Figure 3.3). If the British had not been there to make the difference, Germany might well have won. It is possible that Britain might not have joined if Germany had not invaded Belgium, although Belgium was not the main cause of Britain entering the war. For some people, like Sir Edward Grey and the Foreign Office, the main reason for entering the war was the danger of German control of the Continent. But Britain was a democracy, and the Liberal party in the Cabinet was split. The left Liberals opposed war, but when Germany swept through Belgium and violated Belgian neutrality, it allowed the prowar Liberals to overcome the reluctance of the antiwar Liberals and to repair the split in the British Cabinet.

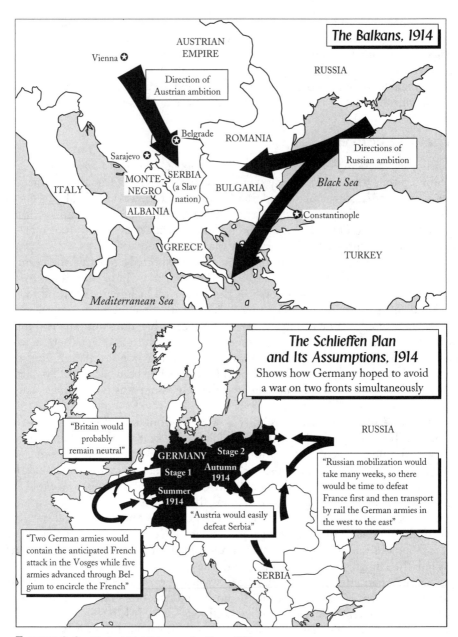

FIGURE 3.3   Flawed Thinking on the Eve of War

Finally, a fourth counterfactual is a war without the United States. By early 1918, Germany might have won the war if the United States had not tipped the military balance by its entry in 1917. One of the reasons the United States became involved was the German submarine campaign against Allied and American shipping. There was also some German clumsiness: Germany sent a message, now known as the Zimmermann telegram, instructing its embassy in Mexico to approach the Mexican government regarding an alliance against the United States. Washington regarded these intercepted instructions as a hostile act. These factors ensured that the United States would enter the war.

Our counterfactual analysis first suggests ways in which the war might not have occurred in 1914, and second, ways in which the war that occurred did not have to become four years of carnage, which destroyed Europe as the heart of the global balance of power. It suggests that World War I was probable, but not inevitable. Human choices mattered.

The Funnel of Choices

History is path dependent. Events close in over time, degrees of freedom are lost, and the probability of war increases. But the funnel of choices available to leaders might open up again, and degrees of freedom could be regained (see Figure 3.4). If we start in 1898 and ask what was the most likely war in Europe, the answer would have been war between France and Britain, which were eyeball to eyeball in a colonial dispute in Africa. But after the British and French formed the Entente in 1904, a Franco-British war looked less likely. The first Moroccan crisis in 1905 and the Bosnian crisis in 1908 made war with Germany look more likely. But some interesting events occurred in 1910. Bethmann Hollweg, the German chancellor, sought détente with Britain. Britain implied that it would remain neutral in any European war if Germany would limit its navy. At that same time, it looked as if renewed colonial friction between Britain and Russia in Asia and between the British and the French threatened a collapse or erosion of the Triple Entente. In other words, in 1910 the funnel of choices started to widen again.

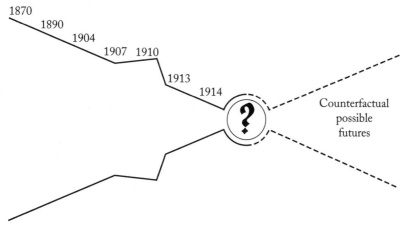

FIGURE 3.4   The Narrowing Funnel of Choices

But the funnel closed once more in 1911 with the second Moroccan crisis. When France sent troops to help the Sultan of Morocco, Germany demanded compensation in the French Congo and sent a gunboat to Agadir on the coast of Morocco. Britain prepared its fleet. French and German bankers lobbied against war, and the Kaiser pulled back. But these events deeply affected public opinion and raised fears about German intentions.

Although the Balkan wars in 1912 and 1913 and the increased pressure on Austria set the scene for 1914, there was also a renewed effort at détente in 1912. Britain sent Lord Haldane, a prominent Liberal politician, to Berlin, and the British and Germans resolved a number of the issues. Also, by this time it was clear that Britain had won the naval arms race. Perhaps the funnel would open up again.

In June 1914, the feeling that relations were improving was strong enough for Britain to send four of its great Dreadnought battleships to Kiel, Germany, for a state visit. If Britain had thought war was about to occur, the last thing it would have done was put four of its prime battleships in an enemy harbor. Clearly, the British were not thinking about war at that point. In fact, on June 28, British and German sailors were walking together along the quay in Kiel when they heard the news that a Serbian terrorist had shot an Austrian archduke in a faraway place called Sarajevo. History has its surprises, and once again, *probable* is not the same as *inevitable*.

Lessons of History Again

Can we draw any lessons from this history? We must be careful about lessons. Analogies can mislead, and many myths have been created about World War I. For example, some say World War I was an accidental war. World War I was not purely accidental. Austria went to war deliberately. And if there was to be a war, Germany preferred a war in 1914 to a war later. There were miscalculations over the length and depth of the war, but that is not the same as an accidental war.

It is also said that the war was caused by the arms race in Europe. But by 1912, the naval arms race was over, and Britain had won. While there was concern in Europe about the growing strength of the armies, the view that the war was precipitated directly by the arms race is too simple.

On the other hand, we can draw some valid warnings from the long slide into World War I. One lesson is to pay attention to the process of a balance-of-power system as well as to its structure or distribution of power. Here the constructivists add an important point that some realists miss. Moderation evolves from the process. Stability is not assured by the distribution of power alone. Another useful lesson is to beware of complacency about peace or believing that the next crisis is going to fit the same pattern as the last crisis: 1914 was supposed to be a repeat of the Bosnian crisis of 1908, though clearly it was not. In addition, the experience of World War I suggests it is important to have military forces that are stable in crisis, without any feeling that one must use them or lose them. The railway timetables were not the major determinants of World War I, but they did make it more difficult for political leaders to buy time for diplomacy.

Today's world is different from the world of 1914 in two important ways: One is that nuclear weapons have made large-scale wars more dangerous, and the other, as constructivists note, is that the ideology of war, the acceptance of war, is much weaker. In 1914, war was thought to be inevitable, a fatalistic view compounded by the social Darwinist argument that war should be welcome because it would clear the air like a good summer storm. On the eve of World War I that was indeed the mood. Winston Churchill's book *The World Crisis* captures this feeling very well:

> There was a strange temper in the air. Unsatisfied by material prosperity, the nations turned fiercely toward strife, internal or external. National passions, unduly exalted in the decline of religion, burned beneath the surface of nearly every land with fierce, if shrouded, fires. Almost one might think the world wished to suffer. Certainly men were everywhere eager to dare.[7]

They dared and they lost, and that is the lesson of 1914.

CHRONOLOGY: THE ROAD TO WORLD WAR I

1905–1906	First Moroccan crisis: Kaiser visits Tangier as Germany attempts to supplant France; settled to France's satisfaction at the Algeciras conference
1908	Austria proclaims annexation of Bosnia and Herzegovina, Slavic territories it had administered since 1878; Serbia threatens war but is powerless without Russian backing; Germany supports Austria-Hungary, deterring Russia
1911	Second Moroccan crisis: German gunboat *Panther* appears at Agadir in attempt to force France into colonial concessions in other areas in return for German recognition of French claims in Morocco
1912	First Balkan War: Bulgaria, Serbia, and Greece defeat Turkey and gain Thrace and Salonika; Austria-Hungary helps create Albania as check to Serbian power
1913	Second Balkan War: Serbia, Greece, and Romania defeat Bulgaria and gain territory at the latter's expense
1914	
June 28	Assassination of Austrian Archduke Franz Ferdinand and his wife at Sarajevo
July 5	Austria seeks and obtains German backing against Serbia
July 23	Austria sends harsh ultimatum to Serbia
July 25	Serbia rejects some terms of ultimatum; seeks Russian support
July 26	British Foreign Minister Sir Edward Grey proposes conference to resolve the crisis; Germany and Austria reject proposal
July 28	Austria declares war on Serbia
July 29	Austrian forces bombard Belgrade; Russia mobilizes against Austria
July 30	Russia and Austria order general mobilization; French troops withdraw 10 kilometers from German border
July 31	Germany delivers ultimatum to Russia, demanding demobilization; Russia does not reply

August 1	Germany declares war on Russia; British fleet mobilizes; France mobilizes as German forces invade Luxembourg
August 2	Germany demands unimpeded passage through Belgium
August 3	Belgium rejects German ultimatum; Germany declares war on France
August 4	German troops march into Belgium; Britain declares war on Germany

STUDY QUESTIONS

1. Was World War I inevitable? If so, why and when? If not, when and how could it have been avoided?

2. How might you apply Waltz's images to the origins of World War I?

3. Which of the following factors do you consider most significant in explaining the outbreak of World War I?
   a. alliance system
   b. public opinion
   c. military doctrine or military leadership (specify countries)
   d. political leadership (specify countries)
   e. economic pressures or forces
   f. misperception
   g. other

4. Thucydides argues that the underlying cause of the Peloponnesian War was the "growth of Athenian power and the fear which this caused in Sparta." To what extent was World War I caused by the growth of German power and the fear this caused in Britain? Or the growth of Russian power and the fear this caused in Germany?

5. To what extent, if any, was World War I "accidental"? Does it make sense to talk about "accidental" wars? What about "unintended" ones?

6. What do realist, liberal, and constructivist approaches add to our understanding of the origins of World War I?

7. What are some "lessons" from 1914 that might help policy makers avoid war today?

NOTES

1. Richard Cobden, *The Political Writings of Richard Cobden* (London: Unwin, 1903; New York: Kraus Reprint, 1969).

2. Winston Churchill, June 22, 1941, to his private secretary Sir John Colville, quoted in Robert Rhodes James, ed., *Churchill Speaks: Winston Churchill in Peace and War: Collected Speeches 1897–1963* (New York: Chelsea, 1980).

3. Bernhard von Bülow, *Memoirs of Prince von Bülow 1909–1919* (Boston: Little, Brown, 1932), pp. 165–166.

4. Kaiser Wilhelm II, quoted in Lebow, *Between Peace and War*, p. 139.

5. Baron Conrad von Hotzendorff, quoted in Sidney Fay, *The Origins of the World War*, vol. 2 (New York: Macmillan, 1929), pp. 185–186.

6. Richard Ned Lebow, *Between Peace and War: The Nature of International Crisis* (Baltimore: Johns Hopkins University Press, 1981), p. 144.

7. Winston Churchill, *The World Crisis* (New York: Scribner's, 1923), p. 188.

SELECTED READINGS

1. Gulick, Edward, *Europe's Classical Balance of Power* (New York: Norton, 1967), pp. 1–34, 184–218.
2. Joll, James, *The Origins of the First World War* (New York: Longman, 1984), pp. 9–147.
3. Kennedy, Paul, "The Kaiser and German *Weltpolitik*," in John C. G. Rohl and Nicholas Sombart, eds., *Kaiser Wilhelm II: New Interpretations, the Corfu Papers* (Cambridge: Cambridge University Press, 1982), pp. 143–168.
4. Lowe, John, *The Great Powers, Imperialism and the German Problem, 1865–1925* (London and New York: Routledge, 1994), pp. 202–239.

FURTHER READINGS

Christiansen, Thomas, and Jack Snyder, "Chain Gangs and Passed Bucks," *International Organization* 44:2 (Spring 1990), pp. 139–168.

Dangerfield, George, *The Strange Death of Liberal England* (New York: Capricorn, 1961).

Ferguson, Niall, *The Pity of War: Explaining World War I* (London: Basic, 1999).

Fischer, Fritz, *World Power or Decline: The Controversy Over Germany's Aims in the First World War* (New York: Norton, 1974).

Howard, Michael, *The Causes of War and Other Essays* (Cambridge, MA: Harvard University Press, 1984).

Kennedy, Paul M., *The Rise of the Anglo-German Antagonism: 1860–1914* (London: Allen & Unwin, 1980).

Kupchan, Charles A., *The Vulnerability of Empire* (Ithaca, NY: Cornell University Press, 1994).

Lebow, Richard Ned, *Between Peace and War: The Nature of International Crisis* (Baltimore: Johns Hopkins University Press, 1981).

Maier, Charles S., "Wargames: 1914–1919," in Robert I. Rotberg and Theodore K. Rabb, eds., *The Origin and Prevention of Major Wars* (New York: Cambridge University Press, 1989), pp. 249–280.

Miller, Steven, Sean M. Lynn-Jones, and Stephen Van Evera, eds., *Military Strategy and the Origins of the First World War* (Princeton, NJ: Princeton University Press, 1991).

Nye, Joseph. S., Jr., *Soft Power: The Means to Success in World Politics* (New York: Public Affairs, 2004).

Organski, A. F. K., and Jacek Kugler, *The War Ledger* (Chicago: University of Chicago Press, 1980).

Rock, Stephen R., *Why Peace Breaks Out: Great Power Rapprochement in Historical Perspective* (Chapel Hill: University of North Carolina Press, 1989).

Sagan, Scott, "1914 Revisited: Allies, Offense, and Stability," *International Security* 11:2 (Fall 1986), pp. 151–176.

Schroeder, Paul W., "World War One as Galloping Gertie: A Reply to Joachim Remak," *Journal of Modern History* 44:3 (1972).

Snyder, Jack L., *Myths of Empire: Domestic Politics and International Ambition* (Ithaca, NY: Cornell University Press, 1991).

Trachtenberg, Marc, *History and Strategy* (Princeton, NJ: Princeton University Press, 1991), chap. 2.

Tuchman, Barbara, *The Guns of August* (New York: Macmillan, 1962).

Turner, L. C. F., *The Origins of World War I* (London: Edward Arnold, 1983).

Walt, Stephen, *The Origins of Alliances* (Ithaca, NY: Cornell University Press, 1987).

Williamson, Samuel R., "The Origin of World War I," in Robert I. Rotberg and Theodore K. Rabb, eds., *The Origin and Prevention of Major Wars* (New York: Cambridge University Press, 1989), pp. 225–248.

Wilson, Keith, *Decisions for War, 1914* (New York: St. Martin's, 1995).

4

The Failure of Collective Security and World War II

Victorious Allied leaders Lloyd George, Clemenceau, and Wilson
shortly before the signing of the Treaty of Versailles, 1919

THE RISE AND FALL OF COLLECTIVE SECURITY

World War I caused enormous social disruption and shock waves of revulsion at the senseless slaughter (Table 4.1). Balance-of-power politics was widely blamed for the war. Woodrow Wilson, the American president during World War I, was a classic

TABLE 4.1   War Deaths, 1914–1918

Country	Deaths
Austria-Hungary	1,250,000
Britain (including empire)	900,000
Bulgaria	100,000
France	1,500,000
Germany	1,750,000
Italy	600,000
Romania	300,000
Russia	1,750,000
Serbia	50,000
Turkey	30,000
United States	112,000

nineteenth-century liberal who regarded balance-of-power policies as immoral because they violated democratic principles and national self-determination. He argued, "The balance of power is the great game now forever discredited. It's the old and evil order that prevailed before this war. The balance of power is a thing that we can do without in the future."[1]

Wilson had a point, because balance-of-power policies do not give priority to democracy or peace. As we have seen, the balance of power is a way to preserve the sovereign state system. States act to prevent any state from becoming preponderant. The resulting balance of power allows for war or violations of self-determination if that is the only way to preserve independence. However, World War I was so devastating, chaotic, and brutal that many people began to think that war to preserve the balance of power was no longer tolerable. But if the world could not afford a balance-of-power system, what would take its place?

Sovereign states could not be abolished, Wilson admitted, but force could be tamed by law and institutions as it was at the domestic level. The liberal solution was to develop international institutions analogous to domestic legislatures and courts so that democratic procedures could be applied at the international level. Some liberals of the day thought that not only was World War I fought to make the world safe for democracy, but in turn democracy could make the world more peaceful. In January 1918, Wilson issued a 14-point statement of America's reasons for entering the war. The fourteenth point was the most important. It called for "a general association of nations to be formed under specific covenants for the purpose of affording mutual guarantees of political independence and territorial integrity to great and small states alike." In effect, Wilson wanted to change the international system from one based on balance-of-power politics to another based on collective security.

The League of Nations

Although critics called Wilson a utopian, he believed that organizing international security could be a practical approach to world politics. He knew mere paper agreements and treaties would not be sufficient; organizations and rules were needed to implement the agreements and enforce the rules. This is why Wilson put so much faith in the idea of a League of Nations. Moral force was important, but a military force was necessary to back it up. Security had to be a collective responsibility. If all nonaggressive states banded together, Wilson believed that the preponderance of power would be on the side of the good. International security would be a collective responsibility in which nonaggressive countries would form a coalition against aggressors. Peace would be indivisible.

How could the states bring about such a new system of collective security? First, make aggression illegal and outlaw offensive war. Second, deter aggression by forming a coalition of all nonaggressive states. If all pledged to aid any state that was a victim anywhere in the world, a preponderance of power would exist on the side of the nonaggressive forces. Third, if deterrence failed and aggression occurred, all states would agree to punish the state that committed aggression. This doctrine of collective security bore some similarities to balance-of-power policies in that states tried to deter aggression by developing a powerful coalition, and if deterrence failed they were willing to use force.

But there were three important differences between the collective-security and balance-of-power approaches. First, in collective security the focus was on the aggressive policies of a state rather than its capacity. This contrasted with balance-of-power politics, in which alliances were created against any state that was becoming too strong; that is, the focus was on the capacity of states. Second, unlike in a balance-of-power system in which coalitions were formed in advance, coalitions in a collective-security system could not be predetermined because it was not known which states would be aggressors. However, once aggression occurred, all states would band against the aggressor. Third, collective security was designed to be global and universal with no neutrals or free riders. If too many countries were neutral, the coalition of the good might appear weak and diminish the coalition's ability to deter or punish the aggressor.

The doctrine of collective security was embodied in the Covenant of the League of Nations, which, in turn, was part of the treaties that ended World War I. Several of the articles of the League of Nations Covenant were especially noteworthy. In Article 10, states pledged to protect all members against aggression. In Article 11, any war or threat of war was declared to be of concern to all states. In Articles 12 and 15, states agreed to submit their disputes to arbitration and not to go to war until three months after arbitration failed. Article 16, the critical article, said any war disregarding the League of Nations procedures would be regarded as a declaration of war against all the members of the League of Nations. The state that started a war would be immediately subject to economic sanctions, and the Council of the League might recommend further military measures.

This sounds straightforward, but there were ambiguities. All members had to agree to apply collective security. Thus each state had a veto. When states signed the Covenant they agreed to abide by Article 16, but in practice it was up to each state to decide what kinds of sanctions to apply and how to implement them; they were not bound by any higher authority. Thus the League of Nations was not a move toward world government in which a higher authority could commit the member states to certain policies. It was not the end of the anarchic system of states, but rather an effort to make the states collectively discipline unruly members of the international system.

Collective security involves two related concepts: *sovereignty* and *international law*. The definition of sovereignty is very simple: legal supremacy within a given territory. As championed by state moralists and established by the League of Nations, the sovereignty of the state is absolute and inviolable; a state government has full authority within its borders. It can limit that authority only with its own consent; that is, if a government signs a treaty allowing another government to have some influence in its domains, which is an agreed limitation rather than an infringement of sovereignty. Thus by signing the pact of the League of Nations, states would voluntarily give up some sovereignty to the international community in return for the guarantees of collective security and international law.

As understood by Wilson and implied in the League of Nations charter, international law transcended national law and hence sovereignty in particular situations. Ever since the Peace of Westphalia in 1648, a central tenet of international law has been that states are sovereign except when they violate international law, in which case they are subject to punishment. Collective security was to international law what the police are to domestic law. However, international law enjoyed far less acceptance among states than domestic law. Many states refused to be constrained by international law and saw compliance as voluntary rather than mandatory.

The United States and the League of Nations

The unwillingness of states to relinquish some sovereignty in exchange for collective security lay at the heart of one of the League's most notable weaknesses: the failure of the United States to join its own creation. The American Senate refused to ratify the Treaty of Versailles, which contained language endorsing the creation of the League of Nations. As a result, the collective-security system had to function without what would have been its biggest player.

Why did the United States hold back when, to a large extent, the League was an American liberal plan to reorder world politics? After World War I, most Americans wanted to return to "normalcy." Many defined "normal" as avoiding involvement in international affairs. Opponents of American involvement in world affairs claimed that the Monroe Doctrine of 1823 limited American interests to the Western Hemisphere, and noted George Washington's warning that the United States should avoid "entangling alliances." The leader of this opposition to the League of Nations, Senator Henry Cabot Lodge of Massachusetts, feared that Article 16 of the Covenant would dilute both American sovereignty and the constitutional power of the Senate to declare war. Lodge suspected the United States might be drawn into distant wars on the basis of the League's decisions to enforce collective security rather than by the Senate's decision or the will of the American people.

The debate between President Wilson and Senator Lodge is sometimes portrayed as a clash between an idealist and a realist, but it can also be seen as a debate between different forms of American moralism. Wilson's obdurate refusal to negotiate terms with Lodge was part of the problem. But Lodge's resistance reflected a long-standing American attitude toward the balance of power in Europe. Opponents of the League believed that European states pursued immoral policies in the name of the balance of power, and that America should not become an active player in such games. In fact, however, the United States was able to ignore the balance of power in the nineteenth century because Americans were enjoying a free ride behind Britain's fleet. Other European countries could not penetrate the Western Hemisphere to threaten Americans. And though the United States was isolationist toward Europe, it was not at all isolationist when it came to interfering in the affairs of its weak neighbors in Central America, Mexico, or Cuba. At the end of World War I Americans were torn between two forms of moralism, and the isolationist impulse toward the European balance of power won. The result was that the country that had tipped the balance of power in World War I refused to accept responsibility for the postwar order.

> My conception of the League of Nations is just this, that it shall operate as the organized moral force of men throughout the world, and that whenever or wherever wrong and aggression are planned or contemplated, this searching light of conscience shall be turned upon them.
>
> —*Woodrow Wilson*[2]

The Early Days of the League

What France wanted more than anything else at the end of World War I was military guarantees that Germany could not rise again. Because the United States would not join the League of Nations, France pressed Britain for a security guarantee and military preparations in case Germany recovered. Britain resisted on the grounds that such an alliance would be against the spirit of collective security because it would identify the aggressor in advance. Moreover, Britain saw France as stronger than Germany, and argued there was no need for an alliance, even on traditional balance-of-power terms. Britain said it was important to reintegrate Germany into the international system, just as the Congress of Vienna had brought France back into the Concert of Europe at the end of the Napoleonic Wars in 1815. War passions had abated more quickly in Britain than in France, and the British felt it was time to appease the Germans by bringing them back into the process.

Unmoved by these arguments, France formed alliances with Poland, which had been reborn at the end of World War I, and with the "Little Entente," the states of Yugoslavia, Czechoslovakia, and Romania, which had emerged out of the former Austro-Hungarian Empire. The French policy fell between two stools: not only were these alliances against the spirit of collective security, but they did not do very much for France in terms of the balance of power. Poland was on bad terms with its neighbors and, as France's ally, acted as a poor substitute for Russia, which had been ostracized because of the Bolshevik Revolution. The Little Entente states were destabilized by ethnic problems and domestic divisions, and as a result were also weak allies.

Germany emerged from World War I enormously weakened (Figure 4.1). It lost 25,000 square miles of territory and 7 million members of its population. Signed in June 1919, the Treaty of Versailles forced Germany to reduce its army to only 100,000 men and prohibited it from having an air force. The treaty contained the famous "war guilt clause," placing the blame for war solely on Germany. Because Germany was responsible, the victors argued Germany should pay for its costs. The reparations bill was $33 billion, a sum Germans thought impossibly high given their damaged economic position. When they initially failed to pay, France sent troops to occupy Germany's Ruhr industrial area until they did. After engaging in passive

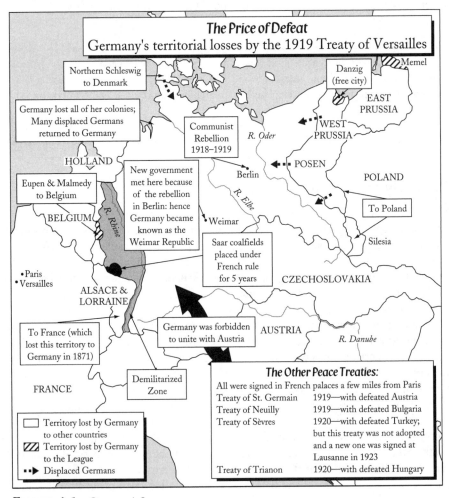

The Price of Defeat
Germany's territorial losses by the 1919 Treaty of Versailles

Northern Schleswig to Denmark

Germany lost all of her colonies; Many displaced Germans returned to Germany

Communist Rebellion 1918–1919

R. Oder

Danzig (free city)

Memel

EAST PRUSSIA

WEST PRUSSIA

POSEN

HOLLAND

Eupen & Malmedy to Belgium

New government met here because of the rebellion in Berlin: hence Germany became known as the Weimar Republic

Berlin

R. Elbe

Weimar

POLAND

To Poland

Silesia

BELGIUM

R. Rhine

Saar coalfields placed under French rule for 5 years

CZECHOSLOVAKIA

• Paris
• Versailles

ALSACE & LORRAINE

Germany was forbidden to unite with Austria

AUSTRIA

R. Danube

To France (which lost this territory to Germany in 1871)

FRANCE

Demilitarized Zone

☐ Territory lost by Germany to other countries
▨ Territory lost by Germany to the League
◾▶ Displaced Germans

The Other Peace Treaties:
All were signed in French palaces a few miles from Paris
Treaty of St. Germain   1919—with defeated Austria
Treaty of Neuilly   1919—with defeated Bulgaria
Treaty of Sèvres   1920—with defeated Turkey; but this treaty was not adopted and a new one was signed at Lausanne in 1923
Treaty of Trianon   1920—with defeated Hungary

FIGURE 4.1   Germany's Losses

resistance, Germany suffered enormous inflation that wiped out the savings of its middle class. That in turn removed one of the sources of internal stability as the Weimar Republic struggled to create democracy.

Italy had never been keen on the Paris peace treaties or the League of Nations. Italy had originally been allied with Germany and Austria-Hungary, but at the beginning of the war, the Italians decided they would get a better payoff from the Allies and switched sides. In the secret Treaty of London signed in 1915, Italy was promised compensation at the expense of the part of the Austro-Hungarian Empire that became postwar Yugoslavia. The Italians expected that these promises would be honored, but Woodrow Wilson objected to such old-fashioned spoils-of-war behavior. In addition, after Benito Mussolini and the fascists took power in 1922, one of their foreign policy aims was to gain glory and finally fulfill the destiny of a new Roman Empire. The goals were inconsistent with the new vision of collective security.

With such a start, it is remarkable the League was able to achieve anything at all. Yet 1924–1930 was a period of relative successes. Plans were made to scale down the reparations Germany had to pay. In 1924, governments signed a protocol on the peaceful settlement of disputes in which they promised to arbitrate their differences. Perhaps most important, in 1925, the Treaty of Locarno allowed Germany to enter the League of Nations and gave Germany a seat on its council.

The Treaty of Locarno had two aspects. In the west, Germany guaranteed that its borders with France and Belgium would be inviolable. Alsace-Lorraine, taken by Bismarck in the War of 1870, had been returned to France by the Treaty of Versailles, and Germany promised to demilitarize a zone along the Rhine. Locarno reaffirmed those results. In the east, Germany promised to arbitrate before pursuing changes in its eastern border with Poland and Czechoslovakia. This second clause should have set off a warning bell, however, for there were now two kinds of borders around Germany—an inviolable part in the west and a negotiable part in the east. But at that time, these agreements looked like progress.

The League managed to settle some minor disputes, such as one between Greece and Bulgaria, and it began a process of disarmament negotiations. Following up on the 1921 Washington Conference, in which the United States, Britain, and Japan had agreed to a measure of naval disarmament, the League organized a preparatory commission for broader disarmament talks, setting the scene for a worldwide conference that finally met (too late) in 1932. In addition, in 1928, states agreed to outlaw war in the Kellogg-Briand Pact, named after the American and French foreign ministers. Most important, the League became a center of diplomatic activity. Although not members, the Americans and the Russians began to send observers to the League meetings in Geneva. The world financial collapse in October 1929 and the success of the National Socialist Party in the 1930 German elections were harbingers of problems to come, yet there was still a sense of progress at the September 1930 annual assembly of the League of Nations. But that optimism about the collective-security system was dispelled by two crises in the 1930s over Manchuria and Ethiopia.

The Manchurian Failure

To understand the Manchurian case, we must understand the situation in Japan. Japan had transformed itself from a potential victim of imperialist aggression in the mid-nineteenth century to a very successful imperialist power by the century's end. Japan defeated Russia in a war during 1904–1905, colonized Korea in 1910, and joined the Allies in World War I. After the war, Japan sought recognition as a major power. Europeans and Americans resisted. At the Paris peace talks in 1919, the Western governments rejected a Japanese proposal that the Covenant of the League affirm the principle of racial equality. This decision mirrored the domestic political sentiment in the American Congress, which, in the 1920s, passed racist laws excluding Japanese immigrants. Simultaneously, Britain ended its bilateral treaty with Japan. Many Japanese thought the rules were changed just as they were about to enter the club of the great powers.

China was the other actor in the Manchurian crisis. The 1911 revolution led to the fall of the Manchu or Qing dynasty that had ruled China since 1644 and established a republic. But the nation quickly fell into chaos as regional civil wars broke out among contending warlords. Manchuria, though part of China, was under the sway of one of these warlords and maintained a quasi-independent status. With Chiang Kai-shek (1887–1975) as chief military adviser to the republic, the Chinese Nationalist movement tried to unify the country, and bitterly criticized the unequal treaties that had humiliated and exploited China ever since the end of the imperialist Opium Wars of the nineteenth century. As the Nationalists gained strength in the 1920s, friction with Japan increased and China declared a boycott against Japanese goods.

Meanwhile in Japan, military and civilian factions contended for dominance. The global economic crisis that began in the late 1920s left Japan, an island nation, extremely vulnerable. The military cliques gained the upper hand. In September 1931, the Japanese army staged an incident along the Manchurian Railway, where they had had a right to station troops since the Russo-Japanese War of 1904–1905. This act of sabotage on the Manchurian Railway provided Japan with a pretext to take over all of Manchuria. Although Japan said its actions were intended to protect the Manchurian Railway, it went further and set up a Japanese-controlled puppet state that was called Manchukuo, installing China's last Manchu emperor, Pu Yi, as its ruler. China appealed to the League of Nations to condemn Japan's aggression, but Japan prevented passage of a resolution asking it to withdraw its troops. In December 1931, the League agreed to send a committee under the British Lord Lytton to investigate the events in Manchuria. Lord Lytton finally reported to the League in October 1932. His report identified Japan as the aggressor, and rejected Japan's pretext as an unjustified intervention. Although his report recommended that the members of the League of Nations not recognize the state of Manchukuo, it did not call for applying Article 16 sanctions against Japan. In February 1933, the Assembly of the League of Nations voted 42 to 1 to accept Lytton's report on the Japanese invasion of Manchuria. The one opposing vote was Japan, which then announced its intention to withdraw from the League of Nations. Overall, the

Manchurian case showed the procedures of the League of Nations to be slow, cautious, and totally ineffective. The Manchurian episode had tested the League, and it failed.

The Ethiopian Debacle

The last great test of the League of Nations' collective-security system came in Ethiopia in 1935. This time sanctions were applied, but the outcome was again failure. Italy had long planned to annex Ethiopia; not only was it near Italy's colonies in Eritrea on the Red Sea, but the fascists felt affronted that the Ethiopians had defeated an Italian effort to colonize them during the imperialist era in the nineteenth century. Fascist ideologists argued that this historic "wrong" should be rectified. Between 1934 and 1935, Italy provoked incidents on the border between Ethiopia and Eritrea. It did so despite the existence of a peace treaty between Ethiopia and Italy, and despite the fact that Italy had signed the Kellogg-Briand Pact outlawing war, and that as a member of the League of Nations, it was committed to arbitrate for three months before doing anything.

In October 1935, Italy invaded Ethiopia. The invasion was a clear-cut case of aggression, and the Council of the League avoided an Italian veto by the procedural device of calling for a special conference to decide what sanctions to impose against Italy. Fifty states attended, and eight days after the invasion the conference recommended to member states that they impose four sanctions: an embargo on the sale of all military goods to Italy, a prohibition against loans to Italy, cessation of imports from Italy, and refusal to sell certain goods that could not be easily bought elsewhere, such as rubber and tin. But three things were missing: Italy was still allowed to buy steel, coal, and oil; diplomatic relations were not broken; and Britain did not close the Suez Canal to Italy, allowing it to continue shipment of materials to Eritrea.

Why didn't the members of the League of Nations do more? There was general optimism that the recommended sanctions would force Italy to withdraw from Ethiopia. Sanctions certainly had an effect on the Italian economy: Italian exports declined by about one-third during the following year, the value of the Italian lira declined, and there were estimates that Italy's gold reserves would be exhausted in nine months. But aside from inflicting economic damage, sanctions did not cause Mussolini to change his policies toward Ethiopia. The anger of Britain and France over Ethiopia was more than offset by their concern for the European balance of power. Britain and France wanted to avoid alienating Italy because Germany, now under Hitler's leadership, was regaining its strength, and Britain and France thought it would be useful to have Italy in a coalition to balance Germany. In 1934, when it looked as though Hitler would annex Austria, Mussolini moved Italian troops to the Austrian border and Hitler backed down. The British and French therefore hoped Mussolini could be persuaded to join a coalition against Germany.

Traditional diplomats did not fight the League of Nations' collective-security system; they reinterpreted it according to the old balance-of-power approach. From a balance-of-power perspective, the last thing they wanted was to become involved in a distant conflict in Africa when there were pressing problems in the heart of Europe.

Distant aggression in Africa, said the traditional realists, was not a threat to European security. Conciliation and negotiation were needed to bring the Italians back into the coalition to balance Germany. Not surprisingly, the British and French began to get cold feet about sanctions. Sir Samuel Hoare and Pierre Laval, the British and French foreign ministers, met in December 1935 and drew up a plan that divided Ethiopia into two parts, one Italian and the other a League of Nations zone. When someone leaked this plan to the press, there was outrage in Britain. Accused of having sold out the League of Nations and collective security, Hoare was forced to resign.

But within three months, British opinion turned again. In March 1936, Hitler denounced the Locarno treaties and marched German troops into the demilitarized Rhineland. Britain and France immediately stopped worrying about Ethiopia. They met with Italy to consult about how to restore the balance of power in Europe. Consequently, the balance of power in Europe prevailed over the application of the collective-security doctrine in Africa. In May 1936, the Italians completed their military victory, and by July the sanctions were removed.

The best line in this tragedy was spoken by the Haitian delegate to the League of Nations: "Great or small, strong or weak, near or far, white or colored, let us never forget that one day we may be somebody's Ethiopia."[3] Within a few years, most European nations fell prey to Hitler's aggression in World War II. The world's first efforts at collective security were a dismal failure.

THE ORIGINS OF WORLD WAR II

World War II overshadows all other wars in terms of its human costs, estimated to be between 35 and 50 million people. The war was noted for advances in weaponry. Tanks and planes that had just been introduced and played an insignificant role in World War I dominated World War II. Radar played a significant role, for example, in the Battle of Britain, one of the turning points in World War II. And at the end of the war, of course, the atomic bomb ushered in the dawn of the nuclear age.

World War II ended with unconditional surrender. Unlike World War I, the Western Allies occupied Germany and Japan and transformed their societies during the occupation. The "German problem" was solved for half a century by dividing Germany. World War II also created a bipolar world in which the United States and the Soviet Union emerged from the conflict much stronger than the world's former great powers. The war represented the end of Europe as the arbiter of the balance of power. Now Europe became an arena where outsiders contended, somewhat like Germany before 1870. The end of World War II in 1945 created the framework for world order until 1989.

Hitler's War?

World War II (1939–1945) is often called "Hitler's war." While true, such an explanation is too simple. World War II was also old business, Act II of the Great War that ended Europe's hegemony in 1918; the interwar period was only an intermission. Hitler wanted war, but not the war we now know as World War II. He wanted a short sharp war, a blitzkrieg. Another reason it was not simply Hitler's war was the war in the Pacific. Hitler had continually, but unsuccessfully, urged the Japanese to attack the British colony of Singapore or to attack Siberia to divert Soviet troops away from Europe. Japan did neither; it surprised Hitler by attacking the American naval base at Pearl Harbor instead. The war in the Pacific, while part of World War II, had different origins and was more a traditional imperial effort at regional hegemony.

On the other hand, we can go too far in emphasizing other causes. Some historians have nearly exonerated Hitler. A. J. P. Taylor argues that while Hitler was a terrible person and a very unpleasant adventurer, he was merely an opportunist stepping into the power vacuums created by the appeasement policies of the Western democracies. But Taylor goes too far. For example, Hitler's 1924 book, *Mein Kampf*, set forth a vague

Hitler greeted by the Reichstag in 1939

> Here, it seems to me, is the key to the problem whether Hitler deliberately aimed at war. He did not so much aim at war as expect it to happen, unless he could evade it by some ingenious trick, as he had evaded civil war at home. Those who have evil motives easily attribute them to others; and Hitler expected others to do what he would have done in their place.
>
> —A. J. P. Taylor, The Origins of the Second World War[4]

plan that Taylor dismisses as Hitler's ranting in resentment of the French invasion of the Ruhr. But Hitler wrote another, secret book in 1928 that repeated many of the arguments in *Mein Kampf*. Even if it was not a detailed plan, it was a clear indication of where he wanted to go.

Taylor also deals too lightly with the "Hossbach memorandum." Colonel Hossbach, an aide to Hitler, took notes at a meeting at Berchtesgaden in 1937 that detailed Hitler's plan to seize foreign territory by 1943, before Germany's preeminence became obsolete. Hitler knew it was important to take opportunities when they arose in the east, and that Austria and Czechoslovakia would be his first targets. Taylor dismisses the importance of this memo by saying it was not an *official* memorandum. Since Taylor wrote, additional evidence has come to light. We know Hitler talked often of this timetable and of these objectives. The Hossbach memorandum generally predicted Hitler's actions.

Hitler's Strategy

Hitler had four options after he came to power in 1933, and he rejected three of them. He could have chosen passivity, accepting Germany's weakened international position. He could have tried expansion through economic growth (like Japan after World War II) and led Germany to international influence through industrial expansion. He could have limited his goals to revision of the Treaty of Versailles and regained some of Germany's 1918 losses. This option seemed likely even if some other leader had come to power in Germany. By the 1930s, the Western democracies were sensitive to the injustice of blaming Germany for *all* of World War I. But these three strategies were rejected by Hitler, who chose instead an expansionist strategy to break out from what he saw as Germany's containment. In his view, Germany, stuck in the middle of Europe, could not live forever encircled. It had to gain land. He would go east for living space, expand his base, and at a later stage go for a larger world role.

Hitler followed this fourth option through four phases. First, he set out to destroy the Versailles framework through a very clever set of diplomatic maneuvers. In October 1933, he withdrew from the League of Nations and from the disarmament conference the League had convened. He blamed the withdrawal on the French, who he said were not willing to cut their forces in the disarmament conference, thereby making it impossible for Germany to continue in the League or the conference. In January of 1934, he signed a treaty with Poland, disrupting the arrangements France had been trying to make with Poland and the smaller eastern European states through the "Little Entente." In March 1935, Hitler denounced the military clauses of the Versailles treaty, saying Germany would no longer be restricted to an army of 100,000. Instead he announced plans to triple the army and build an air force.

The British, French, and Italians met at Stresa (in Italy) to respond to Hitler's activities, but before they could reach a consensus, Hitler invited Britain to enter negotiations on a naval treaty. Britain leapt at the opportunity, thereby disrupting any coordinated response from the Stresa meeting. In March 1936, when events in Ethiopia diverted attention from central Europe, Hitler moved his troops into the Rhineland, which had been demilitarized by the Locarno Pact. He blamed France for forcing him to do this, claiming France had destroyed the Locarno treaty by developing an arrangement with the Soviet Union. He dropped hints that he might return to the League of Nations after the other states in Europe accepted his views about the revisions of the Versailles treaty, a clever maneuver that played on guilt and uncertainty in many Western capitals.

The second phase (1936–1940) was Hitler's expansion into the small countries neighboring Germany. In 1936, Hitler outlined a four-year economic plan for a military buildup in order to be ready for war by 1940. He signed the Axis Pact with Italy and an Anti-Comintern Pact with Japan. (Founded by Lenin in 1919 to foment worldwide Bolshevik-style revolution, the Communist International or Comintern changed its policy in 1935 under Stalin to support so-called "Popular Front" governments, antifascist coalitions comprised of socialists, anarchists, and "bourgeois parties"). Hitler also intervened on the side of the fascists in their war against a left-wing democratically elected popular-front government in Spain. Hitler justified sending troops and bombers to support the fascist general Francisco Franco in the Spanish Civil War (1936–1939) as part of the protection of the West against the threat of bolshevism. In 1937, Spain became a testing ground for Germany's military muscle when Hitler's pilots bombed defenseless civilian populations and annihilated the Basque city of Guernica. Despite widespread international outcry, France, Great Britain, and the United States did little or nothing to defend the loyalists of the Spanish Republic. The following year, Chancellor Schuschnigg of Austria called for a plebiscite on whether Austria should reunite with Germany, hoping that the Austrian people would vote against it before Hitler forced it upon them. But Hitler intervened. In 1938, German troops marched into Vienna, ending Austrian independence.

Czechoslovakia was next. Hitler pressured Czechoslovakia by pushing the issue of national self-determination for the 3 million Germans in the Sudetenland section of Czechoslovakia. This area where Czechoslovakia borders Germany was militarily important because it included the Bohemian mountains, the natural line of defense for Czechoslovakia and the logical place for Czechs to mount their defense against potential German attack. Hitler argued that the post–World War I settlement that put these German-speaking people in Czechoslovakian territory was a violation of their self-determination and another example of the perfidy of the Western countries. He demanded that the German-speaking territory be permitted to leave Czechoslovakia to join the German fatherland. The Czechs became worried and mobilized portions of their reserves. That infuriated Hitler, who vowed to crush Czechoslovakia.

These events also alarmed Britain, which did not want war to break out in Europe. Neville Chamberlain, the British prime minister from 1937 to 1940, made three trips to Germany to try to stave off the war. Chamberlain believed it was not possible for Britain to defend Czechoslovakia because of the distance and because Britain had no troops on the Continent. More important, he did not think Czechoslovakia was worth war and he knew Britain was not ready for war. As the bombing of Guernica had shown, air power was becoming more significant, fear of bombing campaigns was growing, and Chamberlain realized the British air defense and radar systems were not ready for an air war. For this combination of reasons, Chamberlain met with Hitler at Munich in September 1938 and agreed to the partition of Czechoslovakia, giving the Sudetenland to Germany if Hitler would promise to leave the rest of Czechoslovakia alone. Hitler promised, and Chamberlain returned to Britain claiming that he had saved Czechoslovakia and achieved "peace in our time."

Only six months later, in March 1939, German troops rolled into the rest of Czechoslovakia and took the capital city, Prague. A shocked Britain realized Hitler might seek further conquests and that his next target might be Poland. Divided in the eighteenth century, Poland was re-created as a state after World War I and given a corridor to the port of Danzig on the Baltic Sea, though the area included German-speaking people. Once again, Hitler used the same tactics. He claimed that having German-speaking people inside Polish territory was a violation of self-determination, another example of the perfidy of the Versailles treaty. This time, Britain and France tried to deter Hitler by issuing a guarantee to defend Poland.

Hitler then pulled off a brilliant diplomatic coup. Despite having said he would protect the West against bolshevism, Hitler suddenly signed a treaty with Stalin in August 1939. The pact gave Hitler a free hand to do what he wanted in the West. It also included a secret protocol for another partition of Poland. Stalin and Hitler each agreed to take a part. Hitler seized his part by starting a war against Poland on September 1, 1939. This time, he was not looking for another Munich agreement in which the British would step in and give him part of Poland in return for promises of moderation.

> Now Poland is in the position in which I wanted her. . . . I am only afraid that at the last moment some swine or other will submit to me a plan for mediation.
>
> —Adolf Hitler, August 27, 1939[5]

Phase three of Hitler's strategy was short. Germany achieved military mastery on the Continent in 1940 (Figure 4.2). After Hitler took Poland, things

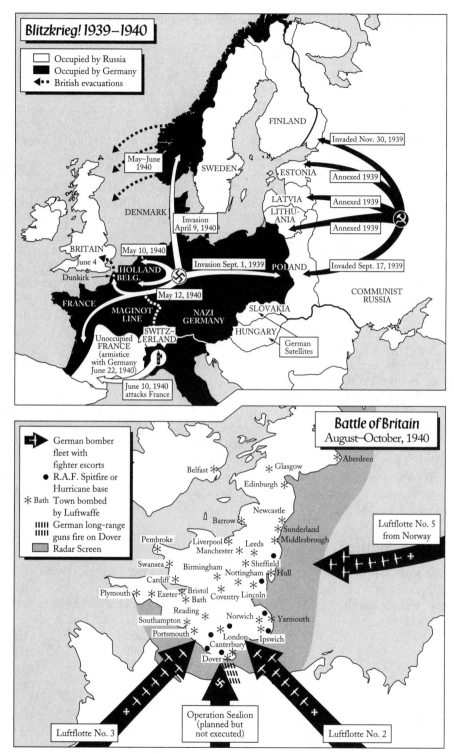

FIGURE 4.2 The Onset of World War II, 1940

were temporarily quiet; this period was called the "phony war." Hitler expected Britain to sue for peace. In the spring of 1940, however, Hitler feared Britain would move troops to Norway. He preempted a British landing in Norway by sending his troops there first. Then he launched his blitzkrieg into Holland, Belgium, and France. Sending his tanks through the supposedly impenetrable Ardennes Forest in May 1940, Hitler took the French and British by surprise. He had skirted the Maginot Line of French fortifications that guarded most of the French border with Germany. German forces drove the British troops back to the port of Dunkirk, where they had to leave their equipment and evacuate what was left of the men across the English Channel. Thus Hitler became master of the European continent west of the Soviet Union through a brilliant set of moves in 1940.

The fourth phase of Hitler's plans, "the phase of overreaching" (1941–1945), unleashed the full-scale war. Hitler had long wanted to move east against the Soviet Union. But he wanted to dispose of Britain first to avoid the possibility of a war on two fronts. If he could gain air supremacy, he could then cross the channel and invade Britain. But Hitler's air force was defeated in the Battle of Britain (July–October 1940). Unable to gain air supremacy, Hitler was faced with a conundrum: Should he put off his plans to attack the Soviet Union?

Hitler decided to attack the Soviet Union even though he had been unable to defeat Britain, thinking he could beat Stalin quickly and then go at Britain once again. Furthermore, he believed that attacking the Soviet Union would deprive the British of any potential alliance with the Soviet Union. In June 1941, Hitler attacked the Soviet Union, a massive mistake. In December 1941, after the Japanese attacked Pearl Harbor, he made another huge mistake: he declared war on the United States. Hitler probably did this to keep Japan locked into the war, since he had been urging Japan to join him, and he took the occasion to unleash his U-boat campaign against American shipping. In doing so, he also unleashed the global war that ended his Third Reich.

The Role of the Individual

What role did Hitler's personality play in causing World War II? It was probably not the crucial factor in the first phase. The Western democracies were so guilt ridden, weak, and internally divided that any clever German nationalist probably would have been able to revise the Versailles system. But the second and third phases that brought mastery over Europe depended on Hitler's skill, audacity, and bellicose ideology. He often overruled his conservative generals and staff. Hitler wanted war and was willing to take risks. The fourth phase, which brought on global war and failure, is also attributable to two aspects of Hitler's personality. First, Hitler's appetite grew with the eating. He was convinced of his own genius, but that conviction led him to two crucial mistakes: invading the Soviet Union before he finished off Britain and declaring war on the United States, which gave Franklin Roosevelt, the American president from 1933 to 1945, a pretext to become engaged in a war in Europe as well as in the Pacific.

Hitler's other great flaw was his racist ideology, which, by promoting the myth of a superior Aryan master race, deprived him of critical assets. For example, when Germany first invaded the Soviet Union, many Ukrainians and others revolted against Stalin's brutality. But Hitler regarded the Slavs as an inferior people, unworthy of an alliance with him against Stalin. He also thought the United States was weak because of its population of blacks and Jews. He used to joke about Roosevelt having a Jewish ancestor. He failed to understand that American pluralism could be a source of strength. Moreover, his anti-Semitism led him to expel some of the scientists crucial to developing the atomic bomb. In short, his individual leadership was one of the crucial causes of World War II. The kind of war it was and its outcome depended very much on Hitler's monomaniacal personality.

Systemic and Domestic Causes

Of course, there were also other causes. World War II was more than just Hitler's war, and that is the value of A. J. P. Taylor's interpretation. There were systemic causes, both structural and procedural. At the structural level, World War I did not solve the German problem. The Versailles treaty was both too harsh because it stirred up German nationalism and too lenient because it left the Germans the capability to do something about it. Furthermore, the absence of the United States and the Soviet Union from the balance of power until very late in the game meant that Germany was undeterred from pursuing its expansionist policies. In addition, the process of the international system was immoderate. Germany was a revisionist state bound on destroying the Versailles treaty system. In addition, the growth of ideologies, the great "isms" of fascism and communism, engendered hatred and hindered communication in the 1930s.

Three domestic-level changes were also particularly important. First, the Western democracies were torn apart by class cleavages and ideological disputes. Coordinated foreign policy making was nearly impossible. For example, when Leon Blum, a French socialist, came to power after 1936, French conservatives used the slogan, "Better Hitler Than Blum." In 1939, the British conservative government sent a mission to Moscow to see whether they could sign a treaty with Stalin, but both the mission and the government were internally divided. Before the British could make up their minds, Hitler had beat them to it. One reason for the delay was the British upper-class reluctance to deal with communists.

A second domestic-level cause of the war was economic collapse. The Great Depression was systemic in the sense that it affected all countries and grew out of the inability of the major capitalist states to establish effective international economic coordination to deal with imbalances in transnational trade and financial flows. But the Depression had powerful effects on domestic politics and class conflict. The enormous amount of unemployment had the political effect of pouring gas on a fire: it contributed to the Nazi takeover in Germany and weakened the governments of the Western democracies.

The third domestic cause was the U.S. policy of isolationism. The United States came out of World War I with the world's strongest economy, but it refused to

> The charismatic nature of Hitler's position as Fuhrer—a quasi-messianic personalized form of rule that arose from the desire for national rebirth and unity in a country traumatized by national humiliation and paralyzed by political collapse—could of its essence not settle into "normality" or routine, or sag into more conservative authoritarianism. Visionary goals of national redemption through European domination and racial purification were at the heart of the regime. These meant constant dynamism and self-perpetuating, intensifying radicalism. The longer the regime lasted, the more megalomaniac were its aims, the more boundless its destructiveness. Its gamble for world supremacy meant an alliance against extremely powerful allies. It was a gamble against the odds, in which the regime asked its own destruction and that of Germany itself. This was Nazism's essential irrationality. Hitler's charismatic leadership implied, therefore, not just an unprecedented capacity for destruction, but also an inbuilt tendency for self-destruction. In this sense the suicide of the German dictator on 30 April 1945 was not merely a welcome but also a logical end to the Third Reich.
>
> —*Ian Kershaw, "Hitler and the Nazi Dictatorship"*[6]

fully accept the responsibilities of that position. In the 1930s, the Great Depression increased internal preoccupation and significantly deepened isolationism. In his first term, President Franklin Roosevelt, along with other Americans, paid little attention to Europe. After his reelection in 1936, Roosevelt began to realize that if Hitler became too strong, he might dominate Europe and eventually threaten the United States. In 1937, Roosevelt began to speak about events in Europe, but the American public did not want to get involved. In 1940, Roosevelt traded destroyers to the British in return for military basing rights in British territories in the Western Hemisphere. In 1941, he persuaded Congress to approve "lend-lease" war supplies to Britain to prevent it from being defeated by Hitler. However, Roosevelt was limited by domestic opinion on how far he could go in resisting Hitler. Only Japan's attack on Pearl Harbor and Hitler's subsequent declaration of war ended America's isolationism.

How do these domestic, personal, and systemic causes fit together? We could say that the deep causes of World War II were systemic—the unfinished business of World War I. The intermediate causes were largely domestic—the social and ideological disruptions that produced Hitler in Germany and the political and economic weaknesses in the democracies. The precipitating cause was Adolf Hitler's strategy for domination (see Figure 4.3).

Was War Inevitable?

Was a second world war inevitable? No, but it became increasingly likely as time passed. In 1926 (after the Locarno treaties), that probability diminished, but after the Great Depression in 1929 and Hitler's ascent to power in 1933, the funnel of choices narrowed until the war became global in 1941 (see Figure 4.4).

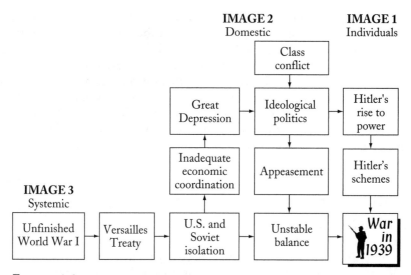

FIGURE 4.3   Courses of World War II

The failure of World War I to solve "the German problem" meant there was already some probability of a second war in 1918. If the Western democracies had chosen to appease Germany in the 1920s and treat it less punitively, the democratic government of the Weimar Republic might have been preserved. Or if the United States had ratified the Treaty of Versailles and stayed in Europe to preserve the balance of power (as it did after 1945), Hitler might not have risen to power. There might have been a war in Europe, but not necessarily the global World War II. In the 1930s, the shock of the economic depression fueled the rise of ideologies that glorified aggression, making war more likely.

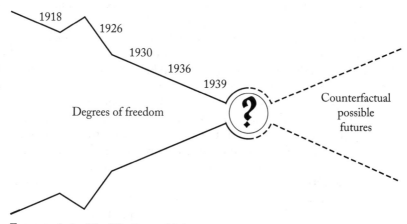

FIGURE 4.4   Was War Inevitable?

Counterfactually, suppose Britain and France had confronted Germany and made an alliance with the Soviet Union early in the 1930s. Or imagine that the United States had joined the League of Nations. Hitler might have been deterred or delayed. He might not have had such dramatic early successes and might have been overthrown by his own generals, who several times had contemplated such a coup. But because these things did not happen, Hitler's personality and strategy became the key precipitating cause. By the late 1930s, once Hitler began to plan war, it became almost inevitable. Even so, some historians believe that if France and Britain had launched an offensive in September 1939, they might have defeated Germany.

The Pacific War

The war in the Pacific had separate origins. Japan's attention was focused on East Asia, and it was not deeply involved in European events. In the 1920s, Japan was far from being a perfect democracy, but it did have a parliamentary system. However, in the 1930s, the military and extreme nationalists gained control of the government. Their policy of imperialist expansion was widely popular. Japan had always worried about maintaining access to the raw materials it had to import to sustain its economy. When the Depression cut Japan's trade, the Japanese feared that if they did not change their situation, they would face a bleak future. Acting as a regional hegemon, Japan tried to create what it called the Greater East Asia Co-Prosperity Sphere (a wonderful euphemism for the conquest of one's neighbors). Japan believed the sphere would allow it to resist threats from Britain and the United States, who were still major naval powers in the Pacific.

Japan first expanded at the expense of China. Japan's brutal war in China brought Japan into diplomatic conflict with the United States, which supported the Chinese Nationalists. After France fell to Hitler in 1940, the Japanese took advantage of the opportunity to seize France's colonies in Southeast Asia, Vietnam, and Cambodia. At this point, the Japanese expansionists had three options. One was to strike westward against the Soviet Union. Since clashes had already occurred between Japanese and Soviet forces along the border in Manchuria, some people thought a Japanese-Soviet war along the Manchurian border was most likely. The second option for the Japanese was to strike south, for although they had already taken the French colonies in Southeast Asia, the biggest prize was the Dutch East Indies (today's Indonesia), which had the oil Japan needed. Option three was to strike east against the United States, by far the riskiest of the three options.

The Japanese eventually chose both options two and three. On December 7, 1941, they struck east against the United States and south toward Indonesia and the Philippines. While the move south was for raw materials, the attack on the United States is more difficult to explain. Given the disparity in power resources, the Japanese knew they could not ultimately win a war against the United States, but they hoped the surprise attack on Pearl Harbor would so demoralize the United States that full-scale war would never erupt. That was a gross miscalculation on the part of the Japanese, but from the perspective of the Japanese

The bombing of Pearl Harbor, December 7, 1941

government, it seemed a better risk than the sure defeat they believed would ensue if they did nothing.

By the fall of 1941, Japanese expansionists no longer considered the Soviet Union a viable target. Hitler's attack on the Soviet Union had removed the Soviet threat to Japan. At the same time, the Americans tried to deter the Japanese from striking south by putting an embargo on oil shipments to Japan. As President Roosevelt put it, "The United States would slip a noose around Japan's neck and give it a jerk now and then." Assistant Secretary of State Dean Acheson was quoted at the time as saying this would not lead to war because "no rational Japanese could believe that an attack on us could result in anything but disaster for his country."[7] But the Japanese felt that if they did not go to war with the United States, they would eventually suffer defeat in any case. With 90 percent of their oil imported, they calculated that their navy could not last for even a year if that supply were cut off; therefore they concluded it was better to go to war than to be slowly strangled.

In addition to restricting Japan's oil supplies, the United States demanded that Japan withdraw from China. The Japanese believed this would cut them off from the area they viewed as their economic hinterland. As a Japanese military officer explained to Emperor Hirohito, the situation was like that of a patient with a serious illness: "An operation, while it might be extremely dangerous, would still offer some hope of saving his life."[8] From their point of view, it was *not* totally irrational for Japan to go to war because it was the least bad of the alternatives they saw. If Germany defeated Britain and American opinion was discouraged by the suddenness of the attack, a negotiated peace might result. A poorly reasoned form of the Japanese leaders' mood was expressed by Vice Army Chief of Staff Tsukuda:

> In general, the prospects if we go to war are not bright. We all wonder if there isn't some way to proceed peacefully. There is no one who is willing to say, "Don't worry, even if the war is prolonged, I will assume all responsibility." On the other hand, it is not possible to maintain the status quo. Hence, one unavoidably reaches the conclusion that we must go to war.[9]

Of course, Japan had the option of reversing its aggression in China and Southeast Asia, but that was unthinkable for the military leaders with their expansionist and bellicose outlook. Thus on December 7, 1941, the Japanese bombed Pearl Harbor (see Figure 4.5).

What about the three levels of analysis as applied to the Pacific war? The *role of the individual* is certainly less pronounced than it was with Hitler in Europe, but individual policy makers nonetheless influenced the trajectory of events. In Japan, expansionist generals and admirals wanted to increase Japan's regional dominance and actively sought an expanded war: west to China; south to Singapore, Indonesia, and the Philippines; and east to U.S. possessions in the Pacific. Military leaders such as Hideki Tojo played a leading role in determining government policy. However, Tojo supported policies identical to those of many other high-ranking military and political leaders. While Hitler had military and industrial support in Germany, he made decisions largely on his own. In Japan, there was a greater diffusion of power at the top and decisions were more the result of consensus among the political and military elite.

The role of the individual was also important for determining U.S. policy. Franklin Roosevelt was willing to impose punitive sanctions in response to Japanese aggression in Southeast Asia, but many in Congress and throughout America were uneasy with Roosevelt's activist and confrontational foreign policy. There was still strong isolationist sentiment in the United States in 1940 and 1941, and many people still rejected U.S. involvement in international politics. If an isolationist like Senators Burton Wheeler of Montana, Gerald Nye of North Dakota, or Hiram Johnson of California had been president, the United States might have tried to appease Japanese aggression rather than confront it, and consequently, Japan may never have felt the need to attack the United States. Of course, Japanese aggression would then have been unchecked, and Japan would have established itself as the regional power in the western Pacific.

In terms of *domestic* and *systemic causes*, we have seen how at a domestic level the increased militarism of Japan's government made war more likely. And as with Europe in the 1930s, the economic collapse in both Japan and the United States affected the foreign policies of both countries. Japan became more expansionist, while until 1940 the United States became even more isolated. In addition, the domestic chaos in Nationalist China continued in the 1930s, making it more

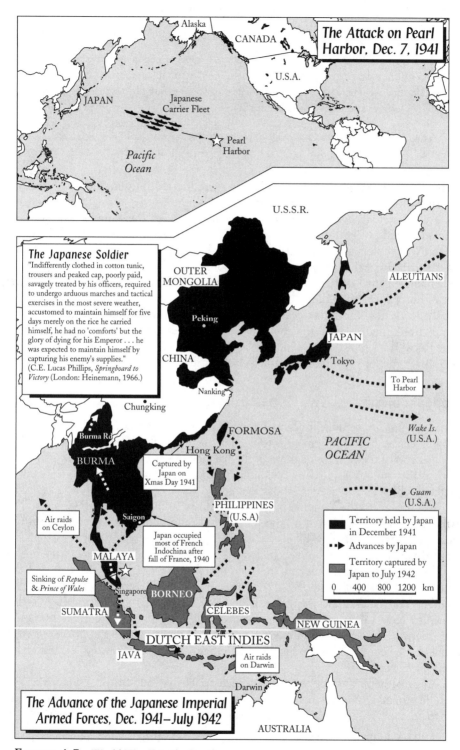

The Attack on Pearl Harbor, Dec. 7, 1941

Alaska
CANADA
U.S.A.
JAPAN
Japanese Carrier Fleet
Pacific Ocean
Pearl Harbor

The Japanese Soldier
"Indifferently clothed in cotton tunic, trousers and peaked cap, poorly paid, savagely treated by his officers, required to undergo arduous marches and tactical exercises in the most severe weather, accustomed to maintain himself for five days merely on the rice he carried himself, he had no 'comforts' but the glory of dying for his Emperor . . . he was expected to maintain himself by capturing his enemy's supplies."
(C.E. Lucas Phillips, *Springboard to Victory* (London: Heinemann, 1966.)

U.S.S.R.
OUTER MONGOLIA
ALEUTIANS
Peking
JAPAN
Tokyo
To Pearl Harbor
CHINA
Nanking
Wake Is. (U.S.A.)
Chungking
FORMOSA
PACIFIC OCEAN
Burma Rd
Hong Kong
Captured by Japan on Xmas Day 1941
BURMA
PHILIPPINES (U.S.A)
Guam (U.S.A.)
Air raids on Ceylon
Saigon
Japan occupied most of French Indochina after fall of France, 1940

Territory held by Japan in December 1941
Advances by Japan
Territory captured by Japan to July 1942
0   400   800 1200 km

MALAYA
Sinking of *Repulse* & *Prince of Wales*
Singapore
BORNEO
SUMATRA
CELEBES
NEW GUINEA
DUTCH EAST INDIES
JAVA
Air raids on Darwin
Darwin

The Advance of the Japanese Imperial Armed Forces, Dec. 1941–July 1942

AUSTRALIA

FIGURE 4.5   World War II in the Pacific

> Even if we should make concessions to the United States by giving up part of our national policy for the sake of a temporary peace, the United States, its military position strengthened, is sure to demand more and more concessions on our part; and ultimately our empire will lie prostrate at the feet of the United States.
>
> —*Records of Japan's 1941 Policy Conferences*

vulnerable to Japanese expansion. That, in turn, increased the influence of the militarists within Japanese domestic politics.

At the system level, the Treaty of Versailles had left the ambitions of Japan in China unsated, while the economic problems of the 1930s made it more difficult for Japan to obtain its needed raw materials by trade alone. And the breakdown between 1931 and 1933 of the already weak League of Nations' collective-security system in Asia removed any institutional constraints on Japan's imperial ambitions. Unlike the war in Europe, both the deep and intermediate causes of the war in the Pacific were largely domestic—the shift toward expansion in Japan and toward greater isolationism in the United States, and the chaos of 1930s China. The precipitating causes were Roosevelt's decision to implement a full embargo in July 1941 and the resulting decision of the Japanese military to attack the United States on December 7.

Appeasement and Two Types of War

What lessons can we draw from this? Some say the key lesson of the 1930s is the evil of *appeasement*. But appeasement is not bad per se; it is a classic tool of diplomacy. It is a policy choice to allow for changes in the balance of power that benefit a rival state. Rather than attempting to deter or contain the aggression of adversaries, a state might prefer to allow its adversaries modest gains. On the eve of the Peloponnesian War, Corinth argued to the Athenians that it should be allowed to absorb Corcyra. The Athenians, however, refused to appease Corinth and chose instead to fight. Given subsequent events, it is possible that Athens would have done better to appease Corinthian ambitions than to challenge them over Corcyra. Appeasement was used successfully in 1815 when the victorious powers appeased the defeated but still strong France. In the 1890s, Britain appeased the rising United States. We could even argue that appeasement might have been the right policy for the Western Allies to have taken toward Germany in the 1920s. One of the great ironies of the interwar period is that the West confronted Germany in the 1920s when it should have been appeased and appeased Germany in the 1930s when it should have been confronted.

Appeasement was the wrong approach to Hitler, but British Prime Minister Neville Chamberlain was not such a coward as the Munich experience makes him out to be. He wanted to avoid another world war. In July 1938, he said,

> When I think of those four terrible years and I think of the 7 million young men who were cut off in their prime and 13 million who were maimed and mutilated,

the misery and suffering of the mothers and fathers, sons and daughters, I must say that there are no winners in a war, but all losers. It is those thoughts which make me feel that it is my prime duty to strain every nerve to avoid repetition of the Great War in Europe.[10]

Chamberlain's sins were not his intentions, but rather his ignorance and arrogance in failing to appraise the situation properly. And in that failure he was not alone.

World Wars I and II are often cast as two quite different models of war: accidental war versus planned aggression. World War I was an unwanted spiral of hostility. To some extent, it might have been avoided with appeasement. As political scientist David Calleo has said, "The proper lesson is not so much the need for vigilance against aggressors, but the ruinous consequences of refusing reasonable accommodation of upstarts."[11] World War II was not an unwanted spiral of hostility—it was a failure to deter Hitler's planned aggression. In that sense, the policies appropriate for preventing World Wars I and II were almost opposite. Accommodation of Germany might have helped forestall World War I and deterrence of Germany might have prevented World War II, but the policies were reversed. In trying to avoid a repetition of World War I, British leaders in the 1930s helped precipitate World War II. At the same time, the efforts of U.S. leaders to deter Japan helped bring on war in the Pacific. Deterrence failed because the Japanese felt cornered in a situation in which the alternative of peace looked worse than risking a war.

Of course, these two models of war are too simple. World War I was not purely accidental, and World War II, in the Pacific at least, was not merely Hitler's planned aggression. The ultimate lesson is to be wary of overly simple historical models. Always ask whether a model is true to the facts of history and whether it really fits the current reality. It helps to remember the story of Mark Twain's cat. As Twain pointed out, a cat that sits on a hot stove will not sit on a hot stove again, but neither will it sit on a cold one. It is necessary to know which stoves are cold and which are hot when using historical analogies or political science models based on World Wars I and II.

CHRONOLOGY: BETWEEN THE WORLD WARS

1919	Peace Conference opens at Versailles; adoption of Weimar Constitution
1920	Creation of the League of Nations
1921–1922	Washington conference on naval armaments
1922	Permanent Court of Justice at The Hague established; Treaty of Rapallo between Germany and the Soviet Union; Mussolini assumes power in Italy
1923	France and Belgium occupy the Ruhr in response to German default on coal deliveries; Nazi Beer Hall *Putsch* aborted
1924	Dawes Plan for reparations accepted; Geneva Protocol for the peaceful settlement of international disputes adopted
1925	Locarno Conference and treaties
1926	Germany admitted to the League of Nations
1928	Kellogg-Briand Pact signed
1930	London Naval Conference

1931	Japanese invasion of Manchuria; failure of the Austrian Credit-Anstalt; Bank of England forced off the gold standard
1932	Disarmament conference; Lausanne Conference on German reparations
1933	Adolf Hitler becomes chancellor of Germany; Reichstag fire; Enabling Act passed establishing Nazi dictatorship; Germany withdraws from the disarmament conference and League of Nations
1934	Soviet Union joins the League of Nations
1935	Germany renounces the disarmament clauses of the Versailles treaty; Franco-Russian alliance formed; Anglo-German naval agreement reached; Italian invasion of Ethiopia; Hoare-Laval Pact
1936	Germany denounced Locarno pacts and reoccupies the Rhineland; Italy wins the war in Ethiopia; League of Nations discredited as a political instrument; Rome-Berlin axis formed; Anti-Comintern Pact formed
1936–1939	Civil war in Spain
1937	Japan launches attacks on Nanjing and other Chinese cities
1938	German invasion and annexation of Austria; Chamberlain meets Hitler at Berchtesgaden, Godesberg, and Munich to resolve the German-Czech crisis; Munich agreement signed
1939	Crisis in Czechoslovakia; Germany occupies all of Czechoslovakia; British and French pledges to Poland and guarantees to Greece and Romania; Italy invades Albania; Russian-German (Molotov–von Ribbentrop) Pact; Germany invades Poland; Britain and France declare war on Germany
1940	Hitler invades France; Battle of Britain; Japan occupies French Indochina
1941	Hitler invades Soviet Union; Japan attacks Pearl Harbor

STUDY QUESTIONS

1. What "lessons" of World War I did policy makers draw at the time? How did it affect their behavior in the interwar period?

2. How did the concept of collective security differ from balance-of-power politics? Is the notion of collective security utopian? If not, how might collective security have worked better during the interwar period?

3. Was World War II inevitable? If so, why and when? If not, when and how could it have been avoided?

4. To what extent can the outbreak of World War II be attributed to the personalities of the leaders involved?

5. What might be some lessons of the interwar period that might help policy makers avoid war today?

6. Was Japan irrational to attack the United States?

NOTES

1. Woodrow Wilson, quoted in Ray S. Baker and William E. Dodd, eds., *The Public Papers of Woodrow Wilson: War and Peace*, vol. 1 (New York: Harper, 1927), pp. 182–183.

2. Woodrow Wilson, quoted in Inis L. Claude, *Power and International Relations* (New York: Random, 1962), p. 104.

3. Quoted in F. P. Walters, *A History of the League of Nations* (London: Oxford University Press, 1952), p. 653.

4. A. J. P. Taylor, *The Origins of the Second World War*, 2nd ed. (Greenwich: Fawcett, 1961), p. 281.

5. Adolf Hitler, quoted in Gordon Craig, *Germany, 1866–1945* (New York: Oxford University Press, 1978), p. 712.

6. Ian Kershaw, "Hitler and the Nazi Dictatorship," in Mary Fulbrook, ed., *German History Since 1800* (London: Edward Arnold, 1997), p. 336.

7. Dean Acheson, quoted in Scott Sagan, "The Origins of the Pacific War," in Robert I. Rotberg and Theodore K. Rabb, eds., *The Origin and Prevention of Major Wars* (New York: Cambridge University Press, 1989), pp. 335–336.

8. Sagan, "The Origins of the Pacific War," p. 325.

9. Tsukuda, quoted in Scott Sagan, "Deterrence and Decision: An Historical Critique of Modern Deterrence Theory" (Ph.D. thesis, Harvard University, 1983), p. 280.

10. Neville Chamberlain, *In Search of Peace: Speeches 1937–38* (London: Hutchinson, n.d.), p. 59.

11. David P. Calleo, *The German Problem Reconsidered: Germany and the World Order, 1870 to the Present* (Cambridge: Cambridge University Press, 1978), p. 6.

Selected Readings

1. Ross, Graham, *The Great Powers and the Decline of the European States System, 1919–1945* (London: Longman, 1983), pp. 109–126.

2. Bell, P. M. H., *The Origins of the Second World War in Europe* (London: Longman, 1986), pp. 14–38.

3. Sagan, Scott, "The Origins of the Pacific War," *Journal of Interdisciplinary History* 18:4 (Spring 1988), pp. 893–922.

4. Taylor, A. J. P., *The Origins of the Second World War* (London: Hamilton, 1961), pp. xi–xxviii, 102–109, 272–278.

5. Bullock, Alan, "Hitler and the Origins of the Second World War," in W. R. Louis, ed., *The Origins of the Second World War: A. J. P. Taylor and His Critics* (New York: Wiley, 1972), pp. 117–145.

Further Readings

Barkin, J. Samuel, and Bruce Cronin, "The State and the Nation: Changing Norms and the Rules of Sovereignty," *International Organization* (Winter 1994), pp. 107–130.

Barnhart, Michael A., *Japan Prepares for Total War: The Search for Economic Security: 1919–1941* (Ithaca, NY: Cornell University Press, 1987).

Bell, P. M. H., *The Origins of the Second World War in Europe* (London: Longman, 1986).

Bullock, Alan, *Hitler: A Study in Tyranny* (New York: Harper & Row, 1964).

Carr, E. H., *The Twenty Years' Crisis 1919–1939: An Introduction to the History of International Relations* (New York: HarperCollins, 1981).

Claude, Inis L., *Power and International Relations* (New York: Random, 1962).

Cohen, Warren, *Empire Without Tears: America's Foreign Relations, 1921–1933* (New York: Knopf, 1987).

Heinrichs, Waldo, Jr., *Threshold of War: Franklin D. Roosevelt and American Entry into World War II* (New York: Oxford University Press, 1988).

Hilderbrand, Klaus, *Foreign Policy of the Third Reich,* trans. Anthony Fothergill (Berkeley: University of California Press, 1973).

Hughes, Jeffrey, "The Origins of World War II in Europe: British Deterrence Failure and German Expansionism," in Robert I. Rotberg and Theodore K. Rabb, eds., *The Origin and Prevention of Major Wars* (Cambridge: Cambridge University Press, 1989), pp. 281–322.

Iriye, Akira, *The Origins of the Second World War in Asia and the Pacific* (London: Longman, 1987).

———, *Pearl Harbor and the Coming of the Pacific War: A Brief History with Documents and Essays* (New York: Bedford/St. Martin's, 1999).

Jervis, Robert, Richard Ned Lebow, and Janice Gross Stein, *Psychology and Deterrence* (Baltimore: Johns Hopkins University Press, 1985).

Kier, Elizabeth, *Imagining War: French and British Military Doctrine Between the Wars* (Princeton, NJ: Princeton University Press, 1997).

Lukacs, John, *Five Days in London, May 1940* (New Haven, CT: Yale University Press, 1999).

Macmillan, Margaret Olwen, *Paris 1919: Six Months That Changed the World* (New York: Random, 2002).

Middlemas, Keith, *The Strategy of Appeasement: The British Government and Germany* (Chicago: Quadrangle, 1972).

Ross, Graham, *The Great Powers and the Decline of the European States System, 1914–1945* (London: Longman, 1983).

Storry, Richard, *A History of Modern Japan* (Baltimore: Penguin, 1960).

Utley, Jonathan, *Going to War with Japan, 1937–1941* (Knoxville: University of Tennessee Press, 1985).

Walters, F. P., *A History of the League of Nations* (London: Oxford University Press, 1952).

Wolfers, Arnold, *Discord and Collaboration: Essays on International Politics* (Baltimore: Johns Hopkins University Press, 1962).

The Cold War

Winston Churchill, Franklin Roosevelt, and Josef Stalin at Yalta, 1945

Given its violent first half, a most remarkable feature of the second half of the twentieth century was the absence of World War III. Instead, there was a *cold war*, a period of intense hostility without actual war. The hostility was so intense that many expected armed conflict between the superpowers. Fighting occurred, but it was on the peripheries and not directly between the United States and the Soviet Union.

115

The Cold War lasted four decades, from 1947 to 1989. The height of the Cold War was from 1947 to 1963, when there were few serious negotiations between the United States and the Soviet Union. There were not even any summit meetings between 1945 and 1955. In 1952, George Kennan, the U.S. ambassador in Moscow, compared his isolation in the American embassy to his experience of being interned during World War II in Berlin. The later phases of the Cold War in the 1970s and 1980s were very different. The Americans and Soviets had many contacts, and they constantly negotiated on arms control treaties. The end of the Cold War occurred quite quickly with the change in Soviet policies after Mikhail Gorbachev came to power in 1985. Soviet hegemony over Eastern Europe collapsed in 1989, and the Soviet Union itself disintegrated in 1991.

DETERRENCE AND CONTAINMENT

What makes the Cold War exceptional is that it was a period of protracted tension that did not end in a war between the two rival superpowers. A variety of explanations for why this was the case will be discussed. Because of its unusual trajectory, the Cold War offers a unique perspective on international relations, and it illuminates the dynamics of two foreign policy choices that were made: the choice to *deter* and the choice to *contain*.

To deter is to discourage through fear, and although frequently associated with the Cold War, deterrence was not a new concept in international politics. Throughout history, countries built armies, formed alliances, and issued threats to deter other countries from attacking. During the Cold War and with the advent of nuclear weapons, the superpowers depended more on discouraging by threat than on denying by defense after an attack occurred. Cold War deterrence was closely tied to the maintenance of large American and Soviet nuclear arsenals, but it was also an extension of balance-of-power logic. Deterrence by nuclear threat was one way each superpower tried to prevent the other from gaining advantage and hence upsetting the balance of power between them. As we shall see, deterrence often aggravated the tension between the United States and the Soviet Union, and it is not necessarily easy to demonstrate that deterrence worked. There is always the danger of spurious causation. If a professor said her lectures kept elephants out of the classroom, it would be difficult to disprove her claim if no elephants ever came to class. We can test such claims by using counterfactuals: How likely is it that elephants would come to class?

The concept of deterrence was linked to the policy of *containment*. During the Cold War, containment referred to a specific American policy of containing Soviet communism so as to promote a liberal economic and political world order. But like deterrence, containment did not originate with the Cold War, even if the term did. Containment has been a primary tool of foreign policy for centuries. In the eighteenth century, the conservative monarchical states of Europe attempted to contain the ideology of liberty and equality espoused by the French Revolution, and even earlier, the Catholic Church in the Counter-Reformation attempted to contain the spread of the

Reformation and the ideals of Martin Luther. There are different forms of containment. It can be offensive or defensive. It can use military power in the form of war or alliances; it can use economic power in the form of trading blocs or sanctions; and it can use soft power in the form of promoting ideas and values. During the Cold War, the United States wavered between an expansive policy of containing communism and a more limited policy of containing the Soviet Union.

THREE APPROACHES TO THE COLD WAR

Who or what caused the Cold War? Almost since it began, those questions have been the subject of fierce debate among scholars and policy makers. There are three main schools of opinion: *traditionalists, revisionists,* and *postrevisionists.*

The *traditionalists* (also known as the orthodox) argue that the answer to the question of who started the Cold War is quite simple: Stalin and the Soviet Union. At the end of World War II, American diplomacy was defensive, while the Soviets were aggressive and expansive. The Americans only slowly awoke to the nature of the Soviet threat.

What evidence do the traditionalists cite? Immediately after the war, the United States was proposing a universal world order and collective security through the United Nations. The Soviet Union did not take the United Nations very seriously because it wanted to expand and dominate its own sphere of influence in Eastern Europe. After the war, the United States demobilized its troops, whereas the Soviet Union left large armies in Eastern Europe. The United States recognized Soviet interests; for example, when Roosevelt, Stalin, and Churchill met in February 1945 at Yalta, the Americans went out of their way to accommodate Soviet interests. Stalin, however, did not live up to his agreements, particularly by not allowing free elections in Poland.

Soviet expansionism was further confirmed when the Soviet Union was slow to remove its troops from northern Iran after the war. Eventually they were removed, but only under pressure. In 1948, the communists took over the Czechoslovakian government. The Soviet Union blockaded Berlin in 1948 and 1949, trying to squeeze the Western governments out. And in 1950, communist North Korea's armies crossed the border into South Korea. According to the traditionalists, these events gradually awakened the United States to the threat of Soviet expansionism and launched the Cold War.

The *revisionists,* who wrote primarily in the 1960s and early 1970s, believe the Cold War was caused by American rather than Soviet expansionism. Their evidence is that at the end of World War II, the world was not really bipolar—the Soviets were much weaker than the United States, which was strengthened by the war and had nuclear weapons while the Soviets did not. The Soviet Union lost up to 30 million people, and industrial production was only half its 1939 level. Stalin told American Ambassador Averell Harriman in October 1945 that the Soviets would turn inward to repair their domestic damage. What is more, say the revisionists, Stalin's external behavior early in the postwar period was quite moderate: In

China, Stalin tried to restrain Mao Zedong's communists from taking power; in the Greek civil war, he tried to restrain the Greek communists; and he allowed non-communist governments to exist in Hungary, Czechoslovakia, and Finland.

Revisionists come in two varieties that stress the first and second levels of explanation. Level one revisionists stress the importance of individuals and claim that Roosevelt's death in April 1945 was a critical event because American policy toward the Soviet Union became harsher after President Harry S. Truman took office. In May 1945, the United States so precipitously cut off the lend-lease program of wartime aid that some ships bound for Soviet ports had to turn around in midocean. At the Potsdam Conference near Berlin in July 1945, Truman tried to intimidate Stalin by mentioning the atomic bomb. In the United States, the Democratic Party gradually shifted from the left and center to the right. In 1948, Truman fired Henry Wallace, his secretary of agriculture, who urged better relations with the Soviets. At the same time, James Forrestal, Truman's new secretary of defense, was a strong anticommunist. These revisionists say these personnel changes help explain why the United States became so anti-Soviet.

The level two revisionists have a different answer. They see the problem not in individuals, but in the nature of U.S. capitalism. Gabriel and Joyce Kolko and William A. Williams, for example, argue that the American economy required expansionism and that the United States planned to make the world safe, not for democracy, but for capitalism. American economic hegemony could not tolerate any country that might try to organize an autonomous economic area. American leaders feared a repeat of the 1930s because without external trade, there would be another Great Depression. According to level two revisionists, the Marshall Plan of aid to Europe was simply a way to expand the American economy. The Soviets were correct to reject it as a threat to their sphere of influence in Eastern Europe. In Williams's words, Americans always favored an open-door policy in the international economy because they expected to walk through it.

The *postrevisionists* of the late 1970s and 1980s, as exemplified by Yale historian John Lewis Gaddis, have yet another explanation that focuses on the structural level. They argue that the traditionalists and revisionists are both wrong because nobody was to blame for starting the Cold War. It was inevitable, or nearly so, because of the bipolar structure of the postwar balance of power. In 1939 there was a multipolar world with seven major powers, but after the destruction wreaked by World War II, only two superpowers were left: the United States and the Soviet Union. Bipolarity plus the postwar weakness of the European states created a power vacuum into which the United States and the Soviet Union were drawn. They were bound to come into conflict and, therefore, say the postrevisionists, it is pointless to look for blame.

The Soviets and the Americans had different goals at the end of the war. The Soviets wanted tangible possessions—territory. Americans had intangible or milieu goals—they were interested in the general context of world politics. Milieu goals clashed with possession goals when the United States promoted the global UN system while the Soviets sought to consolidate their sphere of influence in Eastern Europe. But these differences in style were no reason for Americans to feel sanctimonious, say the postrevisionists, for the United States benefited from the United Nations and, with a majority of allies voting, was not very constrained by it. The Soviets may have had a sphere of influence in Eastern Europe, but the United States also had a sphere of influence in the Western Hemisphere and Western Europe.

The United States and the Soviet Union were both bound to expand, say the postrevisionists, not because of the economic determinism that the revisionists stress, but because of the age-old security dilemma of states in an anarchic system. Neither the Americans nor the Soviets could allow the other to dominate Europe any more than Athens could afford to let the Corinthians gain control of Corcyra's navy. As evidence, postrevisionists cite Stalin's comment to a Yugoslav leader, Milovan Djilas, in 1945: "This war is not as in the past; whoever occupies a territory also imposes on it his own social system. Everyone imposes his own system as far as his army can reach."[1] In other words, in an ideological bipolar world, a state uses its military forces to impose societies similar to its own in order to ensure its security. Roosevelt had said something similar to Stalin in the fall of 1944: "In this global war there is literally no question, political or military, in which the United States is not interested."[2] Given this bipolar structure, say the postrevisionists, a spiral of hostility set in: hard lines in one country bred hard lines in the other. Both began to perceive the enemy as analogous to Hitler in the 1930s. As perceptions became more rigid, the Cold War deepened.

Since the end of the Cold War, a modest flow of documents from formerly inaccessible Soviet archives has given new vigor to the debate over which side started the confrontation. Gaddis, for example, has become increasingly convinced that the USSR was primarily responsible for the onset and the nature of the superpower conflict. He cites the ideological rigidity of Stalin and other Soviet leaders, as well as the Kremlin's equally rigid commitment to maintaining a formal empire in its sphere of influence. Gaddis's move back toward a traditionalist viewpoint has garnered a skeptical reception in some scholarly quarters, guaranteeing that the debate will continue into the foreseeable future.

ROOSEVELT'S POLICIES

Franklin Roosevelt wanted to avoid the mistakes of World War I, so instead of a Versailles-like peace, he demanded Germany's unconditional surrender. He wanted a liberal trade system to avoid the protectionism that had damaged the world economy in the 1930s and contributed to the onset of war. The United States would avoid its tendency toward isolationism that had been so damaging in the 1930s. It would join a new and stronger League of Nations in the form of a United Nations with a powerful Security Council. Cordell Hull, U.S. secretary of state during most of the war, was a committed Wilsonian, and public opinion in the United States was strongly in favor of the United Nations.

To promote his great design, Roosevelt needed to maintain bipartisan domestic support for his international position. Externally, he needed to reassure Stalin that his security needs would be met by joining the United Nations. Roosevelt has been accused of a naive approach to postwar planning. His design was not naive, but some of his tactics were. He placed too much faith in the United Nations, overestimated the likelihood of American isolationism, and, most important, underestimated Stalin. Roosevelt thought he could treat Stalin the way he would treat a fellow American politician, throwing his arm around him, bonding politician to politician.

Roosevelt did not fully realize that Stalin, along with his men, was a totalitarian "who in the name of the people, murdered millions of them; who to defend against Hitler, signs a pact with him, divides the spoils of war with him, and like him, expels, exterminates, or enslaves neighboring peoples; who stands aside and fulminates against the democracies as Germany moves west, and then blames them for not helping enough when Hitler moves east."[4]

Roosevelt misinterpreted Stalin, but Roosevelt did not sell out American interests at the Yalta Conference in 1945, as some later claimed. Roosevelt was not naive in all aspects of his policy. He tried to tie economic aid to political concessions by the Soviets, and refused to share the secrets of the atomic bomb with them. He was simply realistic about who would have troops in Eastern Europe at the end of the war, and, therefore, who would have leverage in that region. Roosevelt's mistakes were in thinking that Stalin saw the world his way, that he understood domestic politics in the United States, and that the same American political skills in which a leader blurred differences and appealed to friendship would work in dealing with Stalin.

> The President acted as if genuine cooperation as the Americans understood the term were possible both during and after the war. Roosevelt apparently had forgotten, if indeed he ever knew, that in Stalin's eyes, he was not all that different from Hitler, both of them being heads of powerful capitalist states whose longterm ambitions clashed with those of the Kremlin.
>
> —*William Taubman, Stalin's American Policy*[3]

STALIN'S POLICIES

Stalin's immediate postwar plans were to tighten domestic control. World War II inflicted tremendous damage on the Soviet Union, not just the terrible losses of life and industry already described, but also to the ideology of communism. Many in the Soviet Union collaborated with the Germans because of their deep resentment over the harshness of communist rule. Germany's invasion seriously weakened Stalin's control. Indeed, Stalin had to increase his appeals to Russian nationalism during the war because the weakened communist ideology was insufficient to motivate his people. Stalin's isolationist policy at the end of the war was designed to cut off external influences from Europe and the United States. Stalin used the United States as an objective enemy, urging the Soviet people to tighten down, to pull in, to mistrust the outsiders. But it does not follow that Stalin wanted the Cold War that actually developed.

Stalin preferred some cooperation, especially if it helped him pursue his goals in Eastern Europe and brought him some economic assistance from the United States. As a good communist, he believed the United States would have to give him economic assistance because the capitalist system had to export capital due to insufficient demand at home. Stalin also believed that in 10 or 15 years, the next crisis of the capitalist system would come along, and at that time the Soviet Union would have recovered and be ready to benefit in the inevitable conflict with the capitalists.

In foreign policy terms, Stalin wanted to protect himself at home, as well as maintain the gains the Soviet Union had made in Eastern Europe from the 1939 pact with Hitler. Stalin also wanted to probe soft spots, something better done when there is no crisis. In 1941, Stalin told the British foreign minister Anthony Eden that he preferred arithmetic to algebra; in other words, he wanted a practical rather than a theoretical approach. When Winston Churchill proposed a formula on the postwar division of influence in the Balkans, that is, some countries under British control, some under Soviet control, and others 50–50, Stalin was quite receptive to the idea. Some of Stalin's early caution in supporting communist governments right away in China, Czechoslovakia, and Hungary fit quite well with this arithmetic rather than algebraic approach to achieving his objectives. Stalin was a committed communist who, although he saw the world within the framework of communism, often used pragmatic tactics.

PHASES OF THE CONFLICT

The early stages of the Cold War can be divided into three phases: 1945–1947—the gradual onset; 1947–1949—the declaration of the Cold War; and 1950–1962—the height of the Cold War.

Neither Stalin nor Truman was looking for a cold war. At the end of World War II, Truman sent Roosevelt's former aide, Harry Hopkins, to Moscow to see if some arrangements could be worked out. Even after the Potsdam Conference, Truman continued to see Stalin as a moderate. Indeed, as late as 1949, he compared Stalin to his old friend Boss Pendergast in Kansas City. In 1946, George Kennan, writing from Moscow as the U.S. embassy's chargé d'affaires, was trying to warn American decision makers about Stalin's true nature and intentions, and Winston Churchill gave a famous speech in Fulton, Missouri, warning that an "iron curtain" was falling across Europe. While Secretary of State James Byrnes was still trying to negotiate a postwar treaty with the Soviets, Truman asked his aide Clark Clifford to prepare a report on what the Soviets were really planning. Clifford talked with a variety of people and concluded that Kennan was right: the Soviets were going to expand whenever they found an inexpensive opportunity. When Truman received the report in December 1946, however, he told Clifford he did not want its results widely known, for he was still trying to follow Roosevelt's great design and had not yet developed a new strategy.

Six issues contributed to eventual change of American strategy and the onset of the Cold War. One was Soviet actions in Poland and Eastern Europe. Poland, of course, had been one of the precipitating causes of World War II, and Americans believed that Stalin broke a clear commitment to hold free elections in Poland after the war. However, it was not clear what Stalin had agreed to do. When Stalin and Roosevelt met at Tehran in 1943, Roosevelt raised the Polish issue, but he appealed to Stalin in the context of the 1944 American election: He had an election coming up, there were many Polish-American voters, and he needed to tell them there would be elections in Poland after the war. Stalin, who never worried about elections in the Soviet Union, did not take Roosevelt's concerns seriously. The February 1945 Yalta agreement was also somewhat ambiguous, and Stalin stretched the meaning as far as he could by setting up a puppet government in Warsaw after Soviet troops had driven out the Germans. The Americans felt cheated, but Stalin felt the Americans would adjust to the reality that Soviet troops had liberated Poland.

In May 1945, the lend-lease aid program was abruptly stopped, and the economic relationship between the United States and the Soviet Union became strained. The precipitous termination of lend-lease was to some extent a bureaucratic mistake, but the overall situation was not improved when in February 1946 the United States refused Soviet requests for loans. The Soviets interpreted those acts as economic leverage for hostile purposes.

Germany was a third problem. At the Yalta meeting, the Americans and the Soviets agreed that Germany should pay $20 billion in reparations, with half going to the Soviet Union. The details of how and when the payments would be made were not worked out at Yalta, although both sides agreed they would be negotiated later. At the Potsdam meeting in July 1945, the Soviets demanded their $10 billion; furthermore, they wanted it from the western zones of Germany that the Americans, British, and French had occupied. Harry Truman, worried about how Germany would be reconstructed, said that if the Soviets wanted to take $10 billion out of Germany, they should take it out of the eastern zone they occupied; if there was anything left over after the reconstruction of the western side of Germany, he would let the Soviets know. Thus began a series of divisions between the Americans and the Soviets about how to reconstruct Germany. The Americans, along with the British and French, created a single currency in the western zones, starting the process of West German integration, which in turn caused the Soviets to tighten control of the eastern zone of Germany.

East Asia was also an issue. The Soviets were neutral in the Pacific until the last week of the war. Then the Soviets declared war on Japan, seizing Manchuria and four islands from the north of Japan. At Potsdam, the Soviets asked for an occupation zone in Japan, like the American occupation zone in Germany. Truman's response was, in effect, that the Soviets arrived at the party late, so no zone. From an American point of view, this seemed perfectly reasonable, but the situation reminded the Soviets of Eastern Europe, where the Americans wanted free elections and influence, but the Soviet armies had arrived there first. So the Soviets saw the Far Eastern situation as analogous to Eastern Europe, while the Americans saw it as one more example of the Soviets pressing for their own expansion.

A fifth issue was the atomic bomb. Roosevelt had decided not to share the secret of the atomic bomb with the Soviet Union. Most historians now agree that Truman dropped the bomb at Hiroshima and Nagasaki primarily to bring a quick end to the war with Japan, not to intimidate the Soviet Union, as some revisionists have claimed. But he did expect the bomb to have some political effects. At the Potsdam meeting when Truman told Stalin that America had an atomic bomb, Stalin remained poker faced and seemingly unimpressed. Of course, Stalin already knew about it from his own spies, but his equanimity was a bit of a jolt to the Americans. In 1946, when the United States set forth the Baruch Plan for UN control of nuclear weapons, Stalin rejected it because he wanted to build his own bomb. As he saw it, a bomb under international control would still be an American bomb, for only the Americans knew how to build it. Stalin believed it would be far better for Soviet security to have their own (which they eventually exploded in 1949).

The sixth issue concerned countries in the eastern Mediterranean and the Middle East, where the British had been influential before World War II. After the war, several things occurred. First, the Soviets refused to remove their troops from northern Iran in March 1946. The United States supported Iran in a debate within the United Nations. The Soviets eventually moved, but not without a good deal of bitterness over the event. The Soviet Union also began to put pressure on Turkey, its neighbor to the south, at the same time that the communists seemed to be winning the civil war in Greece. Once again, the West believed the Soviets were expanding.

These six issues were real, though some misperceptions were involved in almost all of them. Could they have been solved by negotiation and appeasement? Would appeasement have worked? Probably not. Kennan argued that Stalin was intent on probing any soft spots. Appeasement would have been interpreted as a soft spot and invited more probing. In June 1946, Maxim Litvinov, the former Soviet foreign minister, warned an American counterpart against any concessions because the root cause of the tension was "the ideological conception prevailing here that conflict between Communist and capitalist worlds is inevitable." Concessions would merely lead "to the West's being faced, after a more or less short time, with the next series of demands."[5] Appeasement probably would not have worked, but harder bargaining might have limited some of the events that led to the onset of the Cold War. A tactical appeal to Stalin's pragmatism from a firmer American position, plus a willingness to negotiate, might have worked out better in that early period from 1945–1947.

The second phase, the declaration of the Cold War from 1947–1949, followed from the problems in Greece and Turkey (Figure 5.1). Britain, severely weakened by World War II, felt it could no longer provide security in the eastern Mediterranean. The United States had to decide whether to let a vacuum develop or to replace British power by providing assistance to Greece and Turkey. This involved a considerable break from traditional American foreign policy. Truman was not sure that American public opinion would support such a move. There was still fear that isolationism would be the mainstay of America's postwar foreign policy. Truman asked Senator Arthur Vandenberg, the Republican leader from Michigan, whether the Senate would go along with aiding Greece and Turkey. Vandenberg said Truman

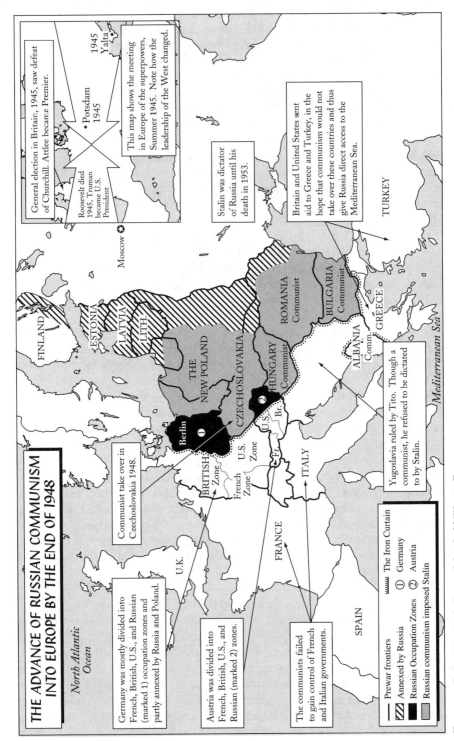

THE ADVANCE OF RUSSIAN COMMUNISM INTO EUROPE BY THE END OF 1948

North Atlantic Ocean

General election in Britain, 1945, saw defeat of Churchill. Attlee became Premier.

Roosevelt died 1945, Truman became U.S. President

Potsdam 1945

1945 Yalta

This map shows the meeting in Europe of the superpowers, Summer 1945. Note how the leadership of the West changed.

Stalin was dictator of Russia until his death in 1953.

Britain and United States sent aid to Greece and Turkey, in the hope that communism would not take over these countries and thus give Russia direct access to the Mediterranean Sea.

Communist take over in Czechoslovakia 1948.

Germany was mostly divided into French, British, U.S., and Russian (marked 1) occupation zones and partly annexed by Russia and Poland.

Austria was divided into French, British, U.S., and Russian (marked 2) zones.

The communists failed to gain control of French and Italian governments.

Yugoslavia ruled by Tito. Though a communist, he refused to be dictated to by Stalin.

Moscow

FINLAND

ESTONIA
LATVIA
LITH.

THE NEW POLAND

CZECHOSLOVAKIA

HUNGARY Communist

ROMANIA Communist

BULGARIA Communist

ALBANIA Comm.

GREECE

TURKEY

Berlin ①

BRITISH Zone

French Zone

U.S. Zone

Fr.

U.S.
Br. ②

ITALY

FRANCE

SPAIN

U.K.

Mediterranean Sea

— Prewar frontiers
///// Annexed by Russia
⬛ Russian communism imposed Stalin
░░ Russian Occupation Zones

----- The Iron Curtain
① Germany ② Austria

FIGURE 5.1 The Early Days of the Cold War in Europe

would have to "scare the hell out of them" to get congressional support for this break in traditional American policy. Thus when Truman explained the policy change, he did not talk about the need to maintain a balance of power in the eastern Mediterranean by providing aid to Greece and Turkey. Instead, he talked about the need to protect free people everywhere. This moralistic, ideological explanation for American assistance became known as the Truman Doctrine.

George Kennan, by then back in the State Department, objected to this ideological approach to formulating foreign policy, arguing that it was too open-ended and would get the United States into trouble. Indeed, there were enormous ambiguities in the policy of containment that flowed from the Truman Doctrine. Was the United States interested in containing Soviet power or communist ideology? At the beginning, containing Soviet power and containing communist ideology seemed to be the same, but later in the Cold War when the communist movement split, the ambiguities became important.

Was Truman wrong to exaggerate the sense of threat and the ideological rationale for the policy change? Some observers feel it is harder to change public opinion in democracies than it is to change policies in totalitarian countries. They argue that exaggeration speeds up the process of change in democracies. It is necessary to tug harder on the reins when trying to turn an unruly team of horses. Regardless of whether the exaggeration was necessary, it helped change the nature of the Cold War.

In June 1947, Secretary of State George Marshall announced a plan for economic aid to Europe. The initial proposal of the Marshall Plan invited the Soviet Union and the Eastern Europeans to join if they wished, but Stalin put strong pressure on the Eastern Europeans not to do so. Stalin saw the Marshall Plan not as American generosity, but as an economic battering ram to destroy his security barrier in Eastern Europe. When Czechoslovakia indicated it would like U.S. aid, Stalin tightened the screws in Eastern Europe, and the communists took full power in Czechoslovakia in February 1948.

Truman heard echoes of the 1930s in these events. He began to worry that Stalin would become another Hitler. The United States advanced plans for West German currency reform; Stalin replied with the Berlin blockade. The United States answered with an airlift and began plans for the North Atlantic Treaty Organization (NATO). Hostility began to escalate in a tit-for-tat fashion.

The most rigid phase of the Cold War occurred after two shocks in 1949: the Soviet Union exploded an atomic bomb, much sooner than some American leaders thought they could, and the Chinese Communist Party took control of mainland China, forcing the Nationalists to retreat to the island of Taiwan. The alarm in Washington was illustrated by a secret government document, National Security Council Document 68 (NSC-68), which forecast a Soviet attack in four to five years as part of a plan for global domination. NSC-68 called for a vast increase in the U.S. defense expenditure. Beset by budget problems, President Truman resisted NSC-68 until June 1950, when North Korea's troops crossed the border into South Korea.

The effect of the Korean War was like pouring gasoline onto a modest fire. It confirmed all the worst Western suspicions about Stalin's expansionist ambitions and led to a huge increase in the American defense budget, which Truman had

> The purpose of NSC-68 was to so bludgeon the mass mind of "top government" that not only could the President make a decision but that the decision could be carried out. Even so, it is doubtful whether anything like what happened in the next few years could have been done had not the Russians been stupid enough to have instigated the attack against South Korea and opened the "hate America" campaign.
>
> —*Secretary of State Dean Acheson, Present at the Creation*[6]

resisted up to that point. Why did Stalin permit North Korea to invade South Korea? Khrushchev gives an explanation in his memoirs: Kim Il Sung, the North Korean leader, pressed Stalin for the opportunity to unify the peninsula. The United States had said Korea was outside its defense perimeter; Secretary of State Dean Acheson had articulated this position and the Joint Chiefs of Staff had planned accordingly. To Stalin, Korea looked like a soft spot. But when North Korea actually crossed into South Korea, Truman responded in an axiomatic rather than a calculating way: Truman remembered Hitler moving into the Rhineland and recalled the axiom that aggression must be resisted everywhere. Calculated plans about defense perimeters were overshadowed by the historical analogies triggered by North Korea's invasion. The United States was able to mobilize the UN Security Council to endorse collective security (which was possible because the Soviet Union was then boycotting the Security Council) and sent troops to Korea under the UN flag to push the communists back above the thirty-eighth parallel that bisected the Korean peninsula.

At first, North Korea's armies swept down the peninsula almost to the tip. In September 1950, however, an American amphibious landing at Inchon, halfway up the peninsula, routed the North Koreans. Had the United States stopped there, it could have claimed victory by restoring the preinvasion status quo, but Truman succumbed to domestic pressures to pursue the retreating communist troops north of the thirty-eighth parallel. As the Americans approached the Yalu River, which divides Korea from China, the Chinese communists intervened, pushing the UN troops back to the middle of the peninsula. There the battle stalemated bloodily for three years until a truce was signed in 1953. The United States had become embroiled with China, and communism appeared to be monolithic. At home, the frustrating war led to domestic division and the rise of McCarthyism, named after the harsh and poorly founded accusations of domestic communist subversion made by Senator Joseph McCarthy of Wisconsin. The Cold War blocs tightened and communication nearly ceased.

INEVITABILITY?

Was the onset of the Cold War inevitable? The postrevisionists are correct if we relax the interpretation of inevitability to mean "highly probable." The bipolar structure made it likely that both sides would be sucked into a power vacuum in Europe and find it diffi-

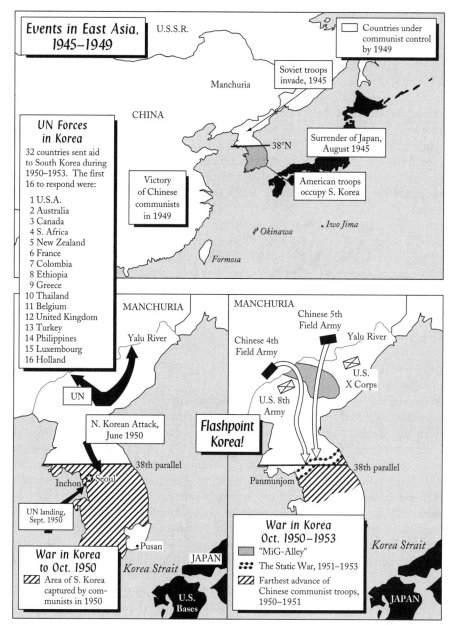

Events in East Asia, 1945–1949

U.S.S.R.

Countries under communist control by 1949

Manchuria

Soviet troops invade, 1945

CHINA

38°N

Surrender of Japan, August 1945

UN Forces in Korea

32 countries sent aid to South Korea during 1950–1953. The first 16 to respond were:

1 U.S.A.
2 Australia
3 Canada
4 S. Africa
5 New Zealand
6 France
7 Colombia
8 Ethiopia
9 Greece
10 Thailand
11 Belgium
12 United Kingdom
13 Turkey
14 Philippines
15 Luxembourg
16 Holland

Victory of Chinese communists in 1949

American troops occupy S. Korea

Okinawa

Iwo Jima

Formosa

MANCHURIA

Yalu River

UN

N. Korean Attack, June 1950

38th parallel

Seoul
Inchon

UN landing, Sept. 1950

War in Korea to Oct. 1950

Area of S. Korea captured by communists in 1950

Pusan

JAPAN

Korea Strait

U.S. Bases

MANCHURIA

Chinese 5th Field Army

Yalu River

Chinese 4th Field Army

U.S. X Corps

U.S. 8th Army

Flashpoint Korea!

38th parallel

Panmunjom

War in Korea Oct. 1950–1953

"MiG-Alley"

The Static War, 1951–1953

Farthest advance of Chinese communist troops, 1950–1951

Korea Strait

JAPAN

FIGURE 5.2   The Early Days of the Cold War in Asia

cult to disengage. The intense ideological climate hampered the working of the United Nations, restricted clear communication, and contributed to the immoderate process of the international system. Under such systemic conditions, conflicts would have arisen over the six issues just identified, or some others, and proven difficult to resolve.

The postrevisionists rely too heavily, however, on systemic explanation. Perhaps some Cold War was inevitable, but its depth was not. After all, there were different phases of the hostility, and since the bipolarity of the system did not change until 1989, structural explanations cannot explain the different phases or depth of the hostility. That is where individuals and domestic politics matter—Roosevelt and Truman, Stalin and Khrushchev. Domestic politics have to be considered to fully understand the extent of the Cold War. The revisionists are right to focus on domestic questions, but they are wrong to focus so strongly on economic determinism. More important was the role of ideology and exaggeration in domestic politics. Stalin used ideology because of Soviet domestic problems after the war, and Truman exaggerated the nature of the communist threat in order to rally support for changing American foreign policy. The use of 1930s analogies helped reinforce rigidity on both sides.

Ironically, alternative strategies at different times might have alleviated the depths of hostility. For example, if the United States had followed Kennan's advice and responded more firmly in 1945–1947, and had tried more pragmatic negotiation and communication from 1947–1950, Cold War tensions might not have mounted to the extent they did in the early 1950s.

LEVELS OF ANALYSIS

The origins of the Cold War can be described in terms of the different images or levels of analysis as illustrated in Figure 5.3.

In the nineteenth century, Alexis de Tocqueville (1805–1859) predicted that Russia and the United States were bound to become two great continental-scale giants in the world. Realists might thus predict that these two would become locked in some form of conflict. And of course, in 1917, the Bolshevik Revolution added an ideological layer to the conflict. When Woodrow Wilson first heard of the Russian Revolution, he congratulated the Russian people for their democratic spirit. But it did not take long before the Americans were accusing the Bolsheviks of regicide, expropriation, and cooperation with Germany in World War I. The United States added a small contingent of troops to an Allied intervention, allegedly to keep the Russians in the war against Germany, but the Soviets saw it as an attempt to strangle communism in its cradle. Despite these differences, the United States and the Soviet Union avoided serious conflict in the interwar period and became allies in the early 1940s. The bipolarity that followed the collapse of all the other great powers in World War II and the resulting power vacuum changed the relationship. Earlier there had been distrust between the two countries, but they distrusted each other at a distance. Before World War II they could avoid each other, but after 1945 they were face to face, Europe was divided, and deep conflict began after 1947. Some people wonder whether the bipolar structure had to have this effect. After all, the Soviet Union was a land-based power, while the United States was a maritime power; why could there not have been a division of labor between the bear and the whale, each staying in its own domain?

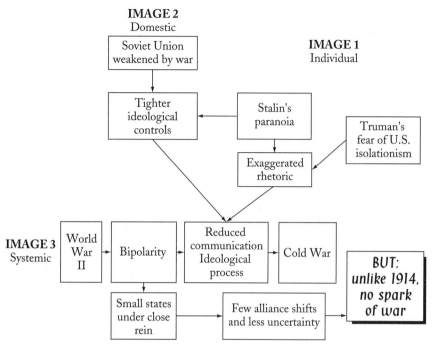

FIGURE 5.3   Causes of the Cold War

The answer is that the key stakes in world politics, the countries that could tip the balance of power, were located on the peripheries of the Soviet Union, particularly Europe and Japan. As George Kennan described the situation after the war, there were four great areas of technological and industrial creativity, which, if they were allied one way or the other, could tip the global balance of power. Those were the United States, the Soviet Union, Europe, and Japan. The fact that Europe and Japan became allied with the United States against the Soviet Union was of profound importance.

Systemic explanations predicted conflict, not how deep it would go (Figure 5.3). For that we need to go beyond systems explanations to look at the societal and individual levels of analysis and constructivist explanations. At the societal level, the two countries were very different from each other. A thumbnail sketch of the Soviet Union's political culture and its expression in foreign policy showed two roots: Russian and communist. Constructivists point out that the Russian political culture emphasized absolutism rather than democracy, a desire for a strong leader, fear of anarchy (Russia had been a large unwieldy empire, and the fear that anarchy and dissent could lead to disintegration was very real), fear of invasion (Russia was a geographically vulnerable land-based power that had invaded and been invaded by its neighbors throughout the centuries), a worry or shame about backwardness (ever since Peter the Great, Russians had been trying to prove their vitality in international competition), and secrecy (a desire to hide the seamy side of Russian life). In addition, the communist system treated class rather than individual rights as the basis for justice. The proper role for a person or for a society was to lead the proletariat or working class toward dominance because this was supposed to be the course of history.

The ideological overlay gave an additional outward thrust to traditional Russian imperialism and resulted in a secret and tightly held foreign policy process. It is interesting to note the strengths and weaknesses of that process. The strengths were evident in 1939 when Stalin was able to quickly sign the nonaggression pact with Hitler. Public opinion did not constrain him, and he did not have to worry about a bureaucracy holding him back. He was free to rush into the pact with Hitler while the British and French were still dithering about whether or not to deal with him. The opposite side of the same coin became evident in 1941, however, when Hitler attacked the Soviet Union. Stalin was unable to believe Hitler would do such a thing and went into a deep depression for more than a week. The result was disastrous for Soviet defenses in the early phases of the war.

In contrast, the American political culture emphasized liberal democracy, pluralism, and fragmentation of power. Instead of shame of backwardness, the United States took pride in its technology and expanding economy. Instead of a fear of invasion, for much of its history, the United States had been able to isolate itself between two oceans (and behind the British navy) while it invaded its weaker neighbors. In terms of secrecy, the United States was so open that governmental documents often reached the press within a matter of days and weeks. Instead of a class basis for conceptions of justice, there was a strong emphasis on individual justice. The foreign policy that resulted from this political culture was moralistic, public, and tended to oscillate between inward and outward orientation. The result was that the American foreign policy process was often inconsistent and incoherent in many of its surface aspects. But there was also an opposite side to this coin. The strengths of openness and pluralism often protected the United States from deeper mistakes.

Thus it is not surprising that these two societies, so differently organized and with such different foreign policy processes, would confuse each other. We saw examples of that in the way both Roosevelt and Truman dealt with Stalin in the 1940s. It was difficult for the Americans to understand the Soviet Union during the Cold War because the Soviet Union was like a black box. American leaders could see what went in and what came out of the box, but not what happened inside. The Americans confused the Soviets as well. The Americans were like a white noise machine that produced so much background noise that it was difficult to hear the true signals clearly. There were too many people saying too many things. Thus the Soviets were often confused about what the Americans really wanted.

U.S. AND SOVIET GOALS IN THE COLD WAR

The Soviets were often accused of being expansionist, of being a revolutionary power rather than a status quo power. The Soviet Union also tended to want tangible or *possession goals* such as territory, whereas the Americans tended to want intangible or *milieu goals*—ways of establishing the general setting of international politics. We can see this in the demands that Stalin, Churchill, and Roosevelt brought to the bargaining table at Yalta. Stalin had very clear objectives at Yalta: Germany and Poland. Churchill wanted the restoration of France to help balance Soviet power in case the Americans went home. Roosevelt wanted the United Nations and an open international economic system. These goals were very different in their tangibility. In some ways, Stalin's postwar goals were classic Russian imperialist goals; he wanted to keep the gains he had made in the treaty with Hitler. His wish list would have been familiar to Peter the Great.

Some Americans thought the Soviets were as expansionist as Hitler in desiring world domination. Others said the Soviets were basically security oriented; their expansion was defensive. There were at least two ways in which Soviet expansionism was not like Hitler's. First, it was not bellicist; the Soviets did not want war. When Hitler invaded Poland, he worried he would be offered another Munich instead of the war he wanted for the glory of fascism. Another difference was that the Soviet Union was cautiously opportunistic, not recklessly adventuresome. Adventurism was seen as a sin against communism because it might disrupt the predicted course of history. During the Cold War, the Soviet Union was never as bellicist or as reckless as Hitler was.

Nonetheless, there are problems in portraying Soviet behavior as purely defensive. As we know from the Peloponnesian War, it is very hard in a bipolar world to distinguish offense from defense. Certain actions may have defensive motives but may look very threatening to the other side. Moreover, there is a long tradition of defensive expansion, or imperialism. For example, in the nineteenth century, Britain originally went into Egypt to protect the sea routes to India. After it took Egypt, it thought it had to take the Sudan to protect Egypt, and then it had to take Uganda to protect the Sudan. After it took Uganda, Britain had to take Kenya to build a railway to protect Uganda. The appetite grows with the eating as the security dilemma is used to justify further and further expansion. Soviet communism added an ideological motive of freeing working classes in all areas of the world, which further legitimized expansion. In short, the Soviet Union was expansionist during the Cold War, but cautiously and opportunistically so.

CONTAINMENT

What about U.S. goals? During the Cold War, the U.S. government wanted to contain the Soviet Union. Yet the policy of containment involved two large ambiguities. One was the question of the ends: whether to contain Soviet power or to contain communism. The second was a question of means: whether to spend resources to prevent any expansion of Soviet power or just in certain key areas that seemed critical to the balance of power. Those two ambiguities in the ends and means of containment were hotly debated in the period before the Korean War. George Kennan dissented from the rather expansive version of containment that Truman proclaimed. Kennan's idea of containment was akin to classical diplomacy. It involved fewer military means and was more selective. A good example was

> It would be an exaggeration to say that American behavior unassisted and alone could exercise a power of life and death over the Communist movement and bring about the early fall of Soviet power in Russia. But the United States has it in its power to increase enormously the strains under which Soviet policy must operate, to force upon the Kremlin a far greater degree of moderation and circumspection than it has had to observe in recent years, and in this way to promote tendencies which must eventually find their outlet in either the break-up or the gradual mellowing of Soviet power.
>
> —George Kennan, *"The Sources of Soviet Conduct"*[7]

Yugoslavia, which had a communist totalitarian government under Josip Tito. In 1948, Tito split with Stalin over Soviet efforts to control Yugoslavia's foreign policy, including its support for the Greek communists. According to an ideologically driven containment policy, the United States should not help Yugoslavia because it was communist. But in a containment policy driven by balance-of-power considerations, the United States should help Yugoslavia as a means of weakening Soviet power. That, in fact, is what the United States did. It provided military aid to a totalitarian communist government despite the fact that the Truman Doctrine proclaimed the goal of defending free peoples everywhere. The United States did this for balance-of-power reasons, and the policy put a big dent in Soviet power in Europe.

After the Korean War, however, Kennan's approach to containment lost ground. Then it looked as though the NSC-68 predictions of Soviet expansionism had been justified. Communism seemed monolithic after the Chinese entered the Korean War, and the rhetoric of containment emphasized the ideological goal of preventing the spread of communism. In this context, the United States made the costly mistake of becoming involved in Vietnam's civil war. For nearly two decades (1955–1973), the United States tried to prevent communist control of Vietnam, at a cost of 58,000 American lives, more than a million Vietnamese lives, $600 billion, and domestic turmoil that undercut support for the policy of containment itself. In addition to containing communism in South Vietnam, the United States feared that a defeat might weaken the credibility of its global military commitments, and thus containment in other parts of the world. Ironically, after the U.S. defeat and withdrawal from Vietnam in 1975, nationalist rivalries among the communist countries in Asia proved to be an effective force for maintaining the balance of power in the region.

THE REST OF THE COLD WAR

In 1952, Dwight Eisenhower was elected president on a campaign pledge to end the Korean War and to roll back communism. The Republican Party argued that containment was a cowardly accommodation to communism. The right approach was to roll back communism. Within six months, however, it became clear that rolling back communism was too risky in terms of precipitating nuclear war. After Stalin died in 1953, the frozen relations of the Cold War thawed slightly. In 1955, there was a U.S.-Soviet summit in Geneva and both sides agreed to the establishment of Austria as a neutral state. In 1956, Khrushchev gave a secret speech exposing Stalin's crimes to the Twentieth Party Congress of the Soviet Union. The secret leaked out and contributed to a period of disarray in the Soviet sphere in Eastern Europe. Hungary attempted to revolt, but the Soviets intervened militarily to keep it within the communist camp.

Khrushchev decided he needed to get the Americans out of Berlin and reach a final settlement of World War II so he could consolidate the Soviet hold on Eastern Europe and begin to take advantage of the decolonization occurring in the Third World. But Khrushchev's style and efforts to negotiate with the United States were reminiscent of the Kaiser's style in trying to force the British to bargain before 1914, full of bluster and deception. Efforts to make the United States come to terms had the opposite effect. Khrushchev failed in the Berlin crisis of 1958–1961 and again in the Cuban Missile Crisis in 1962.

As we see later, the Soviet Union and the United States came so close to the nuclear brink during the Cuban Missile Crisis that they scared each other into a new phase in their relationship. From 1963 to 1978, there was a gradual détente, or relaxation of tensions. In the aftermath of the Cuban Missile Crisis, arms control negotiations produced the Limited Test Ban Treaty that limited atmospheric nuclear tests in 1963 and the Nuclear Non-Proliferation Treaty in 1968. Trade began to grow gradually, and détente seemed to be expanding. The Vietnam War diverted U.S. attention more to the threat from Chinese communism.

From 1969 to 1974, the Nixon administration used détente as a means to pursue the goals of containment. After the Cuban Missile Crisis, the Soviets launched a major military buildup and gained parity in nuclear weapons. The Vietnam War led to the American public's disillusionment with Cold War interventions. Nixon's strategy was (1) to negotiate a strategic arms control treaty with the Soviet Union to cap each nation's nuclear arsenal at relative parity; (2) to open diplomatic relations with China and thus create a three-way balance of power in Asia (rather than pushing the Soviets and the Chinese together); (3) to increase trade so there would be carrots as well as sticks in the U.S.-Soviet relationship; and (4) to use "linkage" to tie the various parts of policy together. The high point of détente occurred in 1972 and 1973, but it did not last very long.

The Middle East War of 1973 and Soviet assistance to anti-Western movements in Africa led to bad feelings about who misled whom. American domestic politics contributed to the decline of détente when American legislators such as Senator Henry Jackson tried to link trade with the Soviet Union to human rights issues, such as the treatment of Soviet Jews, rather than to behavior in balance of power terms. In 1975, when Portugal decolonized Angola and Mozambique, the Soviet Union transported Cuban troops to help keep communist-oriented governments in power there. By the 1976 presidential campaign, President Gerald Ford never used the word *détente*. His successor, Jimmy Carter, tried to continue détente with the Soviet Union during his first two years in office, but the Soviet Union and Cuba became involved in the Ethiopian civil war, the Soviets continued their defense buildup, and in December 1979 the Soviet Union delivered the coup de grâce to détente by invading Afghanistan.

Why was there a resurgence in the level of hostility? One argument is that détente was always oversold, that too much was expected of it. More to the point is that there were three trends in the 1970s that undercut it. One was the Soviet military buildup, in which the Soviets increased their defense spending by nearly 4 percent annually and introduced new heavy missiles that particularly worried American defense planners. Second was the Soviet interventions in Angola, Ethiopia, and Afghanistan. The Soviets thought that these military actions were justified by what they called the changing "correlation of forces" in history, their belief that history was moving in the directions that Marxism-Leninism predicted. Third were changes in American domestic politics, a rightward trend that tore apart the coalition supporting the Democratic Party. The result of the interaction of Soviet acts and U.S. political trends confirmed the view that the Cold War persisted, that détente could not last. However, the renewed hostility in the 1980s was *not* a return to the Cold War of the 1950s. There was a return to the rhetoric of the 1950s, but actions were quite different. Even though President Ronald Reagan talked about the Soviet Union as an "evil empire," he pursued arms control agreements. There was increased trade, particularly in grain, and there were constant contacts between Americans and Soviets. The superpowers even evolved certain rules of prudence in their behavior toward each other: no direct wars, no nuclear use, and discussions of arms and the control of nuclear weapons. It was a different kind of Cold War in the 1980s than in the 1950s.

THE END OF THE COLD WAR

When did the Cold War end? Because the origins of the Cold War were very heavily related to the division of Europe by the United States and the Soviet Union, the end of the Cold War might be dated by when the division ended in 1989. When the Soviet Union did not use force to support the communist government in East Germany and the Berlin Wall was pierced by jubilant crowds in November 1989, the Cold War could be said to be over.

But why did it end? One argument is that containment worked. George Kennan argued right after World War II that if the United States could prevent the Soviet Union from expanding, there would be no successes to feed the ideology, and gradually Soviet communism would mellow. New ideas would arise, people would realize that communism was not the wave of the future, that history was not on its side. In some larger respect, Kennan was right. American military power helped deter Soviet expansion while the soft power of American culture, values, and ideas eroded communist ideology. But the puzzle of timing remains: Why 1989? Why did it last four decades? Why did it take so long to mellow? Alternatively, why didn't it last another ten years? Containment worked, but that does not give the full answer.

Another explanation is "imperial overstretch." The Yale historian Paul Kennedy has argued that empires overexpand until that overexpansion saps the empire's internal strength. With more than a quarter of its economy devoted to defense and foreign affairs (compared to 6 percent for the United States in the 1980s), the Soviet Union was overstretched. But Kennedy went on to say that none of the overexpanded multinational empires in history ever retreated to their own ethnic base until they had been defeated or weakened in a great power war. The Soviet Union, however, was not defeated or weakened in a great power war. A third explanation is that the U.S. military buildup in the 1980s forced the Soviets to surrender in the Cold War. There is some truth to that insofar as President Ronald Reagan's policies dramatized the extent to which the Soviets were imperially overstretched, but it does not really answer the basic question. After all, earlier periods of American military buildup did not have that effect. Why 1989? We must look for deeper causes, because to think that American rhetoric and policy in the 1980s were the prime cause of the Soviet Union's decline may be similar to the rooster who thought that his crowing before dawn caused the sun to come up—another example of the fallacy of spurious causation.

We can gain more exact insights into the timing of the end of the Cold War by looking at our three types of causes: precipitating, intermediate, and deep. The most important precipitating cause of the end of the Cold War was an individual, Mikhail Gorbachev. He wanted to reform communism, not replace it. However, the reform snowballed into a revolution driven from below rather than controlled from above. In both his domestic and foreign policy, Gorbachev launched a number of actions that accelerated both the existing Soviet decline and the end of the Cold War. When he first came to power in 1985, Gorbachev tried to discipline the Soviet people as a way to overcome the existing economic stagnation. When discipline was not enough to solve the problem, he launched the idea of *perestroika*, or "restructuring," but he was unable to restructure from the top because the Soviet bureaucrats kept thwarting his orders. To light a fire under the bureaucrats, he used a strategy of *glasnost*, or open discussion and democratization. Gorbachev believed that airing people's discontent with the way the system was working would put pressure on the bureaucrats and help perestroika work. But once glasnost and democratization let people say what they were thinking, and vote on it, many people said, "We want out. There is no new form of Soviet citizen. This is an imperial dynasty, and we do not belong in this empire." Gorbachev unleashed the disintegration of the Soviet Union, which became increasingly evident after the failed coup by hard-liners in August 1991. By December 1991, the Soviet Union ceased to exist.

Gorbachev's foreign policy, which he called "new thinking," also contributed to the end of the Cold War. This policy had two very important elements. One was changing ideas that constructivists emphasize, such as the concept of common security in which the classical security dilemma is escaped by joining together to provide security. Gorbachev and the people around him said that in a world of increasing interdependence, security was a non-zero-sum game, and all could benefit through cooperation. The existence of the nuclear threat meant all could perish together if the competition got out of hand. Rather than try to build as many nuclear weapons

Bush, Reagan, and Gorbachev in New York, 1987

as possible, Gorbachev proclaimed a doctrine of "sufficiency," holding a minimal number for protection. The other dimension of Gorbachev's foreign policy change was his view that expansionism is usually more costly than beneficial. The Soviet control over an empire in Eastern Europe was costing too much and providing too little benefit, and the invasion of Afghanistan had been a costly disaster. It was no longer necessary to impose a communist social system as a way to ensure security on Soviet borders.

Thus by the summer of 1989, the Eastern Europeans were given more degrees of freedom. Hungary allowed East Germans to escape through its territory into Austria. This exodus of East Germans put enormous pressure on the East German government. Additionally, Eastern European governments no longer had the nerve (or Soviet backing) to put down demonstrations. In November, the Berlin Wall was pierced—a dramatic conclusion to a crescendo of events occurring over a very short period. We can argue that these events stemmed from Gorbachev's miscalculations. He thought communism could be repaired, but in fact, in trying to repair it, he punched a hole in it. And like a hole in a dam, the pent-up pressures began to escape, rapidly increasing the opening and causing the entire system to collapse.

That still leaves the question, "Why 1989? Why under this leader?" To some extent, Gorbachev was an accident of history. In the early 1980s, three old Soviet leaders died, one soon after the other. It was not until 1985 that the younger generation, the people who had come up under Khrushchev, the so-called generation of 1956, had their chance. But if the members of the Communist Party Politburo had chosen one of Gorbachev's hard-line competitors in 1985, it is quite plausible that the declining Soviet Union could have held on for another decade. It did not have to collapse so quickly. Gorbachev's personality explains much of the timing.

As for the intermediate causes, Kennan and Kennedy are both on target. Two important intermediate causes were soft power of liberal ideas, emphasized in constructivist explanations, and imperial overstretch, emphasized by realists. The ideas of openness and democracy and new thinking that Gorbachev used were Western ideas that had been adopted by the generation of 1956. One of the key architects of perestroika and glasnost, Aleksandr Yakovlev, had been an exchange student in the United States and was attracted to American theories of pluralism. The growth of transnational communications and contacts pierced the Iron Curtain and helped spread Western popular culture and liberal ideas. The demonstrated effect of Western economic success gave them additional appeal. While hard military power deterred Soviet expansionism, soft power ate away the belief in communism behind the Iron Curtain. When the Berlin Wall finally fell in 1989, it did not succumb to an artillery barrage, but to an onslaught of civilian hammers and bulldozers.

As for imperial overstretch, the enormous Soviet defense budget began to affect other aspects of Soviet society. Health care declined and the mortality rate in the Soviet Union increased (the only developed country where that occurred). Eventually even the military became aware of the tremendous burden caused by imperial overstretch. In 1984, Marshall Ogarkov, the Soviet chief of staff, realized the Soviet Union needed a better civilian economic base and more access to Western trade and technology. But during the period of stagnation, the old leaders were unwilling to listen and Ogarkov was removed from his post.

Thus the intermediate causes of soft power and imperial overstretch are important, though ultimately we must deal with the deep causes, which were the decline of communist ideology (a constructivist explanation) and the failure of the Soviet economy (a realist explanation). Communism's loss of legitimacy over the postwar period was quite dramatic. In the early period, immediately after 1945, communism was widely attractive. Many communists had led the resistance against fascism in Europe, and many people believed that communism was the wave of the future. The Soviet Union gained a great deal of soft power from their communist ideology but they squandered it. Soviet soft power was progressively undercut by the de-Stalinization in 1956 that exposed his crimes; by the repressions in Hungary in 1956, in Czechoslovakia in 1968, and in Poland in 1981; and by the growing transnational communication of liberal ideas. Although in theory communism aimed to instill a system of class justice, Lenin's heirs maintained domestic power through a brutal state security system involving reform camps, gulags, broad censorship, and the use of informants. The net effect of these repressive measures on the Russian people was a general loss of faith in the system as voiced in the underground protest literature and the rising tide of dissent advanced by human rights activists.

Behind this, there was also decline in the Soviet economy, reflecting the diminished ability of the Soviet central planning system to respond to change in the world economy. Stalin had created a system of centralized economic direction that emphasized heavy metal and smokestack industries. It was very inflexible—all

> In contrast to the way most history is written, Cold War historians through the end of the 1980s were working within rather than after the event they were trying to describe. We had no way of knowing the final outcome, and we could determine the motivations of only some—by no means all—of the major players. . . . We know now, to coin a phrase. Or, at least, we know a good deal more than we once did. We will never have the full story: we don't have that for any historical event, no matter how far back in the past. Historians can no more reconstruct what actually happened than maps can replicate what is really there. But we can represent the past, just as cartographers approximate terrain. And the end of the Cold War and at least the partial opening of documents from the former Soviet Union, Eastern Europe, and China, the fit between our representations and the reality they describe has become a lot closer than it once was.
>
> —*John L. Gaddis, "The New Cold War History"*[8]

thumbs and no fingers—and tended to stockpile labor rather than transfer it to growing service industries. As the economist Joseph Schumpeter pointed out, capitalism is creative destruction, a way of responding flexibly to major waves of technological change. At the end of the twentieth century, the major technological change of the third industrial revolution was the growing role of information as the scarcest resource in an economy. The Soviet system was particularly inept at handling information. The deep secrecy of its political system meant that the flow of information was slow and cumbersome.

Soviet goods and services could not keep up to world standards. There was a great deal of turmoil in the world economy at the end of the twentieth century, but the Western economies using market systems were able to transfer labor to services, to reorganize their heavy industries, and to switch to computers. The Soviet Union could not keep up with the changes. For instance, when Gorbachev came to power in 1985, there were 50,000 personal computers in the Soviet Union; in the United States there were 30 million. Four years later, there were about 400,000 personal computers in the Soviet Union, and 40 million in the United States. Market-oriented economies and democracies proved more flexible in responding to technological change than the centralized Soviet system that Stalin created for the smokestack era of the 1930s. According to one Soviet economist, by the late 1980s, only 8 percent of Soviet industry was competitive at world standards. It is difficult to remain a superpower when 92 percent of industry is subpar.

The end of the Cold War was one of the great transforming events of the twentieth century. It was equivalent to World War II in its effects on the structure of the international system, but it occurred without war. In the next chapters, we turn to what this may mean for international politics in the future.

Following the breakup of the Soviet Union, Russia has undergone a significant transformation. Renouncing the planned economy of the Soviet state, post–Cold War Russia tentatively embarked on a path of democratization and economic liberalization. That road has been fraught with peril, however. Following the advice of the International Monetary Fund, the Russian government at first embraced economic "shock therapy" as a way of making the transition from economic autocracy to liberal democracy. Yet shock therapy so disrupted Russian society that it was quickly shelved in favor of a more gradualist approach. As the economic situation deteriorated, Russian nationalism was rejuvenated.

Theorists such as Michael Doyle, hypothesizing that liberal democracies do not fight wars with one another, have concluded that if Russia makes a successful transition to democracy, it will bode well for international peace. It remains to be seen whether Russian foreign policy will fit the model of the democratic peace, or whether a resurgence of Russian authoritarianism and nationalism will challenge the United States and Western Europe.

Regardless of what the future holds, one major puzzle remains. Just as important as the question of why the Cold War ended is the question of why it did not turn hot. Why did the Cold War last so long without a "hot war" erupting between the two superpowers. Why did it not turn into World War III?

THE ROLE OF NUCLEAR WEAPONS

Some analysts believe that advanced developed societies learned from the lessons of World War I and World War II and simply outgrew war. Others believe that the "long peace" in the second half of the twentieth century stemmed from the limited expansionist goals of the superpowers. Still others credit what they consider the inherent stability of pure bipolarity in which two states (not two tight alliances) are dominant. But for most analysts, the largest part of the answer lies in the special nature of nuclear weapons and nuclear deterrence.

Physics and Politics

The enormous destructive power of nuclear weapons is almost beyond comprehension. A megaton nuclear explosion can create temperatures of 100 million degrees Celsius—four to five times the temperature in the center of the sun. The bomb dropped on Hiroshima in 1945 was relatively small, about the equivalent of 15,000 tons of TNT. Today's missiles can carry 100 times that explosive power or more. In fact, all the explosive power used in World War II could fit in one 3-megaton bomb, and that one bomb could fit in the nose cone of one large intercontinental missile. By the 1980s, the United States and the Soviet Union together had more than 50,000 nuclear weapons.

Some physical effects of nuclear explosions are uncertain. For example, the theory of nuclear winter holds that a nuclear war would create so much carbon and dust in the atmosphere that it would block sunlight, preventing plants from conducting photosynthesis and leading to the end of life as we know it. A National Academy of Sciences study reported that nuclear winter is possible, but highly uncertain. Much would depend on whether the weapons were aimed at cities rather than at other weapons. Burning cities would cause smoke with a high carbon content that would block sunlight, but it is uncertain how long the smoke would stay aloft. If the bombs exploded in the Northern Hemisphere, would the smoke travel to the Southern Hemisphere? Some skeptics argued the worst result would not be nuclear winter, but nuclear autumn—a faint consolation. The certainty is that a large-scale nuclear war would destroy civilization as we know it, at least in the Northern Hemisphere. In their 1983 report on nuclear weapons, the American Catholic bishops engaged in only slight hyperbole when they said, "We are the first generation since Genesis with the capability of destroying God's creation."[9]

Nuclear weapons changed the nature of warfare, but they did not change the basic way in which the world is organized. The world of anarchic states with no higher government above them continued in the nuclear age. In 1946, when the United States proposed the Baruch Plan to establish international control of nuclear weapons, the Soviet Union viewed it as just another American plot. After this failure, Albert Einstein lamented that everything changed except our thinking. Perhaps apocryphally, he is supposed to have said that "physics is easier than politics."

There are both military and political reasons why nuclear weapons did not have a more dramatic effect right after 1945. For one thing, the early atomic weapon did not do significantly more damage than the most deadly uses of mass conventional weapons. The firebombing of the German city of Dresden in 1945 killed more people than the nuclear bombing of Hiroshima. Though one atomic weapon did the work of a entire air attack using conventional bombs, at first there were not that many nuclear weapons in the U.S. arsenal. The United States had only 2 in 1947, and 50 in 1948. Many military planners thought atomic bombs were not totally different, just extensions of conventional warfare.

The emerging U.S.-Soviet rivalry also slowed change in political thinking. The Soviet Union mistrusted the United Nations and saw it as too reliant on the United States. The United States could not coerce the Soviets into cooperation because Europe was a hostage between the Soviets and the Americans. If the United States threatened nuclear attack, the Soviets could threaten to invade Europe with conventional forces. The result was a stalemate. The revolutionary physical effects of nuclear technology were initially not enough to change the ways states behaved in an anarchic system.

The second stage of the nuclear revolution occurred in 1952 when the hydrogen bomb was first tested. Hydrogen bombs rely on the fusion energy released when atoms are fused into one, instead of split apart as in the early fission bombs. The H-bomb vastly increased the amount of destruction possible with a single weapon. The largest human-made explosion on the earth's surface occurred in 1961 when the Soviet Union exploded a 60-megaton hydrogen bomb, 20 times all the explosive power used in World War II.

Ironically, the more important change that accompanied the development of the H-bomb was miniaturization. Fusion made it possible to deliver enormous amounts of destructive power in very small packages. The systems built to deliver the early atomic bombs got bigger and bigger as the bombs increased in size and required more space as the bombs increased in size. The B-36 bomber was a huge eight-engine airplane with one big cavity to hold one bomb. A hydrogen bomb, on the other hand, could put the same potential destruction in a much smaller package. Once that destructive power was mounted in the nose cone of a ballistic missile, an intercontinental nuclear war could occur with only 30 minutes' warning, compared to the eight hours it took a B-36 to fly the same distance.

The increased destructiveness of hydrogen bombs also dramatized the consequences of nuclear war. No longer could warfare be considered merely an extension of politics by other means. Karl von Clausewitz (1780–1831), a nineteenth-century Prussian general and military strategist, said war is a political act, and therefore absolute war is an absurdity. The enormous destructive power of nuclear weapons meant there was now a disproportion between the military means and virtually all the political ends a country might seek. This disjunction between ends and means caused a paralysis in the use of the ultimate force in most situations. Nuclear weapons have not been used since 1945, thus the view that nuclear weaponry is muscle-bound. It is just too powerful, too disproportionate.

The H-bomb had five significant political effects, even though it did not reorganize the anarchic way in which the world goes about its business. First, it revived the concept of limited war. The first half of the twentieth century saw a change from the limited wars of the nineteenth century to the two world wars, which took tens of millions of lives. At midcentury, analysts were referring to the twentieth century as "the century of total war." But war in the second half of the century was more like the old wars of the eighteenth and nineteenth centuries; for instance, though the Korean and Vietnam wars each cost more than 55,000 American deaths, they remained limited in scope and scale. In Vietnam and Afghanistan, the United States and the Soviet Union each accepted defeat rather than use their ultimate weapon.

Second, crises replaced central war as the moments of truth. In the past, war was the time when all the cards were face up on the table. But in the nuclear age, war is too devastating and the old moments of truth are too dangerous. During the Cold War, the Berlin crisis, the Cuban Missile Crisis, and the Middle East crises of the early 1970s played the functional equivalent of war, a time to see the true correlation of forces in military power. Third, nuclear weapons made deterrence (discouragement by fear) the key strategy. It was now critical to organize military might to produce fear in advance so attack would be deterred. In World War II, the United States relied on its ability to mobilize and gradually build a war machine after the war started, but that mobilization approach no longer worked when a nuclear war could be over in a matter of hours.

A fourth political effect was the development of a de facto regime of superpower prudence. The two superpowers, despite their bitter ideological differences, developed one key common interest: avoiding nuclear war. During the Cold War, the United States and the Soviet Union engaged in proxy or indirect peripheral wars, but in no case did the two nations go head to head. In addition, the two sides developed spheres of influence. While the Americans talked about rolling back communism in Eastern Europe in the 1950s, in practice, when the Hungarians revolted against their Soviet rulers in 1956, the United States did not rush in to help them for fear of nuclear war. Similarly, with the exception of Cuba, the Soviets were relatively careful about incursions into the Western Hemisphere. Both countries adhered to a developing norm of nonuse of nuclear weapons. Finally, the superpowers learned to communicate. After the Cuban Missile Crisis, Washington and Moscow developed "hotlines" to allow instant communication between the Soviet and American leaders. Technology made it easier to cooperate in times of crisis by making communication between leaders in the bipolar system more flexible and personal. Simultaneously, the codification of a number of arms control treaties, starting with the Limited Test Ban Treaty in 1963, and frequent arms control negotiations became a way to discuss stability in the nuclear system.

Fifth, nuclear weapons in general and the H-bomb in particular were seen by most officials as unusable in time of war. It was not purely a matter of the destructive potential of the H-bomb. There was a stigma attached to the use of nuclear weaponry that simply did not apply to conventional weaponry. By the late 1960s, in fact, engineers and scientists had managed to shrink the payload of nuclear weapons so that some nuclear weapons could have been used by the United States in Vietnam and the Gulf War or by the Soviet Union in Afghanistan without causing the type of unjustifiable damage of an H-bomb. Yet both Americans and Russians refrained from using smaller-payload nuclear weapons and opted instead for destructive tools such as napalm, incendiary bombs, and assorted conventional weapons. In part, it was feared that using any nuclear weapon, no matter how similar to conventional weapons, would open the window to using all nuclear weapons, and that risk was unacceptable. There was yet another dimension. Ever since the first bomb was dropped by the United States on Hiroshima, there was a lingering sense that nuclear weapons were immoral, that they went beyond the realm of what was acceptable in war. Though that normative restraint is hard to measure, it clearly suffused the debates over nuclear weapons and was one reason for the unwillingness of states to use them.

Balance of Terror

Nuclear weapons produced a peculiar form of the balance of power that was sometimes called the "balance of terror." Tests of strength were more psychological than physical. Both sides followed a policy of preventing preponderance by the other, but the result was different from previous systems. Unlike the nineteenth-century balance-of-power system in which five great powers shifted alliances, the Cold War balance was very clearly organized around two very large states, each capable of destroying the other in an instant.

The problems raised by the classical security dilemma were not ended by the terror of nuclear weapons, but the superpowers acted prudently despite their ideological differences. Their prudence was similar to the effects of the constant communications that occurred in managing the multipolar nineteenth-century balance of power. At the same time, the superpowers tried to calculate balances of force, just as in the days when statesmen compared provinces, infantry, and artillery.

The nuclear balance of terror coincided with a period of bipolarity. Some neorealists such as Kenneth Waltz define bipolarity as situations in which two large states have nearly all the power, but that type of pure bipolarity is rare. More often bipolarity has occurred in history when alliances tighten so much that flexibility is lost, as happened in the Peloponnesian War. Even though they were independent states, the alliances around Athens and around Sparta coalesced tightly into a bipolar situation. Similarly, on the eve of World War I the alliance systems became tightly bound into bipolarity.

Waltz argues that bipolarity is a particularly stable type of system because it simplifies communication and calculations. On the other hand, bipolar systems lack flexibility and magnify the importance of marginal conflicts such as the Vietnam War. The conventional wisdom in the past was that bipolarity either erodes or explodes. If so, why did bipolarity not explode after World War II? Perhaps the prudence produced by nuclear weapons provided the answer, and the stability that Waltz attributed to pure bipolarity was really the result of the bomb. The very terror of nuclear weapons may have helped produce stability through the "crystal ball effect." Imagine that in August 1914 the Kaiser, the Czar, and the Emperor of Austria-Hungary looked into a crystal ball and saw a picture of 1918. They would have seen that they had lost their thrones, their empires had been dismembered, and millions of their people had been killed. Would they still have gone to war in 1914? Probably not. Knowledge of the physical effects of nuclear weapons may be similar to the effect of giving leaders in the post-1945 period a crystal ball. Because few political goals would be proportionate to such destruction, they would not want to take great risks. Of course, crystal balls can be shattered by accidents and by miscalculations, but the analogy suggests why the combination of bipolarity and nuclear weapons produced the longest period of peace between the central powers since the beginning of the modern state system. (The previous record was 1871–1914.)

Problems of Nuclear Deterrence

Nuclear deterrence is a subset of general deterrence, but the peculiar qualities of nuclear weapons changed how the superpowers approached international relations during the Cold War. Nuclear deterrence encourages the reasoning, "If you attack me, I may not be able to prevent your attack, but I can retaliate so powerfully that you will not want to attack in the first place." Nuclear weapons thus put a new twist on an old concept.

NUCLEAR WEAPONS AND THE VIETNAM WAR

When President Kennedy made the first decision to increase significantly the American military presence in 1962–63, . . . he had in mind two things: What would have happened if Khrushchev had not believed him in the Berlin crisis of 1961–62, and what would have happened if Khrushchev did not believe Kennedy in the Cuban Missile Crisis of 1962?

I think we made a mistake in concluding that the Chinese would probably not intervene in the Korean War in 1950, and that influenced the American decision not to invade North Vietnam. The military said they did not think China would come in, but if it did, it would lead to nuclear war, and that decided that.

—*Secretary of State Dean Rusk*[10]

One way to assess the efficacy of nuclear deterrence is by counterfactual analysis. How likely was it that the Cold War would have turned hot in the absence of nuclear weapons? The political scientist John Mueller argues that nuclear weapons were irrelevant, that they were no more than the rooster crowing. He argues that the peoples of Europe had been turning away from war as a policy instrument ever since the horrors of World War I. The cause of peace was the increased recognition of the horror of war, at least in the developed world. According to Mueller, Hitler was an aberration, a rare person who had not learned the lessons of World War I and was still willing to go to war. After World War II, the general revulsion toward war returned more strongly than before. Most analysts, however, believe nuclear weapons had a lot to do with avoiding World War III. Crises over Berlin, Cuba, and perhaps the Middle East might have spiraled out of control without the prudence instilled by the crystal ball effect of nuclear weapons.

That raises a number of questions. One is, "What deters?" Effective deterrence requires both the capability to do damage and a credible threat that the weapons will be used. Credibility depends on the stakes involved in a conflict. For example, an American threat to bomb Moscow in retaliation for a nuclear attack was probably credible. But suppose the United States had threatened to bomb Moscow in 1980 if the Soviets did not withdraw their troops from Afghanistan. The United States certainly had the capability, but the threat would not have been credible because the stakes were too low, and the Soviets could easily have threatened in return to bomb Washington. So deterrence is related not just to capability, but also to credibility.

That problem of credibility leads to a distinction between deterring threats against one's homeland and extending deterrence to cover an ally. For example, the United States could not stop the Soviet Union from invading Afghanistan by nuclear deterrence, but for the four decades of the Cold War it threatened to use nuclear weapons if the Soviet Union invaded the NATO countries of Western Europe. Thus to look for the effects of nuclear weapons in extending deterrence and averting war, we must look at major crises in which the stakes are high.

Can history answer these questions about the effect of nuclear weapons? Not completely, but it can help. From 1945 to 1949, the United States alone had nuclear weapons, but did not use them. So there was some self-restraint even before mutual nuclear deterrence. Part of the reason was small arsenals, a lack of understanding of these new weapons, and the American fear that the Soviets would capture all of Europe with their massive conventional forces. By the 1950s, both the United States and the Soviet Union had nuclear weapons, and American leaders considered their use in several crises. Nuclear weapons were not used in the Korean War, or in 1954 and 1958 when the Chinese communists mobilized forces to invade the Nationalist-held island of Taiwan. Presidents Truman and Eisenhower vetoed the use of nuclear weapons for several reasons. In the Korean War, it was not clear that dropping a nuclear weapon would stop the Chinese, and the United States was concerned about the Soviet response. There was always the danger that the threats might escalate and the Soviets might use a nuclear weapon to help their Chinese ally. So even though the Americans had superiority in the number of nuclear weapons, there was the danger of heading to a larger war involving more than Korea and China.

In addition, ethics and public opinion played a role. In the 1950s, U.S. government estimates of the number of citizens who would be killed by a nuclear attack were so high that the idea was put aside. President Eisenhower, when asked about using nuclear weapons, said, "We can't use those awful things against Asians for the second time in less than ten years. My God!"[12] Even though the United States had more nuclear weapons than the Soviet Union in the 1950s, a combination of factors persuaded the Americans not to use them.

The Cuban Missile Crisis

The key case in nuclear deterrence in the Cold War was the Cuban Missile Crisis of October 1962. This 13-day period was probably the closest call in the nuclear age to a set of events that could have led to nuclear war. If a total outsider, a "man from Mars," had looked at the situation, he would have seen that the United States had a 17-to-1 superiority in nuclear weaponry. We now know the Soviets had only about 20 nuclear weapons on intercontinental missiles that could have reached the United States, but President Kennedy did not know it at the time. Why then didn't the United States try to preempt a Soviet first strike by attacking Soviet missile sites, which were then relatively vulnerable? The answer was that if even one or two of the Soviet missiles had escaped and been fired at an American city, that risk was enough to deter a U.S. first strike. In addition, both Kennedy and

---

THE "GRAVEST ISSUES"

By mid-October 1962, the Cold War had intensified in unforeseen ways. Cuba, which had long been a virtual colony of the United States, had recently moved into the Soviet orbit. In late September U.S. newspapers had begun reporting shipments of Soviet weapons to Cuba. President John F. Kennedy told the American public that, to the best of his understanding, these weapons were defensive, not offensive. Soviet Premier Nikita Khrushchev had given him absolute assurances that this was the case. "Were it to be otherwise," Kennedy said, "the gravest issues would arise."

Shortly before 9:00 A.M. on Tuesday, October 16, Kennedy's Assistant for National Security Affairs, McGeorge Bundy, brought to his bedroom photographs showing that the "gravest issues" had indeed arisen. Taken from very high altitude by a U-2 reconnaissance plane, these photographs showed the Soviets in Cuba setting up nuclear-armed ballistic missiles targeted on cities in the continental United States.

For Kennedy, the presence of these missiles was intolerable. So was the fact that Khrushchev had lied to him. For the next 13 days, Kennedy and a circle of advisers debated how to cope with the challenge. They knew that one possible outcome was nuclear war, and during their discussions Kennedy's civil defense expert offered the chilling information that the U.S. population was frighteningly vulnerable.

—*Ernest May and Philip Zelikow, The Kennedy Tapes*[11]

Khrushchev feared that rational strategies and careful calculations might spin out of their control. Khrushchev came up with a nice metaphor for this in one of his letters to Kennedy: "Be careful as we both tug at the ends of the rope in which we have tied the knot of war."[13]

At a conference in Florida 25 years after the event, Americans who had been involved in President Kennedy's Executive Committee of the National Security Council met with scholars to try to reconstruct the Cuban Missile Crisis. One of the most striking differences among the participants was how much each individual had been willing to take risks. That in turn depended on how likely each thought were the prospects of nuclear war. Robert McNamara, Kennedy's secretary of defense, became more cautious as the crisis unfolded. At the time, he thought the probability of nuclear war in the Cuban Missile Crisis might be one chance out of fifty (though later he rated the risks much higher after he learned in the 1990s that the Soviets had already delivered nuclear weapons to Cuba). Douglas Dillon, who was the secretary of the treasury, said he thought the risks of nuclear war were about zero. He did not see how the situation could possibly progress to nuclear war and as a result was willing to push the Soviets harder and to take more risks than McNamara was. General Maxwell Taylor, the chairman of the Joint Chiefs of Staff, also thought the risk of nuclear war was low, and he complained that the United States let the Soviet Union off too easily in the Cuban Missile Crisis. He argued that Kennedy could have pushed much harder and should have demanded the removal of Cuba's president, Fidel Castro. General Taylor said, "I was so sure we had 'em over a barrel, I never worried much about the final outcome."[14] But the risks of losing control weighed heavily on President Kennedy, who took a very cautious position, indeed, more prudent than some of his advisers would have liked. The moral of the story is that a little nuclear deterrence goes a long way. It is clear that nuclear deterrence made a difference in the Cuban Missile Crisis.

Nonetheless, there are still ambiguities about the missile crisis that make it difficult to attribute the whole outcome to the nuclear component. The public consensus was that the United States won. But the question of how much the United States won and why it won is overdetermined. There are at least three possible explanations. One view is that because the United States had more nuclear weapons than the Soviet Union, the Soviets gave in. A second explanation adds the importance of the relative stakes of the two superpowers in the crisis. Cuba was in America's backyard, but a distant gamble for the Soviets. Therefore, Americans not only had a higher stake in Cuba than the Soviets, but could also bring a third factor to bear: conventional forces. An American naval blockade and the possibility of an American invasion of Cuba also played a role. The psychological burden was on the Soviets because higher stakes and readily available conventional forces gave the Americans more credibility in their deterrent position.

Finally, although the Cuban Missile Crisis is called an American victory, it was also a compromise. The Americans had three options in the Cuban Missile Crisis. One was a shoot-out, that is, to bomb the missile sites; the second was a squeeze-out by blockading Cuba to persuade the Soviets to take the missiles out; the third

Kennedy and Khruschev meeting in Vienna in 1961

was a buyout by offering to trade something the Soviets wanted, such as removal of American missiles from Turkey. For a long time, the participants did not say much about the buyout aspects of the solution, but subsequent evidence suggests that a quiet American promise to remove its obsolete missiles from Turkey was probably more important than was thought at the time. We can conclude that nuclear deterrence mattered in the crisis and that the nuclear dimension certainly figured in Kennedy's thinking. On the other hand, the number of weapons was less important. It was not the ratio of nuclear weapons that mattered so much as the fear that even a few nuclear weapons could wreak such devastation.

Moral Issues

After the Cuban Missile Crisis there was a relative easing of the tension in the Cold War—almost as if the United States and the Soviet Union had stumbled to the brink of a cliff, looked over, and pulled back. In 1963, a hotline allowing direct communication between Washington and Moscow was installed, an arms control treaty limiting atmospheric nuclear tests was signed, Kennedy announced the United States would be willing to trade more with the Soviet Union, and there was some relaxation of tension. Through the late 1960s, the United States was preoccupied with the Vietnam War, yet there were still arms control efforts. Intense fear of nuclear war returned after the Soviet Union invaded Afghanistan in 1979. During "the little cold war" from 1980 to 1985, strategic arms limitation talks stalled, rhetoric became particularly harsh, and military budgets and the number of nuclear weapons increased on both sides. President Ronald Reagan talked about nuclear war fighting, and peace groups pressed for a freeze and ultimate abolition of nuclear weapons.

In the climate of heightened anxiety, many people asked a basic question: "Is nuclear deterrence moral?" As we saw earlier, just war theory argues that certain conditions must be met in making moral judgments. Self-defense is usually regarded as a just cause, but the means and consequences by which a war is fought are equally important. In terms of the means, civilians must be distinguished from combatants; in terms of consequences, there has to be some proportionality, some relationship of the ends and the means.

Could nuclear war possibly fit the just war model? Technically, it could. Low-yield nuclear weapons such as artillery shells and depth charges might be used against radar systems, submarines, ships at sea, or deep underground command bunkers. In that case, we could discriminate between combatants and noncombatants and keep the effects relatively limited. If the fighting stopped there, we could fit nuclear weapons within just war theory. But would fighting stop there or would it

---

In 1962 President Kennedy insisted that each member of the National Security Council read Barbara Tuchman's *The Guns of August*. The book is the story of how the nations of Europe inadvertently blundered into World War I. The author begins by quoting Bismarck's comment that "some damned foolish thing in the Balkans" would ignite the next war. She then related the series of steps—following the assassination on June 28, 1914, of the Austrian heir apparent, Archduke Franz Ferdinand, by Serbian nationalists—each small and insignificant in itself, that led to the most appalling military conflict in the history of the world. Time and again, at the brink of hostilities, the chiefs of state tried to pull back, but the momentum of events dragged them forward.

President Kennedy reminded us of the 1914 conversation between two German chancellors on the origins of that war. One asked, "How did it happen?" and his successor replied, "Ah, if we only knew." It was Kennedy's way of stressing the constant danger of miscalculation.

—Robert McNamara, Blundering into Disaster[15]

escalate? Escalation is the great risk, for what could be worth a hundred million lives or the fate of the earth?

During the Cold War, some people answered, "It's better to be Red than dead." But that may have been the wrong way to pose the question. Alternatively, we might ask: Is it ever justifiable to run a small risk of a large calamity? During the Cuban Missile Crisis, John Kennedy was reputed to have said he thought the chances of conventional fighting were perhaps one in three. And there was some smaller risk of nuclear escalation. Was he justified in taking such a risk? We can ask the counterfactual: if Kennedy had not been willing to take the risk in Cuba, would Khrushchev have tried something even more dangerous? What if a Soviet success had led to a later nuclear crisis or an even larger conventional war, for example, over Berlin or the Panama Canal?

Nuclear weapons probably played a significant role in preventing the Cold War from turning hot. During the 1980s, the American Association of Catholic Bishops said that nuclear deterrence could be justified on a conditional basis as a tolerable interim measure until something better was developed. But how long is the interim? So long as nuclear knowledge exists, some degree of nuclear deterrence will exist. Although the weapons produced prudence during the Cold War, complacency is a danger. It took the United States and the Soviet Union some time to learn how to control nuclear weapons, and it is far from clear that such control systems will exist among new aspirants to nuclear status such as North Korea and Iran. Moreover, terrorist groups might have no use for controls.

Concern about the proliferation of nuclear weapons continues. While 189 states have signed the Nuclear Non-Proliferation Treaty, India and Pakistan exploded weapons in 1998, and countries such as Iraq, Iran, Libya, and North Korea pursued nuclear weapons despite having signed the treaty. Also of concern is the spread of unconventional arsenals such as biological and chemical weapons; Libya and Iraq, for example, constructed chemical weapons facilities, and Iraq used them in its war with Iran (1980–1988). After the Gulf War in 1991, UN inspectors uncovered and destroyed major Iraqi nuclear, biological, and chemical weapons programs. The fear that such programs could be reconstituted was one of the causes of the Iraq War in 2003. Newspaper accounts of nuclear material making its way out of the former Soviet Union and into the international black market demonstrate that these weapons can still cause tension and bring nations to the brink of war. In 2004, it was disclosed that a Pakistani nuclear scientist, A. Q. Khan, had sold nuclear secrets to a number of countries, including Libya, Iran, and North Korea. Moreover, the reports that terrorist groups such as the Japanese Aum Shinrikyo cult and Osama bin Laden's Al Qaeda network were investigating the production of nuclear and biological weapons indicate that they may someday become available to nonstate actors as well.

The continued international worry about weapons of mass destruction has both a moral and a realist dimension. The moral opprobrium against nuclear weapons is shared not just by states that do not have the capacity or desire to make such weapons, but even by states that continue to have them, such as the United States, France, and Russia. Chemical and biological weapons have been condemned since

World War I, when the use of mustard gas led to widespread outcries in both Allied and Axis countries. The realist dimension is simple: Weapons of mass destruction carry great risk of escalation and enormous potential for devastation. Whenever these weapons are present, the dynamics of conflict change. Weak states with nuclear or unconventional weapons are better able to threaten strong states, while strong states with these weapons can more effectively threaten and deter adversaries. At the same time, the risk that these devices will be used if a crisis spins out of control raises the level of tension, whether it is between the United States and North Korea or between India and Pakistan. And the threat of use by terrorists adds a chilling dimension in which deterrence is not a sufficient response. The Cold War may be over, but the era of nuclear and unconventional weapons is not.

CHRONOLOGY: THE COLD WAR YEARS

1943	Tehran meeting between Stalin, Churchill, and Roosevelt
1944	
July	Bretton Woods Conference: Creation of International Monetary Fund and World Bank
August	Dumbarton Oaks Conference: Creation of United Nations
October	Moscow meeting between Churchill and Stalin: Spheres of influence plan for the Balkans
1945	
February	Yalta Conference between Stalin, Churchill, and Roosevelt
April	Roosevelt dies
May	Germany surrenders
April–June	San Francisco Conference–UN Organization Charter
July	First test of A-bomb; Potsdam Conference: Truman, Churchill/Attlee, Stalin
August	Hiroshima and Nagasaki destroyed by A-bombs; USSR enters war in Asia; Japan surrenders
1946	Churchill's Iron Curtain speech; resumption of Greek civil war
1947	
March	Truman Doctrine announced
June	Marshall Plan announced
October	Creation of Cominform by Moscow
1948	
February	Coup by Czech Communist Party
March	Partial blockade of Berlin begins
June	Berlin airlift begins; Yugoslavia ousted from Cominform
November	Truman reelected president
1949	
April	North Atlantic Treaty signed in Washington
May	End of the Berlin blockade

August	USSR explodes first A-bomb
September	Federal Republic of Germany created
October	People's Republic of China proclaimed; German People's Republic proclaimed
1950	
February	Sino-Soviet pact signed in Moscow
April	NSC-68 drafted
June	Beginning of Korean War
1952	First U.S. H-bomb exploded; Eisenhower elected president; Dulles becomes secretary of state
1953	
March	Death of Stalin
June	East Berlin uprising
July	Armistice in Korea
August	First Soviet H-bomb test
September	Khrushchev becomes first secretary of Soviet Communist Party
1954	Chinese bombardment of Quemoy and Matsu
1955	West Germany admitted to NATO; Warsaw Pact signed; Austrian State Treaty signed; Austria neutralized
1956	
February	Khrushchev denounces Stalin at Twentieth Party Congress
June	Poznan uprising in Poland
October	Start of Hungarian uprising
November	USSR intervenes in Budapest
1957	
August	Launching of first Soviet ICBM
October	Sputnik satellite launched
1958	
February	Launching of first U.S. satellite
August	China threatens Taiwan
1959	
January	Victory of Fidel Castro in Cuba
September	Khrushchev visits United States
1960	
February	First French A-bomb test
May	American U-2 shot down over USSR; Paris summit fails
1961	
April	Failure of Bay of Pigs landing in Cuba
June	Khrushchev and Kennedy meet in Vienna
August	Building of the Berlin Wall
October	Incidents at Checkpoint Charlie in Berlin; tensions increase
1962	Cuban Missile Crisis

1963

June	Kennedy visits Berlin, declares *"Ich bin ein Berliner"* ("I am a Berliner") as a gesture of solidarity
October	Kennedy signs Limited Test Ban Treaty; USSR, United States, and United Kingdom outlaw tests in the atmosphere, underwater, and in space
November	Kennedy assassinated; Johnson sworn into office

1964

August	Tonkin Gulf Act passes Congress, escalating U.S. involvement in Vietnam
October	Khrushchev ousted, replaced by Brezhnev and Kosygin
November	China detonates first atomic bomb

1966

March	Anti–Vietnam War rallies held in United States and Europe
April	Beginning of Chinese Cultural Revolution

1967

January	United States, USSR, and 60 other nations agree to Outer Space Treaty limiting military uses of space
June	China explodes first H-bomb

1968

January	Prague Spring reforms begin in Czechoslovakia; Tet Offensive in Vietnam
July	Treaty on the Non-proliferation of Nuclear Weapons (NPT) by United States, USSR, and 58 other countries
August	Soviet invasion of Czechoslovakia
November	Nixon elected president
December	U.S. forces reach peak of 535,000 in Vietnam

1969	Strategic Arms Limitation Talks (SALT) begin between United States and USSR

1970

February	Paris Peace Talks begin between United States and North Vietnam
April	U.S. troops invade Cambodia; Four U.S. college students killed by National Guardsmen at Kent State University at antiwar rally

1971	People's Republic of China joins United Nations

1972

February	Nixon visits China
May	SALT I signed, freezing number of ICBMs and SLBMs in place for five years

1973

January	Paris Accords establish ceasefire and political settlement of Vietnam War
May	East and West Germany establish formal diplomatic relations
September	Chilean socialist government of Salvador Allende overthrown in U.S.-backed military coup
October	Yom Kippur War between Israel and Arab states; United States and USSR nearly drawn into conflict; Arab oil embargo against the United States that lasts until March 1974

1974	Nixon resigns over Watergate; Gerald Ford sworn in as president

1975

April	United States leaves Vietnam after fall of Saigon
July	U.S. and Soviet astronauts link up in space; United States and USSR sign Helsinki Accords, pledging acceptance of European borders and protection for human rights

1976   Jimmy Carter elected president

1979

January	United States and People's Republic of China establish full diplomatic relations
June	SALT II agreement limiting long-range missiles and bombers signed by Carter and Brezhnev
July	Sandinista forces overthrow Somoza dictatorship in Nicaragua
December	USSR invades Afghanistan; United States imposes sanctions and intention to boycott Moscow Olympics

1980   Carter Doctrine states that Persian Gulf is a vital U.S. interest

1981

January	Lech Walesa leads Polish Solidarity union in illegal strike; Ronald Reagan inaugurated; U.S. hostages released from Iran
December	Martial law imposed in Poland

1982   Reagan outlines Strategic Arms Reduction Treaty (START) to reduce ICBMs and number of strategic nuclear weapons on both sides

1983

March	Reagan proposes Strategic Defense Initiative (SDI), popularly called "Star Wars," to develop missile defense technology
November	United States begins deployment of INF Pershing II missiles in West Germany

1985   Mikhail Gorbachev becomes Soviet General Secretary; Nuclear and Space Talks (NST) open in Geneva, based on START model

1986

October	At Reykjavik Summit Reagan refuses Gorbachev's proposal to make significant arms reductions if United States gives up SDI
November	Secret funding of Nicaraguan contras through arms sales to Iran becomes public

1987   At Washington Summit Reagan and Gorbachev agree to eliminate INF and work toward completing a START agreement

1988

April	USSR agrees to withdraw from Afghanistan by February 1989
June	Gorbachev tells Communist Party leaders that elements of communist doctrine must change
August	Cuba withdraws troops from Angola
November	George H.W. Bush elected president

1989

June	Chinese army assaults prodemocracy demonstrators in Tiananmen Square
November	Berlin Wall falls; thousands of East Germans cross to Western side

1990

May–June	Washington Summit between Bush and Gorbachev
October	Germany reunifies into one nation
November	Treaty of Conventional Armed Forces in Europe cuts size of land armies
December	Lech Walesa elected president of Poland

1991

July	Bush and Gorbachev sign START, pledge to destroy thousands of nuclear weapons
August	Coup against Gorbachev fails, but power flows to Russian President Boris Yeltsin
September	All SAC bombers, tankers, and Minuteman II ICBMs taken off alert
December	Soviet Union dissolves; United States recognizes Armenia, Belarus, Kazakhstan, Kyrgyzstan, Russia, and Ukraine

STUDY QUESTIONS

1. When did the Cold War begin? When did it end? Why? What do realist, liberal, and constructivist approaches contribute to your answers?

2. Was the Cold War inevitable? If so, why and when? If not, when and how could it have been avoided?

3. Why were leaders unable to restore a concert system after World War II? What sort of system evolved?

4. How important were first and second image considerations in the development of the Cold War? What were the views of American and European leaders on the Soviet Union and its international ambitions? What were Soviet views of the United States and the rest of the West?

5. Some historians argue that the real question is not why the Cold War occurred, but why it did not escalate into a "hot" war. Do you agree? Why didn't a hot war begin?

6. What is *containment*? How did this American policy emerge, and how was it implemented? What were Soviet responses?

7. How are nuclear weapons different from conventional weapons? Has the advent of nuclear weapons fundamentally changed the way nations behave?

8. Is Mueller correct that nuclear weapons are not the cause of the obsolescence of major wars among developed states? What other factors does he consider?

9. Is nuclear deterrence morally defensible? Or, in the words of one theorist, is it morally analogous to tying infants to the front bumpers of automobiles to prevent traffic accidents on Memorial Day? Might some strategies of deterrence be more ethical than others?

10. What is the relation of nuclear weapons to international relations apart from nuclear deterrence? How useful are they?

11. Why did the Cold War end? What roles did hard and soft power play?

NOTES

1. Milovan Djilas, *Conversations With Stalin*, trans. Michael B. Petrovich (San Diego: Harcourt Brace Jovanovich, 1962), p. 114.

2. Ralph B. Levering, *The Cold War, 1945–1972* (Arlington Heights, IL: Harlan Davidson, 1982), p. 15.

3. William Taubman, *Stalin's American Policy* (New York: Norton, 1982), p. 36.

4. Levering, *The Cold War*, p. 37.

5. Ibid., p. 131.

6. Dean Acheson, *Present at the Creation* (New York: Norton, 1969), p. 375.

7. George Kennan, "The Sources of Soviet Conduct," *Foreign Affairs* 25:4 (July 1947), p. 581.

8. John L. Gaddis, "The New Cold War History," *Foreign Policy Research Institute Footnotes* 5:5 (June 1998).

9. United States Catholic Conference, "The Challenge of Peace: God's Promise and Our Response," *Origins* 13:1 (May 19, 1983), p. 1.

10. Secretary of State Dean Rusk, *The New York Times,* April 30, 1985, p. 6.

11. Ernest R. May and Philip D. Zelikow, eds., *The Kennedy Tapes: Inside the White House During the Cuban Missile Crisis* (Cambridge MA: Belknap & Harvard University Press, 1997), p. 1.

12. Stephen E. Ambrose, *Eisenhower* (New York: Simon & Schuster, 1983), p. 184.

13. Ronald R. Hope, ed., *Soviet Views on the Cuban Missile Crisis: Myth and Reality in Foreign Policy Analysis* (Washington, DC: University Press of America, 1982), p. 48.

14. James Blight and David Welch, *On the Brink: Americans and Soviets Reexamine the Cuban Missile Crisis* (New York: Hill & Wang, 1989), p. 80.

15. Robert McNamara, *Blundering into Disaster: Surviving the First Century of the Nuclear Age* (New York: Pantheon, 1986), p. 14.

SELECTED READINGS

1. Kennan, George F., "The Sources of Soviet Conduct," *Foreign Affairs* 25:4 (July 1947), pp. 566–582.

2. Schlesinger, Arthur, Jr., "The Origins of the Cold War," *Foreign Affairs* 46:1 (October 1967), pp. 22–53.

3. Yergin, Daniel, *The Shattered Peace* (Boston: Houghton Mifflin, 1977), pp. 69–86.

4. Gaddis, John L., *Russia, the Soviet Union, and the United States* (New York: Wiley, 1978), chaps. 6 and 7.

5. Mueller, John, "The Essential Irrelevance of Nuclear Weapons," and Jervis, Robert, "The Political Effects of Nuclear Weapons," *International Security* 13:2 (Fall 1988), pp. 80–90.

6. Khong, Yuen F., "The Lessons of Korea and the Vietnam Decision of 1965," in George W. Breslauer and Philip E. Tetlock, eds., *Learning in U.S. and Soviet Foreign Policy* (Boulder, CO: Westview, 1991), pp. 302–349.

7. Gaddis, John Lewis, *We Now Know: Rethinking Cold War History* (New York: Oxford University Press, 1997).

FURTHER READINGS

Allan, Charles T., "Extended Conventional Deterrence: In from the Cold and out of the Nuclear Fire?" *Washington Quarterly* 17:3 (Summer 1994), pp. 203–233.

Allison, Graham, and Philip Zelikow, *Essence of Decision: Explaining the Cuban Missile Crisis,* 2nd ed. (New York: Longman, 1999).

Beschloss, Michael, *The Conquerors* (New York: Simon & Schuster, 2002).

Blight, James G., and David A. Welch, *On the Brink: Americans and Soviets Reexamine the Cuban Missile Crisis* (New York: Hill & Wang, 1989).

Bundy, McGeorge, *Danger and Survival* (New York: Random, 1988).

Dallek, Robert, *An Unfinished Life: John F. Kennedy, 1917–1963* (Boston: Little, Brown, 2003).

Fursenko, Aleksandr, and Timothy Naftali, *"One Hell of a Gamble": Khrushchev, Castro & Kennedy, 1958–1964* (New York: Norton, 1997).

Gaddis, John, *The Cold War: A New History* (New York: Penguin, 2006).

———, *Strategies of Containment: A Critical Appraisal of Postwar American National Security Policy* (New York: Oxford University Press, 1982).

Gray, Colin S., *Weapons Don't Make War: Policy, Strategy, and Military Technology* (Lawrence: University Press of Kansas, 1993).

Herring, George C., *America's Longest War: The United States and Vietnam, 1950–75*, 3rd ed. (New York: McGraw-Hill, 1996).

Kagan, Donald, *On the Origins of War* (New York: Doubleday, 1995).

Kennan, George F., *Memoirs (1925–1950)* (Boston: Little, Brown, 1967).

Kennedy, Robert, *Thirteen Days* (New York: Norton, 1968).

Kolko, Gabriel, and Joyce Kolko, *The Limits of Power: The World and United States Foreign Policy, 1945–1954* (New York: Harper & Row, 1972).

Lafeber, Walter, *America, Russia, and the Cold War 1945–1996* (New York: McGraw-Hill, 1997).

Larson, Deborah W., *Origins of Containment: A Psychological Explanation* (Princeton, NJ: Princeton University Press, 1985).

Lebow, Richard Ned, and Thomas Risse-Kappen, eds., *International Relations Theory and the End of the Cold War* (New York: Columbia University Press, 1995).

Legvold, Robert, "Soviet Learning in the 1980s," in George W. Breslauer and Philip E. Tetlock, eds., *Learning in U.S. and Soviet Foreign Policy* (Boulder, CO: Westview, 1991), pp. 684–732.

Mandelbaum, Michael, *The Nuclear Revolution* (Cambridge: Cambridge University Press, 1986).

Mastny, Vojtech, *Russia's Road to the Cold War: Diplomacy, Warfare, and the Politics of Communism, 1941–1945* (New York: Columbia University Press, 1979).

May, Ernest R., and Philip D. Zelikow, eds., *The Kennedy Tapes: Inside the White House During the Cuban Missile Crisis* (Cambridge, MA: Belknap & Harvard University Press, 1997).

Nye, J. S., "Nuclear Learning and U.S.-Soviet Security Regimes," *International Organization* 41:3 (Summer 1987).

Remnick, David, *Lenin's Tomb: The Last Days of the Soviet Empire* (New York: Random, 1993).

Taubman, William, *Khrushchev: The Man and His Era* (New York: Norton, 2003).

———, *Stalin's American Policy: From Entente to Détente to Cold War* (New York: Norton, 1982).

Williams, William, *The Tragedy of American Diplomacy* (Cleveland: World, 1959).

Wohlforth, William C., ed., *Witnesses to the End of the Cold War* (Baltimore: Johns Hopkins University Press, 1996).

Yergin, Daniel, *Shattered Peace: The Origins of the Cold War and the National Security State* (Boston: Houghton Mifflin, 1977).

Intervention, Institutions, and Regional and Ethnic Conflicts

UN General Assembly meeting

Major war became less likely after the end of the Cold War, but regional and domestic conflicts persist and there will always be pressures for outside states and international institutions to intervene. Of the 111 conflicts that occurred between the end of the Cold War and the beginning of the new century, 95 were purely intrastate (civil wars) and another 9 were intrastate with foreign intervention. More than 80 state actors were involved, as well as two regional organizations, and more than 200 nongovernmental parties.[1]

ETHNIC CONFLICTS

These communal conflicts are often called *ethnic wars*—wars in which belligerents define themselves in part along cultural lines such as language, religion, or similar characteristics. An ethnic group involves a group name, shared historical memories, and shared symbols.

Most ethnic wars occur where established mechanisms for mediating conflicts break down. The inability of governments to mediate conflict frequently occurs in the aftermath of collapsed empires, such as the European colonial empires in Africa or the Soviet Empire in the Caucasus and Central Asia. Such "failed states" either never had a strong government or their governments were undermined by economic conditions, loss of legitimacy, or outside intervention. Thus even though the end of the bipolar conflict of the Cold War led to the withdrawal of foreign troops from Afghanistan, Cambodia, Angola, and Somalia, communal war continued. And in the former Yugoslavia, which held together to preserve its independence in a bipolar world, the death of President Tito and the end of the Cold War weakened the ability of the central government to mediate ethnic conflicts.

Constructivists point out that ethnicity is not an immutable fact that inevitably leads to war. It is socially constructed in the sense that symbols, myths, and memories can be altered over time. For example, in Rwanda, which suffered a genocide in 1994, people spoke the same language and had the same skin color, but there were economic class differences between the Tutsi people who had migrated into the area with a cattle-based culture centuries earlier and the larger number of agricultural Hutu people. Over time, intermarriage and social change had blurred some of the distinctions, but they were reinforced during colonial rule. In the 1994 genocide in which 750,000 Tutsis were killed, many Hutus who urged moderation or who appeared to be Tutsi were also murdered.

The breakup of the former federation of Yugoslavia in 1991 also led to ethnic conflicts. Some of the worst fighting occurred between Serbs, Croats, and Muslims in Bosnia, the most heterogeneous of the Yugoslav republics. (See box.) But one can also regard the conflict as one between rural areas where old identities and myths were strongest, and urban communities where many people had intermarried and come to identify themselves as "Yugoslavs" rather than as Croats, Serbs, or Muslims. Once Yugoslavia collapsed and fighting broke out, some of these people had new identities thrust upon them. As one man told me in 1993, "All my life I considered myself a Yugoslav, not a Muslim. Now I am a Muslim because that has been forced upon me." Or when I asked a Bosnia Croat military commander during a battle in Mostar how he knew whom to shoot because people on the street looked so similar, his reply was that before the war, you would have to know their name, but now uniforms made it easy. Some theorists attribute ethnic conflicts to deep and ancient hatreds or grand clashes of civilizations, but the ethnic distinctions are better described by Sigmund Freud's term "the narcissism of small differences."

WAR IN FORMER YUGOSLAVIA AND ITS AFTERMATH, 1991–2005 TIMELINE

Summer 1991

Slovenia and Croatia declare independence from Yugoslavia. Ethnic Serbs and Croats begin fighting in Croatia. UN imposes arms embargo on all members of the former Yugoslav Republic.

Spring 1992

Bosnia-Herzegovina (44% Muslim, 31% Serbian, 17% Croatian) declares independence and is recognized by the West. Bosnian Serbs declare independent Serbian Republic within Bosnia. Ethnic tensions explode and war erupts in Bosnia. UN expels Serb-led Yugoslavia.

Summer 1992

Reports of "ethnic cleansing"—a policy of killing or driving away inhabitants to create ethnically "pure" areas—against Muslims in Bosnia.

Winter 1992–1993

UN humanitarian convoys to Muslim enclaves in Bosnia are blocked by Serb forces. UN declares several Bosnian cities "Safe Areas." Vance-Owen Peace Plan, proposing to divide Bosnia along ethnic lines, is rejected by Bosnian Serb Parliament. Croatians, originally fighting with Muslims against Serbs, begin their own ethnic cleansing campaign.

Fall 1993

Bosnian army makes some territorial gains against Croatian separatists. Breakaway Serbian Republic of Bosnia orders a general mobilization among all Bosnian Serb refugees.

February 4, 1994

Marketplace bombing in Sarajevo leaves 68 people dead and more than 200 wounded, ignites public outcry against this and other atrocities.

Summer 1994

Bosnian government army makes advances against separatist Serbs, recapturing some of the territory around Bihac, in Bosnia's northeast corner.

Fall 1994

Serb forces recapture the region around Bihac. In retaliation, NATO bombs runways of Serb-controlled airport in Krajina. Serbs hold more than 300 UN troops hostage.

July 11, 1995

UN "Safe Area" Srebrenica in eastern Bosnia taken by Serbs; 6,000 Muslim men killed in worst massacre in Europe since WWII.

August–September 1995

Croatian forces capture Krajina area from Serbs and force local Serbs to flee in massive ethnic-cleansing operation. NATO air attacks on Bosnian Serb objectives. Warring parties agree to talk peace.

November 1995

Bosnia, Serbia, and Croatia sign the Dayton Peace Accord to end the war in Bosnia. NATO peacekeeping forces sent to Bosnia.

(Continued)

Continued

March 1998

Slobodan Milosevic sends troops to quell unrest in Kosovo. A guerrilla war with the Kosovo Liberation Army ensues. Milosevic rejects calls for international involvement.

September 1998

NATO issues ultimatum to Milosevic: Ease crackdown on Kosovar Albanians or face airstrikes.

March 1999

Kosovo Albanians and Yugoslavia fail to reach an agreement in Paris. NATO airstrikes begin throughout Yugoslavia. Thousands of Kosovo Albanians flee to Albania, creating a massive refugee crisis.

May 1999

UN war crimes tribunal indicts Milosevic as war criminal.

June 1999

NATO suspends bombing after 78 days when Serbia begins to withdraw troops from Kosovo.

September 2000

Vojislav Kostunica wins more votes than Milosevic, but the federal elections commission says Kostunica did not receive a majority. Kostunica supporters reject the findings, and begin a campaign of strikes and civil disobedience to force Milosevic to step down.

October 2000

A huge rally in front of the Parliament ends with protestors storming the building and setting it on fire. A day later Milosevic concedes defeat, and Kostunica is sworn in as president.

March–April 2001

Authorities try to arrest Milosevic. Commandos raid his compound and a gun battle ensues with Milosevic's bodyguards. After 36 hours, Milosevic is arrested and taken into custody. UN chief prosecutor Carla Del Ponte announces a second arrest warrant for Milosevic for crimes committed in Bosnia.

June–July 2001

Milosevic is handed over to The Hague tribunal to investigate charges of war crimes.

February 2002

Milosevic's trial in the Hague begins.

November 2005

10 years after the Dayton Accord was signed, international peacekeepers remain deployed to the Balkans and final status issues remain unresolved.

March 2006

Milosevic found dead in his prison cell; medical experts say he died of natural causes.

Why do people kill over small differences? Most often they do not. Humans always differentiate themselves into groups, and sometimes the differences are accompanied by prejudice and hatred. But such differences rarely lead to large-scale violence. While no two conflicts are exactly the same, a common dynamic is that ethnic symbols and myths create divisions; economic rivalries or the weakening of state authority create fears for group survival. Elites or leaders then mobilize support by appealing to ethnic symbols, and any number of events, (such as Bosnia's declaration of independence in 1992 or the death of Rwanda's president in an April 1992 plane crash,) can spark the fighting.

Political scientist John Mueller stresses the role of violent groups who achieve their ends by manipulating ethnic myths and fears. In his view, the entire concept of "ethnic warfare" is misguided because it implies a Hobbesian war of all against all, whereas so-called ethnic conflicts are "waged by small groups of combatants, groups that purport to fight and kill in the name of some larger entity."[2] Mueller argues that the minority that resorts to violence destroys the space for the moderate middle, and pathological and criminal elements thrive in the resulting chaos. Stuart Kaufman emphasizes the role of symbolic politics. Political entrepreneurs and extremist groups use the emotional power of ethnic symbols to reconstruct the larger group's preferences. The classic security dilemma that we described in Chapter 1 arises among rational actors when lack of trust and inability to enforce agreements under anarchic conditions causes serious conflicts to erupt. But in Kaufman's view, many ethnic conflicts "erupted because one or both sides preferred conflict to cooperation."[3] In failed states such as Sierra Leone and Liberia, uneducated and unemployed young men developed a vested economic interest in looting and plundering. In addition to the problem that rational actors face in the structural conditions of anarchy, the security dilemmas involved in the early stages of ethnic conflict often grow out of the manipulation of emotional symbols by those who prefer violence.

INTERVENTION AND SOVEREIGNTY

Where failed states exist or genocide is threatened, some analysts believe outsiders should ignore sovereignty. In 2005, the United Nations High-Level Panel on Threats, Challenges and Changes endorsed the "norm that there is a collective international responsibility to protect . . . civilians from the effects of war and human rights abuses." According to the UN panel, this responsibility is "exercisable by the Security Council, authorizing military intervention as a last resort, in the event of genocide and other large-scale killing, ethnic cleansing or serious violations of humanitarian law which sovereign Governments have proved powerless or unwilling to prevent."

Intervention is a confusing concept, partly because the word is both descriptive and normative. It not only describes what is happening, but it also casts value judgments. Thus discussions of intervention often involve moral issues. Nonintervention in the internal affairs of sovereign states is a basic norm of international law.

Nonintervention is a powerful norm because it affects both order and justice. Order sets a limit on chaos. International anarchy—the absence of a higher government—is not the same as chaos if basic principles are observed. Sovereignty and nonintervention are two principles that provide order in an anarchic world system. At the same time, nonintervention affects justice. Nation-states are communities of people who deserve the right to develop a common life within their own state boundaries. Outsiders should respect their sovereignty and territorial integrity. But not all states fit this ideal. Sovereignty is a concept that has been applied to many states where it fits poorly. For example, group and clan fighting meant that no government was effectively in control in Sierra Leone, Liberia, and Somalia at the beginning of the twenty-first century. Even children were pressed into battle. Thus there is often a tension between justice and order that leads to inconsistencies about whether to intervene.

Defining Intervention

In its broadest definition, *intervention* refers to external actions that influence the domestic affairs of another sovereign state (Figure 6.1). Some analysts use the term more narrowly to refer to *forcible* interference in the domestic affairs of another state. The narrow definition is merely one end of a spectrum of influences ranging from low coercion to high coercion (see Figure 6.1). At the low end of the scale, intervention may be simply a speech designed to influence domestic politics in another state. For example, in 1990 President George H. W. Bush appealed to the Iraqi people to overthrow Saddam Hussein, and in 1999, Saddam appealed to the peoples of several Arab states to overthrow their leaders. Such speeches are designed to interfere in the domestic politics of another state—often without much effect. In the 1980s, the U.S. government established Radio Martí to broadcast its messages against Fidel Castro in Cuba, but Castro was still in power at the turn of the new century.

Economic assistance can also influence the domestic affairs of another country. For example, during the Cold War U.S. economic aid to El Salvador and Soviet aid to Cuba were designed to influence domestic affairs in those states. Though a form

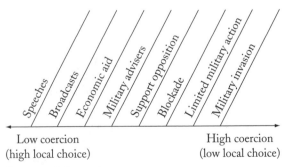

Low coercion
(high local choice)

High coercion
(low local choice)

FIGURE 6.1   Defining Intervention

of illegal economic assistance, bribing high-level foreign officials can induce them to pursue a third party's preferred policies. During the Cold War, American and Soviet intelligence agencies often poured resources into foreign elections in an attempt to engineer a favorable outcome. Similarly, in the 1970s, the government of South Korea spent a great deal of money to help elect U.S. politicians who were more favorable to its interests.

A little further along the spectrum of coercion is the provision of military advisers. In the late 1950s, during the early days of the Vietnam War, the United States began its intervention first with economic and later with military assistance. Similarly, the Soviet Union and Cuba provided military aid and advisers to Nicaragua and other "client" states. Another form of intervention is support for the opposition. For example, in the early 1970s, the United States channeled money to the opponents of Salvador Allende, the democratically elected president of Chile, and at various times the Soviet Union channeled money to peace groups in Western European countries. More recently, the United States has provided financial assistance to nascent democratic movements to several former Soviet bloc countries, including Ukraine.

Toward the coercive end of the spectrum is limited military action. For example, in the 1980s the United States bombed Libya in response to its support of terrorism, and the Soviet Union helped one faction fighting a civil war in South Yemen. In 1998, the United States launched cruise missile attacks into Sudan and Afghanistan in reprisal for terrorist attacks against American embassies in East Africa. And it used air and ground support for local forces to overthrow the Taliban government in Afghanistan after the September 2001 terrorist attacks on American soil. Full-scale military invasion or occupation is the upper end of the spectrum of coerciveness. Examples include U.S. actions in the Dominican Republic in 1965, Grenada in 1983, Panama in 1989, and Iraq in 2003; and the Soviet Union's actions in Hungary in 1956, Czechoslovakia in 1968, and Afghanistan in 1979. It is not merely great powers that intervene with force. For example, in 1979 Tanzania sent troops into Uganda, and Vietnam invaded Cambodia. In 1997, tiny Rwanda intervened militarily in the affairs of its troubled large neighbor, Congo. Some interventions are multilateral, but often one state takes the lead. For example, the United States led the 1995 UN intervention in Haiti and NATO's 1999 intervention in Kosovo, and Nigeria led a group of West African states that intervened in Liberia and Sierra Leone in the 1990s.

The broad definition of intervention therefore includes the whole range of behavior, from not very coercive to highly coercive. The degree of coercion involved in intervention is important because it relates to the degree of choice that the local people have, and thus the degree of outside curtailment of local autonomy.

Sovereignty

Sovereignty was a vital concept of the Westphalian system and was reinforced by the Covenant of the League of Nations and the Charter of the United Nations. It is also at the heart of debates about the legitimacy of intervention. While sovereignty implies absolute control of a territory in a legal sense, de facto control by a government within its borders is often a question of degree.

For several reasons, even popular and effective governments rarely have full control over everything that happens within their borders. One reason is international economic interdependence. For example, when the Socialist Party came to power in France in 1981, it wanted to make major changes in French economic policies. But the Socialists found that the French economy was so interdependent with the other European economies that when they tried to make changes unilaterally, capital fled abroad and the value of the French franc dropped. Ultimately, France's Socialists returned to a common economic policy with the other European states. Interdependence did not limit French legal sovereignty, but it certainly limited de facto control. France was too economically interdependent to pursue a fully autonomous economic policy. Similarly, in 1998, the Asian financial crisis created uncertainties in world markets that forced sovereign governments as physically distant as Russia and Brazil to devalue their currencies and change economic policy. We shall look further at the challenges that economic globalization poses for sovereignty in the next chapter.

Economic interdependence is only one of several factors impinging on sovereignty. A massive influx of refugees can disrupt even stable states. Refugees from Haiti and Cuba who fled to the United States led to political debates in Washington in 1993 and 1994, while Rwandan refugees poured into neighboring Burundi and Congo, exacerbating ethnic conflict there. Drug and arms trafficking can also undermine sovereignty. The influx of arms into northern Pakistan from Afghanistan throughout the 1980s and 1990s limited the ability of the Pakistani government to control its northern territory, while the illegal influx of drugs into the United States from abroad has created problems of law and order domestically. States may be sovereign in the legal sense, but outside actors affect internal affairs.

Conversely, intervention may sometimes increase autonomy. Some poor states may have low de facto autonomy because they have very low capabilities. Some kinds of intervention may actually increase capabilities and thus real autonomy in the future. Economic or military assistance may help a state become more independent in the long term—for example, the UN intervened in Cambodia in the 1990s to help it develop institutional capabilities after two decades of civil strife. These are some of the complications in the relationship of sovereignty, autonomy, and intervention.

Judging Intervention

For skeptics, moral judgments do not matter, but *realists, cosmopolitans,* and *state moralists* have different views of intervention. For realists, the key values in international politics are order and peace, and the key institution is the balance of power; they believe that intervention can be justified when it is necessary to maintain the balance of power and to maintain order. This approach to intervention was utilized throughout the Cold War by both superpowers, in order to maintain the two respective spheres of influence: the American sphere of influence in the Western Hemisphere and the Soviet sphere of influence in Eastern Europe. For example, in

1965, the United States intervened in the Dominican Republic and in the 1980s in Central America on the grounds that there should be no more communist governments in the Western Hemisphere, and the Soviet Union intervened to preserve communist governments in Eastern Europe. The Soviets articulated a right to intervention in 1968 with the Brezhnev Doctrine, which claimed that they had a right to intervene to preserve socialism in their sphere of influence. Realists might justify such interventions on the grounds that they preserved order and prevented the possibility of misunderstandings and miscalculations that might escalate to war, particularly nuclear war.

In contrast, *cosmopolitans* value justice. For them, the key international institution is a society of individuals. Therefore, intervention can be justified if it promotes individual justice and human rights; it is permissible to intervene on the side of the "good." But how is "good" to be defined? During the Cold War, liberal cosmopolitans argued that intervention was justified against right-wing regimes such as the Marcos dictatorship (1965–1986) in the Philippines or the apartheid regime in South Africa (1948–1990), while conservative cosmopolitans said that intervention was justified against left-wing governments. In the 1980s, some Americans proclaimed a Reagan Doctrine when defending the United States' right to intervene against the Sandinista government in Nicaragua and against the communist governments in Angola and Mozambique because of their violation of democratic rights. In the 1990s, with the end of the Cold War, cosmopolitans urged humanitarian intervention in Somalia (1992) to halt widespread starvation, in Haiti (1994) to restore a democratically elected leader to power, in Bosnia (1995) to stop a civil war, and in Kosovo (1999) to stop "ethnic cleansing" triggered by the government of Slobodan Milosevic in Serbia. Similarly, they called for U.S. intervention in conflicts in Liberia (2003) and the Darfur region of Sudan (2006). What cosmopolitans, left and right, shared is the view that intervention is justified if it promotes individual justice and human rights.

For *state moralists*, the key value in international politics is the autonomy of the state and its people. The key institution is a society of states with certain rules and international law. Of these precepts, the most important is nonintervention in the sovereign territory of another state. Consequently, state moralists believe that intervention is justified only to defend a state's territorial integrity or to defend its sovereignty against external aggression. However, the real world is sometimes more complicated. External aggression is often ambiguous. For example, in June 1967, Israel preemptively attacked Egypt in response to its decision to deny Israel access to vital shipping lanes and mass troops along its border. Who was the aggressor, the Egyptians who massed their forces on the border and appeared to be preparing an attack on Israel, or the Israelis who struck just before the Egyptians could attack?

Exceptions to the Rule

In *Just and Unjust Wars*, Michael Walzer, a political scientist who presents the state moralist position, discusses four situations that could morally justify war or military intervention in the absence of overt aggression. The first exception to a strict rule is preemptive intervention, exemplified by the Israeli attack in 1967. If there is a clear and sufficient threat to a state's territorial integrity and political sovereignty, it must act right away or it will have no chance to act later. But the threat must be imminent. Such an argument would not justify, for example, the Soviet intervention in Afghanistan. There is a distinction between preemptive wars and preventive wars. A *preemptive strike* occurs when war is imminent. A *preventive war* occurs when leaders believe merely that war is better now than later. As we have seen, views regarding preventive war influenced the German general staff in 1914, which feared that if Germany waited until 1916 to launch a war, Russia would be too strong for the Schlieffen Plan to work. Walzer's first exception to nonintervention would not have allowed a preventive war because there was no clear and present danger to Germany. And as we saw earlier with our counterfactual examples, many other things might have changed the situation between 1914 and 1916. During the buildup to the 2003 Iraq War, U.S. officials blurred this classic distinction by claiming that a preventive strike against Iraq was preemptive even though the threat of an Iraqi attack against the United States or its allies was not imminent.

The second exception to the strict rule against intervention occurs when intervention is needed to balance a prior intervention. This rule goes back to John Stuart Mill and the nineteenth-century liberal view that a people has the right to determine its own fate. If an intervention prevents local people from determining their own fate, a counterintervention nullifying the first intervention can be justified because it restores the local people's right to decide. Mill's argument permits intervention only as far as it counterbalances a prior intervention; more than that is not justifiable. The overriding principle is to allow the local people to solve their own problems. The United States sometimes used this as a justification for its involvement in Vietnam. In 1979, China intervened in Vietnam by crossing the border, but China pulled its troops back within a few weeks. China argued that it was countering Vietnam's intervention in Cambodia.

The third exception to the rule against intervention is when it is necessary to rescue people who are threatened with massacre. If such people are not saved from total destruction, there is no point to nonintervention as a sign of respect for their autonomy or rights. In 1979, Tanzania invaded Uganda when a dictatorial leader was slaughtering large numbers of people, and it justified its intervention as rescuing people threatened by massacre. Vietnam used a similar pretext for its late 1978 invasion of Cambodia. Still, massacres or genocide do not necessarily lead states or the international community to intervene. Note the reluctance of the United States to send troops to Rwanda in 1994, to Bosnia between 1992 and 1995, to Liberia in 1996, to Sierra Leone in 1999, and to Congo in 2003. In 2005, in the troubled Darfur region of Sudan, support for a military intervention to stop the killing of various ethnic groups was limited to a modest, regional peacekeeping operation led by the African Union.

The fourth exception to nonintervention is the right to assist secessionist movements when they have demonstrated their representative character. In other words, if a group of people within a country has clearly demonstrated that it wants to be a separate country, it is legitimate to assist its secession because doing so helps the group pool its rights and develop its autonomy as a nation. But when does a secessionist movement become worthy of assistance? Is their success the way to judge their worthiness? Part of Mill's argument was that to become a legitimate nation, a people must be able to seek its own salvation and fight for its own freedom. Such a view is consistent, at least, with the principle of nonintervention and a society of states, but it is deficient as a moral principle because it suggests that might makes right.

Problems of Self-Determination

The problem of intervention on behalf of secessionist movements is defining *what* is a people? Who shares a common life? How do outsiders know whether a people really agreed to pool their rights in a single community or state? *Self-determination* is generally defined as the right of a people to form its own state. This is an important principle, but there is always the question of who determines. Consider Somalia, whose people, unlike many other African states, had roughly the same linguistic and ethnic background. Neighboring Kenya was formed by colonial rule from dozens of different peoples or tribes, with different linguistic backgrounds and customs. Part of northern Kenya was inhabited by Somalis. Somalia said the principle of national self-determination should allow the Somalis in the northeastern part of Kenya and the Somalis in the southern part of Ethiopia to secede because they were one Somali nation. Kenya and Ethiopia refused, saying they were still in the process of building a nation. The result was a number of wars in northeast Africa over the Somali nationalist question. The ironic sequel was that Somalia itself later fragmented in a civil war among its clans and warlord leaders.

Voting does not always solve problems of self-determination. First, there is the question of where one votes. Take the question of Ireland. For many years, Catholics objected that if a vote were held within the political area of Northern Ireland, the two-thirds Protestant majority would rule. Protestants replied that if a vote were held within the geographical area of the entire island, the two-thirds Catholic majority would rule. Eventually, after decades of strife, outside mediation helped. But this still does not address the question of when one votes. In the 1960s, the Somalis wanted to vote right away; Kenya wanted to wait 40 or 50 years while it went about its nation-building, or reshaping tribal identities into a Kenyan identity.

Does secession harm those left behind? What about the resources the secessionists take with them, or the disruption they create in the country they leave? For example, after the dismantlement of the Austrian Empire in 1918, the Sudetenland was incorporated into Czechoslovakia even though the people spoke German. After the Munich Agreement in 1938, the Sudeten Germans seceded from Czechoslovakia and joined Germany, but that meant the mountainous frontier went under German control, which was a terrible loss for Czech defenses. Was it right to allow self-determination for the Sudeten Germans, even if it meant stripping Czechoslovakia of its military defenses? When eastern Nigeria decided it wanted to secede and form the state of Biafra in the 1960s, other Nigerians resisted in part because Biafra included most of

Nigeria's oil. They argued that the oil belonged to all the people of Nigeria, not just the eastern area. Indonesia has made the same argument about secessionist demands in its oil-rich province of Aceh.

After 1989, the issue of self-determination became acute in Eastern Europe and the former Soviet Union. Throughout the former Soviet Union, different ethnic groups claimed the right of self-determination, just as many of them had done between 1917 and 1920. In the Caucasus, Azerbeijanis, Armenians, Georgians, Abkhazians, and Chechens all demanded states on the basis of self-determination.

As we have seen, in the former state of Yugoslavia, different ethnic and religious groups seceded and claimed self-determination. The Slovenes, Serbs, and Croats managed to carve out independent republics in the early 1990s, but the Muslims in Bosnia-Herzegovina were less successful. While both Serbia and Croatia had small ethnic minorities, Bosnia was more ethnically diverse and its population included large minorities of Serbs and Croats. After 1992, Bosnian Muslims were subjected to a campaign of ethnic cleansing by both Croatian and Serb forces. The war in Bosnia was devastating for the civilian population, and war-crimes tribunals were convened in The Hague, starting in 1996, to convict those responsible for the massacres. Yet for much of the conflict, the United Nations, the North Atlantic Treaty Organization (NATO), and the European Union were divided over how to respond. Part of what made the war in Bosnia so complicated for the international community was the problem of assessing how much of the fighting could be attributed to tensions among Bosnian Croats, Serbs, and Muslims and how much of the violence was caused by Serbia's intervention. If it was not simple aggression by Serbia, then the only grounds for intervention would be to prevent a massacre. As with Rwanda, the international community was united in its condemnation of the Balkan violence, but was unable to agree on effective joint action until late in the conflict, in 1995, when a NATO peacekeeping force was sent to the troubled area.

Questions of self-determination continue to plague the Balkans even though the Dayton Accords stopped the Bosnian civil war between Muslims and Serbs in 1995. In Kosovo, a province of Serbia with a large ethnic Albanian Muslim population, an independence movement had been gaining momentum since the death of Yugoslav communist leader Josip Tito in 1980. In 1997 an armed insurgent group known as the Kosovo Liberation Army began attacks on Serbian security forces within Kosovo, prompting a retaliatory crackdown by Serbian President Milosevic.

American and European diplomats monitored the situation carefully as human rights conditions deteriorated in the province, and it became clear that the Clinton administration was unwilling to let Kosovo become another Bosnia, where thousands of Muslims had been massacred. After negotiations and sanctions against Serbia failed to make a difference, the United States and NATO bombed Serbia for 78 days in the spring of 1999. Milosevic pulled Serb troops out of Kosovo in June, and NATO deployed an international stability force to the troubled province. Though the killing has stopped, an agreement regarding the "final status" of Kosovo remains elusive.

Self-determination turns out to be an ambiguous moral principle. Woodrow Wilson thought it would solve problems in central Europe in 1919, but it created as many as it solved. Adolf Hitler used the principle to undermine fragile states in the 1930s. With less than 10 percent of the world's states being homogeneous, it is clear that treating self-determination as a primary rather than secondary moral principle could have disastrous consequences for many parts of the world.

The best hope for the future is to ask *what* is being determined as well as *who* determines it. In situations where groups have difficulties living together, it may be possible to allow a degree of autonomy in the determination of internal affairs. Internal self-determination could allow degrees of cultural, economic, and political autonomy similar to that which exists in countries like Switzerland or Belgium. Where such loosening of the bonds is still not enough, it may be possible in some cases to arrange an amicable divorce as happened when Czechoslovakia peacefully divided into two sovereign countries on January 1, 1993. But absolute demands for self-determination are more likely to become a source of violence unless handled extremely carefully.

THE VIETNAM WAR

A good example of misunderstanding self-determination was the Vietnam War, which cost more than 58,000 American and some three million Vietnamese lives over two decades between 1957 and 1975. Under the leadership of Ho Chi Minh, Vietnam successfully fought French efforts to recolonize it after World War II, and in 1954 an international conference in Geneva partitioned the country into a communist North Vietnam with its capital in Hanoi, and a noncommunist South Vietnam with its capital in Saigon (today, Ho Chi Minh City). The Vietnam War began as a civil war between these two governments, with the South Vietnamese government opposing the North's efforts to "unify the country." With the support of the United States, the South successfully blocked a referendum on reunification that had been agreed to at Genevea.

AMERICAN INTERVENTION IN VIETNAM

The U.S. sent its troops into Vietnam to reverse the verdict of a local struggle, which meant, in turn, imposing a ghastly cost in death and suffering upon the Vietnamese. As it turned out, the U.S. could not reverse that verdict finally; it could only delay its culmination.

Those of us who opposed American intervention yet did not want a communist victory were in the difficult position of having no happy ending to offer—for the sad reason that no happy ending was possible any longer, if ever it had been. And we were in the difficult position of urging a relatively complex argument at a moment when most Americans, pro- and antiwar, wanted blinding simplicities.

—Irving Howe and Michael Walzer, "Were We Wrong About Vietnam?"[4]

The United States saw the conflict in Cold War terms, as aggression by a communist government against a noncommunist government. It feared that if South Vietnam fell, other noncommunist governments in Southeast Asia would topple like a row of dominoes. The North Vietnamese government and its southern allies (the Viet Cong) viewed the war as a continuation of the struggle against the French for independence and self-determination. After fifteen years of fighting, direct U.S. involvement ended with the signing of a peace treaty in Paris in 1973. The war between the North and South continued until Hanoi succeeded in uniting the country in 1975. But rather than a toppling of dominoes, a unified Vietnam wound up fighting with its communist neighbors, Cambodia and China. If the United States had correctly interpreted the conflict as being more about nationalism and self-determination than communism, it might have seen the conflict in terms of the balance of power and used a metaphor of checkers rather than dominoes to guide its policy. Ironically, the communist government of Vietnam and the United States today enjoy good relations.

CHRONOLOGY: AMERICAN INVOLVEMENT IN VIETNAM (1954–1975)

(Main sources: The History Place, "Vietnam War Timeline"; and PBS: *The American Experience,* "Vietnam Timeline.")

1954	In response to the French defeat at Dien Bien Phu, President Dwight Eisenhower articulates the "Domino Theory," warning that if Vietnam fell to the communists, other states in Southeast Asia would follow
1955	
October 26	Diem becomes president of the Republic of Vietnam (South Vietnam)
1956	
Summer	Following the French withdrawal, the U.S. Military Assistance Advisor Group begins training South Vietnamese military forces
July	Vietnam fails to hold elections, as per the Geneva Convention Agreements of 1954
1961	*By year's end, U.S. assistance to the South exceeds $1 million a day*
January	Soviet Premier Nikita Khrushchev announces Soviet support for "wars of national liberation"; Ho Chi Minh interprets this as a green light to escalate the communist assault on South Vietnam
May	President John F. Kennedy deploys 400 Green Berets to serve as "advisers" to the South Vietnamese military regarding counterinsurgency warfare
1962	
May	On a visit to South Vietnam, McNamara declares, "We are winning the war"
December	Following a trip to Saigon, U.S. Senate Majority Leader Michael Mansfield becomes the first U.S. policy maker to question further American involvement in Vietnam; in a confidential memorandum to

President John F. Kennedy he argues that the United States should withdraw its support of Diem

1963   *As of December 31, roughly 16,000 U.S. military advisers are stationed in Vietnam*

November 1   With the tacit approval of the United States, South Vietnamese troops surround the presidential palace in Saigon; on November 2, Diem and his brother, Nhu, are captured and assassinated

November 22–24   Following the assassination of Kennedy, Johnson assumes the office of the presidency and tells Lodge that the United States will "not lose" Vietnam during his administration

1964   *The cost of U.S. support to the Vietnamese Army exceeds $2 million per day; by December 31, 23,000 U.S. miltary advisers are deployed to South Vietnam*

August 2   The "Gulf of Tonkin" incident occurs when three North Vietnamese patrol boats open fire on the USS *Maddox* in the Gulf of Tonkin

August 4   Johnson announces retaliatory air strikes against the North; two aircraft are shot down, and the North claims its first American prisoner of war (POW)

August 7   Congress overwhelmingly approved the Gulf of Tonkin resolution authorizing Johnson to "take all necessary steps, including the use of armed force . . . to prevent further aggression"

1965   *As of January, public support for U.S. involvement in Vietnam is roughly 80 percent; By the end of the year, roughly 184,000 U.S. troops are deployed to Vietnam*

March   Johnson orders the start of Operation Rolling Thunder, a three-year bombing campaign characterized by gradual escalation of the use of force

April 1   Johnson authorizes additional troop deployments and American combat patrols in South Vietnam; the decision is not disclosed to the public for two months

December   McNamara warns Johnson that time favors the North and that U.S. combat deaths could top 1,000 per month; late in the month, the second bombing pause begins

1966   *As of year's end, roughly 390,000 U.S. military personnel are deployed to Vietnam*

Late January   U.S. commences six weeks of "search and destroy" missions to root out the Viet Cong; the U.S. bombing campaign restarts and B-52s are introduced in April

1967   *U.S. troop levels reach roughly 463,000 by year's end, and combat deaths total roughly 16,000*

August   In testimony before the Senate Armed Services Committee, McNamara calls the U.S. bombing campaign ineffective

November 29   McNamara resigns as secretary of defense, in part because of his increasing discomfort with Johnson's war policies

1968	*U.S. troop levels rise to 495,000 by year's end; more than 1,000 U.S. troops are killed each month, and the total number of U.S. troops killed in Vietnam tops 30,000*
January	North Vietnam launches the Tet Offensive, a series of attacks against South Vietnamese cities, including Saigon; though U.S. forces defeated the communist insurgents, the size of their offensive caused the American press and public to question Pentagon claims that the enemy was nearly defeated; following the Tet Offensive, polls showed that only 26 percent of Americans supported Johnson's war policy
March 31	Johnson announces that he will not seek reelection; additionally, he calls for a partial halt to U.S. bombing and encourages the North Vietnamese to attend peace talks
May 10	The "Paris Peace Talks" begin with the United States represented by Averell Harriman and the North represented by Foreign Minister Xuan Thuy; negotiations between both sides continue on-and-off for the next five years
July 1	General Creighton W. Abrams is announced as Westmoreland's replacement
1969	*Total combat deaths are roughly 40,000*
Late January	Paris Peace Talks resume
March 17	Nixon orders secret bombing campaign against North Vietnamese supply depots in Cambodia
April	U.S. troop levels reach their highest point—543,400
May 14	Nixon offers a peace agreement to the North, which is quickly rejected
June	Nixon and Secretary of Defense Melvin Laird announce a U.S. policy of "Vietnamization," by which the United States will begin withdrawing forces and handing over more responsibilities to South Vietnamese troops
1970	*U.S. troops drop to 280,000 by December 31*
February	Kissinger begins two years of secret talks with Le Duc Tho
April 30	Nixon announces an expansion of the U.S. war effort into Cambodia
June 24	U.S. Senate votes to repeal the Gulf of Tonkin resolution
December 22	Congress passes the Cooper-Church Amendment, banning the use of defense spending for U.S. military operations in Laos or Cambodia
1971	U.S. troop levels decrease to roughly 156,000 by year's end; total combat deaths exceed 45,000
June 13–18	*The New York Times* and *The Washington Post* publish the Pentagon Papers, a series of classified memorandums detailing U.S. decision making regarding Vietnam
June 18–22	The U.S. Senate passes a nonbinding resolution calling for the withdrawal of all U.S. forces from Vietnam by year's end

1972

April   Nixon orders B-52s to bomb Hanoi and Haiphong, with the intent of pressuring the North to make further concessions at the peace talks

July   Paris Talks resume

October   Kissinger announces "peace is at hand" after reaching a broad agreement with Le Duc Tho; South Vietnamese president Thieu, however, rejects the U.S. proposal that communist forces be permitted to remain in South Vietnam

December   Peace talks collapse after the North balks at dozens of amendments submitted by Thieu; Nixon orders a series of "Christmas bombings" to force the North back to the negotiation table

December 26 The North returns to talks following the cesssation of bombing

1973   *By year's end, all U.S. troops are withdrawn from Vietnam; the death toll is finalized at 47,244 U.S. military personnel.*

January   Kissinger and Le Duc Tho reach a revised agreement, which the U.S. forces Thieu to accept; Thieu calls the agreement "tantamount to surrender"

January 23   Nixon announces the cease-fire, stating that it will "end the war and bring peace with honor in Vietnam and Southeast Asia"

March 29   The United States completes its military withdrawal from Vietnam

1974

December   North Vietnam launches a new offensive against the South, taking the Mekong Delta region; the United States responds diplomatically

1975

April 30   As North Vietnamese troops enter Saigon, the last U.S. government personnel evacuate the embassy; within hours, the North declares the end of the Vietnam War

Motives, Means, and Consequences

If consistency about self-determination is difficult, what other principles can be used to judge interventions? Three dimensions of judgment are related to the just war tradition: motives, means, and consequences. All three are important because judging interventions by one dimension alone may yield an incomplete understanding of the conflict. For example, judging intervention by consequences alone is equivalent to saying "might makes right." Obviously, more than consequences must be considered.

On the other hand, good intentions alone do not justify an intervention. For example, the writer Norman Podhoretz argued that the United States was right to intervene in Vietnam because the Americans were trying to save the South Vietnamese from totalitarian rule. Here is an analogy. Suppose a friend offers to drive your child home one night. It is a rainy night; your friend drives too fast and skids off the road and your daughter is killed. Your friend says, "My intentions were purely good. I wanted to get her home early for a good night's rest before the SATs." You, however, are no doubt more concerned with the consequences of her actions. Likewise, Podhoretz's argument that the American action in Vietnam was what he called "imprudent but moral" fails to account for consequences. In evaluating interventions, we have to consider more than the motivation; appropriate means and good consequences must be considered as well.

In the Vietnam War, it was not enough that the United States tried to save South Vietnam from the horrors perpetrated by North Vietnamese communists. Even if the cause was just, the means used are a different proposition. Some questions to ask are, were there alternatives? Was intervention a last resort? Were there efforts to protect innocent life? Was it proportional—did the punishment fit the crime, so to speak—or was it excessive? Were there procedures to ensure impartiality? To what extent was there attention to international multilateral procedures that might have checked the human tendency to weight these considerations in one's own favor? What about the consequences? What about the prospects for success? What about the danger of unintended consequences because a local situation was not well enough understood, because of the difficulty of differentiating between civilians and guerrillas? As obvious as it seems, we must still emphasize the need to be careful about situations where there is enormous complexity and very long causal chains. Motives, means, and consequences must all be considered before judgments can be made.

Consider how the policy of containment led to intervention in Vietnam. As we have seen, in the early stages just after World War II, the issue was whether the United States should step into Britain's place in the eastern Mediterranean to defend Turkey and Greece against possible Soviet encroachment. U.S. policymakers struggled with how to frame this intervention to the American people. Secretary of State George Marshall was quite cautious. Others, such as Undersecretary Dean Acheson and Senator Arthur Vandenberg, pushed for a moral argument to appeal to the American people's belief in a universal right to freedom. Consequently, when President Truman explained his actions in the Truman Doctrine, he talked of protecting free people everywhere.

The diplomat George Kennan, who had warned against Stalin's aggressive plans, became disillusioned as containment became highly ideological. He argued that the United States was trying to contain Soviet power; therefore, anything that balanced Soviet power without intervening directly with American troops was for the good. But those who took the more ideological view said the United States should contain communism directly, through more aggressive means. Over time, the argument for balancing Soviet power gave way to a broader view of containment as keeping the world free from communism. In Vietnam, this view caused leaders to underestimate national differences among communist states. The United States began to think it had to contain Chinese and Soviet power and the spread of communist ideology. By the time the doctrine of containment moved from the eastern Mediterranean in 1947 to Southeast Asia in the 1950s, it had become a justification for an overly ambitious and ill-fated intervention.

In conclusion, although the simple absolute principle of nonintervention is frequently breached in practice, the norm of nonintervention remains important. Exceptions to nonintervention must be judged on a case-by-case basis by looking at the motives, means, and consequences. The same principles can be applied to the Iraq War, as we will see shortly.

INTERNATIONAL LAW AND ORGANIZATION

Sovereignty and nonintervention are enshrined in international law and organization. People sometimes have problems understanding international law and organization because they use a domestic analogy. But international organization is not like domestic government, and international law is not like domestic law. International organizations do not act as an incipient world government for two reasons. First, the sovereignty of member states is protected in the charters of most international organizations. Article 2.7 of the Charter of the United Nations says, "Nothing in the Charter shall authorize the United Nations to intervene in matters within domestic jurisdiction." In other words, the organization is not an effort to replace the nation-states.

Domestic Analogies

The other reason that international organization is not incipient world government is because of its weakness. There is an international judiciary in the form of the International Court of Justice, which consists of 15 judges elected for nine-year terms by the United Nations, but the International Court of Justice is not a world supreme court. States may refuse its jurisdiction, and a state may refuse to accept its judgments, even if the state has accepted the court's jurisdiction. In the 1980s, for example, the Reagan administration refused to accept an International Court of Justice ruling that the United States had acted illegally in mining the harbors of Nicaragua.

If we imagine the UN General Assembly as the equivalent of Congress, it is a very strange kind of legislature. It is based on the principle of one state, one vote, but that principle does not reflect either democracy or power relations in the world. Democracy rests on the principle of one person, one vote. In the UN General Assembly, the Maldive Islands with 100,000 people in the southern Indian Ocean has one vote and China, a country with more than a billion people, has one vote. That means a Maldive Islander has 10,000 times the voting power of a Chinese in the UN General Assembly, which does not fit well with the democratic criteria for legislatures. Nor is it a very good reflection of power, because the Maldive Islands has the same vote in the General Assembly as the United States or India or China. So there is an oddity about the General Assembly that makes states unwilling to have it pass binding legislation. UN General Assembly resolutions are just that: resolutions, not laws.

Finally, we might imagine that the secretary-general of the United Nations is the incipient new president of the world. But that is also misleading. The secretary-general is a weak executive. If the secretary-general has power, it is more like the soft power of a Pope than the combination of hard and soft power a president possesses. Trying to understand international organizations by analogy to domestic government is a sure way to get the wrong set of answers.

International law is not like domestic law. Domestic law is the product of legislatures and customs, sometimes called common law. Domestic law involves provisions for enforcement, adjudication by individuals (you can go to a court yourself and bring suit), and orderly revision by legislation. Public international law is similar in the sense that it consists of treaties, which are agreements among states, and customs, which are the generally accepted practices of states. But it differs dramatically in enforcement and adjudication. On enforcement, there is no executive to make a state accept a court decision. International politics is a self-help system. In the classic ways of international law, enforcement was sometimes provided by the great powers. For example, in the Law of the Sea, a custom developed that a state could claim a 3-mile jurisdiction out into the oceans. In the nineteenth century when Uruguay claimed broader territorial seas to protect the fisheries off its coasts, Britain, the great naval power of the day, sent gunboats within 3 miles of the coast. So customary law was enforced by the great power. You might ask, "Who enforced the law against Britain if Britain violated the law?" The answer is that enforcement in self-help systems is a one-way street.

Adjudication in international law is by states, not by individuals (though the European Court at Strasbourg is a regional exception). Instead of any of the world's billions of citizens bringing cases to the international court, only the states can bring cases, and they are unlikely to bring cases unless they want to get them off their docket or think they have a reasonable chance of winning. Thus the court has had relatively few cases. In the 1990s, special tribunals were established to try war criminals from the Bosnian and Rwandan conflicts, and in 2002 a large number of states established an International Criminal Court to try war and genocide criminals if their national governments failed to try them. However, a number of significant states, including the United States and China, refused to ratify the treaty because they felt it infringed on their sovereignty. In addition, there are problems about how customary rules should be interpreted even when a principle is agreed on. Take the principle of expropriation. It is accepted that a state can nationalize a corporation from another country that operates on its territory, but it must pay compensation for what the corporation is worth. But who is to say what is just compensation? Many of the less developed countries have argued that low compensation is adequate; rich countries usually want higher levels.

Finally, even when the UN General Assembly has passed resolutions, there is a good deal of ambiguity about what they mean. They are not binding legislation. The only area in the UN Charter in which a state must legally accept a decision is Chapter VII, which deals with threats to peace, breaches of the peace, and acts of aggression. If the Security Council (not the General Assembly) finds that there has been an act of aggression or threats to peace warranting sanctions, then member states are bound to apply the sanctions. That is what happened in 1990 when Iraq invaded Kuwait, and in 2001 after the United States was the target of transnational terrorist attacks.

The other way in which new law is sometimes created is through large intergovernmental conferences that negotiate draft treaties for governments to sign. Such conferences are often very large and unwieldy. For example, in the 1970s the Law of the Sea Conference involved more than a hundred participating states trying to draft principles for a 12-mile territorial sea, an exclusive economic zone for fisheries out to 200 miles, and designating the manganese nodules on the bottom of the ocean as the common heritage of all. The trouble was that some states agreed to only parts of the text, leaving the outcome unclear in international law. Nonetheless, in 1995, when the United States wanted to resist possible Chinese claims to the seas around the Spratly Islands, it appealed to the international Law of the Sea.

International law basically reflects the fragmented nature of international politics. The weak sense of community means there is less willingness to obey or restrain oneself out of a sense of obligation or acceptance of authority. The absence of a common executive with a monopoly on the legitimate use of force means that sovereign states are in the realms of self-help, and force, and survival. And when matters of survival come up, law usually takes second place.

Predictability and Legitimacy

Nonetheless, international law and organization are an important part of political reality because they affect the way states behave. States have an interest in international law for two reasons: predictability and legitimacy.

States are involved in conflicts with each other all the time. The vast range of international transactions, both public and private, includes trade, tourism, diplomatic missions, and contacts among peoples across national boundaries. As interdependence grows, those contacts grow and there are increasing opportunities for friction. International law allows governments to avoid conflict at a high level when such friction arises. For example, if an American tourist is arrested for smuggling drugs in Mexico, a British ship collides with a Norwegian ship in the North Sea, or a Japanese firm claims that an Indian company has infringed its patents, the governments may not want to spoil their other relations over these private collisions. Handling such issues by international law and agreed principles depoliticizes them and makes them predictable. Predictability is necessary for transactions to flourish and for the orderly handling of the conflicts that inevitably accompany them.

Legitimacy is a second reason why governments have an interest in international law. Politics is not merely a struggle for physical power, but also a contest over legitimacy. Power and legitimacy are not antithetical, but complementary. Humans are neither purely moral nor totally cynical. It is a political fact that the belief in right and wrong helps move people to act, and therefore legitimacy is a source of power. If a state's acts are perceived as illegitimate, the costs of a policy will be higher. States appeal to international law and organization to legitimize their own policies or delegitimize others, and that often shapes their tactics and outcomes. And legitimacy enhances a state's soft power.

In major conflicts of interest, international law may not restrain states, but it often helps shape the flow of policy. Law is part of the power struggle. Cynics may say these are just games that lawyers play; but the fact that governments find it important to make legal arguments or to take the resolutions of international organizations into account shows they are not completely insignificant. To put it in an aphorism: "When claims to virtue are made by vice, then at least we know virtue has a price." Simply put, governments may be trapped by their own legal excuses.

An example is UN Security Council Resolution 242. Passed at the end of the 1967 Middle East War, it called for a return to prewar boundaries. Over the years, it had the effect of denying the legitimacy of the Israeli occupation of the territories it captured during that war. That put Israel on the defensive in the United Nations. The Arab states lost the war, but were nonetheless able to put pressure on Israel. In 1976, when the Arab coalition tried to expel Israel from the United Nations, the United States spent a good deal of political capital lobbying before the General Assembly to prevent Israel's expulsion, another indication that symbols of legitimacy in international organizations are part of a power struggle.

When vital issues of survival are at stake, a state will use its most effective form of power, which is military force. And that may explain the limited success of efforts of international law and organization to deal with the use of force. It is one thing to handle drug smuggling, collision of ships at sea, or patent infringement by international law; it is another to put the survival of one's country at risk by obeying international law. That was the problem with collective security in the 1930s, but a modified form of collective security was re-created in the UN charter.

United Nations: Collective Security and Peacekeeping

The classical balance of power did not make war illegal. The use of military force was accepted, and it often ensured the stability of the system. During the nineteenth century, with changes in technology making war more destructive, and with the rise of democracy and peace movements, there were several efforts to organize states against war. Twenty-six states held a peace conference at The Hague in 1899. In 1907, another Hague conference was attended by 44 states. The approach taken in these conferences was very legalistic. The conferees tried to persuade all states to sign treaties of arbitration so disputes would be handled by arbitration rather than force. They also tried to codify rules of war in case arbitration did not work.

As we have seen, after World War I the League of Nations was an attempt to develop a coalition of states that would deter and punish aggressors. In the eyes of Woodrow Wilson and those who thought as he did, World War I had been largely an accidental and unnecessary war caused by the balance of power, and such wars could be prevented by an alliance of all states for collective security. If the League of Nations was designed to prevent World War I after the fact, the United Nations was designed in 1943–1945 to prevent World War II. Forty-nine states met in San Francisco in 1945 to sign a charter that included innovations to repair the deficiencies of the League. Unlike the balance-of-power system of the nineteenth century, the offensive use of force was now illegal for any state that signed the UN Charter, with three exceptions: any use of force had to be for either self-defense, collective self-defense, or collective security.

The UN designers also created a Security Council composed of five permanent members and a rotating pool of nonpermanent members. The Security Council can be seen as a nineteenth-century balance-of-power concept integrated into the collective security framework of the UN. The Security Council can pass binding resolutions under Chapter VII of the charter. If the five great power policemen do not agree, they each have a veto, which is like a fuse box in a house lighting system. Better a veto that makes the lights go out than the house burn down in the form of a war against a great power, argued the UN founders.

During the Cold War, the UN collective security system did not work. In the Cold War ideological cleavage, there was little agreement on what was a legitimate use of force, and great problems arose in defining aggression. For example, how should one weigh covert infiltration against forces crossing a border first? In 1956 Israel suffered from covert attacks by Egyptian-backed guerrillas, yet Israeli conventional forces crossed the border into Egypt first. Depending on your side in the Cold War, you took different views regarding who was the initial aggressor. For two decades during the Cold War, UN committees tried to define aggression. They came up with a vague and generally ineffective rule: A list of acts of aggression was followed by the proviso that the Security Council could determine that other acts also constituted aggression. Even when armed force had been used, the council could choose not to declare that there had been any aggression. So as far as the United Nations was concerned, aggression was committed when the Security Council said so. Everything depended on a consensus in the Security Council, and that was rare during the Cold War.

The impasse over collective security gave rise to the concept of UN preventive diplomacy and peacekeeping forces. Rather than identifying and punishing the aggressor, which is the basic concept of collective security, the United Nations would assemble independent forces and interpose them between the warring powers. The model was developed during the Suez Canal crisis of 1956.

In July 1956, President Gamal Nasser of Egypt nationalized the Suez Canal (Figure 6.2). Sir Anthony Eden, the British prime minister, saw this as a major threat to Britain. He regarded Nasser as a new Hitler, and he drew analogies to the 1930s. He worried about the fact that Nasser had accepted Soviet arms—this, of course, being at the height of the Cold War. Britain developed a secret plan with France to support Israel if it invaded Egypt (which had been sending guerrillas across the Israeli border). The UN Security Council called for a cease-fire. Britain and France used their vetoes to prevent the cease-fire. They wanted the intervention to continue until they could eliminate Nasser.

A LETTER TO PRESIDENT DWIGHT EISENHOWER

In the nineteen-thirties Hitler established his position by a series of carefully planned movements. These began with occupation of the Rhineland and were followed by successive acts of aggression against Austria, Czechoslovakia, Poland and the West. His actions were tolerated and excused by the majority of the population of Western Europe. . . .

Similarly the seizure of the Suez Canal is, we are convinced, the opening gambit in a planned campaign designed by Nasser to expel all Western influence and interests from Arab countries. He believes that if he can get away with this, and if he can successfully defy eighteen nations, his prestige in Arabia will be so great that he will be able to mount revolutions of young officers in Saudi Arabia, Jordan, Syria and Iraq. (We know that he is already preparing a revolution in Iraq, which is most stable and progressive.) These new Governments will in effect be Egyptian satellites if not Russian ones. They will have to place their united oil resources under the control of a United Arabia led by Egypt and under Russian influence. When that moment comes Nasser can deny oil to Western Europe and we here shall be at his mercy.

—British Prime Minister Anthony Eden, 1956[5]

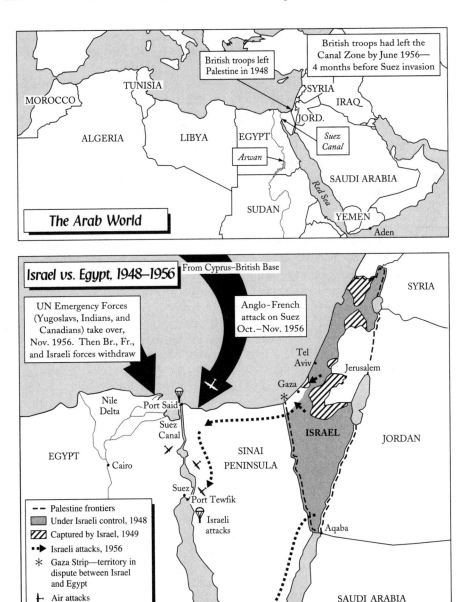

FIGURE 6.2 The United Nations Peacekeeping and Collective Security

Dag Hammarskjöld, the UN secretary-general, working with Canadian foreign minister Lester Pearson, devised a plan to separate the Israelis and the Egyptians by inserting a UN peacekeeping force. A resolution in the General Assembly, where there was no veto, authorized a UN force in the Sinai region.

The United States did not support its European allies, worrying that their intervention would antagonize Arab nationalists and increase the opportunities for the Soviet Union in the Middle East. On November 15, the first UN expeditionary force was inserted into the Sinai between the opposing forces, and later in December, the United Nations took on the task of clearing the ships that had been sunk in the canal.

This peacekeeping model has become an important role for the United Nations. It has been used 55 times in the past half century, compared to two formal collective security operations (Korea in 1950, Iraq in 1991). At the beginning of 2006, 17 UN peacekeeping operations were in the field. Thus even though the Cold War prevented the United Nations from implementing the formal doctrine of collective security, it did not prevent the innovation of using international forces to keep two sides apart. In collective security, if a state crosses a line, all the others are to unite against it and push it back. In preventive diplomacy and peacekeeping, if a state crosses a line, the United Nations steps in and holds the parties apart without judging who is right or wrong. During the Cold War, one of the basic principles of UN peacekeeping was that the forces always came from small states, not from the Soviet Union or the United States, so that the great powers would be kept out of direct conflict. Preventive diplomacy and peacekeeping was an important innovation that still plays a significant role in regulating international conflicts. But it is not collective security.

Iraq's 1990 invasion of Kuwait was the first post–Cold War crisis. Since the Soviet Union and China did not exercise their vetoes, UN collective security was used for the first time in 40 years. There were three reasons for this remarkable resurrection. First, Iraq committed an extraordinarily clear-cut aggression, very much like the 1930s, which reminded leaders of that failure of collective security. The second reason was the feeling that if UN collective security failed in such a clear case, it would not be a principle for order in a post–Cold War world. Third, the small states in the United Nations supported the action because most of them were fragile and had disputable postcolonial boundaries. The arguments Saddam Hussein used to justify his invasion of Kuwait threatened most of the other small states as well. To paraphrase the Haitian delegate to the League of Nations quoted earlier, they did not want to become someone else's Kuwait.

Will UN collective security be a basis for a new world order? Only rarely. The permanent members of the Security Council, for example, were not able to agree on resolutions to authorize either the Kosovo or Iraq wars in 1999 and 2003. There are important problems. First, the UN system works best when there is clear-cut aggression; it is much more difficult to apply in civil wars. Second, collective security will work if there is no veto, but if the United States, Russia, China, Britain, or France cannot reach agreement, collective security will be hamstrung once more. Moreover, in 1945, UN collective security was not designed to be applicable against the five great powers with vetoes in the Security Council. Third, collective security works when UN member states provide the necessary financial and military resources, but it is difficult to imagine collective security working if the states with large military forces do not contribute. Collective security was a miserable

The United Nations System

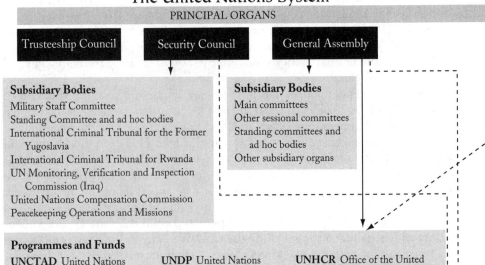

Notes: Solid lines from a Principal Organ indicate a direct reporting relationship; dashes indicate a non-subsidiary relationship. [1]The UN Drug Control Programme is part of the UN Office on Drugs and Crime. [2]UNRWA and UNIDIR report only to the GA. [3]The World Trade Organization and World Tourism Organization use the same acronym. [4]IAEA reports to the Security Council and the General Assembly (GA). [5]The CTBTO Prep.Com and OPCW report to the GA. [6]Specialized agencies are autonomous organizations working with the UN and each other through the coordinating machinery of the ECOSOC at the intergovernmental level, and through the Chief Executives Board for coordination (CEB) at the inter-secretariat level.

FIGURE 6.3   The United Nations System

Economic and Social Council	International Court of Justice	Secretariat

Functional Commissions
Commissions on:
Human Rights
Narcotic Drugs
Crime Prevention and
Criminal Justice
Science and Technology
for Development
Sustainable Development
Status of Women
Population and Development
Commission for Social
Development
Statistical Commission
Regional Commissions
Economic Commission for
Africa (ECA)
Economic Commission for
Europe (ECE)
Economic Commission for
Latin America and the
Caribbean (ECLAC)
Economic and Social
Commission for Asia and
the Pacific (ESCAP)
Economic and Social
Commission
for Western Asia (ESCWA)
Other Bodies
Permanent Forum on
Indigenous Issues (PFII)
United Nations Forum on
Forests Sessional and
standing committees
Expert, ad hoc and related
bodies
Related Organizations
WTO³ World Trade
Organization
IAEA⁴ International Atomic
Energy Agency
CTBTO PREP.COM⁵
PrepCom for the
Nuclear-Test-Ban-
Treaty Organization
OPCW⁵ Organization for the
Prohibition of
Chemical Weapons

Specialized Agencies⁶
ILO International Labour
Organization
FAO Food and Agriculture
Organization of the
United Nations
UNESCO United Nations
Educational, Scientific
and Cultural
Organization
WHO World Health
Organization
WORLD BANK GROUP
IBRD International Bank
for Reconstruction and
Development
IDA International
Development
Association
IFC International Finance
Corporation
MIGA Multilateral
Investment Guarantee
Agency
ICSID International
Centre for Settlement
of Investment Disputes
IMF International Monetary
Fund
ICAO International Civil
Aviation Organization
IMO International Maritime
Organization
ITU International Tele-
communication Union
UPU Universal Postal Union
WMO World Meterological
Organization
WIPO World Intellectual
Property Organization
IFAD International Fund for
Agricultural
Development
UNIDO United Nations
Industrial development
Organization
WTO³ World Tourism
Organization

Departments and Offices
OSG Office of the Secretary-
General
OIOS Office of International
Oversight Services
OLA Office of Legal Affairs
DPA Department of Political
Affairs
DDA Department for
Disarmament Affairs
DPKO Department of Peace-
keeping operations
OCHA Office for the
Coordination of
Humanitarian Affairs
DESA Department of
Economic and Social
Affairs
DGACM Department for
General Assembly and
Conference
Management
DPI Department of Public
Information
DM Department of
Management
OHRLLS Office of the High
Representitive for the
Least Developed
Countries, Landlocked
Developing Countries
and Small Island
Developing States
UNSECOORD
Office of the United
Nations security
Coordinator
UNODC United Nations
Office on Drugs and
Crime

UNOG UN Office at Geneva
UNOV UN Office at Vienna
UNON UN Office at Nairobi

Published by the UN Department of
Public Information DPI/2342—
March 2004

failure in the 1930s, was put on ice during the Cold War, and then, like Lazarus, rose from the dead in the Persian Gulf in 1990. But it was only a minor miracle, for, as we see in Chapter 9, collective security is only part of what will be needed for world order in the future.

The United Nations has political effects, even when collective security cannot be applied, because the presumption against force written into the UN charter places the burden of proof on those who want to use force. It affects states' soft power, as the United States discovered in 2003. The failure to obtain a second UN resolution did not prevent the United States from going to war with Iraq, but it limited the amount of help received and made the war and its aftermath more costly. In addition, the Security Council provides an important forum for the discussion of international violence, dramatizing the practice of collective concern and directing attention to important matters in times of crisis. It sometimes crystallizes viewpoints, raising the costs of aggressive uses of force, and acts as a safety valve for diplomacy. Finally, the role of the UN peacekeeping forces is limited but useful. These trip wires and buffer zones are devices that states have found in their interests again and again.

With the end of the Cold War came more opportunities for the United Nations. The United Nations played a role in the decolonization of Namibia, in monitoring human rights in El Salvador, in the elections in Nicaragua, in the administration in Cambodia, and in overseeing peacekeeping forces. Its recent peacekeeping record is mixed. UN peacekeepers helped in Haiti and Cambodia in the 1990s, but failed to prevent genocide in Rwanda or to stop civil war in Angola. They played a crucial role in Cyprus for three decades, but in Bosnia they had to be replaced by a stronger NATO force. Neutral interposition of troops does not always work well in ethnic conflicts. Indeed, some political scientists argue that neutral interventions may lengthen the duration of civil wars, causing greater bloodshed and loss of life. On the other hand, the UN still plays an important legitimizing role while countries like Australia take the lead in providing forces to stabilize a chaotic situation like East Timor. And the failure of the United States and Britain to obtain a second Security Council resolution explicitly authorizing their use of force in 2003 greatly increased the cost of their occupation of Iraq.[6] Even though the original doctrines of collective security do not fit as neatly as once thought, it would be a mistake to dismiss international law and the United Nations. They are part of the political reality of the anarchic state system. It is a mistake to be too cynical or too naive about international organization and law. States do not live by law alone, but they do not live completely without it.

At the beginning of the twenty-first century, the UN is clearly not the "parliament of man" that some of its founders hoped for when it was created in 1945. With an annual regular budget of less than $2 billion a year and a central staff of 9,000 members, the organization has fewer resources than many colleges and universities. Even when the special budget for peacekeeping operations (roughly $3 billion) and the annual budgets of all the specialized agencies and development funds (see Figure 6.3) are added together, the total comes out around $11 billion, or about 2 percent of what the United States spends on defense. The budget for human rights activities is smaller than that of the Zurich Opera House, and the budget of the UN's World Health Organization is similar to that of one medium-sized hospital.[7]

Many observers have called for the reform of UN institutions. The 15 members of the Security Council have the legal power to authorize the use of force, and 5 permanent members (China, the United States, Russia, Britain, and France) have had veto power since 1945. In 2005, a High Level Panel appointed by Secretary-General Kofi Annan suggested enlarging the Council to 24 members, and adding India, Brazil, Japan, and Germany as permanent members. The plan failed, however, when China objected to Japan's inclusion, regional rivals raised objections, and African states demanded more seats. The panel made a number of other useful suggestions for reform, including a Peacebuilding Commission to oversee the reconstruction of failed states, revision of the Human Rights Commission to exclude states that violate human rights, clearer criteria for pre-emptive use of force and humanitarian intervention, and an agreed definition of terrorism. Except for the Peacebuilding Commission, and a modest new Human Rights Council, the General Assembly has been slow in implementing the recommendations

The UN remains an assembly of 191 sovereign states trying through diplomacy to find a common denominator for dealing with international problems while protecting their national interests (Figure 6.3). Yet it also represents a central point for focusing on issues of security, international development, humanitarian assistance, environmental degradation, drugs, transnational crime, health and diseases, and global common spaces that require international collaboration. Despite its flaws, it remains the only universal organization that creates a focal point for international diplomacy. It is sometimes said that if the UN did not exist, it would have to be reinvented. Given the diversity of cultures and national interests in the world today, it is not clear that it could be.

CONFLICTS IN THE MIDDLE EAST

Torn by strife for the last half century, the Middle East has been the stage for, perhaps, the world's most notorious regional conflicts. It best fits the realist view of international politics, but despite this, it is also an area where international law and organization have played significant roles. What is the cause of so much conflict? Nationalism, religion, and balance-of-power politics each provide part of the answer.

The Iran-Iraq War (1980–1988) offers a good example. Why did Iraq invade its larger neighbor? One reason was the Islamic revolution that overthrew the Shah of Iran. Under the Shah, Iran had claimed the whole waterway between Iran and Iraq. But after the 1979 Iranian Revolution deposed the Shah, Iran was torn apart by domestic strife, and Iraq's president, Saddam Hussein, saw an opportune time to attack. Moreover, revolutionary Iran was causing problems inside Iraq. Iraqi Muslims were divided between Sunnis and Shi'ites, and Saddam Hussein was a secular head of state. The Shi'ite fundamentalists in Iran urged the Iraqi Shi'ites to rise up against Saddam Hussein. This transnational religious appeal failed when Saddam Hussein killed many Iraqi Shi'ite leaders. But Iraq also miscalculated. Iranians are not Arabs, and there was a large Arabic-speaking minority in the part of Iran adjacent to Iraq. Iraqis thought they would be welcomed as liberators in the Arabic-speaking part of Iran, but that was not the case. Instead, Iraq's attack helped unite the Iranians.

After this pair of miscalculations, the war bogged down into a long drawn-out affair, instead of the short profitable war Saddam Hussein had intended. Iraq decided it wanted to withdraw, but Iran refused to let go. Having been attacked, it was not going to let Iraq decide when to quit. The Ayatollah Khomeini, spiritual leader of Iran, said Iran would not end the war until the downfall of Saddam Hussein. For most of the decade, the rest of the world looked on. Conservative Arab countries like Saudi Arabia and Jordan supported Iraq against Iran because they were more afraid of Iranian revolutionary power. But, as we have seen, Arab Syria, a secular and radical regime in many ways similar to Iraq, supported Iran for balance-of-power reasons. Damascus was worried about the rising strength of its neighbor Iraq, rather than more distant Iran.

Outsiders also took sides. The United States, worried about the growth of Iranian power, provided covert assistance to Iraq. Israel secretly shipped U.S.-built weapons to Iran, even though fundamentalists in Iran were calling for the abolition of Israel. Israel's covert weapons assistance can be explained by balance-of-power considerations. Israel feared both Iraq and Iran, but Iraq was a closer threat, and on the principle of "the enemy of the enemy is my friend," Israel provided assistance to Iran. So a war that started from miscalculations rooted in religion, nationalism, and ambition was expanded by balance-of-power concerns into an intractable, nearly decade-long conflict.

The Questions of Nationalism

How does nationalism cause war? Indeed, what is nationalism and what is a nation? Constructivists point out that the concept of a nation is problematic. The dictionary defines a *nation* as a group claiming common identity and the right to be a state. But what kinds of groups does that encompass? What is the source of the common identity? One claim is ethnic similarity, but the United States is ethnically diverse and yet one nation. Another claim is linguistic similarity, but Switzerland is linguistically diverse and yet one nation. Others say religion can be the basis of a nation, and some states, such as Israel and Pakistan, are largely based on religious identity. The point is that when a group of people with a common identity calls itself a nation, there can be various sources of that identity. As the French thinker Ernest Renan put it: "The essential element of a nation is that all its individuals must have many things in common, but they must also have forgotten many things."[8] Nations are also called "imagined communities" because they are too large for everyone to know each other, and imagination plays a large role.

Nationalism is tricky because it is not merely a descriptive term, it is also prescriptive. When words are both descriptive and prescriptive, they become political words used in struggles for power. Nationalism has become a crucial source of state legitimacy in the modern world. Therefore, claims to nationhood become powerful instruments. If a people can get others to accept its claim to be a nation, it can claim national rights and use such claims as a weapon against its enemies. For example, in the 1970s the Arab states successfully lobbied in the UN General Assembly to pass a resolution that labeled Zionism as racism. Their intent was to deprive Israel of the legitimacy of calling itself a nation. To be labeled as racist is bad; to be labeled as nationalist is generally good. To argue that Israel was not a nation was to use words as weapons that would deprive Israel of legitimacy and weaken its soft power.

The analytic problem with the argument was that religion can be a basis of national identity. It is also true that a religious basis can make it more difficult for minorities outside the religion to share the national identity. Life can be more difficult for Muslims in Israel than for Jews, just as daily life can be more trying for Hindus in Pakistan than for Muslims. But it does not follow that because a people uses religion to call itself a nation that the state is racist. The UN General Assembly finally annulled the resolution by a second vote in 1991.

In the eighteenth century, nationalism was not all that important. Why have claims to nationalism become so important now? After all, as constructivists showed, humans are capable of multiple crosscutting loyalties—above and below the state level—and these loyalties can change. Loyalties tend to change when the usual patterns of life are disrupted. The idea of the nation often starts among the most disrupted, with people who are marginal figures in their own cultures and less certain about their identity. These are often people who are jolted out of normal patterns, who start to ask questions. National claims often start with intellectuals or with deviant religious groups. For example, the early Arab nationalists in the nineteenth century were often Christians rather than Muslims. Gradually their concern about a new identity developed broader support as industry and urbanization disrupted the traditional patterns and loyalties of rural societies.

The disruptions that mobilize people for new identities can come from internal or external forces. Modern nationalism was greatly stimulated by the French Revolution. The rise of the middle class disrupted traditional political and social patterns. Rising political groups no longer wanted the state of France to be defined by the king but to be defined in terms of the nation, all the people. And externally, as Napoleon's armies marched across Europe, they disrupted society and mobilized nationalist feelings among German-speaking peoples and other groups. By the middle of the century, there was widening support for the idea that each nation should have a state. This ideal culminated in the unification of Germany and Italy. Ironically, as we saw in Chapter 2, Bismarck was a conservative who did not try to unite all German speakers, only those he could control for the Prussian crown. Nonetheless, he harnessed nationalism for his purposes, and the unification of Germany and Italy became a model of success.

World War II weakened the European colonial empires, and decolonization was one of the major movements in Asia and Africa over the next three decades. The metropolitan societies had been weakened by the war itself, and elites in the colonized areas began to use the idea of nationalism against the crumbling European empires. But if the nineteenth-century model of states based on language and ethnicity had been used to organize the postcolonial world, it would have led to thousands of mini-states in Africa and many parts of Asia. Instead, the postcolonial elites asserted the right of the state to make a nation, just the opposite of the nineteenth-century pattern. The local leaders argued that they needed to use the state machinery the colonists had established—the budget, the police, the civil service—to shape a nation out of smaller tribal groups. The same ideology of nationalism came to be used to justify two things that are almost the opposite of each other—nation makes state or state makes nation—because *nationalism* is a political word with an instrumental use. In that sense, national identities are socially constructed. (Even in the seemingly classic "nation makes state" case of France, the state used education and police to bring laggard regions like Brittany into line.)

In the early romantic days of colonial liberation movements, there was often a successful blurring of these differences in "pan" movements. Europe in the nineteenth and early twentieth centuries saw the rise of pan-Slavism, claiming a common identity of all Slavic-speaking peoples. The modern Middle East saw pan-Arabism, and Africa, pan-Africanism. Early opponents of alien rule argued that since colonized people all suffered alike from the external colonizers, they should form pan-African or pan-Arab nations. But when it came to the actual business of governing, as opposed to liberating or resisting colonialism, the business of government required the instruments of state such as budgets, police, and civil service. And those instruments existed not on a "pan" basis, but on the basis of the artificial boundaries created by colonial rule. So, as the romanticism gradually wore away, identity based on the state began to replace that of the pan movements. Nonetheless, the romanticism of the pan movements often lingered on as a disruptive force.

The Middle East has often seen appeals to pan-Arabism and odd situations in which countries suddenly announce that they are forming a union, as Egypt and Syria did in forming the United Arab Republic in 1958, or countries as disparate as Libya and Morocco did in 1989. Over time, however, the forces of the state have prevailed over these pan-nationalist movements. For example, Egyptian nationalism focused on the state gradually became stronger in public opinion than pan-Arabism. But the gradual process is far from complete. Much of the postcolonial world saw enormous disruption of the normal patterns of life because of economic change and modern communications. Political leaders tried to control this postcolonial discontent. Some used national appeals, some used pan-Arab appeals, and others used fundamentalist religious appeals, all contributing to the complexity of the forces that create conflict in regions like the Middle East. The failure of states in the region to

modernize effectively explains why some of their citizens turned toward the fundamentalism and terrorism promoted by the Al Qaeda network.

The Arab-Israeli Conflicts

The Arab-Israeli conflict has produced six wars between two groups of people asserting different national identities, but claiming the same postage-stamp-size piece of
land. The Israeli claim dates to biblical times when the area was controlled by
Jews before the Romans asserted their authority in the first century B.C. In modern
historical times, Israelis have pointed to several events tied to World Wars I and II to
justify the existence of Israel. During World War I, the British issued the Balfour
Declaration, a letter written by the British government to Lord Rothschild of the
British Zionist Federation promising that the British government would work for a
Jewish homeland in Palestine. After World War II, Israelis argue, the horrors of
Hitler's Holocaust proved the need for a Jewish state. In 1948, Jewish settlers were
willing to accept a partition of Palestine, but the Arab people in the area were not.
The United Nations recognized the new Jewish state, but the Israelis had to fight to
preserve it from concerted Arab attack. This, the Israelis say, is the historical origin
and justification of the state of Israel.

His Majesty's Government views with favour the establishment in Palestine of a national
home for the Jewish people, and will use their best endeavours to facilitate the achievement
of this object, it being clearly understood that nothing shall be done which may prejudice
the civil and religious rights of existing, non-Jewish communities in Palestine, or the rights
and political status enjoyed by Jews in any other country.

—*The Balfour Declaration, November 2, 1917*

The Palestinian Arabs respond that they also have lived in the area for many
centuries. At the time of World War I, when the Balfour Declaration was issued,
90 percent of the people living in the area of Palestine were Arabs. Indeed, as late as
1932, 80 percent of the people were Arabs. They argue that Britain had no right to
make a promise to the Jews at the Arabs' expense. What is more, the Arabs continue, the Holocaust may have been one of history's greatest sins, but it was committed by Europeans. Why should Arabs have to pay for it?

Both sides seem to have valid points. In World War I, the area that is now
Palestine was ruled by the Turks, and the Ottoman Empire was allied with
Germany. Turkey's defeat, its empire was dismembered, and its Arab territories
became mandates under the League of Nations. France ruled Syria and Lebanon;
Britain called the area it received between the Jordan River and the Mediterranean
"Palestine," and the area it governed across the Jordan River "Trans-Jordan."

In the 1920s, Jewish immigration to Palestine increased slowly, but in the
1930s, after the rise of Hitler and intensified anti-Semitism in Europe, it began to

rapidly increase. By 1936, nearly 40 percent of Palestine was Jewish, and the influx led the Arab residents to riot. The British established a royal commission, which recommended partition into two states. In May 1939, with World War II looming, Britain needed Arab support against Hitler's Germany, so Britain promised the Arabs it would restrict Jewish immigration. But restriction was hard to enforce after the war. Because of the Holocaust, many in Europe were sympathetic to the idea of a Jewish homeland, and there was a good deal of smuggling Jewish refugees. In addition, some of the Jewish settlers in Palestine engaged in terrorist acts against their British rulers. Britain, meanwhile, was so financially and politically exhausted from World War II and the decolonization of India that it announced in the fall of 1947 that come May 1948, it would turn Palestine over to the United Nations.

In 1947, the United Nations recommended a partition of Palestine. Ironically, it would have been better for the Arabs if they had accepted the UN partition plan, but instead they rejected it. That led to outbreaks of local fighting. In May 1948 Israel declared itself independent, and Israel's Arab neighbors attacked to try to reverse the partition. The first war lasted for eight months of on-and-off fighting. Even though the Arabs outnumbered the Israelis 40 to 1, they were poorly organized and hampered by disunity. After a cease-fire and UN mediation, Jordan controlled the area called the West Bank and Egypt controlled Gaza, but most of the rest of the Palestinian mandate was controlled by the Israelis; in fact, more than they would have had if the Arabs had accepted the UN plan of 1947.

The war produced a flood of Palestinian refugees, a sense of humiliation among many Arabs, and a broad resistance to any idea of permanent peace. The Arabs did not want to accept the outcome of the war because they did not want to legitimize Israel. They believed time was on their side. Arab leaders fostered pan-Arab feelings and the belief that they could destroy Israel in another war. King Abdullah of Jordan was assassinated when he tried to sign a separate peace treaty with Israel in 1951, further decreasing the likelihood of a peaceful settlement between the Arab states and the new Israeli government.

The second Arab-Israeli war occurred in 1956. In 1952, Gamal Abdel Nasser and other young nationalist officers overthrew King Farouk of Egypt and seized power. They soon received arms from the Soviet Union and maneuvered to gain control of the Suez Canal, a vital commercial shipping channel linking Europe and Asia. Egypt harassed Israel with a series of guerrilla attacks. As we saw earlier, Britain and France, angry about the canal and worried about Nasser dominating the Middle East, colluded with Israel to attack Egypt. However, the United States refused to help Britain, and the war was stopped by a UN resolution and peacekeeping force that was inserted to keep the sides apart. But there was still no peace treaty.

The third war, the Six-Day War of June 1967, was the most important because it shaped the subsequent territorial problems at the heart of today's Middle East peace problem. Nasser and the Palestinians continued to harass the Israelis with guerrilla attacks, and Egypt closed the Straits of Tiran, which cut off Israeli shipping from the Red Sea. Nasser was not quite ready for war, but he saw the prospect of a Syrian-Israeli war looming and thought he would do well to join. Nasser asked the United Nations to remove its peacekeeping forces from his border. Israel, watching Nasser prepare for war, decided not to wait, but to preempt Egypt's likely attack. The Israelis caught the Egyptian air force on the ground and went on to capture not only the whole Sinai Peninsula, but also the Golan Heights from Syria and the West Bank from Jordan.

At that point the superpowers stepped in to press the two sides to accept a cease-fire. In November 1967, the UN Security Council passed Resolution 242, which said Israel should withdraw from occupied lands in exchange for peace and recognition. But Resolution 242 contained some deliberate ambiguities. Depending on which of the several language versions of the resolution one read, it did not say *all* territories, just "territories," implying that some might not have to be returned. It was also ambiguous about the status of the Palestinians, who were not recognized as a nation but were described as refugees. Again, the basic issue was not settled.

The fourth war, the War of Attrition, was a more modest affair. In 1969–1970, Nasser, with support from the Soviet Union, organized crossings of the Suez Canal and other harassments. These provoked an air war in which Israeli and Egyptian pilots fought a number of air battles. Eventually the air war tapered off into a stalemate.

The fifth war was the Yom Kippur War of October 1973. After Nasser died, he was succeeded by Anwar Sadat, who realized that Egypt could not destroy Israel. He decided that some psychological victory was necessary before he could make any conciliatory moves toward peace. Sadat decided to attack across the Suez Canal, but not to try to recapture all of the Sinai Peninsula. Sadat colluded with the Syrians and achieved an effective surprise. In the first stages, the war went well for the Egyptians, but the Israelis vigorously counterattacked.

Once again, the superpowers stepped in and called for a cease-fire. Secretary of State Henry Kissinger flew to Moscow, but while he was there the Israelis surrounded the Egyptian armies. The Soviets felt they had been cheated. They mobilized their forces in the southern part of the Soviet Union and sent the United States a letter suggesting that the superpowers introduce their own forces directly. The United States responded by raising the nuclear alert level in the United States, and the Soviets dropped their demand. The Israelis also backed down under American pressure and released the noose around the Egyptian army.

The war was followed by a series of diplomatic maneuvers in which the United States negotiated a partial drawback by Israel. UN observers were placed in the Sinai and on the Golan Heights. The most dramatic result of the war, however, was delayed. In 1977, Sadat went to Israel and announced that Egypt was ready to negotiate a separate peace. In 1978 and 1979, with President Jimmy Carter's mediation, Israel and Egypt negotiated the Camp David Accords, which returned the Sinai to Egypt and provided for talks about local autonomy in the West Bank. The Camp David Accords meant that the largest Arab state had quit the coalition confronting Israel, and Egyptian nationalism had prevailed over pan-Arabism. Sadat broke the pan-Arab coalition, but a few years later he was assassinated by religious extremists who objected to his policy.

The sixth war was Israel's invasion of Lebanon in 1982. Initially, Lebanon had been delicately balanced between Christian and Muslim Arabs. The Muslims, in turn, were divided among Sunnis, Shi'ites, and Druzes. The Palestine Liberation Organization (PLO) was a major presence in Lebanon, and the Christians were also split into factions. Lebanon was once cited as a haven of stability in the Middle East, the one area of true pluralism and diversity, but as Lebanon began to break apart into civil war, it presented increasing opportunities for outside intervention. Syria began to impose order in the north, and in 1978 Israel went into southern Lebanon as far as the Litani River.

In June 1982, Israeli Defense Minister Ariel Sharon decided to go further. First he said Israel would go only 25 miles into Lebanon to protect the northern parts of Israel, but in fact Israeli troops marched farther north and besieged Beirut for ten weeks. The siege led to the evacuation of the PLO from Beirut, and a Lebanese Christian leader, Bashir Gemayel, signed a peace treaty with Israel. However, Gemayel was soon assassinated, the treaty collapsed, and Lebanon fell further into chaos. In 1985, the Israelis withdrew from most of Lebanon except a buffer zone in the south, which they finally evacuated in 2000.

The violent recent history of the Middle East shows how regional conflicts based on ethnicity, religion, and nationalism can become embittered and difficult to resolve. Hard-liners reinforce each other. Arab governments were slow to make peace because they did not want to legitimize Israel, and in their rejection they reinforced the domestic position of those Israelis who did not want to make peace with the Arabs. The extremists formed a de facto transnational coalition that made it very difficult for moderates who wanted to find a compromise. In 1973 and 1977 Sadat took risks, but eventually paid for them with his life. A decade later, Israeli Prime Minister Yitzhak Rabin also took risks for peace and was assassinated by a Jewish religious extremist. In such a world of extremes, trust and cooperation are difficult, and the Prisoner's Dilemma provides an accurate model of regional politics.

During the bipolar Cold War era, wars in the Middle East tended to be short, in part because the superpower role was so prominent. On the one hand, each superpower supported its clients, but when it looked like the clients might pull the superpowers toward the nuclear brink, they pulled their clients back. The pressures for cease-fires came from outside. In 1956, it was the United States via the United Nations; in 1967, the United States and the Soviet Union used their hotline to arrange a cease-fire; in 1973, the United States and the Soviet Union stepped in; and in 1982, the United States pressed Israel to draw back from Lebanon. While in many instances the Cold War exacerbated regional conflicts, it also placed a safety net underneath them. With the end of the Cold War, the smaller states have increasingly looked to the United Nations to provide that safety net, but it was unclear to be seen how effective the UN safety net could be. In 1990–1991, responding to Iraq's invasion of Kuwait, the United Nations passed its first post–Cold War test.

The 1991 Persian Gulf War and Its Aftermath

The Persian Gulf crisis started on August 2, 1990, when Saddam Hussein invaded Kuwait. Iraq had always claimed that Kuwait was an artificial creation of the colonial era and should not be a separate state. In 1961, it tried to take over Kuwait but was deterred by Britain. However, as we have seen, the idea that colonial boundaries are meaningless promised to create enormous havoc in other regions of the postcolonial world, which may explain why so many countries in the United Nations rejected the Iraqi reasoning.

In any case, there were deeper economic and political reasons. Iraq had been economically devastated by its eight-year war with Iran. It had an $80 billion debt, which was increasing at the rate of $10 billion every year. At the same time, Iraq sat next to a gold mine—Kuwait—with enormous oil surpluses and a small population. In addition, Iraq was angry with Kuwait over Kuwait's oil policy. Iraq argued that Kuwait ignored OPEC guidelines for oil production and that every dollar reduction in the price of a barrel of oil cost Iraq $1 billion per year. Capturing Kuwait, therefore, looked like a solution to Iraq's economic problems.

Politically, Saddam Hussein was worried about the security of Iraq. He believed that everybody was out to undercut his country. After all, in 1981 the Israelis had bombed his nuclear research reactor, and with the decline of the Soviet Union, it looked as though the United States and Israel were becoming ever more powerful. In a speech in Amman, Jordan, in February 1990, Saddam said the Soviet Union was in decline and could no longer counter the Americans and the Israelis. Saddam believed he would have to do it himself. He undertook a number of actions designed to test the Americans. Ironically, the United States was trying to appease Saddam Hussein, to bring him back into the community of responsible nations, and to use Iraq as an effective balance to Iranian power in the region. The inconsistency of American policy misled Saddam Hussein, and he believed he could get away with the invasion of Kuwait without suffering serious reprisals.

Saddam was wrong. A series of UN resolutions applied the doctrine of collective security against Iraq. Why did the United States and others respond as they did? One argument is that it was all for oil. Oil exports to the United States and other leading Western industrialized nations made the Persian Gulf an abnormally important region, but there was more to the 1990 crisis than oil. For example, Britain was deeply involved in the war, but Britain did not import any gulf oil. There was also concern about collective security and echoes of the failure to stand up to German aggression in the 1930s. And there was also a third dimension: preventive war. Saddam Hussein was building weapons of mass destruction. He had a nuclear weapons program with covertly imported materials; he had chemical weapons and was developing biological weapons. If he were to have, in addition to this, the revenues that came from Kuwait's oil, the world would face a larger, stronger, more devastating Iraq later in the decade. Some reasoned that if there were to be a war, better now than later.

But others argued that the war was unnecessary because economic sanctions could force Iraq to evacuate its troops from Kuwait. The counterfactual is hard to prove, but historically sanctions have rarely achieved their intended effect in a short time frame. In November, the United States doubled the size of its troop deployment in Saudi Arabia in the prelude to war. Why did Saddam Hussein not escape at the last minute by saying he would withdraw or find some other ruse? Partly, his miscalculation seemed to be, as he told the American ambassador in August 1990, that the United States had no stomach for high casualties and would not commit itself to a long, drawn-out war. In that sense, he was a victim of the Vietnam analogy. And partly, Saddam may have been driven by pride and an inability to back down after being at the center of the world stage.

What did the Gulf War solve? It briefly revived the doctrine of UN collective security, but as we have seen, questions exist about how typical this regional conflict was. The cease-fire set a precedent whereby UN inspectors visited Iraq and destroyed its nuclear and chemical facilities. But it left Saddam Hussein in place. President Bush decided not to occupy Baghdad because he thought Saddam Hussein might be removed by his own people, and he was concerned that neither the American public nor the UN coalition would tolerate a costly occupation.

In the aftermath of the Gulf War, the Israeli government and the PLO made significant progress toward peace and normalized relations. Using the political leverage it accrued from the war, the Bush administration pressured the PLO and the government of Yitzhak Shamir to meet along with other Arab governments in Madrid in late 1991 and in Washington in 1992. While these talks stalled, back-channel negotiations between Israeli officials and PLO officials outside Oslo, Norway, led to the Declaration of Principles signed in Washington, D.C., in September 1993 between the PLO and the government of Yitzhak Rabin. The declaration was followed by a series of agreements for the withdrawal of Israeli troops from the Gaza Strip and from Palestinian towns and villages in the West Bank. The PLO was recognized by Israel as the legitimate voice of the Palestinian people, and the reins of local autonomy, including policing, were handed over to PLO leader Yasir Arafat and the PLO in several stages after 1994.

Historic handshake between Rabin and Arafat with Clinton's encouragement, 1993

At the same time, King Hussein of Jordan negotiated a peace treaty with the Rabin government, which was signed in Washington in 1994. During the Gulf War, Jordan had equivocated in its support for the U.S.-led coalition, and King Hussein calculated that normalizing relations with Israel would put him back into the good graces of the United States and the oil-producing states in the Middle East. The PLO had backed Saddam Hussein and Iraq during the Gulf War and, as a result, had seen its once generous donations from Kuwait, Saudi Arabia, and the other oil states diminish. With its financial situation desperate, the PLO relaxed its opposition to a negotiated settlement.

In spite of the peace negotiations, many Israelis remained skeptical about the policy of ceding occupied territory to a Palestinian state. Ultraconservative Israelis considered Rabin a traitor, and in November 1995 he was assassinated by one of them. The PLO government and Arafat were perceived by some Palestinians as corrupt and authoritarian, thereby giving strength to opposition groups such as the fundamentalist Hamas, which sought to disrupt the peace process. Terrorist bombings by Arab extremists opposed to the peace process affected the 1996 Israeli elections, and the new Likud government, led by Benjamin Netanyahu (1996–1999) slowed the peace process. Nonetheless, Netanyahu signed the Wye River Accords with the PLO in 1998, and a subsequent Labor government under Prime Minister Ehud Barak offered significant concessions in negotiations with Yasir Arafat at Camp David in the summer of 2000. After the Camp David negotiations failed, and despite efforts to revive talks, violence broke out again in September 2000. At the start of the Camp David talks, President Clinton told both Arafat and Barak that there was some danger that if they reached agreement, they would be killed by their own extremists, but that if they failed to reach agreement, many people, all younger than they, would be killed on both sides. Unfortunately, he was right. During the last days of his presidency, Clinton made a last-ditch attempt to broker a settlement between Barak and Arafat, which culminated in the failed Taba Talks in late January 2001.

The context of the Israeli-Palestinian conflict changed greatly over the next year. Ariel Sharon, a decorated war hero with a reputation for tough military tactics, replaced Barak as Israel's prime minister in February 2001. By electing Sharon, the Israeli public signaled its fatigue with negotiations and preference for a more aggressive response to the wave of Palestinian suicide bombings that had taken place inside Israel since September 2000. Sharon made it immediately clear that he considered Arafat a terrorist, and that a peace settlement was not possible with Arafat.

The international context of the conflict also changed in 2001. When George W. Bush took office in January, he promoted a realist foreign policy agenda that emphasized the importance of Great Power relations with China and Russia. Bush criticized Clinton's involvement in the peace process and made it clear that he would take a hands-off approach to the conflict. Eight months later, Bush's foreign policy dramatically shifted after the terrorist attacks of September 11, 2001. Fighting terrorism became the administration's focus.

In Afghanistan, in October through December 2001, American air power and Special Forces helped turn the tide in the civil war. The American military intervention allowed the Northern Alliance to overthrow the fundamentalist Taliban government that had provided sanctuaries to Osama bin Laden and his al Qaeda terrorist network, the perpetrators of the September 11 terrorist attacks on New York and Washington. The American action was widely supported by NATO allies and legitimized by a UN resolution.

In 2002, however, as the Bush administration prepared to go to war against Iraq, international support began to fade. In terms of the distinction drawn earlier in this chapter, the United States called its actions against Iraq "preemptive," but many countries saw the United States' proposed invasion as a "preventive" war of choice because the threat posed by Iraq was not imminent. In September 2002, following a speech in which Bush called on the UN to enforce previous Security Council resolutions against Iraq, the United States obtained a UN Security Council resolution demanding that Saddam Hussein cooperate fully with international inspectors to prove that he was complying with resolutions passed a decade earlier assuring that he had given up his nuclear, biological and chemical weapons programs. Saddam allowed inspectors to return to Iraq for the first time in four years; simultaneously, the United States moved forward with a large buildup of troops in neighboring Kuwait and Qatar, and Congress passed a resolution authorizing the use of force against Saddam Hussein. In December 2002 and again in February 2003, the inspectors reported partial but not complete compliance and asked for more time to complete their task. Concerned about the approach of hot weather and the readiness of its forces, the United States felt that another delay would cause its efforts to lose momentum. After failing to obtain a second Security Council resolution authorizing an attack against Iraq, the United States, Great Britain, and a small coalition argued that the earlier resolutions provided a legal basis, and invaded Iraq in March 2003. Within three and a half weeks, Baghdad was occupied and Saddam had fled.

But winning the war proved much easier than winning the peace. While the occupation was initially welcomed in some of the Shia and Kurdish areas of the country, many of the former Sunni ruling groups and some Shia formed an insurgency against the occupation. They were aided by foreign terrorists, such as the Jordanian-born Al Qaeda operative Abu Musab al-Zarqawi, who crossed into Iraq and sought to continue their radical jihad against the United States. The Bush administration had not planned for enough troops to manage the looting that followed the collapse of Saddam's regime, or the insurgency that followed the invasion. The ensuing violence slowed reconstruction efforts that could have helped generate popular support and soft power. Additionally, the failure to obtain a second UN resolution meant that many countries believed that the invasion lacked legitimacy, as a result, their participation in the reconstruction effort was limited.

The costs of the war for American soft power were compounded when inspectors failed to find any weapons of mass destruction after the war. Two of the three reasons given for the war before the invasion—Saddam's weapons of mass destruction and an alleged connection between Saddam and the 9/11 events—turned out to be based on false intelligence and political exaggeration. That left the third cause: the hope that removing Saddam's brutal dictatorship would lead to a democratic Iraq, which would begin a democratic transformation of the Middle East.

Three rounds of national elections were successfully held in Iraq in 2005, but as we saw earlier, elections are not sufficient to produce a liberal democracy where societies are divided along ethnic and religious lines, institutions are weak, and there is little sense of overarching community that makes minorities willing to acquiesce in the rule of the majority. While it may take a decade or more to judge the final effects of the Iraq war, in 2006 polls showed that many Americans were beginning to believe that the costs had outweighed the benefits. Whatever the original intentions, the failure to plan carefully for appropriate means contributed to negative consequences.

Meanwhile, the Arab-Israeli conflict continued. In the spring of 2002, as the United States began making an international case for war with Iraq, Saudi Arabia and other U.S. allies insisted that President Bush first turn his attention to the Israeli-Palestinian situation, which had reached crisis proportions. In retaliation for a spate of terrorist attacks during the winter of 2001–2002, Israeli troops reoccupied towns and cities in the West Bank and held Arafat's compound in Ramallah under siege for months in the spring of 2002.

As the violence continued throughout the spring, the United States announced that in conjunction with a "Quartet"—the European Union, Russia, and the UN—it had developed a "Road map" for peace with cooperative, reciprocal measures to be implemented by both sides. Israel, however, said it would proceed with unilateral plans to construct a security fence to separate the West Bank from Israel to prevent suicide bombers from entering. The United States articulated its support for the Road map most clearly in June, when Bush stated that the United States sought a permanent two-state solution to the conflict by 2005.

The removal of Saddam Hussein from power in Iraq in the spring of 2003 significantly improved Israel's security among its neighbors. The absence of a strong external military threat to Israel in the region led to a renewed push for progress on the Israeli-Palestinian issue. In a move that was acceptable to both the United States and Israel, Arafat appointed Mahmoud Abbas, also known as Abu Mazen, prime minister of the Palestinian Authority. At the same time, Hamas, a party that rejected recognition of the legitimacy of Israel, began to increase its strength among Palestinians. The Quartet Road map was released, calling for a two-state solution and outlining a three-phase process for achieving this goal. Abbas negotiated a three-month cease-fire among the Palestinian militant groups, and Sharon, Abbas, and Bush met in Aqaba, Jordan, in June 2003 for peace talks. These were the first face-to-face talks between an Israeli and Palestinian leader since Bush and Sharon had come to power. The cease-fire failed to hold, however, and plans for a second round of talks were cancelled. Israel continued construction of a security fence.

In the fall of 2003 unofficial Israeli and Palestinian negotiators met in Geneva to work out a model comprehensive peace deal. Known as the Geneva Accord, this agreement followed the outlines of the Clinton proposals from Camp David and Taba, but it went even further by resolving the difficult questions of the status of Jerusalem, Israeli settlements, and the limited Palestinian "right of return" for the families of refugees who had fled in 1948. While the Geneva Accord carried no legal standing, it demonstrated that knowledgeable, concerned parties on both sides could agree on even the toughest issues. U.S. Secretary of State Colin Powell met with the accord negotiators despite strong protests from the Israeli government. As more than one observer noted, the episode showed that it was easier to identify a solution to the Israel-Palestine conflict than to identify a way to get there.

The death of PLO leader Yasir Arafat in November 2004 was followed by the election of Abbas to the presidency of the Palestinian Authority. Sharon faced down opposition from settlers, split the Likud Party and withdrew Israeli forces from Gaza in the summer of 2005. While this represented progress, it did not lead to implementation of the road map or resolution of the longer-standing issues in the conflict. In January 2006, Sharon was incapacitated by a major stroke, and Hamas won the Palestinian elections further adding to the political uncertainty and slowing agreement on peace. In March, Ehud Olmert, Sharon's former deputy, led a new centrist Kadima Party to victory in Israeli elections, but both Israelis and Palestinians remained internally divided about how to resolve their conflict.

The Middle East illustrates the same dynamics of the individual, the state, and the international system we have seen in other conflicts. At one level, individuals such as Arafat, Rabin, Sharon, Sadat, and King Hussein determined whether there would be peace accords. Terrorists and assassins also played key roles. The states of the region frequently act in a manner consonant with the realist model—seeking power and security in competition with other states—but international law and organizations have helped shape the political struggles, as have individual and non-state actors. Issues such as religion, ethnicity, economic underdevelopment, and population pressures continue to make Middle Eastern politics volatile. Throughout the region, autocratic governments are faced with fundamentalist challenges to their authority, and many of these threaten to explode into civil war, as they have in Algeria and the Sudan. We can expect further conflict in the Middle East.

Chronology: The Arab-Israeli Conflict

1897	Publication of Herzl's *The Jewish State*; First World Zionist Congress meets
1915	MacMahon–Sharif Husain agreements leading to Arab revolt against Turks in return for British assurances on independent Arab state
1916	Sykes-Picot agreement secretly establishing Anglo-French spheres of influence in the Middle East
1917	Balfour Declaration stating that the British government favored "the establishment in Palestine of a national home for the Jewish people . . . it being understood that nothing shall be done which may prejudice the civil and religious rights of existing non-Jewish communities in Palestine"
1922	Great Britain given the Palestine Mandate by the League of Nations
1936	Formation of Arab High Committee with aim of uniting all Arabs in opposition to Jewish claims
1937	Palestinian Arab revolt against British authority; Peel Commission report proposes partition into three states: one Arab, one Jewish, and a British-administered territory; scheme adopted by the World Zionist Congress and rejected by the Pan-Arab Congress

1939	British White Paper calls for independent Palestine in ten years
1945	Egypt, Iraq, Jordan, Lebanon, Saudi Arabia, and Yemen create the Arab League
1947	British government refers Palestine dispute to the United Nations; UN General Assembly votes for partition of Palestine into Jewish and Arab states with Jerusalem under UN trusteeship; UN partition plan accepted by Jews but rejected by Arabs
1948	Fighting between Arabs and Jews in Palestine; British mandate ends; Jewish provisional government under David Ben-Gurion proclaims the state of Israel; Israel recognized by the United States and the Soviet Union
1948–1949	War between Israel and the Arab League
1949	Israel admitted to the United Nations
1952	Free Officer revolt led by Gamal Abdel Nasser in Egypt
1955	Soviet-Egyptian arms deal concluded; Baghdad Pact created with Great Britain, Iran, Iraq, Turkey, and Pakistan as members
1956	Suez Crisis: Israeli forces invade the Sinai; Britain and France bomb and land paratroopers in the Suez Canal zone
1957	Eisenhower Doctrine: President granted congressional authority for U.S. intervention in event of communist aggression in the Middle East
1958	Antimonarchical revolt in Iraq; crisis in Lebanon and Jordan; American Marines land in Beirut
1964	Formation of the Palestine Liberation Organization (PLO)
1967	Six-Day War: Israel occupies the Sinai, Gaza Strip, West Bank, and the Golan Heights; adoption of UN Resolution 242 calling for Israeli withdrawal from occupied Arab lands in return for peace within negotiated permanent borders; Palestinian demands referred to only as the "refugee" problem
1969	War of Attrition
1970	"Black September" in Jordan: Jordanian army expels Palestinian commandos from Jordan; death of Nasser: Anwar Sadat becomes Egyptian president
1973	Yom Kippur War: Egypt and Syria launch surprise attack against Israel
1973–1974	Arab oil embargo
1974	Military disengagement accords between Israel and Egypt and Syria
1975	Sinai Agreement between Israel and Egypt permits reopening of Suez Canal
1977	Egypt's Sadat becomes first Arab head of state to recognize Israel and to address Israeli Knesset in Jerusalem
1978	Camp David Summit with Carter, Begin, and Sadat
1979	Climax of Iranian revolution: Shah forced into exile, Ayatollah Khomeini returns to Tehran as new Iranian leader; Egyptian-Israeli peace treaty signed in Washington, D.C.; American embassy overrun by Iranians and staff taken hostage; Soviet forces invade Afghanistan
1980	Carter Doctrine: United States will use force to counter Soviet aggression in the Persian Gulf region; Iraqi forces invade Iranian territory; beginning of Iran-Iraq War; Iraq invades Iran
1981	Sadat assassinated in Cairo
1982	Israeli forces invade Lebanon

1983	Multinational peacekeeping force arrives in Beirut; attacks against American embassy and Marine barracks
1987	Beginning of Palestinian uprising (*intifada*) in Gaza Strip and West Bank
1988	Jordan's King Hussein renounces Jordanian sovereignty over West Bank; PLO declares independent Palestinian states on West Bank and Gaza
1990	Iraq invades Kuwait; UN Security Council votes sanctions
1991	Iraq expelled from Kuwait in Gulf War
1991–1992	Arab-Israeli peace talks in Madrid and Washington, D.C.
1993	Oslo negotiations and Declaration of Principles between Israel and the PLO
1994	Jordanian-Israeli peace treaty signed in Washington, D.C.; PLO-Israeli agreement for Palestinian control of Gaza and Jericho
1995	Rabin assassinated in Tel Aviv
1996	Likud leader Netanyahu elected prime minister after terrorist bombings in Israeli cities undermines support for Peres, Rabin's Labor successor
1997	Israel cedes 80 percent of West Bank town of Hebron to Palestinians
1998	United States brokers Israeli-PLO Wye River Accords, which cede additional 13 percent of West Bank to Palestinians; U.S. President Clinton addresses Palestinian Assembly in Gaza
1999	Death of Jordan's King Hussein; Labor leader Barak elected Israeli prime minister
2000	Camp David negotiations fail; Second Intifada begins
2001	Ariel Sharon elected Israeli prime minister
2002	Israel reoccupies towns in West Bank and Gaza and begins construction of a security fence between the West Bank and Israel; UN Security Council passes a resolution demanding that Israel withdraw from Palestinian towns
2003	The United States, the European Union, Russia, and the UN release the three-phase "Road map" calling for an independent Palestinian state and full peace by 2005; Arafat appoints Mahmoud Abbas (also known as Abu Mazen) prime minister; Abbas, Sharon, and Bush meet in Jordan in June for peace talks; Abbas resigns after cease-fire collapses and talks break down
2004	Death of Arafat; Abbas becomes president of the Palestinian Authority
2005	Israel completes unilateral withdrawal from Gaza and continues construction of security fence despite protests that it takes Palestinian land
2006	Sharon is incapacitated as a result of a major stroke
	Hamas wins Palestinian election; Ehud Olmert and new Kadima Party come first in Israeli election

STUDY QUESTIONS

1. What is ethnic conflict? When is it likely to occur?
2. When is intervention justified? Is self-determination always a justification?
3. Is there a difference between international law and morality? How important is international law?
4. How does the United Nations differ from the League of Nations?

5. What are the respective claims of the Palestinians and the Israelis to the territory Israel now encompasses? Which group has a better argument, in your opinion, or are they equally valid?

6. What was the UN Palestine partition proposal? Why did the Arabs reject this plan?

7. What were the causes of the Middle East wars of 1956, 1967, 1973, and 1982? Were they inevitable? If so, when and why? Is another Arab-Israeli war inevitable?

8. The 1967 war yielded the present configuration of the Arab-Israeli dispute. What happened in that war? What was the famous Security Council Resolution 242?

9. Sadat claimed that he had to go to war in 1973 to go to peace with Israel afterward. Assess this argument. What parallels can you draw between Nasser's success in 1956 and Sadat's in 1973?

10. How successful have the UN peacekeeping operations in the region been? What have been their limitations?

11. How did the 1991 Gulf War and the 2003 Iraq War differ? What reasons were given for each war? What is the difference between preemptive and preventive war?

12. What do realism, liberalism, and constructivism each contribute to your understanding of the Middle Eastern conflicts?

NOTES

1. Peter Wallensteen and Margareta Sollenberg, "Armed Conflict 1989–2000," report no. 60, in Margareta Sollenberg, ed., *States in Armed Conflict 2000* (Uppsala, Sweden: Uppsala University, Department of Peace and Conflict Research, 2001), pp. 10–12.

2. John Mueller, "The Banality of Ethnic War," *International Security* 25 (Summer 2000), p. 42.

3. Stuart Kaufman, *Modern Hatreds* (Ithaca, NY: Cornell University Press, 2001), p. 220.

4. Irving Howe and Michael Walzer, "Were We Wrong About Vietnam?" *The New Republic,* August 18, 1979, p. 18.

5. Anthony Eden, quoted in Robert R. Bowie, *Suez 1956* (New York: Oxford University Press, 1974), p. 124.

6. "Binding the Colossus," *The Economist,* November 22, 2003, pp. 25–26.

7. Linda Fasulo, *An Insider's Guide to the UN* (New Haven, CT: Yale University Press, 2004), p. 115.

8. Ernest Renan, quoted in Hans Kohn, *Nationalism: Its Meaning and History* (Princeton, NJ: Van Nostrand, 1955), p. 137.

SELECTED READINGS

1. Mill, John Stuart, "A Few Words on Non-Intervention," in John Stuart Mill, *Collected Works,* vol. 21 (Toronto: University of Toronto Press, 1963), pp. 109–124.

2. Fasulo, Linda, *An Insider's Guide to the UN* (New Haven, CT: Yale University Press, 2004), pp. 1–89.

3. Kaufman, Stuart, *Modern Hatreds* (Ithaca, NY: Cornell University Press, 2001), Chaps. 1, 2, and 6.

4. McGarry, John, and Brendan O'Leary, eds., *The Politics of Ethnic Conflict Regulation* (London: Routledge, 1993), pp. 1–38.

5. Lewis, Bernard, *The Crisis of Islam* (New York: Modern Library, 2003).

FURTHER READINGS

Anderson, Benedict, *Imagined Communities* (London: Verso, 1983).

Bowie, Robert R., *Suez 1956* (New York: Oxford University Press, 1974).

Chayes, Abram, and Antonia Handler Chayes, *The New Sovereignty: Compliance with International Regulatory Agreements* (Cambridge, MA: Harvard University Press, 1995).

Cordesman, Anthony, *The Iraq War* (Washington, DC: Center for Strategic and International Studies, 2003).

Coulon, Jocelyn, *Soldiers of Diplomacy: The United Nations, Peacekeeping and the New World Order* (Toronto: University of Toronto Press, 1998).

Deutsch, Karl W., *Nationalism and Its Alternatives* (New York: Knopf, 1959).

Diamond, Larry, *Squandered Victory: The American Occupation and the Bungled Effort to Bring Democracy to Iraq* (New York: Times Books, 2005).

Durch, William J., *U.N. Peacekeeping, American Politics and the Uncivil Wars of the 1990s* (New York: St. Martin's, 1996).

Finnemore, Martha, *The Purpose of Intervention* (Ithaca, NY: Cornell University Press, 2003).

Gause, F. Gregory, "Can Democracy Stop Terrorism?" *Foreign Affairs* 84:5 (September/October 2005), pp. 62–76.

Gellner, Ernest, *Nations and Nationalism* (Oxford: Blackwell, 1983).

Goodrich, Leland M., Edvard Hambro, and Anne Patricia Simons, *Charter of the United Nations: Commentary and Comments* (New York: Columbia University Press, 1969).

Gordon, Michael, and Bernard Trainor, *The Generals' War: The Inside Story of the Conflict in the Gulf* (Boston: Little, Brown, 1995).

Gordon, Philip, and Jeremy Shapiro, *Allies at War: America, Europe and the Crisis Over Iraq* (New York: McGraw-Hill, 2004).

Haas, Ernst, "Nationalism: An Instrumental Social Construction," *Millennium* 22:3 (Winter 1993), pp. 505–545.

Hehir, J. Bryan, "World of Faultlines: Sovereignty, Self-Determination, Intervention," *Commonwealth* 119:16 (September 25, 1992), pp. 8–10.

Henkin, Louis, *How Nations Behave: Law and Foreign Policy*, 2nd ed. (New York: Columbia University Press, 1979).

Herring, George, *America's Longest War: The United States and Vietnam, 1950–1975* (New York: Knopf, 1986).

Ignatieff, Michael, *Virtual War: Kosovo and Beyond* (New York: Holt, 2000).

Jacobson, Harold K., *Networks of Interdependence: International Organizations and the Global Political System* (New York: Knopf, 1979).

Kohn, Hans, *Nationalism: Its Meaning and History* (Princeton, NJ: Van Nostrand, 1955).

Krasner, Stephen D., *Sovereignty: Organized Hypocrisy* (Princeton, NJ: Princeton University Press, 1999).

Mayall, James, *Nationalism and International Society* (Cambridge UK: Cambridge University Press, 1990).

Moynihan, Daniel P., *On the Law of Nations* (Cambridge, MA: Harvard University Press, 1990).

Murray, William, and Robert Scales, *The Iraq War: A Military History* (Cambridge, MA: Harvard University Press, 2003).

Nye, Joseph S., and Roger K. Smith, eds., *After the Storm: Lessons of the Gulf War* (Queenstown, MD: Madison Books and Aspen Strategy Group, 1992).

Podhoretz, Norman, *Why We Were in Vietnam* (New York: Simon & Schuster, 1982).

Power, Samantha, *A Problem from Hell: America and the Age of Genocide* (New York: Basic, 2002).

Quandt, William B., ed., *The Middle East: Ten Years After Camp David* (Washington, DC: Brookings Institution, 1988).

Safran, Nadav, *From War to War: A Study of the Arab-Israeli Confrontation 1948–1967* (New York: Pegasus, 1969).

Sifry, Micah L., and Christopher Cerf, *The Gulf War Reader: History, Documents, Opinions* (New York: New York Times Books, 1991).

Vincent, R. J., *Nonintervention and International Order* (Princeton, NJ: Princeton University Press, 1974).

Walzer, Michael, *Just and Unjust Wars: A Moral Argument with Historical Illustrations* (New York: Basic, 1977).

———, *Arguing About War* (New Haven, CT: Yale University Press, 2004).

Woodward, Bob, *Plan of Attack* (New York: Simon & Schuster, 2004).

Woodward, Susan L., *Balkan Tragedy: Chaos and Disillusion After the Cold War* (Washington, DC: Brookings Institution, 1995).

Globalization and Interdependence

Oil wells in the Middle East

With the end of the Cold War in 1989, a number of observers argued that economic issues would become more central in world politics. Networks of economic interdependence that span the globe have increased as costs of communication and transportation have declined and shrunk the effects of distance. The role of markets has also increased as a result of new information and transportation technologies, as well as changed attitudes about the role of governments and states. Nearly half of all industrial production today is produced by multinational enterprises whose decisions about where to locate production have a powerful effect on domestic economies and politics. As the economist Dani Rodrik points out, globalization is "exposing a deep fault line between groups who have the skills and mobility to flourish in global markets" and those who don't, "such as workers, pensioners, and environmentalists, with governments stuck in the middle."[1] Some theorists see a new competition—"geo-economics"—replacing geopolitics and predict that economic sanctions and embargoes will become the key instruments of international politics.

It is important to keep these changes in perspective. Security can be taken for granted in peaceful times, but all markets operate within a political framework. Global markets depend on an international structure of power. Security is like oxygen: easy to take for granted until you begin to miss it, and then you can think about nothing else. Similarly, economic sanctions have been popular instruments because they avoid the use of force, but their effectiveness is mixed. Studies suggest they have achieved their intended effects in fewer than half of the cases in which they have been tried. Multilateral sanctions were one factor in ending apartheid in South Africa and putting pressure on Serbia and Libya in the 1990s, but they failed to oust Iraqi troops from Kuwait or return an elected president to power even in a poor country such as Haiti. Moreover, globalization and economic interdependence were already growing rapidly when states followed relatively liberal policies toward trade, investment, and migration in the nineteenth century. This did not stop two world wars and an economic depression in the first half of the twentieth century from occurring and interrupting elements of these long-term trends.

THE DIMENSIONS OF GLOBALIZATION

Globalization—defined as worldwide networks of interdependence—does not imply universality. For example, at the beginning of the twenty-first century half of the American population used the World Wide Web, compared to one-hundredth of one percent of the population of South Asia. Most people in the world today do not have telephones. Even in an era of cheap cell phones, hundreds of millions of people live as peasants in remote villages with only slight connections to world markets or the global flow of ideas. Indeed, globalization is accompanied by increasing gaps, in many respects, between the rich and the poor. It does not imply either homogenization or equity.

Even among rich countries, there is a lot less globalization than meets the eye. A truly globalized world market would mean free flows of goods, people, and capital, and similar interest rates. In fact, we have a long way to go. For example, even in North America, Toronto trades ten times as much with Vancouver as with Seattle, though the distance is the same and tariffs are minimal. Globalization has made national boundaries more porous, but not irrelevant. Nor does globalization mean the creation of a universal community. In social terms, contacts among people with different religious beliefs and other deeply held values have often led to conflict: witness the great crusades of medieval times (eleventh through thirteenth century) or the current notion of the United States as "the Great Satan," held by some Islamic fundamentalists in the Middle East. Clearly, in social as well as economic terms, homogenization does not follow necessarily from globalization.

Globalization has a number of dimensions, though all too often economists write as if it and the world economy are one and the same. But other forms of globalization also have significant effects on our daily lives. The oldest form of globalization is environmental. For example, the first smallpox epidemic is recorded in Egypt in 1350 B.C. It reached China in 49 A.D.; Europe after 700; the Americas in 1520; and Australia in 1789. The plague or Black Death originated in Asia, but its spread killed a quarter to a third of the population of Europe in the fourteenth century. Europeans carried diseases to the Americas in the fifteenth and sixteenth centuries that destroyed up to 95 percent of the indigenous population. In 1918, a flu pandemic caused by a bird virus killed some 40 million people around the world, far more than the recently concluded world war. Some scientists today predict a repeat of an avian flu pandemic. Since 1973, 30 previously unknown infectious diseases have emerged, and other familiar diseases have spread geographically in new drug-resistant forms. In the 20 years after HIV/AIDS was identified in the 1980s, it killed 20 million people and infected another 40 million around the world. Some experts project double that number by 2010. The spread of foreign species of flora and fauna to new areas has wiped out native species, and may result in economic losses of several hundred billion dollars a year. On the other hand, not all effects of environmental globalization are adverse. For instance, both Europe and Asia benefited from the importation of such new world crops as the potato, corn, and the tomato, and the "green revolution" agricultural technology of the past few decades has helped poor farmers throughout the world.

Global climate change will affect the lives of people everywhere. Thousands of scientists from more than 100 countries recently reported that there is new and strong evidence that most of the warming observed over the last 50 years is attributable to human activities, and average global temperatures in the twenty-first century are projected to increase between 2.5 and 10 degrees Fahrenheit. The result could be more severe variations in climate, with too much water in some regions and not enough in others. The effects in North America will include stronger storms, hurricanes, floods, droughts, and landslides. In Europe, warming sea temperatures could alter the flow of the Gulf Stream and result in severe local cooling trends. Rising temperatures have lengthened the freeze-free season in many regions and led to a 10 percent decrease in global snow cover since the 1960s. Glaciers are melting. The rate at which the sea level rose in the last century was ten times faster than the average rate over the last three millennia. As Harvard scientist James McCarthy notes, "What is different now is that Earth is populated with 6 billion people and the natural and human systems that provide us with food, fuel, and fiber are strongly influenced by climate."[2] As climate change accelerates, "future change may not occur as smoothly as it has in the past." It does not matter whether carbon dioxide is placed in the atmosphere from China or the United States; it still affects global warming.

Military globalization consists of networks of interdependence in which force, or the threat of force, is employed. The world wars of the twentieth century are a case in point. During the Cold War, the global strategic interdependence between the United States and the Soviet Union was acute and well recognized. Not only did it produce world-straddling alliances, but either side could have used interconti-nental missiles to destroy the other within the space of 30 minutes. It was distinc-tive not because it was totally new, but because the scale and speed of the potential conflict arising from military interdependence were so enormous. Today, Al Qaeda and other transnational actors have formed global networks of operatives, challeng-ing conventional approaches to national defense.

Social globalization is the spread of peoples, cultures, images, and ideas. Migra-tion is a concrete example. In the nineteenth century, some 80 million people crossed oceans to new homes—far more than in the twentieth century. At the beginning of the twenty-first century, 32 million residents of the United States (11.5 percent of the population) were foreign-born. In addition, some 30 million visitors (students, businesspeople, tourists) enter the country each year. Ideas are an equally important aspect of social globalization. Four great religions of the world—Buddhism, Judaism, Christianity, and Islam—have spread across great distances over the last two millennia, as has the scientific method and the Enlightenment worldview over the past few centuries. Political globalization (a part of social global-ization) is manifest in the spread of constitutional arrangements, the increase in the number of countries that have become democratic, and the development of interna-tional rules and institutions. Those who think it is meaningless to speak of an inter-national community ignore the importance of the global spread of political ideas such as the antislavery movement in the nineteenth century, anticolonialism after World War II, and the environmental and feminist movements today. Of course, the world is a long way from a global community replacing citizens' loyalties to clans, tribes, and states, but such transnational political ideas affect how nations construct their national goals and how they use their soft power.

What's New About Twenty-First-Century Globalization?

While globalization has been going on for centuries, its contemporary form is "thicker and quicker." Globalization today is different from the nineteenth century, when European imperialism provided much of its political structure, and higher transport and communications costs meant fewer people were involved directly with people and ideas from other cultures. But many of the most important differences are closely related to the information revolution. As the columnist Thomas Friedman argues, contemporary globalization goes "farther, faster, cheaper and deeper."[3]

Economists use the term *network effects* to refer to situations in which a prod-uct becomes more valuable once many other people also use it. One telephone is useless, but its value increases as the network grows. This is why the Internet is causing such rapid change. The Nobel Prize–winning economist Joseph Stiglitz argues that a knowledge-based economy generates "powerful spillover effects, often spreading like fire and triggering further innovation and setting off chain reactions of new inventions. . . . But goods—as opposed to knowledge—do not always spread like fire."[4] Moreover, as interdependence has become thicker and quicker, the rela-tionships among different networks have become more important. There are more interconnections among the networks. As a result, "system effects"—by which small perturbations in one area can spread throughout a whole system—become more important.

As government officials fashion foreign policies, they encounter the increasing thickness of globalism—the density of the networks of interdependence—which means that the effects of events in one geographical area, or the economic or ecological dimension, can have profound effects in other geographical areas, on the military or social dimensions. These international networks are increasingly complex and their effects are therefore increasingly unpredictable. Moreover, in human systems, people are often hard at work trying to outwit each other, to gain an economic, social, or military advantage precisely by acting in an unpredictable way. As a result, globalization is accompanied by pervasive uncertainty. There will be continual competition between increased complexity and uncertainty, on the one hand; and efforts by governments, corporations, and others to comprehend and manipulate to their benefit these increasingly complex interconnected systems. Frequent financial crises or sharp increases in unemployment could lead to popular movements to limit interdependence.

Quickness also adds to uncertainty and the difficulties of shaping policy responses. As mentioned, modern globalization operates at a much more rapid pace than its earlier forms. Smallpox took nearly three millennia to spread to all inhabited continents, finally reaching Australia in 1775. AIDS took less than three decades to spread from Africa all around the world. And to switch to a metaphorical virus, in 2000 the "love bug" computer virus, invented by hackers in the Philippines, needed only three days to straddle the globe. From three millennia to three decades to three days: that is the measure of the quickening of globalization.

Direct public participation in global affairs has also increased in rich countries. Ordinary people invest in foreign mutual funds, gamble on offshore Internet sites, and travel and sample exotic cuisine that used to be the preserve of the rich. Friedman termed this change the *democratization* of technology, finance, and information because diminished costs have made what were previous luxuries available to a much broader range of society. *Democratization* is not quite the right word, however, because in markets, money votes, and people start out with unequal stakes. There is no equality, for example, in capital markets, despite the new financial instruments that permit more people to participate. A million dollars or more is often the entry price for large hedge fund investors. *Pluralization* might be a more accurate description of this trend, suggesting the vast increase in the number and variety of participants in global networks. In 1914, according to the English economist John Maynard Keynes, "The inhabitant of London could order by telephone, sipping his morning tea in bed, the various products of the whole earth, in such quantity as he might see fit, and reasonably expect their early delivery upon his doorstep."[5] But Keynes's Englishman had to be wealthy to be a global consumer. Today, supermarkets and Internet retailers extend that capacity to the vast majority of people in postindustrial societies.

This vast expansion of transnational channels and contacts at multicontinental distances means that more policies are up for grabs internationally, including regulations and practices—ranging from pharmaceutical testing to accounting and product standards to banking regulation—that were formerly regarded as the prerogatives of national governments.

What the information revolution has added to contemporary globalization is a quickness and thickness in the network of interconnections that make them more complex. But such "thick globalism" is not uniform: it varies by region and locality, and by issue.

Political Reactions to Globalization

Domestic politics channel responses to change. Some countries imitate success, as exemplified by democratizing capitalist societies from South Korea to Eastern Europe. Some accommodate change in distinctive and ingenious ways. For instance, small European states such as the Netherlands and Scandinavia have maintained relatively large governments and emphasized compensation for disadvantaged sectors, while the Anglo-American industrialized countries have, in general, emphasized markets, competition, and deregulation. Capitalism is far from monolithic, with significant differences between Europe, Japan, and the United States. There is more than one way to respond to global markets and to run a capitalist economy.

In other societies like Iran, Afghanistan, and Sudan, conservative groups have resisted globalization strongly, even violently. Reactions to globalization help stimulate fundamentalism. Domestic institutions and divisions—economic or ethnic— can lead to domestic conflict, which can reformulate ethnic and political identities in profound and often unanticipated ways. As we saw in the last chapter, in Bosnia, political elites appealed to traditional identities of people in rural areas to overwhelm and dissolve the cosmopolitan identities that had begun to develop in the cities, with devastating results. And Iran has seen struggles between Islamic fundamentalists and their more liberal opponents—who are also Islamic but more sympathetic to Western ideas.

As mentioned earlier, rising inequality was a major cause of the political reactions that halted a previous wave of economic globalization early in the twentieth century. The recent period of globalization, like the half century before World War I, has also been associated with increasing inequality among and within some countries. The ratio of incomes of the 20 percent of people in the world living in the richest countries, compared to the 20 percent living in the poorest countries, increased from 30 to 1 in 1960 to 74 to 1 in 1997. By comparison, it increased between 1870 and 1913 from 7 to 1 to 11 to 1. In any case, inequality can have political effects even if it is not increasing. According to the economist Robert Wade, "The result is a lot of angry young people, to whom new information technologies have given the means to threaten the stability of the societies they live in and even to threaten social stability in countries of the wealthy zone."[6] As increasing flows of information make people more aware of inequality, it is not surprising that some choose to protest.

The political consequences of these shifts in inequality are complex, but the economic historian Karl Polanyi argued powerfully in his classic study *The Great Transformation* that the market forces unleashed by the Industrial Revolution and globalization in the nineteenth century produced not only great economic gains, but also great social disruptions and political reactions. There is no *automatic* relationship between inequality and political reaction, but the former can give rise to the latter. Particularly when inequality is combined with instability, such as financial crises and recessions that throw people out of work, such reactions could eventually lead to restrictions on the pace of globalization of the world economy.

Protests against globalization are, in part, a reaction to the changes produced by economic interdependence. From an economist's view, imperfect markets are inefficient, but from a political view, some imperfections in international markets can be considered "useful inefficiencies" because they slow down and buffer political change. As globalization removes such inefficiencies, it becomes the political prisoner of its economic successes. In addition, as global networks become more complex there are more linkages among issues that can create friction.

Power and Interdependence

Liberals sometimes argue that interdependence means peace and cooperation, but unfortunately it is not that simple. Struggles over power go on, even in a world of interdependence. Because the coalitions are more complex and different forms of power are used, the conflicts are often like playing chess on several boards at the same time. Conflicts in the twenty-first century involve *both* guns and butter. The Chinese leader Mao Zedong (1893–1976) once said that power grows out of the barrel of a gun. After the oil crisis of 1973, the world was reminded that power can also grow out of a barrel of oil—as we shall see shortly.

THE CONCEPT OF INTERDEPENDENCE

Interdependence is often a fuzzy term used in a variety of conflicting ways, like other political words such as *nationalism, imperialism,* and *globalization.* (Indeed, as we discussed, globalization is the subset of interdependence that occurs at global distances). Leaders and analysts have different motives when they use political words. The leader wants as many people marching behind his or her banner as possible. Political leaders blur meanings and try to create a connotation of a common good: "We are all in the same boat together, therefore we must cooperate, therefore follow me." The analyst, on the other hand, makes distinctions to understand the world better. He or she distinguishes questions of *good* and *bad* from *more* and *less.* The analyst may note that the boat we are all in may be heading for one person's port but not another's, or that one person is doing all the rowing while another steers or has a free ride.

As an analytical word, *interdependence* refers to situations in which actors or events in different parts of a system affect each other. Simply put, interdependence means mutual dependence. Such a situation is neither good nor bad in itself, and there can be more or less of it. In personal relations, interdependence is summed up by the marriage vow in which each partner is interdependent with another "for richer, for poorer, for better, or for worse." And interdependence among nations sometimes means richer, sometimes poorer, sometimes for better, sometimes for worse. In the eighteenth century, Jean-Jacques Rousseau pointed out that along with interdependence comes friction and conflict. His "solution" was isolation and separation. But this is seldom possible in a globalized world. When countries try isolation, as with the cases of North Korea and Myanmar (formerly Burma), it comes at enormous economic cost. It is not easy for nations to divorce the rest of the world.

Sources of Interdependence

Four distinctions illuminate the dimensions of interdependence: its sources, benefits, relative costs, and symmetry. Interdependence can originate in physical (natural) or social (economic, political, or perceptual) phenomena. Both are usually present at the same time. The distinction helps clarify the degree of choice in situations of reciprocal or mutual dependence.

Military interdependence is the mutual dependence that arises from military competition. There is a physical aspect in the weaponry, especially dramatic since the development of nuclear weapons and the resulting possibility of mutually assured destruction. However, an important element of perception is also involved in interdependence, and a change in perception or policy can reduce the intensity of the military interdependence. As we saw in Chapter 5, Americans lost little sleep over the existence of British and French nuclear weapons during the Cold War because there was no perception that those weapons would ever land on American soil. Similarly, Westerners slept a bit easier in the late 1980s after Gorbachev announced his "new thinking" in Soviet foreign policy. It was not so much the number of Soviet weapons that made the difference, but the change in the perception of Soviet hostility or intent. Indeed, American public anxiety about the Soviet nuclear arsenal virtually evaporated after the final collapse of the USSR, despite the fact that at the twentieth century's close thousands of poorly guarded Soviet warheads were at risk of falling into the hands of terrorists or states such as Iran and North Korea.

Generally speaking, economic interdependence is similar to military interdependence in that it is the stuff of traditional international politics and has a high degree of social, especially perceptual, origin. Economic interdependence involves

---

ECOLOGICAL AND ECONOMIC INTERDEPENDENCE

"For the first time in more than a decade, the developing countries have an issue where they have some real leverage," said an official from a Caribbean nation. "They had none during the debt negotiations. But they are part of the environment, so they have leverage now. And they are using it. It's their negotiating strategy."

Poor nations, he said, see leverage because the north, the main polluter, wants them to cut emissions, stop deforesting and make other changes. But to adapt to those changes, they argue, they need funding and technology.

—*The New York Times, March 17, 1992*[7]

policy choices about values and costs. For example, in the early 1970s there was concern that the world's population was outstripping global food supplies. Many countries were buying American grain, which in turn drove up the price of food in American supermarkets. A loaf of bread cost more in the United States because the Indian monsoons failed and because the Soviet Union had mishandled its harvest. In 1973, the United States, in an effort to prevent price rises at home, decided to stop exporting soybeans to Japan. As a result, Japan invested in soybean production in Brazil. A few years later, when supply and demand were better equilibrated, U.S. farmers greatly regretted that embargo because the Japanese were buying their soybeans from a cheaper source in Brazil. Social choices as well as physical shortages affect economic interdependence in the long run. It is always worth considering the long-term perspective when making short-term choices.

Benefits of Interdependence

The benefits of interdependence are sometimes expressed as *zero-sum* and *nonzero-sum*. In a zero-sum situation, your loss is my gain and vice versa. In a *positive-sum* situation, we both gain; in a *negative-sum* situation, we both lose. Dividing a pie is zero-sum, baking a larger pie is positive-sum, and dropping it on the floor is negative-sum. Both zero-sum and nonzero-sum aspects are present in mutual dependence.

Some liberal economists tend to think of interdependence only in terms of joint gain, that is, positive-sum situations in which everyone benefits and everyone is better off. Failure to pay attention to the inequality of benefits and the conflicts that arise over the distribution of relative gains causes such analysts to miss the political aspects of interdependence. Both sides can gain from trade, for example, if Japan and Korea trade computers and television sets, but how will the gains from trade be distributed? Even if Japan and Korea are both better off, is Japan a lot better off and Korea only a little better off, or vice versa? The distribution of benefits—who gets how much of the joint gain—is a zero-sum situation in which one side's gain is the other's loss. The result is that there is almost always some political conflict in economic interdependence. Even when there is a larger pie, people can fight over who gets the biggest slices. Even if interdependent countries enjoy a joint gain, there may be conflict over who gets more or less of the joint gain.

Some liberal analysts mistakenly think that as globalization makes the world more interdependent, cooperation will replace competition. Their reason is that interdependence creates joint benefits, and those joint benefits encourage cooperation. That is true, but economic interdependence can also be used as a weapon— witness the use of trade sanctions against Serbia, Iraq, and Libya. Indeed, economic interdependence can be more usable than force in some cases because it may have more subtle gradations. And in some circumstances, states are less interested in their absolute gain from interdependence than in how the relatively greater gains of their rivals might be used to hurt them.

Some analysts believe that traditional world politics was always zero-sum. But that is misleading about the past. Traditional international politics could be positive-sum, depending on the actors' intentions. It made a difference, for example, whether Bismarck or Hitler was in charge of Germany. If one party sought aggrandizement, as Hitler did, then indeed politics was zero-sum—one side's gain was another's loss. But if all parties wanted stability, there could be joint gain in the balance of power. Conversely, the politics of economic globalization has competitive zero-sum aspects as well as cooperative positive-sum aspects.

In the politics of interdependence, the distinction about what is domestic and what is foreign becomes blurred. For example, the soybean situation mentioned earlier involved the domestic issue of controlling inflation at home, as well as American relations with Japan and Brazil. In the late 1990s, on the other hand, an Asian financial crisis depressed world commodity prices, which helped the American economy continue to grow without encountering inflationary pressures. In 2005, when the American Secretary of the Treasury, John Snow, visited China, he pleaded with the Chinese to increase consumer credit because the United States saw it "as going directly to the thing we have most on our minds—the global imbalances." Chinese leaders replied that the Americans "need to get their own house in order by reducing their fiscal deficits."[8] Were Snow and his Chinese counterparts commenting on domestic or foreign policy?

Or, to take another example, after Iran's 1979 revolution curtailed oil production, the American government urged citizens to cut their energy consumption by driving 55 miles per hour and turning down thermostats. Was that a domestic or a foreign policy issue? Should the United States allow strip mining of coal if the coal is to be exported? Do those who import that coal pay the additional costs that accompany the destruction of the environment in West Virginia? Interdependence thoroughly mixes domestic and foreign issues, which gives rise to much more complex coalitions, more intricate patterns of conflict, and a different distribution of benefits than in the past.

Interdependence also affects domestic politics in a different way. In 1890, a French politician concerned with relative economic gains pursued a policy of holding Germany back. Today a policy of slowing economic growth in Germany is not good for France. Economic interdependence between France and Germany means that the best predictor of whether France is better off economically is when Germany is growing economically. Now with the two countries sharing a common currency, it is in the self-interest of the French politicians that Germany do well economically and vice versa. The classical balance-of-power theory, which predicts that one country will act only to keep the other down lest the other gain preponderance, is not valid. In economic interdependence, states are interested in absolute gains as well as gains relative to other states.

Costs of Interdependence

The costs of interdependence can involve short-run sensitivity or long-term vulnerability. *Sensitivity* refers to the amount and pace of the effects of dependence; that is, how quickly does change in one part of the system bring about change in another part? For example, in 1987, the New York stock market crashed suddenly because of foreigners' anxieties about U.S. interest rates and what might happen to the price of bonds and stocks. It all happened very quickly; the market was extremely sensitive to the withdrawal of foreign funds. In 1998, weakness in emerging markets in Asia had a contagious effect that undercut geographically distant emerging markets in Russia and Brazil.

A high level of sensitivity, however, is not the same as a high level of vulnerability. *Vulnerability* refers to the relative costs of changing the structure of a system of interdependence. It is the cost of escaping from the system or of changing the rules of the game. The less vulnerable of two countries is not necessarily the less sensitive, but rather the one that would incur lower costs from altering the situation. During the 1973 oil crisis, the United States depended on imported energy for only about 16 percent of its total energy uses. On the other hand, in 1973 Japan depended about 95 percent on imported energy. The United States was sensitive to the Arab oil boycott insofar as prices shot up in 1973, but it was not as vulnerable as Japan was. In 1998, the United States was sensitive but not vulnerable to East Asian economic conditions. The financial crisis there cut half a percent off the U.S. growth rate, but with a booming economy the United States could afford it. Indonesia, on the other hand, was both sensitive and vulnerable to changes in global trade and investment patterns. Its economy suffered severely and that in turn led to internal political conflict.

Vulnerability involves degree. When the shah of Iran was overthrown in 1979, Iranian oil production was disrupted at a time when demand was high and markets were already tight. The loss of Iran's oil caused the total amount of oil on the world markets to drop by about 5 percent. Markets were sensitive, and shortages of supply caused a rapid increase in oil prices. But Americans could reduce 5 percent of their energy consumption simply by turning down their thermostats and driving 55 miles per hour. It appears that the United States was sensitive but not very vulnerable if it could avoid damage by such simple actions.

SENSITIVITY INTERDEPENDENCE

. . . The Bank of Japan is under pressure to raise interest rates—for the fourth time since last May—to bolster the sagging yen. Fear of inflation are [sic] also lingering, due to a severe shortage of labor, soaring land prices and rapid growth in the nation's money supply.

The adjustment to higher short-term interest rates in Tokyo last week took place in the American financial markets a few weeks ago, as United States rates bobbed upward and stock prices slid under similar pressures.

"Tokyo's markets rode the Shinkansen to catch up with Amtrak," said Mr. Okumura, referring to Japan's famous bullet train and the well-known American railroad. "Tokyo has only caught up with movements that took place in New York several weeks ago, and now everyone is watching the situation in Germany."

—*The New York Times, February 26, 1990*[9]

Vulnerability, however, depends on more than aggregate measures. It also depends on whether a society is capable of responding quickly to change. For example, the United States was less adept at responding to changes in the oil markets than Japan. Furthermore, private actors, large corporations, and speculators in the market may each look at a market situation and decide to hoard supplies because they think shortages are going to grow worse. Their actions will drive the price even higher because it will make the shortages greater and put more demand on the market. Thus degrees of vulnerability are not quite as simple as they first look.

Vulnerability also depends on whether substitutes are available and whether there are diverse sources of supply. In 1970, Lester Brown of the World Watch Institute expressed alarm about the increasing dependence of the United States, on imported raw materials, and therefore its vulnerability. Of 13 basic industrial raw materials, the United States was dependent on imports for nearly 90 percent of aluminum, chromium, manganese, and nickel. He predicted that by 1985 the United States would be dependent on imports in 10 of the basic 13.[10] He thought this would lead to a dramatic increase in U.S. vulnerability as well as a drastic increase in strength for the less developed countries that produced those raw materials.

But in the 1980s, raw materials prices went down, not up. What happened to his prediction? In judging vulnerability, Brown failed to consider the alternative sources of raw materials and the diversity of sources of supply that prevented producers from jacking up prices artificially. Moreover, technology improves. Yesterday's waste may become a new resource. Companies now mine discarded tailings because new technology has made it possible to extract copper from ore that was considered depleted waste years ago. Today's reduced use of copper is also due to the introduction of fiber-optic cables made from silicon, whose basic origin is sand. Thus projections of U.S. vulnerability to shortages of raw materials were inaccurate because technology and alternatives were not adequately considered.

Some analysts refer to advanced economies today as information-based in the sense that computers, communications, and the Internet are becoming dominant factors in economic growth. Such economies are sometimes called "lightweight" economies because the value of information embedded in products is often far greater than the value of the raw materials involved. Such changes further depreciate the value of raw materials in world politics. One of the few exceptions is oil, which still plays a significant role in most advanced economies, particularly for transportation. This in turn contributes to the strategic significance of the Persian Gulf, where a large portion of the world's currently known oil reserves are located.

Symmetry of Interdependence

Symmetry refers to situations of relatively balanced versus unbalanced dependence. Being less dependent can be a source of power. If two parties are interdependent but one is less dependent than the other, the less dependent party has a source of power as long as both value the interdependent relationship. Manipulating the asymmetries of interdependence can be a source of power in international politics. Analysts who say that interdependence occurs only in situations of equal dependence define

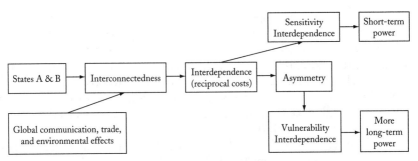

FIGURE 7.1   Chart demonstrating the asymmetric nature of interdependence

away the most interesting political behavior. Such perfect symmetry is quite rare; so are cases of complete imbalance in which one side is totally dependent and the other is not dependent at all. Asymmetry is at the heart of the politics of interdependence (see Figure 7.1).

Asymmetry often varies according to different issues. In the 1980s, when President Reagan cut taxes and raised expenditures, the United States became dependent on imported Japanese capital to balance its federal government budget. Some argued that this gave Japan tremendous power over the United States. But the other side of the coin was that Japan would hurt itself as well as the United States if it stopped lending to the United States. In addition, Japanese investors who already had large stakes in the United States would have found their investments devalued by the damage done to the American economy if Japan suddenly stopped lending to the United States. Japan's economy was a little more than half the size of the American economy, and that meant the Japanese needed the American market for their exports more than vice versa, although both needed each other and both benefited from the interdependence. A similar relationship has developed today between the United States and China. America accepts Chinese imports, and China holds American dollars and bonds, in effect making a loan to the United States. Neither side is in a hurry to break that interdependence.

Moreover, security was often linked to other issues in the U.S.-Japanese relationship. After World War II, Japan followed the policy of a trading state and did not develop a large military capability or gain nuclear weapons. It relied on the American security guarantee to balance the power of the Soviet Union and China in the East Asian region. Thus when a dispute seemed to be developing between the United States and Japan over trade in 1990, the Japanese made concessions to prevent weakening the overall security relationship.

When there is asymmetry of interdependence in different issue areas, a state may try to link or unlink issues. If each issue could be thought of as a separate poker game, and all poker games were played simultaneously, one state might have most of the chips at one table and another state might have most of the chips at another table. Depending on a state's interests and position, it might want to keep the games separate or create linkages between the tables. Therefore, much of the political conflict over interdependence involves the creation or prevention of linkage. States want to manipulate interdependence in areas in which they are strong and avoid being manipulated in areas in which they are relatively weak. Economic sanctions are often an example of such linkage. For example, in 1996 the United States threatened sanctions against foreign companies that invested in Iran, but when faced with European threats of retaliation through other linkages, the United States backed down.

By setting agendas and defining issue areas, international institutions often set the rules for the trade-offs in interdependent relationships. States try to use international institutions to set the rules that affect the transfer of chips among tables. Ironically, international institutions can benefit the weaker players by keeping some of the conflicts in which the poorer states are relatively better endowed separated from the military table, where strong states dominate. The danger remains, however, that some players will be strong enough to overturn one or more of the tables. With separate institutions for money, shipping, pollution, and trade, if the militarily strong players are beaten too badly there is a danger they may try to kick over the other tables. Yet when the United States and Europe were beaten at the oil table in 1973, they did not use their preponderant military force to kick over the oil table because, as we see later, a complex web of linkages held them back.

The largest state does not always win in the manipulation of economic interdependence. If a smaller or weaker state has a greater concern about an issue, it may do quite well. For instance, because the United States accounts for nearly three-quarters of Canada's foreign trade while Canada accounts for about one-quarter of the U.S. foreign trade, Canada is more dependent on the United States than vice versa. Nonetheless, Canada often prevailed in a number of disputes with the United States because Canada was willing to threaten retaliatory actions, such as tariffs and restrictions that deterred the United States. The Canadians would have suffered much more than the United States if their actions had led to a full dispute, but Canada felt it was better to risk occasional retaliation than to agree to rules that would *always* make it lose. Deterrence via manipulation of economic interdependence is somewhat like nuclear deterrence in that it rests on a capability for effective damage and credible intentions. Small states can often use their greater intensity and greater credibility to overcome their relative vulnerability in asymmetrical interdependence.

A natural outgrowth of rising interdependence is the proliferation of trade pacts. The European Union is the most sophisticated of these agreements and requires its member states to forfeit not just some economic sovereignty, but political sovereignty as well. By early 1994, the United States, Mexico, and Canada had ratified the North American Free Trade Agreement (NAFTA). For Mexico and Canada, NAFTA was appealing because it bound their economies more tightly to the larger U.S. economy and, in so doing, increased their access to U.S. markets and their ability to export their products to the United States. For the United States, NAFTA expanded the realm of U.S. exports and made it easier for U.S. companies to do business in Canada and Mexico.

Regional pacts such as NAFTA may increase interdependence and lessen the asymmetry in a relationship. By agreeing to intertwine its economy with that of

Mexico, the United States assumed some of the liabilities of the Mexican economy along with the benefits of easier access. When the value of the Mexican peso plummeted in 1994, the Clinton administration rushed in early 1995 to shore up the flagging currency and assembled a multibillion-dollar aid package. At a time when the U.S. Congress was deadlocked over increased domestic spending for services such as health care, the administration saw little choice but to rescue the peso. With greater interdependence, even strong countries can find themselves sensitive to economic developments beyond their borders. In 1997, when Southeast Asia suffered its financial crisis, the United States was less vulnerable than in the Mexican case and responded primarily through multilateral institutions. Nevertheless, fears of an economic domino effect in which collapse of some developing economies would undermine confidence in others meant that the United States and other advanced economies could not continue to stand idly by.

Leadership and Institutions in the World Economy

By and large, the rules of the international economy reflect the policies of the largest states (Figure 7.2). In the nineteenth century, Great Britain was the strongest of the major world economies. In the monetary area, the Bank of England adhered to the gold standard, which set a stable framework for world money. Britain also enforced freedom of the seas for navigation and commerce, and provided a large open market for world trade until 1932. After World War I, Britain was severely weakened by its fight against the Kaiser's Germany. The United States became the world's largest economy, but it turned away from international affairs in the 1930s. The largest player in the world economy behaved as if it could still take a free ride rather than provide the leadership its size implied. Some economists believe that the Great Depression of the 1930s was aggravated by bad monetary policy and lack of American leadership. Britain was too weak to maintain an open international economy, and the United States was not living up to its new responsibilities.

After World War II, the lessons of the 1930s were on the minds of American leaders, and in 1944 an international conference at Bretton Woods, New Hampshire, established institutions to maintain an open, international economy. The International Monetary Fund (IMF) lends money, usually to developing countries and new market economies, to help when they have difficulties with their balance of payments or with paying interest on their debts. The IMF generally conditions its loans on the recipient country reforming its economic policies, for example reducing budget deficits and price subsidies. While its policies are sometimes controversial and not always effective, the IMF played a role in helping the Russian economy in the early 1990s as well as in the Asian financial crisis later in the decade. The International Bank for Reconstruction and Development (the World Bank) lends money to poorer countries and new market economies for development projects. (There are also regional development banks for Asia, Latin America, Africa, and Eastern Europe.)

The General Agreement on Tariffs and Trade (GATT), later transformed into the World Trade Organization (WTO), established rules for liberal trade and has served as

MAJOR INTERNATIONAL ECONOMIC INSTITUTIONS

International Monetary Fund (IMF) (Source: IMF)

Location: Washington, DC
Founded: 1945, as a result of the International Monetary and Financial Conference held at Bretton Woods, NH, in 1944
Members: 184 countries
Staff: Approx. 2,680 from 139 countries
Budget: $312 billion USD (sustained by member payments based on a quota system)

Organizational Structure:
- Board of Governors, with one representative from each member, which meets annually
- International Monetary and Finance Committee, consisting of 24 members, which meets twice a year
- Executive Board, consisting of 24 members, which carries out daily business of the IMF

System of Voting: Majority—Weighted based on size of membership quota (payment)
Primary Goals:
- Promoting international monetary cooperation
- Facilitating the expansion and balanced growth of international trade
- Promoting exchange stability
- Assisting in the establishment of a multilateral system of payments
- Making its resources available (under adequate safeguards) to members experiencing balance-of-payments difficulties

The World Bank (Source: The World Bank)

Location: Washington, DC
Founded: 1945, as a result of the International Monetary and Financial Conference held at Bretton Woods, NH, in 1944
Members: 184 countries
Staff: Approx. 10,000 employees stationed around the world
Budget: $14 billion USD in trust funds and contributions (sustained by member contributions and investments); disbursed roughly $22 billion in loans (2004)

Organizational Structure:
- Board of Governors, with one representative from each member, which meets annually
- President from the largest shareholder (the United States) elected to a renewable five-year term and responsible for overseeing the Board of Directors
- Board of Directors consisting of 24 members who meet twice weekly
- Executive Directors carry out daily operations and decision making

System of Voting: Majority—Weighted based on size of each member's economy

Subagencies:
- International Bank for Reconstruction and Development
- International Development Association
- International Finance Corporation
- Multilateral Investment Guarantee Agency
- International Center for the Settlement of Investment Disputes

Primary Goals:
- Reducing poverty through efforts to promote economic growth and employment
- Debt relief for developing and least developed countries
- Improving the quality of governance and capacity of governing institutions
- Reducing the spread of diseases, including HIV/AIDS and malaria
- Increasing child access to primary education
- Reducing environmental degradation

FIGURE 7.2   Chart providing overview of various major international economic institutions

<u>**The World Trade Organization (WTO)**</u> (Source: The WTO)

Location: Geneva, Switzerland
Founded: 1995, as a result of the Uruguay Round of multilateral trade negotiations
                (formerly known as Generalized Agreement on Tariffs and Trade [GATT]
                which entered force in 1948)
Members: 149 countries
Staff: 630 (Secretariat Staff)
Budget: 168 million Swiss francs ($129 million USD) (sustained by member pay-
                ments apportioned based on individual member total share of world trade)

Organizational Structure:
- General Council, with one representative from each member, which convenes
  several times a year to negotiate agreements; also convenes as the Dispute
  Settlement Body and Trade Policy Review Body
- Appellate Body, consisting of seven permanent members who hear disputes referred
  to it by the Dispute Settlement Body (i.e. General Council)
- Secretariat, led by a Secretary, which has no formal decision-making powers
  and thus works to facilitate the daily business of the General Council and
  various subcommittees

System of Voting: Consensus based—One member, one vote

Primary Goals:
- Administering WTO trade agreements
- Providing a forum for multilateral trade negotiations
- Handling trade disputes
- Monitoring national trade policies
- Providing technical assistance and training to developing countries
- Cooperating with other international development organizations

<u>**Organization for Economic Cooperation and Development (OECD)**</u> (Source: The
OECD)

Location: Paris, France
Founded: 1960, as an economic counterpart to NATO; was preceded by the
                Organization for European Economic Cooperation founded after
                World War II to coordinate the Marshall Plan
Members: 30 countries (mostly developed nations)
Staff: 2,000 (Secretariat Staff)
Budget: 330 million euros ($400 million USD) (generated by members payments
                based on the size of each member's economy)

Organizational Structure:
- Council, with one representative from each member, which provides guidance
  regarding OECD activities and establishes the group's annual budget
- Secretary General, who oversees the Council and the Secretariat, which is responsible
  for the group's daily operations

System of Voting: Consensus based

Primary Goals:
- Promoting good governance
- Conducting economic surveys and offering economic policy recommendations
- Promoting economic development
- Providing a forum for multilateral discussion of economic, development, social, and
  governance challenges related to globalization

FIGURE 7.2   *Continued*

the locus for a series of rounds of multilateral negotiations that have lowered trade barriers. The Organization for Economic Cooperation and Development (OECD) serves as a forum for thirty of the most developed countries to coordinate their international economic policies. Since the mid-1970s, the leaders of the seven largest economies, which account for two-thirds of world production, have met at annual summit conferences (expanded in the 1990s to include Russia) to discuss conditions of the world economy. These institutions helped reinforce government policies that allow rapid growth of private transnational interactions. The period has seen a rapid increase in economic interdependence. In most of the period after 1945, trade grew between 3 and 9 percent per year, faster even than the growth of the world product. International trade, which represented 10 percent of the U.S. GDP in 1960, more than doubled to 22 percent of the U.S. GDP by the 1990s and was roughly 25 percent of GDP in 2004. Large multinational corporations with global strategies became more significant as international investments increased by nearly 10 percent per year.

Critics have argued that the major international economic institutions are biased in favor of rich rather than poor countries. The IMF and World Bank, for example, have weighted voting that gives a preponderant influence to the United States, Europe, and Japan. The Fund has always been directed by a European and the Bank by an American. The United States is able to run fiscal and trade deficits with only the mildest of criticism, but when poor countries incur similar debts, IMF bureaucrats insist on a return to market discipline as a condition for help. One reason is that the poor countries often need the IMF's help to borrow money, but the United States can borrow without the IMF. In other words, the institutions reflect the underlying power of the asymmetrical interdependence of financial markets. Abolishing the IMF would not change that underlying power reality in financial markets. If anything, leaving matters to private bankers and fund managers might make it even more difficult for poor countries to borrow.

The World Trade Organization does not have weighted voting. It provides a forum in which 149 countries can negotiate trade agreements on a nondiscriminatory basis, as well as panels and rules to help arbitrate their trade disputes. Critics argue that the agreements countries negotiate within its framework (such as the current Doha "development round" of multilateral trade talks) have allowed rich countries to protect areas such as agriculture and textiles from developing-country competition and thus are unfair to the poor. The critics' descriptions are correct, and the protectionist policies hurt poor countries. But the causes of such protectionism lie in the domestic politics of the rich countries, and might be even greater if the WTO did not play a role. Again, international institutions can alleviate but not remove the underlying power realities. If anything, the fact that the United States and Europe have abided by costly decisions made against them by WTO panels suggests that institutions can make a difference, even if at the margin.

Even among the rich and powerful countries, there are problems in managing a transnational economy in a world of separate states. In the 1980s and again after 2001, the United States became a net debtor when it refused to tax itself to pay its bills at home and instead borrowed money from abroad. Some analysts believed this was setting the scene for a repeat of the 1930s, that the United States would experience decline as Britain had. But the United States did not decline and turn inward, and other countries continued to be willing to lend it money because they had confidence in its economy and it suited their interests. China, for example, continues to hold large reserves in dollars as a means to facilitate its exports to the United States.

Financial volatility, however, remains a potential problem. In 1999 most members of the European Union created a European monetary unit with a single currency, the euro, which some think may come to rival the dollar as another world reserve currency. In addition, global financial markets have grown dramatically in recent years, and their volatility poses risks to stability. Much will depend on the willingness of their governments to pursue policies that maintain stability in the international economic system. In any case, the global political and economic system is more complicated and complex than before. More sectors, more states, more issues, and more private actors are involved in the complexity of interdependent relationships. It is increasingly unrealistic to analyze world politics as occurring solely among a group of large states, solid as billiard balls, bouncing off each other in a balance of power.

Realism and Complex Interdependence

What would the world look like if three key assumptions of realism were reversed? These assumptions are that states are the only significant actors, military force is the dominant instrument, and security is the dominant goal. Reversed, we can postulate a very different world politics: (1) States are not the only significant actors—transnational actors working across state boundaries are also major players; (2) force is not the only significant instrument—economic manipulation and the use of international institutions are the dominant instruments; and (3) security is not the dominant goal—welfare is the dominant goal. We can label this antirealist world *complex interdependence*. Social scientists call complex interdependence an "ideal type." It is an imaginary concept that does not exist in the real world, but as we have seen, neither does realism perfectly fit the real world. Complex interdependence is a thought experiment that allows us to imagine a different type of world politics.

Both realism and complex interdependence are simple models or ideal types. The real world lies somewhere between the two. We can ask where certain country relationships fit on a spectrum between realism and complex interdependence. The Middle East is closer to the realist end of the spectrum, but relations between the United States and Canada and relations between France and Germany today come much closer to the complex interdependence end of the spectrum. Different politics and different forms of the power struggle occur depending on where on the spectrum a particular relationship between a set of countries is located. In fact, countries can change their position on the spectrum. During the Cold War, the U.S.-Soviet relationship was clearly near the realist end of the spectrum, but with end of the Cold War the Russia-U.S. relationship moved closer to the center between realism and complex interdependence (see Figure 7.3).

A prime example of the interaction in the real world between complex interdependence and realism is the U.S. relationship with China (Figure 7.3). As with

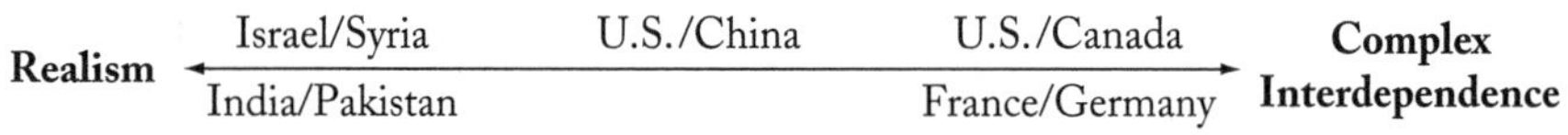

Realism	Israel/Syria	U.S./China	U.S./Canada	**Complex**
	India/Pakistan		France/Germany	**Interdependence**

FIGURE 7.3   Chart showing spectrum from realism to complex interdependence

Japan, U.S. imports from China far outstrip U.S. exports. The result is a significant trade deficit. While the bilateral trade relationship between the United States and China is asymmetrical in China's favor, the United States is not particularly vulnerable to potential Chinese trade embargoes because it could compensate for the potential loss of Chinese goods by purchasing them elsewhere, and China has strong domestic incentives to export to the United States. On the other hand, the potential size of the Chinese market for American goods and the domestic demand for Chinese goods in the United States mean that the ability of the U.S. government to act against China is somewhat constrained by transnational actors, including U.S. multinational corporations that have pressured the U.S. government not to implement sanctions against China for unfair trade practices and human rights violations. At the same time, the rapid growth of China's economic and military strength had a strong effect on the perceptions of the balance of power in East Asia, and contributed to the reinvigoration of the U.S.-Japan security alliance starting in 1995.

Before the 2003 Iraq War, columnist Robert Kagan argued that many European countries were less willing to confront dangerous dictators like Saddam Hussein because they had become accustomed to the peaceful conditions of complex interdependence that prevailed inside Europe and tended to generalize them to the realist world outside Europe, where they were less appropriate. In his words, "Americans were from Mars, and Europeans were from Venus." Of course this clever phrase was too simple (witness the role of Britain in the Iraq War), but it captured different perceptions across the Atlantic. It also illuminated a larger point. In their relations with each other, all advanced democracies form Kantian islands of peace in the sea of Hobbesian realism. In its relations with Canada, Europe, and Japan, even the United States is from Venus. It is equally mistaken to pretend that the whole world is typified by Hobbesian realism or by Kantian complex interdependence.

THE POLITICS OF OIL

As mentioned earlier, oil is the most important raw material in the world, in both economic and political terms, and it is likely to remain the key source of energy well into this century. The United States consumes a quarter of the world's oil (compared to 8 percent for China, though Chinese consumption is growing rapidly.) Even with high Chinese growth, the world is not running out of oil anytime soon. More than a trillion barrels of reserves have been proven, and more is likely to be found. But two-thirds of the proven reserves are in the Persian Gulf and are therefore vulnerable to political disruption, which could have devastating effects on the world economy. Oil was not the primary cause of the two Gulf wars in the simple sense of seizing and owning it, but the strong positive relationship between the stability of Middle East oil supplies and global economic stability was a major consideration of policy makers when they debated policy toward Iraq. As one wag put it, if the gulf produced broccoli instead of oil, the wars might not have occurred. Thus oil not only is important in itself, but is also an issue that illustrates aspects of both realism and complex interdependence.

Interdependence in a given area often occurs within a framework of rules, norms, and institutions that are called a *regime*. The international oil regime has changed dramatically over the decades. In 1960, the oil regime was a private oligopoly with close ties to the governments of the major consuming countries. Oil at that time sold for about $2 a barrel, and seven large transnational oil companies, sometimes called the "seven sisters," determined the amount of oil that would be produced. The price of oil depended on how much the large companies produced and on the demand in the rich countries where most of the oil was sold. Transnational companies set the rate of production, and prices were determined by conditions in rich countries. The strongest powers in the international system in traditional military terms occasionally intervened to keep the system going. For example, in 1953, when a nationalist movement tried to overthrow the Shah of Iran, Britain and the United States covertly intervened to return the Shah to his throne. The oil regime was then largely unchanged.

As mentioned earlier, after 1973 there was a major change in the international regime governing oil. The producing countries set the rate of production and therefore had a strong effect on price, rather than price being determined solely by the market in the rich countries. There was an enormous shift of power and wealth from rich to relatively poor countries. Confidential documents released in 2004 showed that in response to the Arab oil embargo of 1973, the United States had considered the use of force to seize Persian Gulf oil fields, as realist theory might have predicted. But it did not do so, and the regime changed in favor of the weaker countries. How could such a dramatic change be explained?

A frequently offered explanation is that the oil-producing countries banded together and formed the Organization of Petroleum Exporting Countries (OPEC). The trouble with this explanation is that OPEC was formed in 1960 and the dramatic change did not occur until 1973. Oil prices fell despite OPEC, so there is more to the story. There are three ways to explain these changes in the international oil regime: the overall balance of power, the balance of power in the oil issue, and international institutions.

Realists look at changes in the balance of power resting primarily on military force, particularly with regard to the Persian Gulf, the major oil-exporting region of the world. Two changes affected that balance: the rise of nationalism and decolonization. In 1960, half the OPEC countries were colonies of Europe; by 1973, they were all independent. Accompanying the rise in nationalism was a rise in the costs of military intervention. It is much more expensive to use force against a nationalistically awakened and decolonized people. When the British and Americans intervened in Iran in 1953, it was not very costly, but if the Americans had tried to keep the Shah on his throne in 1979, the costs would have been prohibitive.

Relative changes in U.S. and British power also affected the balance of power in the Persian Gulf. When OPEC was formed and earlier, Britain was to a large extent the policeman of the Persian Gulf. In 1961, it prevented an earlier Iraqi effort to annex Kuwait. But by 1971 Britain was economically weakened, and the British government was trying to cut back on its international defense commitments. In 1971, Britain ended what used to be called its role "east of Suez." That may sound a bit like 1947, when Britain was unable to maintain its role as a power in the eastern Mediterranean. At that time, the United States stepped in to help Greece and Turkey, and formulated the Truman Doctrine. But in 1971, the United States was not well placed to step in to replace Britain as it did in 1947. The United States was deeply embroiled in Vietnam and unwilling to accept an additional major military commitment in the Persian Gulf. As a result, President Nixon and then National Security Adviser Kissinger designed an American strategy that relied heavily on regional powers. Their chosen instrument was Iran. By using Iran as the regional hegemon, they thought they could replace the departing British policeman cheaply. A realist would point to these changes in the overall structure of power, particularly the balance of power in the Persian Gulf region, to explain the change in the oil regime.

A second way of explaining the change is a modified form of realism that focuses on the relative market power of various nations. Between 1950 and 1973 serious changes occurred in global oil consumption that altered U.S. dependence on foreign oil. Specifically, the United States, until 1971, was the largest oil producer in the world. But American production peaked in 1971; American imports began to grow thereafter and the United States no longer had any surplus oil. During the two Middle East wars of 1956 and 1967, the Arab countries tried an oil embargo, but their efforts were easily defeated because the United States was producing enough oil to supply Europe when it was cut off by the Arab countries. Once American production peaked in 1971 and the United States began to import oil, the power to balance the oil market switched to countries like Saudi Arabia and Iran. No longer was the United States the supplier of last resort that could make up any missing oil.

A third way to explain the difference in the oil regime after 1973 relies less on realism than on changes in the role of international institutions, particularly the multinational corporations and OPEC. The "seven sisters" gradually lost power over this period. One reason was their *obsolescing bargains* with the producer countries. When a multinational corporation goes into a resource-rich country with a new investment, it can strike a bargain in which the multinational gets a large part of the joint gains. From the point of view of the poor country, having a multinational come in to develop its resources will make it better off. Even if it gets only 20 percent of the revenues and the multinational gets 80 percent, the poor country has more than it had before. So at the early stages when multinationals have a monopoly on capital, technology, and access to international markets, they strike a bargain with the poor countries in which the multinationals get the lion's share. But over time, the multinationals inadvertently transfer resources to the poor countries, not out of charity but in the normal course of business. They train locals. The Saudis, Kuwaitis, and others learn how to run oil fields, pumping stations, and loading docks. Locals develop expertise in marketing and so forth.

Eventually the poor countries want a better division of the profits. The multi-national could threaten to pull out, but now the poor country can threaten to run the operation by itself. So over time, the power of the multinational company, particularly in raw materials, diminishes in terms of its bargaining with the host country. That is the "obsolescing bargain." From the 1960s to 1973, the multinationals inadvertently transferred technology and skills that developed the poor countries' capacity to run oil operations themselves.

There were other developments. The seven sisters were joined by "little cousins" when new transnational corporations entered the oil market. Although they were not as large as the seven sisters, they were still big, and they began to strike their own deals with the oil-producing countries. Thus when an oil-producing country wanted to get out of the hands of the seven sisters, it could strike a deal with smaller independent multinationals. That again reduced the bargaining power of the largest multinationals.

Institutionally, there was a modest increase in the effectiveness of OPEC as a cartel. Cartels restricting supply had long been typical in the oil industry, but in the past they had been private arrangements of the seven sisters. Cartels generally have a problem because there is a tendency to cheat on production quotas when markets are soft and the price drops. Cartels work best when there is a shortage of oil, but when there is a surplus, people want to sell their oil and tend to cut the price in order to get a bigger share of the market. With time, market forces tend to erode cartels. OPEC represented an effort to shift from a private to a governmental cartel of the oil-producing countries. In its early years, OPEC had trouble exercising power because there was plenty of oil. As long as oil was in surplus, the OPEC countries had incentives to cheat to get a larger share of the market. OPEC was unable to enforce price discipline from the year it was founded, 1960, until the early 1970s. But after oil supplies tightened, OPEC's role in coordinating the bargaining power of the producers increased.

The Middle East War of 1973 gave OPEC a boost, a signal that now it could use its power. The Arab countries cut off access to oil during the 1973 war for political reasons, but that created a situation in which OPEC could become effective. Iran, which is not an Arab country, was allegedly the American instrument for policing the Persian Gulf, but the Shah of Iran moved to quadruple oil prices and the other OPEC countries followed suit. Over the long term, OPEC could not maintain permanently high prices because of market forces, but there was a stickiness on the downside that was an effect of the OPEC coalition.

A more important institutional factor was the role the oil companies played in "smoothing the pain" in the crisis itself. At one point in the crisis, Henry Kissinger, by now secretary of state, said that if the United States faced "strangulation," force might have to be used. Fifteen percent of traded oil was cut, and the Arab embargo reduced oil exports to the United States by 25 percent. However, oil companies made sure that no one country suffered much more than any other. They redistributed the world's traded oil. When the United States lost 25 percent of its Arab oil imports, the companies shipped it more Venezuelan or Indonesian oil. They smoothed the pain of the embargo so the rich countries all lost about 7–9 percent of their oil, well below the strangulation point. They helped prevent the economic conflict from becoming a military conflict.

Why did they do this? It was not out of charity. Transnational companies are long-run profit maximizers; that is, they want to maximize their profit in the long term. To do so, they want stability and market access. The multinational companies feared situations in which they would be nationalized in a country if they refused to sell to that country. For example, Prime Minister Edward Heath of Britain demanded that the head of British Petroleum sell only to Britain and not to other countries. The head of British Petroleum replied that if he followed such an order, the company would be nationalized by those other countries, which would destroy British Petroleum. The British prime minister backed down. Essentially, because the oil companies were long-run profit maximizers, they tried to stabilize the market rather than have the pain strike any one country strongly. By reducing the threat of strangulation, they reduced the probability that force would be used.

In short, oil is an illustration of an issue that falls between the ideal types of realism and complex interdependence. Changes in three dimensions—the overall balance of power, the issue structure of power, and the institutions within the oil issue area—help explain the dramatic difference between the oil regime of 1960 and the oil regime after 1973.

Oil as a Power Resource

How powerful was the oil weapon at the turning point of 1973? By cutting production and embargoing sales to countries friendly to Israel, Arab states were able to bring their issues to the forefront of the U.S. agenda. They also created temporary disarray in the alliances between Japan, Europe, and the United States. In order to protect their oil supplies, France and Japan took independent positions. The oil weapon encouraged the United States to play a more conciliatory role in arranging the settlement of the Arab-Israeli dispute in the aftermath of the Yom Kippur War. On the other hand, the oil weapon did not change the basic policy of the United States in the Middle East. The Americans did not suddenly switch from their alliance with Israel to support of the Arab cause. Oil was a power resource that had an effect, but not a strong enough effect to reverse American policy.

Why was the oil weapon not more effective? Part of the answer is reciprocity in interdependence. Saudi Arabia, which became the key country in oil markets, had large investments in the United States. If the Saudis damaged the U.S. economy too much, they would also hurt their own economic interests. In addition, Saudi Arabia depended on the United States in the security area. In the long run, the United States was the only country able to keep a stable balance of power in the Persian Gulf region. The Saudis knew this and they were careful about how far they pushed the oil weapon.

What was the role of force as a power resource in the oil crisis of 1973? There was no overt use of force. There was no military intervention because strangulation never occurred. Moreover, the Saudis were benefiting from the long-run security guarantee provided by the United States. Thus force played a background role.

There was an indirect linkage between the security interdependence and the oil interdependence. Force was too costly to use overtly, but it played a role as a power resource in the background.

This complex set of factors persists. Oil remains an exception among raw materials, and this contributed in part to the two Gulf Wars and to the continuing strong U.S. naval presence in the Persian Gulf. But oil prices are sensitive to global market forces and multinationals' exploration for new supplies in Central Asia and other regions has increased supply. Prices at the end of the century had returned to historical lows before the 1973 crisis.

The nightmare oil scenarios predicted during the 1970s failed to materialize. The U.S. Department of Energy, for instance, forecast that oil would cost more than $100 a barrel by 2000.[11] A number of factors helped keep these predictions from coming true. On the demand side, policy measures and price increases led to more efficient use of energy. For example, the Corporate Average Fuel Efficiency law in the United States mandated that automakers manufacture cars that achieved minimum standards for gas mileage. This is an example of a domestic policy that had a clear intended effect on foreign policy. (In addition, cost-conscious drivers who had felt the pinch of high gasoline prices also contributed to this effect.)

On the supply side, the emergence of non-OPEC oil sources that were unavailable during the Cold War meant that OPEC faced more competition on the world market. By the late 1990s Russia became a major oil supplier to the West. The Caspian Sea reserves also offered another promising outlet outside OPEC's control. Advances in technology led geologists to gain access to oil that had previously been impossible to reach, exposing the limitations of the projections that were made in the 1970s about global reserves.

But in 2005, oil prices spiked again, partly in response to disruptions from war and hurricanes, but also because of projections of rising demand. Two growing giants will influence the future of energy markets: China and India. As the two most populous nations on earth, both are experiencing rapid increases in demand for energy as they modernize and industrialize. Both countries are making mercantilist efforts to buy and control foreign oil supplies, though the lessons of the 1970s crisis should teach them that oil markets tend to spread supplies and even out the pain no matter who owns the oil. China also has vast coal reserves as well as natural gas in its western Xinjiang province, but it will increasingly rely on imports to meet its growing needs. Both countries also face serious environmental challenges from their use of fossil fuels that may have global implications in terms of air pollution, and climate change. In any event, their rapid economic growth will contribute significantly to the global demand for oil.

The United States will also likely continue to rely on imported oil to meet its energy needs, and this means that the biggest global oil-producing regions, such as the Persian Gulf, will still play a key role in geopolitics. Despite new sources such as Russia, experts anticipate that Saudi Arabia and its neighbors will meet two-thirds of the increased global oil demand that takes place between now and 2030.[12] Because Saudi Arabia is the world's number one producer, any major changes in its political system could have dramatic consequences.

Prices could rise suddenly for rich and poor countries alike if conflicts disrupt supplies from the Persian Gulf. The drama regarding oil is not over. While raw materials are less crucial in information age economies than in the industrial age, oil still matters. And while growing global networks of economic interdependence produce joint gains, they can also create political problems. Power politics just becomes more complex in an era of economic globalization.

STUDY QUESTIONS

1. What are the major types of globalization? Is globalization an irreversible process? How is contemporary globalization different from past periods of globalization?

2. What are the implications of globalization in the cultural realm? Does globalization necessarily result in global cultural homogenization? More specifically, will globalization ultimately lead to universal "Americanization"?

3. What kinds of political responses has globalization sparked? What is the relationship between antiglobalization sentiment and economic inequality in the international sphere?

4. What is complex interdependence? Is it a descriptive model? Where do we find complex interdependence most developed today?

5. What makes economic interdependence a source of power? How do sensitivity and vulnerability differ?

6. What were the underlying and immediate causes of the 1973 oil crisis? Why didn't it occur earlier—say, in 1967? Was it a unique event or the beginning of a revolution in international politics? Why was force not used? Could it be used today?

7. Liberal theory was optimistic that increasing international commerce would seriously decrease the attractiveness of military force as a tool in international politics. What does the international oil regime indicate, to either support or falsify this thesis?

8. Under classical realist assumptions, we would not expect to see cooperation among states under conditions of anarchy. How can you explain the degree of cooperation achieved by states in international economic relations? Do institutions play a role?

NOTES

1. Dani Rodrik, *Has Globalization Gone Too Far?* (Washington, DC: Institute for International Economics, 1997), p. 2.

2. James J. McCarthy, "The Scope of the IPCC Third Assessment Report," *Climate Report* (Winter 2001), p. 3.

3. Thomas Friedman, *The Lexus and the Olive Tree: Understanding Globalization* (New York: Farrar, Straus & Giroux, 1999), pp. 7–8.

4. Joseph Stiglitz, "Weightless Concerns," *Financial Times* (London), February 3, 1999, p. 14.

5. John Maynard Keynes, *The Economic Consequences of the Peace* (New York: Penguin, 1988), p. 11.

6. Robert Wade, "Winners and Losers" and "Of Rich and Poor," *The Economist*, April 28, 2001, pp. 72–74, 80.

7. "North-South Divide Is Marring Environmental Talks," *The New York Times*, March 17, 1992, p. 8.

8. Edmund Andrews, "Snow Urges Consumerism on China Trip," *The New York Times*, October 14, 2005, p. 1.

9. "German Shift Felt in Japan," *The New York Times*, February 26, 1990, p. D1.

10. Lester Brown, *World Without Borders* (New York: Random, 1972), p. 194.

11. "Still Holding Customers Over a Barrel," *The Economist*, October 25, 2003, pp. 61–63.

12. Ibid.

SELECTED READINGS

1. Keohane, Robert O., and Joseph S. Nye, Jr., *Power and Interdependence,* 2nd ed. (Glenview, IL: Scott Foresman, 1989), chaps. 1–3.

2. David Held et al., *Global Transformations: Politics, Economics and Culture* (Stanford, CA: Stanford University Press, 1999), chaps. 1–3.

3. Thomas Friedman, *The World Is Flat: A Brief History of the Twenty-First Century* (New York: Farrar, Straus & Giroux, 2005), chaps. 1, 11–13.

4. Joseph S. Nye, Jr., and John D. Donahue, eds., *Governance in a Globalizing World* (Washington, DC: Brookings Institution, 2000), chaps. 1–2.

FURTHER READINGS

Adler, Emmanuel, and Peter Haas, "Epistemic Communities, World Order, and the Creation of a Reflective Program," *International Organization* 46:1 (1992), pp. 367–390.

Baldwin, David A., *Economic Statecraft* (Princeton, NJ: Princeton University Press, 1985).

Bhagwati, Jagdish, *In Defense of Globalization* (New York: Oxford University Press, 2004).

Cairncross, Frances, *The Death of Distance: How the Communications Revolution Will Change Our Lives* (Boston: Harvard Business School Press, 1997).

Castaneda, Jorge, "Can NAFTA Change Mexico?" *Foreign Affairs* 72:4 (October 1993), pp. 66–80.

Coglianese, Cary, "Globalization and the Design of International Institutions," in Joseph S. Nye, Jr., and John D. Donahue, eds., *Governance in a Globalizing World* (Washington DC: Brookings Institution, 2000).

Cohen, Benjamin J., *The Question of Imperialism: The Political Economy of Dominance and Dependence* (New York: Basic, 1973).

Diamond, Jared, *Guns, Germs and Steel: The Fates of Human Societies* (New York: Norton, 1998).

Falk, Richard, and Andrew Strauss, "Toward Global Parliament," *Foreign Affairs* 80:1 (January/February 2001).

Florida, Richard, "The World Is Spiky," *Atlantic Monthly* (October 2005), pp. 48–51.

Foreign Affairs Editors' Choice, *Globalization: Challenge and Opportunity* (New York: Council on Foreign Relations, 2002).

Galtung, Johan, "A Structural Theory of Imperialism," *Journal of Peace Research* 18:2 (1971), pp. 81–118.

Giddens, Anthony, *Runaway World: How Globalization Is Reshaping Our Lives* (New York: Routledge, 2000).

Gilpin, Robert, *The Political Economy of International Relations* (Princeton, NJ: Princeton University Press, 1987).

Grieco, Joseph, "Anarchy and the Limits of Cooperation," *International Organization* 42:2 (Summer 1988), pp. 485–508.

Haggard, Stephan, *Pathways from the Periphery* (Ithaca, NY: Cornell University Press, 1990).

Held, David, ed., *Debating Globalization* (Cambridge, UK: Polity, 2005)

Held, David, and Anthony G. McGrew, *Governing Globalization: Power, Authority, and Global Governance* (Cambridge, UK: Polity, 2002).

Hufbauer, Gary C., Jeffrey J. Schott, and Kimberly A. Elliott, *Sanctions Reconsidered*, 2nd ed. (Washington, DC: Institute for International Economics, 1990).

Inkeles, Alex, *One World Emerging? Convergence and Divergence in Industrial Societies* (Boulder, CO: Westview, 1998).

Jervis, Robert, *System Effects: Complexity in Political and Social Life* (Princeton, NJ: Princeton University Press, 1997).

Joy, Bill, et al., "Why the Future Doesn't Need Us," *Wired*, April 2000.

Kahler, Miles, and David Lake, eds., *Governance in a Global Economy: Political Authority in Transition* (Princeton, NJ: Princeton University Press, 2003).

Kapur, Devesh, "The IMF: A Cure of a Curse?" *Foreign Policy* no. 111 (Summer 1998), pp. 114–129.

Keohane, Robert O., *After Hegemony* (Princeton, NJ: Princeton University Press, 1984).

Kindleberger, Charles P., *The World in Depression, 1929–1939* (Berkeley: University of California Press, 1973).

Krasner, Stephen D., ed., *International Regimes* (Ithaca, NY: Cornell University Press, 1983).

Krugman, Paul, *Pop Internationalism* (Cambridge, MA: MIT Press, 1996).

LaFeber, Walter, *Michael Jordan and the New Global Capitalism* (New York: Norton, 1999).

Lake, David A., "Leadership, Hegemony, and the International Economy," *International Studies Quarterly* 37:4 (Winter 1993–1994), pp. 459–490.

Llosa, Mario Vargas, "Globalization at Work: The Culture of Liberty," *Foreign Policy* (January/February 2001).

Longworth, Richard, "Government Without Democracy," *American Prospect* (Summer 2001).

Mallaby, Sebastian, *The World's Banker: A Story of Failed States, Financial Crises, and the Wealth and Poverty of Nations* (New York: Penguin, 2004).

Narlikar, Amrita, *The World Trade Organization: A Very Short Introduction* (Oxford: Oxford University Press, 2005).

Polanyi, Karl, *The Great Transformation* (New York: Rinehart, 1944).

Reich, Robert B., *The Work of Nations: Preparing Ourselves for 21st-Century Capitalism* (New York: Knopf, 1991).

Rodrik, Dani, *Has Globalization Gone Too Far?* (Washington, DC: Institute for International Economics, 1997).

———, "Sense and Nonsense in the Globalization Debate," *Foreign Policy* (Summer 1997), pp. 19–37.

Sassen, Saskia, *Losing Control? Sovereignty in an Age of Globalization* (New York: Columbia University Press, 1996).

Scholte, Jan Aart, *Globalization: A Critical Introduction* (New York: St. Martin's, 2000).

Stiglitz, Joseph, *Globalization and Its Discontents* (New York: Norton, 2002).

Strange, Susan, *The Retreat of the State: The Diffusion of Power in the World Economy* (New York: Cambridge University Press, 1996).

Thompson, Dennis, "Democratic Theory and Global Society," *Journal of Political Philosophy* (June 1999).

Védrine, Hubert, and Dominique Moisi, *France in an Age of Globalization* (Washington, DC: Brookings Institution, 2001).

Vernon, Raymond, *Sovereignty at Bay: The Multinational Spread of U.S. Enterprises* (New York: Basic, 1971).

Yergin, Daniel, *The Prize: The Epic Quest for Oil, Money, and Power* (New York: Simon & Schuster, 1991).

Yergin, Daniel, and Joseph Stanislaus, *The Commanding Heights: How the Battle Between Government and the Marketplace Is Remaking the Modern World* (New York: Simon & Schuster, 1998).

The Information Revolution, Transnational Actors, and the Diffusion of Power

Space Telescope

POWER AND THE INFORMATION REVOLUTION

An information revolution is currently transforming world politics. Four centuries ago, the English statesman-philosopher Francis Bacon wrote that knowledge is power. At the start of the twenty-first century, a much larger part of the population both within and among countries has access to this power. Governments have always worried about the flow and control of information, and the current period is not the first to be strongly affected by changes in information technology. In the fifteenth century, Johann Gutenberg's (1398–1468) invention of movable type, which allowed printing of the Bible and its accessibility to large portions of the European population, is often credited with playing a major role in the onset of the Reformation. Pamphlets and committees of correspondence paved the way for the American Revolution. As constructivists point out, rapid changes in information flows can lead to important changes in identities and interests.

The current information revolution is based on rapid technological advances in computers, communications, and software that in turn have led to dramatic decreases in the cost of processing and transmitting information. Computing power doubled every 18 months for 30 years, and by the beginning of the twenty-first century it cost one-thousandth of what it did in the early 1970s. If the price of automobiles had fallen as quickly as the price of semiconductors, a car today would cost five dollars.

In 1993, there were about 50 websites in the world; by the end of the decade, that number had surpassed 5 million. Between 2000 and 2005, global Internet usage grew by 170 percent, with Africa and the Middle East experiencing the largest gains. Communications bandwidths are expanding rapidly, and communications costs continue to fall even more rapidly than computing power. As late as 1980, phone calls over copper wire could carry only one page of information per second; today a thin strand of optical fiber can transmit 90,000 *volumes* in a second. In terms of current dollars, the cost of a brief transatlantic phone call had fallen from $250 in 1930 to considerably less than a dollar at the beginning of the new century. Now with voice over the Internet, it can be virtually free. Webcams allow people to have personal videoconferences from the comfort of their home office. In 1980, a gigabyte of storage occupied a room; now an Apple iPod that fits in your pocket comes with 60 gigabytes of storage.

The key characteristic of the information revolution is not the *speed* of communications between the wealthy and powerful: for more than 130 years, virtually instantaneous communication has been possible between Europe and North America. The crucial change is the enormous reduction in the *cost* of transmitting information. For all practical purposes, the actual transmission costs have become negligible; hence the amount of information that can be transmitted worldwide is effectively infinite. The result is an explosion of information, of which documents are a tiny fraction. By one estimate, there are 1.5 billion gigabytes of digital magnetically stored information (or 250 megabytes for each inhabitant of the earth), and shipments of such information are doubling each year. At the beginning of the twenty-first century, computer users sent roughly 4 trillion e-mail messages per year, and the World Wide Web contained about 170 terabytes of information on its surface, which is equivalent to 17 times the volume of printed material in the Library of Congress. This dramatic change in the linked technologies of computing and communications, sometimes called the "third industrial revolution," is changing the nature of governments and sovereignty and creating a diffusion of power.

Lessons from the Past

We can get some idea of where we are heading by looking back at the past of the developed world. In the first industrial revolution around the turn of the nineteenth century, the application of steam to mills and transportation had a powerful effect on the economy, society, and government. Patterns of production, work, living conditions, social class, and political power were transformed. Public education arose as literate trained workers were needed for increasingly complex and potentially dangerous factories. Police forces such as London's "bobbies" were created to deal with urbanization. Subsidies were provided for the necessary infrastructure of canals and railroads.

The "second industrial revolution," around the turn of the twentieth century—electricity, synthetics, and the internal combustion engine—brought similar economic and social changes. The United States went from a predominantly agrarian to a primarily industrial and urban nation. In the 1890s, most Americans still worked on farms or as servants. A few decades later, the majority lived in cities and worked in factories. Social class and political cleavages were altered as urban labor and trade unions became more important. And again, with lags, the role of government changed. The bipartisan progressive movement ushered in antitrust legislation, early consumer protection regulation by the forerunner of the Food and Drug Administration, and economic stabilization by the Federal Reserve Board. The United States rose to the status of a great power in world politics. Some expect the third industrial revolution to produce analogous transformations in the economy, society, government, and world politics.

These historical analogies help us understand some of the forces that will shape world politics in the twenty-first century. Economies and information networks have changed more rapidly than governments have. The political scales of sovereignty and authority have not yet grown to a similar scale. As the sociologist Daniel Bell notes, "If there is a single overriding sociological problem in postindustrial society—particularly in the management of transition—it is the management of scale."[1] Put more simply, the basic building blocks of world politics are being transformed by the new technology. If we focus solely on the hard power of nation-states, we will miss the new reality.

We are still at an early stage of the current information revolution, and its effects on economics and politics are uneven. As with steam in the late eighteenth century and electricity in the late nineteenth century, productivity growth lagged as society had to learn to fully utilize the new technologies. Social institutions change more slowly than technology. For example, the electric motor was invented in 1881, but it was nearly four decades before Henry Ford pioneered the reorganization of factory assembly lines to take full advantage of electric power. Similar lags were true for information technology and computers. The increase in productivity of the American economy began to register only as recently as the mid-1990s.

The advent of truly mass communications and broadcasting a century ago, which was facilitated by newly cheap electricity, provides some lessons about possible social and political effects today. It ushered in the age of mass popular culture. The effects of mass communication and broadcasting, though not the telephone, tended to have a centralizing political effect. While information was more widespread, it was more centrally influenced even in democratic countries than in the age of the local press. President Roosevelt's use of radio in the 1930s worked a dramatic shift in American politics. These effects were particularly pronounced in countries where they were combined with the rise of totalitarian governments that were able to suppress competing sources of information. Indeed, some scholars believe totalitarianism could not have been possible without the mass communications that accompanied the second industrial revolution.

In the middle of the twentieth century, people feared that the computers and communications of the current information revolution would create the central governmental control dramatized in George Orwell's novel *1984*. Mainframe computers seemed set to enhance central planning and increase the surveillance powers of those at the top of a pyramid of control. Government television would dominate the news. Through central databases, computers can make government identification and surveillance easier, and commercialization has already altered the early libertarian culture and code of the Internet. Nonetheless, the technology of encryption is evolving, and programs like Gnutella and Freenet enable users to trade digital information anonymously. They promise greater space for individuals than the early pessimists envisioned, and the Internet is more difficult for governments to control than was the technology of the second information revolution.

As computing power has decreased in cost and computers have shrunk in size and become more widely distributed, their decentralizing effects have outweighed their centralizing effects. The Internet creates a system in which power over information is much more widely distributed. Compared with radio, television, and newspapers, controlled by editors and broadcasters, the Internet creates unlimited communication one-to-one (via e-mail), one-to-many (via a personal homepage or blog), many-to-one (via electronic broadcast) and, perhaps most important, many-to-many (an online chat room or message board). Comparing these electronic methods of communication to previous advances in communication, political scientist Pippa Norris wrote: "Internet messages have the capacity to flow farther, faster, and with fewer intermediaries."[2] Central surveillance is possible, but governments that aspire to control information flows through control of the Internet face high costs and ultimate frustration. Rather than reinforcing centralization and bureaucracy, the new information technologies have tended to foster network organizations, new types of community, and demands for different roles for government.

What this means is that world politics will not be the sole province of governments. Both individuals and private organizations, ranging from corporations to NGOs to terrorists, will be empowered to play direct roles in world politics. The spread of information means that power will be more widely distributed and informal networks will undercut the monopoly of traditional bureaucracy. The speed of Internet time means all governments, both here and overseas, will have less control of their agendas. Political leaders will enjoy fewer degrees of freedom before they must respond to events, and then will have to share the stage with more actors. Constructivists warn that we will have to avoid being mesmerized by terms such as *balance of power* and *hegemony*, and measures of strength that compare only the hard power of states run by centralized governments. Realist images of sovereign states balancing and bouncing off each other like billiard balls will blind us to the new complexity of world politics.

A New World Politics?

The effects of the third information revolution on central governments are still in their early stages. Peter Drucker and Heidi and Alvin Toffler argue that the information revolution is bringing an end to the hierarchical bureaucratic organizations that typified the age of the industrial revolution.[3] In civil societies, as decentralized organizations and virtual communities develop on the Internet, they cut across territorial jurisdictions and develop their own patterns of governance.

If these prophets are right, the result would be a new cyberfeudalism, with overlapping communities and jurisdictions laying claim to multiple layers of citizens' identities and loyalties. In short, these transformations suggest the reversal of the modern centralized state that has dominated world politics for the past 350 years. Instead of "international" politics, we may have a broader "world politics." A medieval European might have owed equal loyalty to a local lord, a duke, a king, and the Pope. A future European might owe loyalty to Brittany, Paris, Brussels, as well as to several cybercommunities concerned with religion, work, and various interests.

While the system of sovereign states is still the dominant pattern in international relations, we can begin to discern a pattern of crosscutting communities and governance that resembles the situation before the Peace of Westphalia formalized the state system in 1648. Transnational contacts across political borders were typical in the feudal era, but were gradually constrained by the rise of centralized nation-states. Now sovereignty is changing. Three decades ago, transnational contacts were already growing, but they involved relatively small numbers of elites involved in multinational corporations, scientific groups, and academic institutions. Now the Internet is creating low costs that open transnational communications to millions of people.

Sovereignty and Control

The issue of sovereignty is hotly contested in world politics today. Many political leaders resist anything that seems to diminish national autonomy. They worry about the political role of the United Nations in limiting the use of force, the economic decisions handed down by the World Trade Organization, and efforts to develop environmental institutions and treaties. In their eyes, the notion of an international community of opinion is illusory.

But the debate over the fate of the sovereign state has been poorly framed. As the constructivist political scientist John Ruggie put it, "There is an extraordinarily impoverished mind-set at work here, one that is able to visualize long-term challenges to the system of states only in terms of entities that are institutionally substitutable for the state."[4] A better historical analogy is the development of markets and town life in the early feudal period. Medieval trade fairs were not substitutes for the institutions of feudal authority. They did not tear down the castle walls or remove the local lord, but they did bring new wealth, new coalitions, and new attitudes summarized by the maxim "town air brings freedom."

Medieval merchants developed the *Lex Mercatoria* ("Merchant Law") that governed their relations largely as a private set of rules for conducting business. Similarly, today, everyone from hackers to large corporations is developing the code and norms of the Internet partly outside the control of formal political institutions. The development of transnational corporate intranets behind firewalls and encryption "represent(s) private appropriations of a public space."[5] These private systems, such as corporate intranets or worldwide newsgroups devoted to specific issues such as the environment, do not frontally challenge the governments of sovereign states; they simply add a layer of relations that sovereign states do not effectively control. People will participate in transnational Internet communities without ceasing to be loyal citizens, but their perspectives will be different from those of typical loyal citizens before the Internet.

Even in the age of the Internet, the roles of political institutions are likely to change gradually. After the rise of the territorial state, other successors to medieval rule such as the Italian city-states and the Hanseatic League in northern Europe persisted as viable alternatives, able to tax and fight for nearly two centuries. The real issue today is not the continued existence of the sovereign state, but how its centrality and functions are being altered. "The reach of the state has increased in some areas but contracted in others. Rulers have recognized that their effective control can be enhanced by walking away from some issues they cannot resolve."[6] All countries, including the largest, are facing a growing list of problems that are difficult to control within sovereign boundaries—financial flows, drug trade, climate change, HIV/AIDS, refugees, terrorism, and cultural intrusions—to name a few. Complicating the task of national governance is not the same as undermining sovereignty. Governments adapt. However, in the process of adaptation they change the meaning of sovereign jurisdiction, control, and the role of private actors.

Take, for example, the problems of controlling U.S. borders. In one year, 475 million people, 125 million vehicles, and 21 million import shipments come into the country at 3,700 terminals in 301 ports of entry. It takes five hours to inspect a fully loaded 40-foot shipping container, and more than 5 million enter each year. In addition, millions of undocumented immigrants have simply walked or ridden across the Mexican and Canadian borders. As September 11, 2001, illustrated, terrorists can easily slip across borders, and it is easier to bring in a few pounds of a deadly biological or chemical agent than to smuggle in the tons of illegal heroin and cocaine that arrive annually. The only way for the Department of Homeland Security to cope with such flows is to expand intelligence sharing with and cooperation inside the jurisdiction of other states, and to rely on private corporations to develop transparent systems for tracking international commercial flows so enforcement officials can conduct "virtual" audits of inbound shipments before they arrive. Today, customs officers are working throughout Latin America to help businesses implement security programs that reduce the risk of being exploited by drug smugglers, and cooperative international mechanisms are being developed for policing trade flows. The sovereign state adapts, but in doing so it transforms the meaning and exclusivity of governmental jurisdiction. Legal borders do not change, but they blur in practice.

National security—the absence of threat to major values—is another example. Damage done by climate change or imported viruses can be larger in terms of money or lives lost than the effects of some wars. But even if one restricts the definition of national security more narrowly to organized violence, the nature of military security is changing. As the U.S. Commission on National Security in the Twenty-First Century pointed out, the country has not been invaded by foreign armies since 1814, and the military is designed to project force and fight wars far from our shores. But the U.S. military was not well equipped to protect us against an attack on the homeland by terrorists using civilian aircrafts as weapons of great destruction. The United States suffered more casualties from the transnational terrorist attacks on September 11, 2001, than from the Japanese government's attack on Pearl Harbor in 1941.

Today, attackers may be governments, groups, individuals, or some combination. The Al Qaeda 0network that attacked the United States on September 11, 2001, involved individuals and groups from many countries and is alleged to have had cells in as many as 50 (including the United States). But some aggressors may be anonymous and not even come near the targeted country. In 1998, when Washington complained about seven Moscow Internet addresses involved in the theft of Pentagon and NASA secrets, the Russian government replied that phone numbers from which the attacks originated were inoperative. The United States had no way of knowing whether the Russian government had been involved. More than 30 nations have developed aggressive cyberwarfare programs, but as anyone with a computer knows, any individual can also enter the game. With a few keystrokes, an anonymous source anywhere in the world might break into and disrupt (private) power grids of major cities or (public) emergency response systems. A hacker in Malaysia who turns off the electricity in Chicago can do great damage from halfway around the world. And government firewalls are not enough. Every night, American software companies send work electronically to India and other countries where software engineers can work while Americans sleep and send it back the next morning. Someone outside America's borders could also embed trapdoors deep in computer code for use at a later date. Nuclear deterrence, border patrols, and stationing troops overseas to shape regional power balances will continue to matter in the information age, but they will not be sufficient to ensure national security.

Competing interpretations of sovereignty arise even in the domain of law. Since 1945, human rights provisions have coexisted in the Charter of the United Nations alongside provisions that protect the sovereignty of states. As we saw in Chapter 6, Article 2.7 says nothing shall authorize the United Nations to intervene in matters within domestic jurisdiction. Yet the development of a global norm of antiracism and repugnance at the South African practice of apartheid led a large majority at the UN to abridge this principle. More recently, the NATO intervention in Kosovo in 1999 was the subject of heated debate among international lawyers with some claiming it was illegal because it was not explicitly authorized by the UN Security Council and others arguing it was legal under the evolving body of international humanitarian law. Another example of this complexity was the 1998 detention of General Augusto Pinochet in Britain in response to a Spanish request for extradition based on human rights violations and crimes committed while he was president of Chile.

Information technology, particularly the Internet, has eased the tasks of coordination and strengthened the hands of human rights activists, but political leaders, particularly in formerly colonized countries, cling to the protections legal sovereignty provides against outside interventions. The world is likely to see these two partly contradictory bodies of international law continue to coexist for years to come.

For many people, the national state provides an important source of the political identity that is important to them. As we saw in Chapter 6, people are capable of multiple crosscutting identities—family, village, ethnic group, religion, nationality, cosmopolitan—and which one predominates often depends on the context. In many preindustrial countries, subnational identities at the tribe or clan level prevail. In some postindustrial countries, including the United States and European countries, cosmopolitan identities such as "global citizen" or "custodian of planet Earth" are beginning to emerge. It is still too early to understand the full effects of the Internet, but the shaping of identities can move in contradictory directions at the same time—up to Brussels, down to Brittany, or fixed on Paris—as circumstances dictate.

A fascinating use of the Internet to wield soft power can be found in the politics of diaspora communities. In the words of communications expert David Bollier, "The Internet has been a godsend to such populations because it enables large numbers of geographically isolated people with a shared history to organize into large virtual communities."[7] The Internet enables them to present attractive alternative ideas to those back home. Internet connections between foreign nationals and local citizens helped spark protests in Beijing against anti-Chinese riots taking place in Indonesia in 1998. The frustration of ethnic Chinese living in Indonesia was transferred to Beijing with remarkable speed. Similarly, in Zimbabwe, the Internet was crucial in spreading news about government actions during disputed elections.

One example of a diaspora group that has effectively used the Internet and other media sources to affect political outcomes in its home country is the Ghanaian expatriate community. In the elections of 2000, the first opportunity for Ghanaians to change their government through democratic means, the diaspora network was crucial in mobilizing support and money for the opposition candidate. Online community networks such as the Ghana Cyber Group (GCG), established in 1999 in New York, mobilized the diaspora in the United States to aggressively campaign for regime change in Ghana. The GCG is in the process of establishing a network among 2.5 million Ghanaian expatriates to increase the flow of capital to their home country.[8]

The Internet has also allowed protests to be quickly mobilized by freewheeling amorphous groups, rather than hierarchical organizations. In the Vietnam era, planning a protest required weeks and months of pamphlets, posters, and phone calls, and it took four years before the size of the first rallies of 25,000 reached half a million in 1969. In contrast, 800,000 people turned out in the United States and 1.5 million in

Europe on one weekend in February 2003 to protest the looming war in Iraq.[9] Protests do not represent the "international community," but they do often affect the attitudes of editorial writers, parliamentarians, and other influential people in important countries whose views are summarized by that vague term.[10] The continual contest for legitimacy illustrates the importance of soft power.

The result may be greater volatility rather than consistent movement in any one direction. The many-to-many and one-to-many characteristics of the Internet seem "highly conducive to the irreverent, egalitarian, and libertarian character of the cyber-culture." One effect is "flash movements"—sudden surges of protest—triggered by particular issues or events, such as antiglobalization protests or the sudden rise of the anti–fuel tax coalition that captured European politics in the autumn of 2000 or the protests around the world during the 2003 Iraq War.[11] Politics becomes more theatrical and aimed at global audiences. The Zapatista rebels in Mexico's Chiapas province relied less on bullets than on transnational publicity, much of it coordinated on the Internet, to pressure the Mexican government for reforms. In 2004, activists used cell phones to organize peaceful revolutions in the former Soviet states of Georgia and Ukraine. Political scientist James Rosenau has tried to summarize such trends by inventing a new word, *fragmegration*, to express the idea that both integration toward larger identities and fragmentation into smaller communities can occur at the same time. But one need not alter the English language to realize that apparently contradictory movements can occur simultaneously. They do not spell the end of the sovereign state, but they do make its politics more volatile and less self-contained within national shells.

TRANSNATIONAL ACTORS

As we have seen, a characteristic of the global information age is the increased role of *transnational actors*—nonstate entities acting across international borders (Figure 8.1). Traditional international politics is discussed in terms of states. We use shorthand expressions like "Germany wanted Alsace" or "France feared Britain." That shorthand is a useful simplification, especially in the classical period of international politics. In the eighteenth century, the monarch spoke for the state. If Frederick the Great wanted something for Prussia, Frederick was Prussia. In the nineteenth century, a broader elite class controlled foreign policy decisions, but even on the eve of World War I, European diplomacy was a relatively narrowly held cabinet-level affair. In addition, in the classical period of international politics the agenda was more limited. Military security issues dominated the agenda, and they were handled primarily by the foreign office.

Qualitatively, transnational actors have played a role for centuries, but the quantitative shift in the last half of the twentieth century marks a significant change in the international system. In a world of global interdependence, the agenda of international politics is broader, and everyone seems to want to get into the act. In the United States, for example, almost every domestic agency has some international role. The Department of Agriculture is interested in international food issues; the Environmental Protection Agency is interested in acid rain and global warming; the Coast Guard is interested in ocean dumping; the Department of Commerce is interested in trade; the Treasury Department is interested in exchange rates. The State Department does not control all these issues. Every bureau of the U.S. government has its own little foreign ministry. In fact, if we look at the representation of the United States abroad, only a minority of the Americans in most embassies are from the State Department.

In complex interdependence, societies interact at many points. There is too much traffic for one intersection or for one cop at one intersection. These interactions across state borders outside the central control of the foreign policy organs are called transnational relations. They include but are not limited to migration of populations, the rapid transfer of capital from one country to another that occurs daily in the world stock and money markets, illicit trafficking in weapons and drugs, and certain forms of terrorism. Governments can try to control these activities, and in the case of terrorism or smuggling they need to, but control often comes at a very high price. For example, the Soviet Union closely controlled transnational relations, and the Soviet economy suffered gravely for it. In circumstances with high degrees of interdependence and a great number of transnational actors, we can be led astray by the shorthand that was so useful in the classical period. We say things like "Japan agreed to import more" or "America opposed broad claims to the continental shelf under the ocean," but looking more carefully, we notice that Japanese firms acted transnationally to export more or that some U.S. citizens lobbied internationally to promote a broad definition of the continental shelf.

This complexity of interests has always existed, but it is greater in economic and social issues than in the traditional military security issues. Security issues are often more collectively shared. The survival of a people as a whole is obviously a collective good. Social and economic issues are often less broadly shared; there are more differences of interest. Thus, with the rise of economic interdependence and the rise of economic issues on the agenda of international politics, we find that our traditional shorthand less adequately describes the political process.

Let me illustrate with the case of oil we examined in Chapter 7. I said the consumer nations wanted low prices and the producer nations wanted high prices in 1973. But the politics was a lot more complex than that. Producing interests inside the consumer countries wanted high oil prices. Small Texas oil producers were not at all unhappy that OPEC raised oil prices, for they had the same economic interests as the Arabs, not the same as the consumers freezing in New England. Producers of nuclear energy were not unhappy to see oil prices rise because that might help nuclear energy become a more competitive energy source. The declining coal industry in Europe and unemployed coal miners were not unhappy about the rise of oil prices either. Neither were ecologists who believed higher prices would curtail consumption and pollution. So inside the consumer countries there were enormous differences in the interests over oil prices. In a situation of interdependence, politics looks different if we lift the veil of national interest and national security. One of the reasons why consumer countries did not use more extreme measures such as force was that the sensitivity

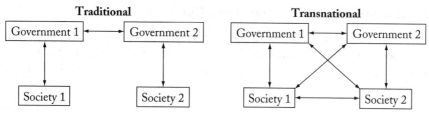

FIGURE 8.1   Traditional versus transnational world politics

interdependence that led to high energy prices was regarded as good by important political actors inside the consumer countries. There was a de facto transnational coalition that was not unhappy with higher oil prices.

Of course, the existence of contradictory interests inside nations is not new. In the nineteenth-century United States, politics was marked by differences between Southern farmers and Northern industrialists over tariffs. When President George W. Bush raised tariffs on steel in 2002, he pleased companies and unions that produce steel, but hurt those companies, such as car manufacturers, who use it. As we saw in Chapter 2, domestic politics has always been important to foreign policy, but with the expansion of participation in domestic politics it becomes more so. Moreover, as some of those domestic interests develop the capability to communicate and interact directly with other interests in other countries, they develop a different type of world politics.

Two forms of world politics are illustrated by Figure 8.1. The traditional form of international politics is the outside shell in the left-hand diagram of the figure. Traditional international politics follows the regular solid lines. If people in Society 1 want to put pressure on Government 2, they ask Government 1 to talk to Government 2. But in transnational relations, people in Society 1 put pressure on Government 2 directly, or people in Society 1 may put pressure on people in Society 2 directly. The additional lines in the right-hand diagram are individuals or nongovernmental organizations (NGOs) going across national boundaries. When we talk about the politics of interdependence, we must not assume that everything is captured by the traditional model of government-to-government relations. One of the distinguishing characteristics of complex interdependence is the significance of other actors in addition to the states.

The traditional shorthand is not wrong. It remains the best first approximation even for the politics of interdependence. States usually are the major actors. But if you restrict your attention to states alone, you may be misled about the politics of interdependence. States may look invulnerable in the aggregate, but a more careful look shows that some parts of states are highly vulnerable while other parts are not. And those vulnerable parts may act transnationally to remedy their situation. In short, states remain the most important actors in international politics, but as constructivists remind us, when you have said that, you have not said everything that is important to know about the politics and conflicts of interdependence.

Nongovernmental Organizations (NGOs)

Private organizations also increasingly cross national boundaries (Figure 8.2). Transnational religious organizations opposed to slavery date back to 1775, and the nineteenth century saw the founding of the Socialist International, the Red Cross,

---

Human Rights Watch (Source: Human Rights Watch)
Website: http://www.hrw.org
Founded: 1978
Headquarters: New York
Budget: $21.7 million USD (private donations)

Overview:
- Largest U.S.-based human rights organization
- "Shames" human rights offenders by documenting human rights abuses in more than 70 countries, generating media attention regarding abuses and lobbying governments and institutions to diplomatically pressure offending governments
- Was part of a coalition for groups and individuals that won the Nobel Peace Prize in 1997 for work related to the Campaign to Ban Landmines

International Crisis Group (Source: International Crisis Group)
Website: http://www.crisisgroup.org
Founded: 1995
Headquarters: Brussels
Budget: Approx. $12 million USD (40% government grants, 43% private foundations, 16% private individuals and businesses)

Overview:
- Analyzes countries "at risk of outbreak, escalation or recurrence of violent conflict" and offers policy recommendations, targeted to policy makers, regarding ways to diffuse tensions and resolve the conflicts
- Crisis Group Board includes influential figures from politics, diplomacy, business, and media who help shape the group's operations and lobby for implementation of its policy recommendations

Amnesty International
Website: http://www.amnesty.org
Founded: 1961
Headquarters: London
Budget: $41.7 million USD (private donations)

Overview:
- Mobilizes a network of 1.8 million members in more than 150 countries to help prevent and end "grave abuses of the rights to physical and mental integrity, freedom of conscience and expression, and freedom from discrimination" and promote human rights

Doctors Without Borders (Medecins San Frontieres) (Source: Doctors Without Borders)
Website: http://www.msf.org
Founded: 1971
Headquarters: Geneva
Budget: $439.9 million USD (81% private donations, 19% government grants)

FIGURE 8.2   Overview of Select Non-Governmental Organizations (NGOs)

Overview:
- International humanitarian aid organization assisting more than 70 countries
- Assistance provided to "populations in distress, to victims of natural or man-made disasters and to victims of armed conflict, without discrimination and irrespective of race, religion, creed or political affiliation"

Bill and Melinda Gates Foundation (Source: Bill and Melinda Gates Foundation)

Website:	http://www.gatesfoundation.org
Founded:	2000
Headquarters:	Seattle
Staff:	250
Budget:	Approx. $28.8 billion USD (endowment)

Overview:
- Founded by Microsoft founder Bill Gates and his wife, Melinda
- Works to "promote greater equity in four areas: global health, education, public libraries, and support for at-risk families"

The Carter Center (Source: The Carter Center)

Website:	http://www.cartercenter.org
Founded:	1982
Headquarters:	Atlanta
Budget:	Approx. $36 million USD (donations from individuals, foundations and corporations)

Overview:
- Founded by former U.S. President Jimmy Carter and his wife, Rosalynn
- Works to strengthen democracies, mediate conflicts, and eliminate disease worldwide

Oxfam International (Source: Oxfam International)

Website:	http://www.oxfam.org
Founded:	1942
Headquarters:	Oxford, UK
Budget:	Approx. $2.6 billion USD (40% government grants, 43% private foundations, 16% private individuals and businesses)

Overview:
- A "confederation of 12 organizations, working together with over 3,000 partners in more than 1,000 countries to find solutions to poverty, suffering and injustice"

International Committee of the Red Cross (ICRC) (Source: ICRC)

Website:	http://www.icrc.org
Founded:	1863
Headquarters:	Geneva
Budget:	$704.1 million (government funds, donations from individuals, corporations, and other entities)

Overview:
- Tasked by the Geneva Convention with responsibility for "visiting prisoners, organizing relief operations, re-uniting separated families and similar humanitarian activities *during armed conflicts*"
- An "impartial, neutral and independent organization whose exclusively humanitarian mission is to protect the lives and dignity of victims of war and internal violence and to provide them with assistance"

FIGURE 8.2   *Continued*

Greenpeace
Website:	http://www.greenpeace.org
Founded:	1971
Headquarters:	Amsterdam
Budget:	Approx. $42 million USD (private donations)

Overview:
- Mobilizes 2.8 million supporters in more than 40 countries to support efforts against climate change, degradation of the oceans, whaling, and genetic engineering
- Supports efforts to preserve ancient forests, eliminate toxic chemicals, and encourage sustainable trade

---

FIGURE 8.2   *Continued*

peace movements, women's suffrage organizations, and the International Law Association, among others. Before World War I, there were 176 international nongovernmental organizations. In 1956, they numbered nearly a thousand; in 1970 nearly 2,000. More recently, there has been an explosion in the number of NGOs, increasing from 6,000 to approximately 26,000 during the 1990s alone. And the numbers do not tell the full story, because they represent only formally constituted organizations. Many NGOs claim to act as a "global conscience" representing broad public interests beyond the purview of individual states, or that states are wont to ignore. Though they are not democratically elected, they sometimes help develop new norms by directly pressing governments and business leaders to change policies, and indirectly by altering public perceptions of what governments and firms should be doing. In terms of power resources, these new groups rarely possess much hard power, but the information revolution has greatly enhanced their soft power.

Governments now have to share the stage with actors who can use information to enhance their soft power and press governments directly, or indirectly by mobilizing their publics. Given the power of credible editors and cue givers who can cut through the avalanche of available information in the Internet age, a rough way to gauge the increasing importance of transnational organizations is to look at the number of mentions these organizations receive in mainstream media publications. By this measure, the biggest NGOs have become established players in the battle for the attention of influential editors. For example, after Human Rights Watch released its "2003 World Report," which included strong criticism of the U.S. government for its conduct in the war on terrorism, articles appeared in 288 newspapers and magazines over the next ten days mentioning the organization.[12]

News coverage over the past decade has reflected the growth of this general sector; the use of the term "nongovernmental organization" or "NGO" has increased 17-fold since 1992. In addition to Human Rights Watch, other NGOs such as Amnesty International, the International Red Cross, Greenpeace, Doctors Without Borders (Medecins Sans Frontieres), and Transparency International have undergone exponential growth in terms of mainstream media mentions.

Not only is there a great increase in the number of transnational and governmental contacts, but there has also been a change in type. Earlier transnational flows were heavily controlled by large bureaucratic organizations such as multinational corporations or the Catholic Church that could profit from economies of scale. Such organizations remain important, but the lower costs of communication in the Internet era have opened the field to loosely structured network organizations with little headquarters staff, and even to individuals. These nongovernmental organizations and networks are particularly effective in penetrating states without regard to borders. Because they often involve citizens who are well placed in the domestic politics of several countries, they are able to focus the attention of the media and governments on their preferred issues. The treaty banning landmines, as mentioned earlier, was the result of an interesting mixed coalition of Internet-based organizations working with middle-power governments such as Canada and some individual politicians and celebrities such as the late Princess Diana. In 2005, rock stars, NGOs, and political leaders worked together to press for debt relief for heavily indebted poor countries.

Environmental issues are another example. The role of NGOs was important as a channel of communication across delegations in the global warming discussions at Kyoto in 1997. Industry, unions, and NGOs competed in Kyoto for the attention of media from major countries in a transnational struggle over the agenda of world politics.

Geographical communities and sovereign states will continue to play the major role in world politics for a long time to come, but they will be less self-contained and more porous. They will have to share the stage with actors who can use information to enhance their soft power and press governments directly or indirectly by mobilizing their publics. Governments that want to see rapid development will find that they have to give up some of the barriers to information flow that historically protected officials from outside scrutiny. No longer will governments that want high levels of development be able to afford the comfort of keeping their financial and political situations inside a black box, as Burma and North Korea have done. That form of sovereignty proves too expensive. Even large countries with hard power, such as the United States, find themselves sharing the stage with new actors and having more trouble controlling their borders. Cyberspace will not replace geographical space and will not abolish state sovereignty, but like the town markets in feudal times, it will coexist and greatly complicate what it means to be a sovereign state or a powerful country.

Transnational Terrorism

Another type of nonstate actor that has attracted the attention of governments is the transnational terrorist. Terrorism is not new in world politics. It is a method of violence with roots stretching far back in history. Terror means great fear, and governments as varied as the French First Republic (1792–1804) and Stalin's Soviet Union have used it to control their populations. Terrorism was also used by anarchists and other transnational revolutionaries in the nineteenth century, as we saw in Chapter 3. They killed half a dozen heads of state, and World War I was triggered in part by such a terrorist turned assassin.

What is new today is that technology is putting into the hands of deviant individuals and groups destructive powers that were once reserved primarily to governments. In the twentieth century, heads of government such as Stalin and Hitler could kill large numbers of people. If terrorists are able to obtain weapons of mass destruction in the twenty-first century, they will develop similar capabilities. That is why some observers refer to terrorism as the privatization of war. Moreover, technology has made the complex systems of modern societies more vulnerable to large-scale attack. As Walter Laquer argues, "This trend toward increased vulnerability was occurring even before the Internet sped it along."[13]

The current generation of Islamist extremists may have a goal of forcing people to accept a distorted seventh-century version of Islam, but they are very adept at using the Internet for distribution of their message. That means there is nothing to smuggle across borders and less chance of getting caught. Terrorism involves theater and a competition for audience. In May 2004, a shocking video of Al Qaeda operative Abu Musab al Zarqawi decapitating Nicholas Berg in Iraq was downloaded millions of times on the Internet and stimulated copycat beheadings by other groups. When one website is shut down, today's generation of terrorists is adept at switching to other sites, including some they temporarily hijack.

One of the hardest things for terrorists to do is to organize trustworthy cells across borders that cannot be taken down by intelligence and police agencies. By moving from the physical sanctuaries of the 1990s to virtual sanctuaries on the Internet, the terrorists reduce their risk. No longer does recruiting occur only in physical locations like mosques and jails. Instead, alienated individuals in isolated national niches can make contact with a new virtual community of fellow believers around the world. The number of jihadist websites is reported to have grown from a dozen in the late 1990s to more than 4,500 today. Such websites not only recruit; they also train. They include detailed instructions on how to make bombs from fertilizer, how to cross the border into Iraq, how to plant and explode devices to kill American soldiers. And experts use chat rooms and message boards to answer trainees' questions. Plans and instructions are then sent through coded messages. Of course, such websites can be monitored by governments. Some sites are shut down, others left open to monitor. But the cat and mouse game between police agencies and terrorists is a close one.

The Al Qaeda terrorist network's September 11 attacks on the United States, which claimed roughly 3,000 lives, conformed to a trend of increasing lethality (even as the number of attacks had been declining). Previous terrorist events such as the bombing of an Air India flight in 1985 killed 325 people, and the 1995 truck bombing of the federal building in Oklahoma City killed 168. Terrorism in the 1970s and 1980s was driven largely by ideology or nationalism, but by the 1990s, extreme religious beliefs increasingly provided its context. Traditional terrorists, whether left-wing, right-wing, or nationalist-separatists, often had some scruples about indiscriminately killing innocent people, but such differentiations between the "enemy" and innocent civilians seem less prevalent today. When such attitudes are combined with a willingness to sacrifice their own lives, the new terrorists can wreak enormous destruction. While those responsible for the September 2001 attacks were motivated by a certain type of Islamic fundamentalism, it is worth remembering that the worst previous incident in the United States (Oklahoma City) was purely homegrown, and that radical groups willing to use terror can be secular, cults, or attached to the fringes of several religions.

What is terrorism? Under American law it is premeditated, politically motivated violence against noncombatant targets by subnational groups. The UN has passed conventions to suppress terrorist bombings, assassinations, hostage taking, and the financing of terrorism. A Security Council resolution in September 2001 that obligated all 189 member states to deny terrorists safe harbor helped legitimate American actions in Afghanistan. Nonetheless, the General Assembly found it difficult to agree on a resolution defining terrorism. Arab governments led by Egypt and Syria blocked any text that did not exempt groups such as the Palestinians from being defined as terrorists. In their eyes, the Palestinian resistance to Israeli occupation of the West Bank was legitimate national resistance, and the responses used by the Israeli government were killing innocent Palestinian civilians. As skeptics sometimes put it, "One man's terrorist is another man's freedom fighter."

When President George W. Bush addressed the UN General Assembly in 2001, he said the world must unite in "opposing all terrorists, not just some of them. No national aspiration, no remembered wrong can ever justify the deliberate murder of the innocent." His statement was consistent with the just war doctrine discussed in Chapter 6, and with international law. Some acts of nonstate political resistance perhaps should not be considered terrorism—for example, much of the antiapartheid struggle in South Africa did not kill civilians. But even if a political group can argue that the absence of democratic procedures for change make violence necessary in a "war of national liberation," the taking of innocent life is not morally or legally acceptable under just war doctrine. Similarly, if states deliberately kill noncombatants to terrorize a population, it is a war crime. If terrorism is defined as the substate use of violence for political purposes, states are excluded (by definition), but they are not thereby exculpated if they engage in similar immoral and illegal behavior. For all the difficulties at the margins of defining terrorism, the core evil of deliberately killing innocent people for political purposes is broadly condemned by the moral codes of all major religions as well as by international law. In 2004, a High-Level-Panel appointed by the UN Secretary-General agreed unanimously that terrorism is any action intended to cause death or serious bodily harm to civilians or noncombatants for the purpose of intimidation.

Transnational terrorism is to the twenty-first century somewhat like piracy was to an earlier era. Some governments gave pirates and privateers safe harbor to earn revenues or to harass their enemies. Today some states harbor terrorists in order to attack their enemies or because they are too weak to control such groups. The American campaign against the Taliban government of Afghanistan, and the various UN resolutions, may make state-sponsored terrorism less likely in the future. At the same time, the technology of miniaturization of explosives, the vulnerability of modern systems such as air travel, and the increasing ease of communication via the Internet provide opportunities for nonstate actors to do great harm across borders even without state support. Ironically, the common threat felt by many peoples may enhance the appreciation of the role of states and the importance of their cooperation in providing security. The anarchy of the interstate system is usually more bearable than the chaotic anarchy of a nonstate actor's war of all against all.

INFORMATION AND POWER AMONG STATES

The information revolution is making world politics more complex by empowering nonstate actors, for better and worse, and reducing control by central governments. It is also affecting power among states. Here the United States benefits, and many poorer countries lag behind. While some poor countries such as China, India, and Malaysia have made significant progress in entering the information economy, more than half of all Internet users in 2005 lived in either Europe or North America. In the information age the world remains a mixture of agricultural, industrial, and service-dominated economies. The postindustrial societies and governments most heavily affected by the information age coexist and interact with countries thus far less affected by the information revolution.

Will this digital divide persist for a long time? Decreasing costs may allow poor countries to leapfrog or skip over certain stages of development. For instance, wireless communications are already replacing costly landlines, and voice recognition technologies can give illiterate populations access to computer communications. The Internet may help poor farmers better understand weather and market conditions before they plant crops, and more information may diminish the role of predatory intermediaries. Distance learning and Internet connections may help isolated doctors and scientists in poor countries. But what poor countries need most is basic education and infrastructure.

Technology spreads over time, and many countries are keen to develop their own Silicon Valleys. But it is easier to identify the virtual keys to the high-tech kingdom than to open the actual gates. Well-developed communications infrastructure, secure property rights, sound government policies, an environment that encourages new business formation, deep capital markets, and a skilled workforce, many of whom understand English (the language of 80 percent of all Web pages), will come to some poor countries in time, but not quickly. Even in India, which meets some of the criteria, software companies employ hundreds of thousands, but half of India's 1 billion people remain illiterate.

The information revolution has an overall decentralizing and leveling effect, but will it also equalize power among nations? As it reduces costs and barriers of entry into markets, it should reduce the power of large states and enhance the power of small states and nonstate actors. But in practice, international relations are more complex than such technological determinism implies. Some aspects of the information revolution help the small; but some help the already large and powerful. There are several reasons why.

First, size still matters. What economists call barriers to entry and economies of scale remain in some of the aspects of power that are related to information. For example, soft power is strongly affected by the cultural content of what is broadcast or appears in movies and television programs. Large established entertainment industries often enjoy considerable economies of scale in content production and distribution. The dominant American market share in films and television programs in world markets is a case in point. It is hard for newcomers to compete with Hollywood (though India's "Bollywood" has a wide following). Moreover, in the information economy, there are "network effects" with increasing returns to scale. As we know, one telephone is useless. The second adds value, and so forth as the network grows.

Second, even though it is now cheap to disseminate existing information, the collection and production of new information often requires major investment. In many competitive situations, *new* information matters most. In some dimensions, information is a nonrival public good: One person's consumption does not diminish that of another. Thomas Jefferson used the analogy of a candle. If I give you a light, it does not diminish my light. But in a competitive situation, it may make a big difference if I have the light first and see things before you do. Intelligence collection is a good example. America, Russia, Britain, and France have capabilities for collection and production that dwarf those of other nations. Published accounts suggest the United States spends some $44 billion a year on intelligence. In some commercial situations, a fast follower can do better than a first mover, but in terms of power among states, it is usually better to be a first mover than a fast follower. It is ironic, but no accident, that for all the discussion of the Internet shrinking distance, firms still cluster in Silicon Valley, a congested little area south of San Francisco, because of what is called "the cocktail party effect." What makes for success is informal access to new information before it becomes public. Douglas McGray notes, "In an industry where new technology is perpetually on the verge of obsolescence, firms must recognize demand, secure capital and bring a product to market quickly or else be beaten by a competitor."[14] Market size and proximity to competitors, suppliers, and customers still matter in an information economy.

Third, first movers are often the creators of the standards and architecture of information systems. As in Robert Frost's famous poem, once the paths diverge in the wood and one is taken, it is difficult to get back to the other. Sometimes, crude low-cost technologies open shortcuts that make it possible to overtake the first mover, but in many instances, the path-dependent development of information systems reflects the advantage of the first mover. The use of the English language and the pattern of top-level domain names on the Internet is a case in point. Partly because of the transformation of the American economy in the 1980s, and partly because of large investments driven by Cold War military competition, the United States was often the first mover and still enjoys a lead in the application of a wide variety of information technologies.

Fourth, as we have seen, military power remains important in critical domains of international relations. Information technology has some effects on the use of force that benefit the small and some that favor the already powerful. The off-the-shelf commercial availability of formerly costly military technologies benefits small states and nongovernmental actors and increases the vulnerability of large states. For example, today anyone can order 1-meter-resolution satellite images of what goes on in other countries inexpensively from commercial companies. Commercial firms and individuals can go to the Internet and get access to satellite photographs that were top secret and cost governments billions of dollars just a few years ago. When a nongovernmental group felt that American policy toward North Korea was too alarmist a few years ago, it published private satellite pictures of North Korean rocket launch pads. Obviously, other countries can purchase similar pictures of American bases.

Global positioning devices that provide precise locations, once the property of the military alone, are readily available at stores such as Wal-Mart. What's more, information systems create vulnerabilities for rich states by adding lucrative targets for terrorist (including state-sponsored) groups. It's conceivable in the next 25 years that a sophisticated adversary (such as a small country with cyberwarfare resources) will decide it can blackmail the United States. There is also the prospect of free-lance cyberattacks.

Other trends, however, strengthen already powerful nations. Information technology has produced a revolution in military affairs. Space-based sensors, direct broadcasting, high-speed computers, and complex software provide the ability to gather, sort, process, transfer, and disseminate information about complex events that occur over a wide geographic area. This dominant-battle-space awareness combined with precision targeting and networking of military systems produces a powerful advantage. As the two Gulf Wars showed, traditional assessments of balances of weapons platforms such as tanks or planes become irrelevant unless they include the ability to integrate information with those weapons. That was the mistake Saddam Hussein made (as well as those in Congress in 1990 who predicted massive American casualties). Many of the relevant technologies are available in commercial markets, and weaker states can be expected to purchase many of them. The key, however, will not be possession of fancy hardware or advanced systems, but the ability to integrate a system of systems. In this dimension, the United States is likely to maintain its lead. In information warfare, even a small edge makes all the difference.

The Information Revolution and Complex Interdependence

The information revolution has not equalized power among states. Thus far it has had the opposite effect, and realists might feel vindicated. But what about reducing the role of governments and the power of all states? Here the changes are more along the lines predicted by liberals and constructivists. Complex interdependence is certainly much greater in the dimension of multiple channels of contact between societies.

The explosion of information has produced a "paradox of plenty."[15] Plenty of information leads to scarcity—of attention. When people are overwhelmed with the volume of information confronting them, they have difficulty discerning what to focus on. Attention rather than information becomes the scarce resource, and those who can distinguish valuable information from background clutter gain power. Editors and cue givers are in increasingly higher demand, and this is a source of power for those who can tell us where to focus our attention. Brand names and the ability to bestow an international "Good Housekeeping" seal of approval will become increasingly more important.

In addition, publics have become more wary and sensitized about propaganda. Propaganda as a form of free information is not new. Hitler and Stalin used it effectively in the 1930s. Milosevic's control of television was crucial to his power in Serbia in the 1990s. In Moscow in 1993, a battle for power was fought at a TV station.

Now credibility is the crucial resource, and an important source of soft power. Reputation becomes even more important than in the past, and political struggles occur over the creation and destruction of credibility. Governments compete for credibility not only with other governments, but with a broad range of alternatives including news media, corporations, nongovernmental organizations, intergovernmental organizations, and networks of scientific communities.

Politics has become a contest of competitive credibility. The world of traditional power politics is typically about whose military or economy wins. Politics in an information age "may ultimately be about whose story wins."[16] Governments compete with each other and with other organizations to enhance their own credibility and weaken that of their opponents. Witness the struggle between Serbia and NATO to frame the interpretation of events in Kosovo in 1999 and the events in Serbia a year later. Prior to the demonstrations that led to the overthrow of Slobodan Milosevic in October 2000, 45 percent of Serb adults were tuned to Radio Free Europe and the Voice of America. In contrast, only 31 percent listened to the state-controlled radio station, Radio Belgrade.[17] Moreover, the domestic alternative radio station, B92, provided access to Western news, and when the government tried to shut it down, it continued to provide such news on the Internet.

Information that appears to be propaganda may not only be scorned, but it may also turn out to be counterproductive if it undermines a country's reputation for credibility. In 2003, exaggerated claims about Saddam Hussein's weapons of mass destruction and ties to Al Qaeda may have helped mobilize domestic support for the Iraq War, but polls showed that the subsequent disclosure of the exaggeration dealt a costly blow to British and American credibility. Under the new conditions more than ever, a soft sell may prove more effective than a hard sell.

The Iraq example illustrates that power does not necessarily flow to those who can withhold information. Under some circumstances, private information can cripple the credibility of those who have it. As the Nobel Prize winner George Ackerloff has pointed out, sellers of used cars have more knowledge about their defects than potential buyers. Moreover, owners of bad cars are more likely to sell than owners of good ones. These facts lead potential buyers to discount the price they are willing to pay in order to adjust for unknown defects. Hence the result of the superior information of sellers is not to improve the average price they receive, but instead to make them unable to sell good used cars for their real value. Unlike asymmetrical interdependence in trade, in which power goes to those who can afford to hold back or break trade ties, information power flows to those who can edit and credibly validate information to sort out what is both correct and important.

THE NEW GLOBAL ACTORS

It is almost as if the world has arrived at a sort of neomedievalism in which the institutions and sources of authority are multifarious. Just as the leaders of the Knights Templars or the Franciscan order outranked all but the most powerful of princes, so too the secretary general of Amnesty International and the chief executive officer of Royal Dutch Shell cast far longer shadows on the international stage than do leaders of Moldavia, Namibia, or Nauru. The state may not be quite ready to wither away, but it's not what it used to be.

—Peter J. Spiro[18]

One implication of the abundance of free information sources, and the role of credibility, is that soft power is likely to become less a function simply of material resources than in the past. When the ability to produce and disseminate information is the scarce resource, limiting factors include the control of printing presses, radio stations, and newsprint. Hard power—for instance, using force to take over the radio station—can generate soft power. In the case of worldwide television, wealth can also lead to soft power. For instance, CNN was based in Atlanta rather than Amman or Cairo because of America's leading position in the industry and in technology. When Iraq invaded Kuwait in 1990, the fact that CNN was basically an American company helped frame the issue worldwide as aggression (analogous to Hitler's actions in the 1930s), rather than as a justified attempt to reverse colonial humiliation (analogous to India's widely accepted "liberation" of the Portuguese colony of Goa in the 1960s). But by 2003, the rise of cable networks in the region, such as al Jazeera and al Arabiya, undercut the American monopoly and provided a local framing of the issues involved in the Iraq War. In an information age, the occupation of Iraq and its coverage were very costly for American soft power.

The close connection between hard and soft power is likely to be somewhat weakened under conditions of complex interdependence in an information age. The power of broadcasting persists, but it will be increasingly supplemented by the Internet with its multiple channels of communication, controlled by multiple actors who cannot use force to control one another. Conflicts will be affected not only by which actors own television networks, radio stations, and websites—once a plethora of such sources exist—but also by who pays attention to which fountains of information and misinformation.

Broadcasting is a type of information dissemination that has long had an impact on public opinion. By focusing on some conflicts and human rights problems, broadcasters have pressed politicians to respond to some foreign conflicts rather than others—for example, Somalia rather than southern Sudan in the 1990s. Not surprisingly, governments have sought to influence, manipulate, or control television and radio stations, and have been able to do so with considerable success since a relatively small number of physically located broadcasting sites were used to reach many people with the same message. However, the shift from broadcasting to "narrowcasting" has major political implications. Cable and the Internet enable senders to segment and target audiences. Even more important for politics is the interactive role of the Internet; it not only focuses attention, but also facilitates coordination of action across borders. Interactivity at low cost allows for the development of new virtual communities: people who imagine themselves as part of a single group regardless of how far apart they are physically from one another.

The Information Revolution and Democratization

As far as countries are concerned, most information shapers are democracies. This is not accidental. Their societies are familiar with free exchange of information and their institutions of governance are not threatened by it. They can shape information because they can also take it. Authoritarian states, typically among the laggards, have considerably more trouble. Governments such as China's can control their citizens' access to the Internet by controlling Internet service and content providers, such as Yahoo and Google, and by monitoring the relatively small percentage of users. It is possible, but costly, to route around such restrictions, and control does not have to be complete to be effective for political purposes. Singapore, a state that combines political control with economic liberalism, has thus far combined its political controls with an increasing role for the Internet. But as societies like Singapore reach levels of development in which a broader range of knowledge workers want fewer restrictions on access to the Net, Singapore runs the risk of losing its creative knowledge workers, its scarcest resource for competing in the information economy.

Traders huddled around computers

Thus Singapore is wrestling with the dilemma of reshaping its educational system to encourage the individual creativity that the information economy will demand, while at the same time attempting to maintain existing social controls over the flow of information. Closed systems become more costly.

Another reason closed systems become more costly is that it is risky for foreigners to invest funds in an authoritarian country where the key decisions are made in an opaque fashion. Transparency is becoming a key asset for countries seeking investments. The ability to keep information from leaving, which once seemed so valuable to authoritarian states, undermines the credibility and transparency necessary to attract investment on globally competitive terms. This point was illustrated by the 1997 Asian financial crisis. Governments that are not transparent are not credible, because the information they offer is seen as biased and selective. Moreover, as economic development progresses and middle-class societies develop, repressive measures become more expensive not only at home, but also in terms of international reputation. Both Taiwan and South Korea discovered in the late 1980s that repressing rising demands for democracy and free expression would be expensive in terms of their reputation and soft power. By beginning to democratize then, they strengthened their capacity—as compared, for instance, with Indonesia—to cope with economic crisis.

Whatever the future effects of interactivity and virtual communities, one political effect of increased flows of free information through multiple channels is already clear: States have lost much of their control over information about their own societies. States that seek to develop need foreign capital and the technology and organization that go with it. Geographical communities still matter most, but governments that want to see rapid development will have to give up some of the barriers to information flows that protected officials from outside scrutiny. No longer will governments that want high levels of development be able to afford the comfort of keeping their financial and political situations inside a national black box.

We are at such an early stage of the information revolution that any conclusions must be tentative. Nevertheless current evidence supports four main arguments. First, some liberals are wrong in their predictions of an equalizing effect of the information and communications revolutions on the distribution of power among states. In part this is because economies of scale and barriers to entry persist with regard to commercial and strategic information; and in part because with respect to free information, larger states are often well placed in the competition for credibility. Second, cheap flows of information have created an enormous change in channels of contact across state borders. Nongovernmental actors operating transnationally have much greater opportunities to organize and propagate their views. Sovereign states are more easily penetrated and less like black boxes. Political leaders will find it more difficult to maintain a coherent ordering of foreign policy issues. Third, the information revolution is changing political processes in a way in which open democratic societies and transnational actors will compete more successfully than authoritarian states for the key power resource of credibility. Finally, soft power is becoming more important in relation to hard power than it was in the past as credibility becomes a key power resource for both governments and NGOs. Although the coherence of government policies may diminish in more pluralistic and penetrated states, those same countries may be better placed in terms of credibility and soft power. In short, geographically based states that realists emphasize will continue to structure politics in an information age, but the constructivists are correct that the processes of world politics within that structure are undergoing profound change.

STUDY QUESTIONS

1. What is the third industrial revolution? How does it differ from previous industrial revolutions?
2. How are the information revolution and the Internet affecting world politics?
3. Which have been stronger—the centralizing or decentralizing effects of advances in information technology?
4. What kind of impact has the information revolution had on state sovereignty? What kind of changes in the international system of states and in global governance is it producing?
5. Has the information revolution brought about an equalizing effect in terms of power and wealth among states?
6. What is the "digital divide"? What implications does it have for developing countries in particular? Has the information revolution brought about an equalizing effect in terms of power and wealth among states?
7. What are the three dimensions of information?
8. What are transnational actors? Are they likely to gain in importance? What are some examples of the power of transnational actors in the information age?
9. What is the role of large states in the governance of the international economy? What is the role of institutions?
10. What has been the relationship between the information revolution and democracy? Have globalization and the information revolution strengthened civil societies in nondemocratic states? What kind of impact have they had on political participation?

NOTES

1. Daniel Bell, *The Coming of Post-Industrial Society: A Venture in Social Forecasting* (New York: Basic, 1999), pp. 94, 97.
2. Pippa Norris, *The Digital Divide: Civic Engagement, Information Poverty, and the Internet Worldwide* (New York: Cambridge University Press, 2001), p. 232.
3. Alvin Toffler and Heidi Toffler, *The Politics of the Third Wave* (Kansas City, MO: Andrews & McMeel, 1995); and Peter Drucker, "The Next Information Revolution," *Forbes*, August 24, 1998, pp. 46–58.
4. John G. Ruggie, "Territoriality and Beyond: Problematizing Modernity in International Relations," *International Organization* (Winter 1993), pp. 143, 155.
5. Saskia Sassen, "On the Internet and Sovereignty," *Indiana Journal of Global Legal Studies* (Spring 1998), p. 551.
6. Stephen Krasner, "Sovereignty," *Foreign Policy* (January/February 2001), p. 24, and Linda Weiss, *The Myth of the Powerless State* (Ithaca, NY: Cornell University Press, 1998).
7. David Bollier, "The Rise of Netpolitik" (PDF document), pp. 21, 23, 24, The Aspen Institute http://www.aspeninstitute.org (accessed March 15, 2006).

8. Ghana Cyber Group, "A Brief History of GCG," http://www.ghanacybergroup.com (accessed March 15, 2006). See also "Net Effect: Africa's Expat Politics," *Foreign Policy* (September/October 2003), p. 51. I am indebted to Alexandra Scacco for calling my attention to this case.

9. Jennifer Lee, "How Protesters Mobilized So Many and So Nimbly," *The New York Times*, February 23, 2003, "Week in Review," p. 4.

10. For various views of what it means, see "What Is the International Community?" in the September 2002 issue of *Foreign Policy*.

11. Norris, *The Digital Divide*, p. 191.

12. Search of Factiva/Dow Jones database, January 14–25, 2003.

13. Walter Laquer, "Left, Right, and Beyond: The Changing Face of Terror," in James F. Hogue and Gideon Rose, eds., *How Did This Happen? Terrorism and the New War*, (New York: Council on Foreign Relations, Public Affairs, 2001), p. 73.

14. Douglas McGray, "The Silicon Archipelago," *Daedalus* 128:2, p. 167.

15. Herbert A. Simon, "Information 101: It's Not What You Know, It's How You Know It," *Journal for Quality and Participation* (July/August 1998), pp. 30–33.

16. John Arquilla and David Ronfeldt, *The Emergence of Neopolitik: Toward an American Information Strategy* (Santa Monica, CA: RAND Corporation, 1999), p. 53.

17. Edward Kaufman, "A Broadcasting Strategy to Win Media Wars," *The Battle for Hearts and Minds* (Washington, DC: Center for Strategic and International Studies, 2003), p. 303.

18. Peter J. Spiro, "New Global Communities, Nongovernmental Organizations in International Decision-Making Institutions," *Washington Quarterly* 18:1 (Winter 1995), pp. 45–46.

SELECTED READINGS

1. Keohane, Robert O., and Joseph S. Nye, Jr., "Power and Interdependence in the Information Age," *Foreign Affairs* (September/October 1998).

2. Litan, Robert, "The Internet Economy," *Foreign Policy* (March/April 2001).

3. Simon, Herbert A., "Information 101: It's Not What You Know, It's How You Know It," *Journal for Quality and Participation* (July/August 1998).

4. Meyer-Schönberger, Viktor, and Deborah Hurley, "Globalization of Communication," in Joseph S. Nye, Jr., and John D. Donahue, eds., *Governance in a Globalizing World* (Washington, DC: Brookings Institution, 2000), pp. 135–151.

5. Matthews, Jessica T., "Power Shift," *Foreign Affairs* (January 1997), pp. 50–66.

6. Florini, Ann, ed., *The Third Force* (Washington, DC: Carnegie Endowment, 2000).

FURTHER READINGS

Adams, James, "Virtual Defense," *Foreign Affairs* (May/June 2001), pp. 98–112.

Arquilla, John, and David Ronfeldt, *The Emergence of Neopolitik: Toward an American Information Strategy* (Santa Monica, CA: RAND Corporation, 1999).

Bell, Daniel, *The Coming of Post-Industrial Society: A Venture in Social Forecasting* (New York: Basic, 1999).

Brown, L. David, and Mark H. Moore, "Accountability, Strategy, and International Nongovernmental Organizations," *Nonprofit and Voluntary Sector Quarterly* 30:3 (September 2001), pp. 569–587.

Drucker, Peter, "The Next Information Revolution," *Forbes*, August 24, 1998, pp. 46–58.

Dyson, Esther, *Release 2.1: A Design for Living in the Digital Age* (New York: Broadway, 1998).

Edwards, Michael, *NGO Rights and Responsibilities* (London: Foreign Policy Centre, 2000).

Feldman, Noah, *After Jihad: America and the Struggle for Islamic Democracy* (New York: Farrar, Straus & Giroux, 2003).

Florini, Ann, ed., *The Third Force* (Washington, DC: Carnegie Endowment, 2000), chap. 1.

Flynn, Stephen, "Beyond Border Control," *Foreign Affairs* (November/December 2000), pp. 57–68.

Guetzkow, Harold, *Multiple Loyalties: Theoretical Approach to a Problem in International Organization* (Princeton, NJ: Princeton University Press, 1955).

Hill, Kevin, and John Hughes, *Cyberpolitics* (New York: Rowman & Littlefield, 1998).

Hoge, James, and Gideon Rose, eds., *How Did This Happen? Terrorism and the New War* (New York: Public Affairs, 2001).

Kaldor, Mary, Helmut Anheier, and Marlies Glasius, eds., *Global Civil Society 2003* (Oxford: Oxford University Press, 2003).

Kamarck, Elaine, and Joseph S. Nye, Jr., eds., *Governance.com: Democracy in the Information Age* (Washington, DC: Brookings Institution, 2002), chap. 1.

Keane, John, *Global Civil Society?* (Cambridge, UK: Cambridge University Press, 2003).

Keck, Margaret, and Kathryn Sikkink, *Activists Beyond Borders: Advocacy Networks in International Politics* (Ithaca, NY: Cornell University Press, 1998).

Keohane, Robert O., and Joseph S. Nye, Jr., *Transnational Relations and World Politics* (Cambridge, MA: Harvard University Press, 1972).

Khagram, Sanjeev, James V. Riker, and Kathryn Sikkink, eds., *Restructuring World Politics: Transnational Social Movements, Networks, and Norms* (Minneapolis: University of Minnesota Press, 2002).

LaFeber, Walter, *Michael Jordan and the New Global Capitalism* (New York: Norton, 1999).

Lennon, T. J., ed., *The Battle for Hearts and Minds: Using Soft Power to Undermine Terrorist Networks* (Cambridge, MA: MIT Press, 2003).

Lessig, Lawrence, *Code and Other Laws of Cyberspace* (New York: Basic, 2000).

Litan, Robert, "The Internet Economy," *Foreign Policy* (March/April 2001).

Matthews, Jessica T., "Power Shift," *Foreign Affairs* (January 1997), pp. 50–66.

Norris, Pippa, *The Digital Divide: Civic Engagement, Information Poverty, and the Internet Worldwide* (New York: Cambridge University Press, 2001).

Nye, Joseph S., Jr., *Soft Power: The Means to Success in World Politics* (New York: Public Affairs, 2004).

Pells, Richard, *Not Like Us* (New York: Basic, 1997).

Perritt, Henry H., Jr., "The Internet as a Threat to Sovereignty?" *Indiana Journal of Global Legal Studies* (Spring 1998), pp. 423–442.

Quinlan, Joseph, and Marc Chandler, "The U.S. Trade Deficit: A Dangerous Illusion," *Foreign Affairs* (May/June 2001).

Roberts, Adam, "The So-Called 'Right' of Humanitarian Intervention," *Yearbook of International Humanitarian Law* (May/June 2001), pp. 98–112.

Roy, Olivier, *Globalized Islam: The Search for a New Ummah* (New York: Columbia University Press, 2004).

Ruggie, John G., "Territoriality and Beyond: Problematizing Modernity in International Relations," *International Organization* (Winter 1993).

Rugh, William A., *American Encounters with Arabs: The "Soft Power" of U.S. Public Diplomacy in the Middle East* (Westport, CT:Praeger, 2006).

Saich, Tony, "Globalization, Governance, and the Authoritarian State: China," in Joseph S. Nye, Jr., and John D. Donahue, eds., *Governance in a Globalizing World* (Washington, DC: Brookings Institution, 2000).

Sassen, Saskia, "On the Internet and Sovereignty," *Indiana Journal of Global Legal Studies* (Spring 1998).

Simon, Herbert A., "Information 101: It's Not What You Know, It's How You Know It," *Journal for Quality and Participation* (July/August 1998).

Smith, Gordon, and Moises Naim, *Altered States: Globalization, Sovereignty and Governance* (Ottawa: International Development Research Centre, 2000).

Sola Pool, Ithiel, *Technologies of Freedom* (Cambridge, MA: Belknap, 1983).

Spiro, Peter, "The New Sovereigntists," *Foreign Affairs* (November/December 2000).

Spruyt, Hendryk, *The Sovereign State and Its Competitors* (Princeton, NJ: Princeton University Press, 1994).

Strange, Susan, *The Retreat of the State* (Cambridge, UK: Cambridge University Press, 1996).

Stern, Jessica, *The Ultimate Terrorists* (Cambridge, MA: Harvard University Press, 1999).

Williamson, Jeffrey, *Globalization and Inequality Then and Now: The Late 19th and Early 20th Centuries Compared* (Cambridge, MA: National Bureau of Economic Research, 1996).

A New World Order?

Rwandan refugees, 1994

ALTERNATIVE DESIGNS FOR THE FUTURE

International politics remains a realm of self-help where states face security dilemmas and force plays a considerable role. There are mitigating devices such as the balance of power and international norms, law, and organization, but they have not prevented all wars. The logic of international conflict as described by Thucydides still applies in some parts of the world today.

With the end of the Cold War, there was a good deal of talk about the prospects for a "new world order." As we later found, there was far less clarity about what that meant. There was a new world order in the sense that the bipolar system established after World War II had broken down. But that was order within the anarchic state system, and it was not necessarily a just order. Others thought a new world order meant escaping from the problems of the anarchic state system. Is such a world possible? British historian Arnold Toynbee wrote at the beginning of the Cold War that the nation-state and the split atom could not coexist on the same planet. In a world of sovereign states, where war is the ultimate form of defense and nuclear bombs are the ultimate weapon, he believed that something had to go, preferably the state. And as we saw in the last two chapters, globalization and the information revolution present new challenges to state sovereignty, for better and for worse.

The territorial state has not always existed in the past, so it need not necessarily exist in the future. Fragmented units and state systems have existed since the days of Thucydides, but the large territorial state as the prime basis of international politics developed only after the Renaissance of the fourteenth and fifteenth century. The Thirty Years' War (1618–1648) still had some features of a feudal war and was thus both the last of the wars of feudalism and the first of the wars of the territorial state. The large territorial state as we know it today has been the dominant institution of modern world politics for only three or four centuries. A number of futurists have predicted the decline of the territorial state. Their new world order involves structures that overcome the anarchic dilemma. Since World War II, there have been five major efforts to develop alternatives that go beyond the nation-state as the model for world politics.

World Federalism. One of the oldest traditions of European thought, federalism posits a solution for the problem of anarchy by way of an international federation: States would agree to give up their national armaments and accept some degree of central government. Federalists often draw analogies to the way the 13 American colonies came together in the eighteenth century. Some believe that history is a record of progress toward larger units. But federalism has not proven to be a very successful design at the global level. Peace is not the only thing people value. People also want justice, welfare, and autonomy, and they do not trust world government to protect them. In addition, few people are convinced that the federal remedy would work, that it would be a cure for the problem of war. Even if the anarchic system of states is part of the cause of war, getting rid of independent states would not necessarily be the end of war. As we have seen, most wars in recent years have been *internal* to states.

Functionalism. Because of the inadequacies of federalism, the idea of international functionalism was developed. Popular in the 1940s, functionalism suggested that economic and social cooperation could create communities that cut across national boundaries and thus eliminate war. Sovereignty would then become less relevant, and though the formal shell of the state would still exist, its hostile content would be drained away. At the end of World War II, functionalist thinking gave rise to some of the specialized UN agencies such as the Food and Agricultural Organization and the World Health Organization. Functionalism exists to some extent today, with a world full of transnational interests, nongovernmental organizations, multinational corporations, and so on. But functionalism has not proven a sufficient design for *world* order, and most states are reluctant to allow themselves to become so interdependent that they become highly vulnerable to others.

Regionalism. Regional integration became very popular in the 1950s and 1960s. Jean Monnet, head of the French Planning Commission, thought the functional approach at a regional level might lock Germany and France together and thereby prevent a resurgence of the conflicts that had led to World Wars I and II. In 1950, Europe started the process with the Schumann Plan, integrating Western European coal and steel industries. After 1957, the Treaty of Rome established the European Common Market, which provided a step-by-step reduction of trade barriers and harmonization of a whole range of agricultural and economic policies that culminated in the creation of the European Union in 1992. As we have seen, other regions have tried to emulate European regionalism, with NAFTA as the most significant example in the Western Hemisphere.

Yet, in 1965 General de Gaulle, then president of France, and later, in the 1980s Margaret Thatcher, then prime minister of Great Britain, set limits on how far regional integration could go. By the mid-1990s there was widespread ambivalence in the countries of the European Union over just how much sovereignty to cede to a regional government. The coins of the new common currency, the euro, began to circulate in 2002, but not in all countries. Efforts to create a new constitution for the European Union faltered when voters in France and the Netherlands rejected a proposed draft in referendums held in 2005. But despite these speed bumps in the road toward greater integration and organizational hurdles resulting from the admission of several Eastern European nations, Europe has changed for the better compared with the earlier periods we have studied. The EU represents an ongoing and dynamic experiment in international relations. As its members continue to painstakingly negotiate a thick web of multilateral institutions that deal with issues from agriculture to a common defense force, a distinctly European identity has emerged. While national differences certainly remain at the policy-making level, public opinion polls show that many EU citizens regard themselves as *European* as well as French, German, or Spanish. This fits with constructivist theory, which emphasizes the role ideas and culture play in the construction of political identities and beliefs. EU members have chosen to increase their complex interdependence in the belief that the cost/benefit ratio favors cooperation over full national independence. In today's Europe, everybody may not be in the same boat, but the boats are lashed together in a variety of ways that are very different from earlier periods. For example, in many areas EU laws now supercede national laws. The European Union represents a new type of international polity but is only a regional one.

Ecologism. In the 1970s, ecologism provided a new brand of hope for a different type of world order. Richard Falk's *This Endangered Planet* argued that two things could provide the basis of a new world order: the growing importance of transnational, nonterritorial actors and growing interdependence under conditions of scarcity. Falk argued there would be a gradual evolution of grassroots, populist values that would transcend the nation-state. Anticolonialism, antiracialism, greater equality, and ecological preservation would lead not only to strengthening of majorities in the United Nations, but to the creation of new regimes for handling the world's dwindling resources. The result would be international norms of peace, justice, and ecological balance and a new form of world order.

Technological change and economic growth have accentuated ecological problems. Global resource supplies have become further stretched, and as biological diversity decreases, further harm has occurred to the oceans and atmosphere that are part of the global commons. Over the last century, governments have signed more than 170 environmental treaties concerning subjects of shared concern, including fisheries, acid rain, ozone depletion, endangered species protection, Antarctica, and ocean pollution. Two-thirds have been signed since the first UN Environmental Conference in Stockholm in 1972. Major UN conferences on the environment and global warming were held in Brazil in 1992 and in Japan in 1997. Environmental issues have also spawned numerous nongovernmental organizations with transnational lobbying efforts. Citizens and politicians in developed countries are expressing increased awareness and concern regarding matters of environmental degradation and protection.

However, Falk overestimated how scarce resources would become and underestimated how much new technologies can compensate for the scarcity there is, and in many countries, ecological concerns take second place to a desire for rapid economic development.

Cyberfeudalism. As we saw in the last chapter, some theorists of organization in the information age—Peter Drucker and Alvin and Heidi Toffler—argued that the information revolution is flattening hierarchies and replacing them with network organizations. They predict that the centralized bureaucratic governments of the twentieth century will become decentralized organizations in the twenty-first century, and more governmental functions will be handled by private markets as well as by nonprofit organizations. Moreover, Internet expert Esther Dyson argues that as decentralized organizations and virtual communities develop on the Internet, they will cut across territorial jurisdictions and develop their own patterns of governance. While nation-states will continue to exist, they will become much less important and less central to people's lives. People will live by multiple voluntary contracts and drop in and out of communities at the click of a mouse. The new pattern of crosscutting communities and governance will become a modern and more civilized analogue to the feudal world that existed before the Westphalian system of states became dominant.

Although we can discern trends in this direction, this vision of how to get beyond the nation-state leaves open questions about how the claims of virtual and geographical communities will conflict, and how issues of violence and security will be handled. Moreover, as we saw in the last chapter, new information technologies can be used for evil as well as good. Today's terrorists use computers and the Internet to recruit members, obtain instructions for building weapons, transfer funds, and expand their networks. And remote hackers can create damage in other countries without ever crossing borders. In such situations, citizens may want stronger, not weaker, states whose governments can provide protection. As Thomas Hobbes pointed out centuries ago, the anarchy of states has its dangers, but they are less than a different type of anarchy in which there is no government to provide protection against nonstate actors.

Contrary to the predictions of these five models, the nation-state has not yet become obsolete. Those who believe it has often use a simple analogy. They say the nation-state today is penetrable both by rockets and electronic messages that can cross its borders in no time. Just as gunpowder and infantry penetrated and destroyed the medieval castle, so have nuclear missiles and the Internet made the nation-state obsolete. But people want three things from their political institutions: physical security, economic well-being, and communal identity. Changes in international processes are shifting the locus of these values slowly, but thus far the nation-state has provided more of all three than any other institution. Multinational corporations, NGOs, and international organizations lack the force to provide for security and the legitimacy to provide a focus for communal identity. Moreover, at this stage of human history, democracy has flourished only within the context of nation-states. Virtual communities are still weaker than geographical ones. So, despite the long tradition of efforts to design alternatives, the territorial state and its challenges remain central to world politics.

States will persist, but the context of world politics is changing. Revolutionary changes in technology make the world seem smaller and more close-knit. Yet at the same time, many people are reacting to rapid change with divisive ethnic, religious, and nationalistic responses. As we saw in Chapter 7, globalization can create economic integration and political fragmentation at the same time.

Communications are changing the world. Diplomacy is carried out in real time. In the Gulf War, both Saddam Hussein and George Bush were watching CNN for the latest news. During the fighting in Afghanistan, both Osama bin Laden and George W. Bush watched CNN and the Arabic station al Jazeera. During the Iraq War, television reporters were embedded with frontline troops and broadcast battles in real time to a global audience. Human rights problems and mass suffering in distant parts of the globe are brought into our living rooms on television. People living on a dollar a day in poor countries are becoming more aware of the lifestyles of people earning millions of dollars a year. According to Kenneth Rogoff, former chief economist of the International Monetary Fund, a high correlation between business and consumer sentiment across the world may sway global economic activity toward a common recession more than in the past. "One reason we have become more synchronized," he said, "is because we are all watching CNN."[1]

But economic integration does not mean political integration. Most people who watched the wars in Afghanistan and Iraq on al Jazeera had different views of events than those who watched them on CNN. Similarly, the World Wide Web makes more information available to more people, but people do not always seek the same types and sources of information. The Internet, cable, and satellite television encourage "narrowcasting" of information to specific groups rather than the common denominator that typified television network broadcasting. The Canadian communications theorist Marshall McLuhan once argued that modern communications was producing what he called a "global village." But the metaphor of a global village can be misleading because global political identity remains weak. In much of the world, national, religious, and ethnic identities seem to be getting stronger, not weaker. Instead of a global village, we have villages around the globe that are more aware of each other. And villages connote parochialism as well as community. This simultaneous process of integration and disintegration has given rise to two popular oversimplified visions of the future of world politics after the end of the Cold War.

The End of History or the Clash of Civilizations?

In 1989, Francis Fukuyama published an article entitled "The End of History." He did not mean that literally, but rather argued that with the demise of communism we had reached the end point of ideological evolution and "the emergence of Western liberal democracy as the final form of human government." Deep ideological cleavages drove international conflict over the twentieth century, and movements such as fascism and communism were responses to the disruption of traditional life by modernization. Industrialization tore people from their villages or small communities and made them available for mobilization by the large ideological movements. Over time, however, liberal capitalism proved more successful in producing a higher level of welfare and citizen participation. The end of the Cold War suggested that liberal capitalism had prevailed. In one sense, Fukuyama is right. There is no longer one single competitor to liberal capitalism as an overarching ideology. And the relations among rich democracies have been profoundly transformed. Neither Germany and France nor the United States and Japan expect or plan for war with each other. Their complex interdependence forms large islands of democratic peace in the world today, along the lines of Kant's liberal predictions.

But in another sense, rather than the "end of history," the post–Cold War world could be described as the *return* of history. The return of history means more normal circumstances in which a single ideological cleavage does not drive the larger conflicts in international politics. Liberal capitalism has many competitors, albeit fragmented ones. China and Russia use capitalism and global markets, yet neither is liberal nor fully capitalist. In other areas, religious fundamentalism challenges the norms and practices of liberal capitalism. We sometimes lump all religious fundamentalisms together, but there are many fundamentalisms. What many have in common is a reaction against and a resistance to secular liberal capitalism. The major response and competitor to liberal capitalism after the Cold War is ethnic, religious, and national communalism.

In 1993, Samuel P. Huntington published an article (later a book) titled "The Clash of Civilizations" that became a well-known counter to Fukuyama's vision. Huntington argued that rather than the fundamental sources of conflict in the new world being primarily ideological or economic, the great divisions that would dominate conflict would be cultural. Building on the work of the British historian Arnold Toynbee, Huntington divided the world into eight great "civilizations" (Western and Latin American, African, Islamic, Sinic, Hindu, Orthodox, Buddhist, and Japanese). He predicted conflict along the fault lines of those civilizations. In contrast to realists who used balance-of-power theory to predict that interstate conflicts would reemerge between Germany and its neighbors, or some liberals who expected the democratic peace to spread around the globe, Huntington proved astute in focusing on culture as a source of conflict.

On the other hand, Huntington oversimplified his vision by adopting Toynbee's rather arbitrary categorization of civilizations. As we saw in Chapter 7, cultures are not homogeneous or static, but overlapping and fluid. More conflicts have occurred within the large "civilizations" in Huntington's map of the world (e.g., within Africa or Islam) than between them. Some observers argue that Osama bin Laden's terrorist attacks and his call for an Islamic jihad against the West prove that Huntington was correct, but one can just as plausibly see the events following September 2001 as a civil war within Islam between extreme fundamentalists and moderates. Many faithful Muslims have more in common with moderate Christians and Jews than with Osama bin Laden.

Both Fukuyama's and Huntington's visions suffer from trying to fit the post–Cold War world into one or the other pattern. But one size does not fit all. As we saw earlier, not only are there multiple cultures, but there are very different types of states in terms of levels of economic modernization. Fukuyama's triumph of liberal capitalism and democratic peace fits well with much of the postindustrial world. Realism has much to tell us about relations among preindustrial and industrializing countries. Huntington's focus on cultural conflict fits better with the preindustrial world and its relations with the rest of the world.

As we saw earlier, ethnic and cultural conflict tends to rise when identities are challenged by major social changes that accompany modernization and globalization. People with similar ethnic characteristics asserting their common identity is a very powerful idea, and when they seek to control a state we call it nationalism. Realists criticize Huntington by pointing out that such nation-states are in tension with the transnational civilizations and religious cultures he focuses on. As we saw in the Middle East, nation-states such as Egypt and Syria proved stronger than pan-Arabism, and are currently struggling against Islamic fundamentalism.

Even when states prevail, nationalism varies in intensity. It is instructive to look at the difference between Eastern and Western Europe. Under communist rule nationalistic and ethnic conflicts in the East were frozen for a half century. The end of the Cold War and the removal of Soviet hegemony thawed many of these tensions. For example, with the end of the Cold War and the demise of its communist government, competition between Serbs, Croats, Muslims, and Kosovar Albanians came to the fore with terrible consequences in Yugoslavia. Throughout the former Soviet Union, many ethnic groups spill across borders, stirring up more potential for further ethnic conflict and revivals of nationalism. Contrast this with post–Cold War Western Europe, where intrastate conflict is negligible and countries that previously held strong national rivalries have formed a larger European Union. What can explain it?

Part of the explanation may be the role of economic growth. When people are better off, the animosities may be less tense. Part of it may be democracy, for when people have a chance to resolve disputes openly, passions can be better managed. Some Western animosities were exorcised through democratic processes—witness the debate that went on in West Germany at the end of World War II that led to changes in the textbooks and the new understanding of German history. And part of the answer lies in the regional institutions that pulled Western Europeans together in a larger framework in which the more extreme nationalist views were discouraged. Fortunately, the desire of many Eastern European countries to join the European Union had an important moderating effect on their leaders and peoples. Indeed, the soft power of the European Union has helped spur significant economic and political reforms in Eastern Europe, at a pace once considered unachievable.

But even in Western Europe, nationalism is far from dead and gone. Many Europeans do not want their national identity submerged completely in a European identity. There are still residual fears between French and Germans. One reason why the French support European integration is to tie the Germans down. In addition, many Western Europeans are concerned about the impact of immigration on their national cultures. They fear migration from the north of Africa as well as from Eastern Europe. Experts point to the September 11 terrorist attacks, and subsequent attacks in Madrid and London, as evidence that European citizens and leaders have failed to adequately address the political and economic grievances of Europe's sizable Muslim immigrant community. And riots throughout France in late 2005 demonstrated that many North African immigrants had not been successfully assimilated into the French economy and society. Simultanesouly, right-wing parties in Western Europe increasingly appeal to xenophobia and provide a warning signal that the problems of nationalism and ethnic tensions are not totally banished from Western Europe. But with declining birth rates and porous borders, Europe cannot cut off all immigration from its poorer neighbors across the Mediterranean Sea. Resolving the tensions between a desire to preserve a European identity and the need to better integrate immigrants into society will therefore be Europe's next challenge.

Technology and the Diffusion of Power

A third vision of the future is less determinate than that of Fukuyama or Huntington, but also comes closer to reality: the view that technology, particularly information technology, is leading to a diffusion of power away from central governments (Table 9.1). Just as the twentieth century was the era of centralizing power in

TABLE 9.1   The Diffusion of Governance in the Twenty-first Century

	Private	*Public*	*Third Sector*
Supranational	Transnational Corporations (e.g. IBM, Shell)	Intergovernmental Organizations (e.g. UN, WTO)	Nongovernmental Organizations (e.g. Oxfam, Greenpeace)
National	National Corporations (e.g. US Airways)	Twentieth-Century Central Government	National Nonprofits (e.g. American Red Cross)
Subnational	Local Businesses	State/Local Government	Local Groups

national capitals, which reached its peak with the totalitarian governments in the Soviet Union and Nazi Germany, economic and information networks are moving some functions of governance to higher and lower levels of government, and some from formal government to the private and nonprofit sectors, as Table 9.1 illustrates.

As we saw in Chapter 8, information is power, and governments of all kinds will find their control eroding during the twenty-first century as information technology gradually spreads and costs continue to decrease. In the middle of the twentieth century, people worried that computers might produce the centralized, authoritarian world of George Orwell's novel *1984*, but the decentralizing effects have proven to be more powerful.

How far and how fast the information revolution causes decentralization will vary across countries, and countervailing forces may arise. But the general proposition that governments are losing their monopoly over foreign policy and that they will have to share the stage in world politics with the nonstate actors described in Chapter 8 seems highly likely.

This diffusion of power can have both positive and negative consequences. A benign vision paints a picture in which technology will encourage economic development and make authoritarian regimes less tenable. The result will be to speed the spread of the islands of democratic peace. A malign vision sees a new feudalism in which destructive individuals, terrorist groups, and otherwise weak states gain access to weapons of mass destruction, creating true anarchy, rather than the anarchy of the interstate system. In such an insecure world, a negative reaction may slow down or reverse economic globalization; citizens may sacrifice democratic liberties in favor of Hobbesian autocratic governments that provide basic personal security.

The benign vision points out that because of transnational communications, there is much more awareness of what is going on in other parts of the globe and groups are better able to organize on a global basis. As we have seen, NGOs are able to mount transnational campaigns for environmental and human rights causes. The Internet provides information to citizens that undercuts the controls of authoritarian regimes.

The most impressive transnational actor, of course, is the multinational corporation. By spreading investments around the world and making profits in different parts of the global market, the transnational corporation is producing a different type of world economy. Governments compete to attract international investments. A large part of international trade is trade within multinational corporations. Honda now produces more automobiles in the United States than it does in Japan, and it transports American-made automobiles back to Japan. The U.S. government has even pressed the European Union to accept Honda vehicles made in the United States. In other words, the United States defined the export of Japanese cars made in the United States to Europe as an American national interest. Similarly, IBM was the largest producer of mainframe computers in Japan; IBM/Japan does its research in Japan and hires Japanese employees. In 2004, IBM sold its personal computer division to the Chinese computer manufacturer Lenovo, furthering the globalized nature of the computer industry. When an American calls a toll-free service number in the United States, the call is likely to be answered by an Indian in Bangalore who has learned to reply with an American accent.

This led former Secretary of Labor Robert Reich to ask, "Who is us?" Should analysts focus on the identity of the headquarters of a company or on where it does its research and production? He argues that in terms of what is good for the people living within the borders of the United States, a foreign company working inside the United States may be more important than an American company working in Japan. Critics have responded to Reich by saying that he is looking further into the future than is currently justified. Most multinational corporations have a predominant national identity, and three-quarters of American production is done by companies with headquarters in the United States. Nonetheless, it is an interesting way of thinking about the future. Transnational investment is helping to confuse identities, to confuse the question of "who is us," and along with ecological interdependence, might affect long-run views of global problems.

If the United States responded by excluding foreign firms from American markets, it would simply create inefficient firms that can no longer compete on a global basis. The trouble with protectionist responses is that they may hurt the protector as much as they hurt the other side. So in the 1990s, the Americans and the Japanese negotiated over domestic impediments to trade. The United States pressed Japan over something strictly within Japanese domestic jurisdiction. Japan had laws restricting supermarket size and other practices restricting access of foreign firms to the distribution system. A number of Japanese politicians and consumers were delighted to have this American pressure because it benefited the Japanese consumer. In a sense, there was a transnational coalition between U.S. producers and Japanese consumers. The Japanese government in turn pressed the United States to reduce its budget deficit, arguing correctly that the U.S. trade deficit was related to the government budget deficit. In other words, Americans and the Japanese officials were dealing with each other not at water's edge, but on matters that were deep within the sovereign jurisdiction of each country.

Proliferation of Weapons of Mass Destruction

The malign vision of the effects of technology on world order focuses on a different dimension of the transnational spread of technology. As we saw in the oil case, companies spread technologies and skills. Technology can also be spread through trade, migration, education, and the flow of ideas. What will this dispersal do to security? Already 40 countries have the potential to make nuclear, chemical, or biological weapons of mass destruction. The technology of chemical weaponry is nearly a century old; nuclear weaponry and ballistic missiles are half-century-old technologies. To some extent, policies of nonproliferation have slowed the rate of spread of nuclear weapons. But the problem of proliferation was exacerbated when the Soviet Union collapsed and its successor states have been less able to control the outflow of technology.

Before the Soviet collapse, eight countries had nuclear weapons. Five were formally declared nuclear weapons states in the 1968 Treaty on the Non-proliferation of Nuclear Weapons (NPT): the United States, the Soviet Union, Britain, France, and China. Three states remained outside the treaty and were widely reputed to have developed nuclear weapons covertly: Israel, India, and Pakistan. In 1998, both India and Pakistan openly tested their nuclear weapons. Three other countries— Iraq, Iran, and North Korea—signed the NPT but were widely viewed as trying to develop weapons anyway. North Korea eventually withdrew from the treaty. Five other countries—South Africa, South Korea, Argentina, Brazil, and Libya—started down that path but changed their minds. Interestingly, more than 30 countries could have produced nuclear weapons but did not; that is, three or four times more states were able to have nuclear weapons than actually had them. That is quite a contrast to President Kennedy's fear when signing the Limited Test Ban Treaty in 1963, that 25 countries would have nuclear weapons by the 1970s.

Why wasn't there more nuclear proliferation? After all, in an anarchic world of sovereign states, nuclear weapons are the ultimate form of self-help. There are four major answers. One was the alliances that arose during the Cold War in which each superpower gave security guarantees to its allies. For example, Germany and Japan did not develop nuclear weapons because they had American security guarantees. American promises to prevent any country from using nuclear blackmail against these allies reassured the Japanese and the Germans that they did not have to develop nuclear weapons. Alliances also made a difference to some of the smaller states. For example, South Korea and Taiwan each began to develop nuclear weapons when it looked as if the United States might withdraw from Asia in the 1970s in the aftermath of Vietnam, but they stopped when the United States protested and promised continued protection. Similarly, the Soviet Union constrained its Eastern European allies and Third World client states from developing nuclear weapons.

Another cause was superpower cooperation. In the early stages of the nuclear era, the superpower attitude on nuclear weaponry was highly competitive. The superpowers tried to use nuclear technology to earn points in the ideological competition. In 1953, President Eisenhower announced with great fanfare the Atoms for Peace program to help other countries develop nuclear technology for peaceful purposes, emphasizing the benign face of the atom to win more points for the United States. Similarly, the Soviet Union extended nuclear assistance to China. But by 1968, the United States and the Soviet Union were able to cooperate to the point that they could agree on a nonproliferation treaty. In 1977, the United States, the Soviet Union, and 13 other countries that supplied nuclear technology set up the Nuclear Suppliers Group to set guidelines on what sorts of nuclear technology could be exported.

A third reason why nuclear proliferation was curbed was the existence of treaties and institutions. Roughly 190 states have now signed the Non-Proliferation Treaty, in which nations agreed not to develop or to transfer nuclear weapons. Non-nuclear states have agreed to have inspectors from the UN's International Atomic Energy Agency in Vienna (which was awarded the 2005 Nobel Peace Prize) visit their peaceful nuclear facilities to ensure that they are not being misused. As we have seen, only a few countries such as Israel, India, and Pakistan did not sign the treaty and a few signatories cheated. Finally, after Iraq lost the Gulf War, American forces and UN inspectors dismantled its nuclear programs.

Two open questions for the post–Cold War world were the future of alliances, institutions, and security guarantees, and whether nuclear technology would flow from the former Soviet Union to would-be proliferators. Neorealists, such as Kenneth Waltz, have argued that the spread of nuclear weapons may be stabilizing because deterrence will work. If nuclear weapons helped prevent the Cold War from becoming hot, why wouldn't their crystal ball effect produce prudence and order in other parts of the world such as the Middle East and South Asia? The trouble with this view is that it rests almost entirely on a rational model of deterrence among coherent unitary actors. But if the real danger of nuclear weapons in the post–Cold War period is likely to be loss of control, then these rational models that provide the basis for confident predictions may be largely irrelevant. Many of the countries that will next develop nuclear weapons have an unstable record caused by coups and by armies splitting.

Transnational Threats and the Concept of Security

Nuclear weapons in the United States and the Soviet Union were equipped with elaborate technological devices—permissive action links—that required a code from a higher authority in order to get access to the weapon. But many of the countries developing new nuclear weapons will not have these elaborate technological devices. The end of the Cold War and the transnational spread of technology may produce a larger prospect of nuclear weapons being used in some of the new countries trying to enter the nuclear race than was true in the last half century. And one of the greatest threats in the future will be transnational terrorists obtaining weapons of mass destruction. We know that bin Laden and the Al Qaeda network were making efforts to obtain such weapons and had made contact with scientists working in Pakistan's nuclear program.

Fissile material is difficult and costly to produce, but terrorists might get access to material stolen from former Soviet states and smuggled abroad. Moreover, nuclear weapons are not the only threat. Biological agents have been developed by states such as Iraq. Even though they are unreliable on the battlefield (think of the effect of wind on an aerosol cloud of anthrax spores), biological weapons are easier to make than nuclear weapons—recipes are available on the Internet—and can be used to create terror among defenseless civilian populations. In 1993, if the transnational terrorists who detonated a truck bomb in the basement garage of New York's World Trade Center had used anthrax or the chemical agent sarin in addition to high explosives, they could have claimed thousands of victims. In 2001, terrorists turned hijacked civilian airliners into gigantic cruise missiles to accomplish that purpose. In contrast, however, if the 9/11 terrorists had had access to a nuclear weapon, they could have killed hundreds of thousands of people. More alarmingly, the problem of transnational actors acquiring weapons of mass destruction is not likely to vanish if the

Al Qaeda network is dismantled. In 1995, a religious cult in Japan, Aum Shinrikyo, killed a dozen people with sarin in the Tokyo subway system. The cult had already begun to expand transnationally, had been carrying out experiments in developing biological weapons, and was investigating nuclear weapons.

Terrorist groups could also wreak havoc by attacking the information systems that control electricity for hospitals, air traffic radar, or banking transactions. Such attacks could be perpetrated with high explosives at the sites of key server computers, but they could also be carried out transnationally by computer hackers tens of thousands of miles away.

Deterrence does not provide adequate protection against terrorist threats because there is sometimes no return address against which to retaliate unless a foreign state can be proven to have assisted the terrorists, as Afghanistan's Taliban regime did. And the worst case of terrorism in the United States before 2001, the bombing of the federal building in Oklahoma City in 1995, was purely homegrown. In other cases, criminal groups may take control of the government of a state but ostensibly behave according to international law and claim the rights of sovereign protection against interference in their internal affairs. In such circumstances, other states may feel justified in intervening. Some situations in Latin America and the Caribbean have come close to this: witness the 1989 American invasion of Panama, the capture of its president Manuel Noriega, and his trial in the United States on drug-smuggling charges. In 2002, President George W. Bush issued a new national security strategy that argued in favor of preemption in the face of terrorist threats, and pledged to attack both terrorist regimes and governments that harbor or support them.

As transnational threats grow, states will not only begin to question the Westphalian norms that make clear distinctions between what is domestic and international, but they will also find themselves broadening their concepts of security and defense. Many new threats will not be susceptible to solution by armies firing high explosives. Close cooperation of intelligence, customs, and police agencies will play a major role, as will private-sector measures of protection and prevention of facilities critical to the global economy. If democracies fail in these tasks, and terrorists using weapons of mass destruction create an anarchy of individuals rather than states, Fukuyama's vision of the future becomes less relevant. If governments rise to the challenge and contain terrorism, more traditional problems of interstate order still remain.

A NEW WORLD ORDER?

Given the contradictory forces at work, what will be the shape of the world order in the early decades of the twenty-first century? The end of the Cold War certainly altered the international system, but claims of the dawning of "a new world order" were undermined by the profoundly different ways people interpret the word *order*. Realists argue that wars arise from the effort of states to acquire power and security in an anarchic world, or one in which there is no ultimate arbiter of order other than self-help and the force of arms. In this view, *order* refers primarily to the structure or distribution of power among states. Liberals and constructivists argue that conflicts and their prevention are determined not only by the balance of power, but by the domestic structure of states; their values, identities, and cultures; and international institutions for conflict resolution. In contrast to realists, liberals argue that institutions such as the United Nations can help prevent conflict and establish order by stabilizing expectations, thereby creating a sense of continuity and a feeling that current cooperation will be reciprocated in the future. Order for liberals, then, is tied to values such as democracy and human rights, as well as to institutions. Finally, constructivists remind us that any order is contested by various parties and thus is never a value-neutral term.

For some, order has sinister connotations. In the view of nativist or nationalist groups such as that led by Pat Robertson in the United States, or by Jean-Marie Le Pen in France, "new world order" suggests a conspiracy among financial and political elites to dominate the world. In this view, multinational corporations, in league with the financial markets of Wall Street, London, and Tokyo, enrich themselves at the expense of the rest. In the view of certain Islamic fundamentalists, order is a purely Western concept designed to dominate the non-Western world.

These differing conceptions of order mean that a "new world order" is tricky to define. None of these schools of thought is adequate by itself in understanding the causes of conflict in the current world. The realist emphasis on the balance of power is necessary but not sufficient when long-term societal changes are eroding the norms of state sovereignty. The view that peace has broken out among the major liberal democracies is accurate, but it is not a panacea when many states, including some rising great powers, are not liberal democracies. The old, bipolar Cold War order provided a stability of sorts. The Cold War exacerbated a number of Third World conflicts, but economic conflicts among the United States, Europe, and Japan were dampened by common concerns about the Soviet military threat, and bitter ethnic divisions were kept under the tight lid of the Soviet presence in Eastern Europe. With the passing of that bipolar order, conflict did not end. It did, however, have different sources.

Future Configurations of Power

As historians and political observers since Thucydides have noted, rapid power transitions are one of the leading causes of great power conflict. Such power transitions were a deep structural cause of recent great power conflicts, including Germany's rise before each world war and the relative rise and resulting rivalry of the United States and the Soviet Union after World War II. There is a strong consensus that the period after the Cold War was one of rapid power transitions with the rise of the United States and China and the decline of Russia. Considerable debate remains over the description and magnitude of the transitions, however, and these debates indicate the unpredictability that makes such transitions a potential source of conflict.

One alternative is *multipolarity*. French President Jacques Chirac, for example, called for a return to a multipolar world. If the term *multipolarity* implies a historical analogy with the nineteenth century, it is highly misleading. That order rested on a balance of power between roughly five equal powers, whereas the great powers after the Cold War are far from equal. Russia has declined faster and further since 1991 than almost anyone expected, though it retains an immense nuclear arsenal. China has risen faster than most anticipated, with a long period of double-digit economic growth, but remains a developing country. Japan and Germany have not become the full-fledged superpowers that some incorrectly predicted in 1990. And India, despite its great economic progress of the past decade, must overcome several hurdles before achieving its full potential as a major world power. The United States is the only military superpower, though the European Union is similar in economic scale.

Some realists warn that the rapid rise of China will present a hegemonic challenge to the United States in the twenty-first century analogous to what the Kaiser's Germany posed to Britain on the eve of World War I. But the historical analogy is flawed. Germany had already surpassed Britain in industrial strength by 1900, while China's economy is only about one-eighth the size of the United States (measured at official exchange rates). Even if China continues to grow at a rapid rate of 9 percent and the United States at 3 percent, China will still be less than half the economic size of the United States in 2025. While conflict between the two countries is possible if the governments mismanage their relations, a hegemonic conflict is far from inevitable.

Some analysts predict the world will be organized around *three economic blocs*— Europe, Asia, and North America. Yet even here, global technological changes and the increase of nonbloc, nonstate actors such as multinational corporations and ethnic groups will resist the capacity of these three blocs to constrain their activities. And we have already discussed the problem with describing the world order as one of civilizations.

In the aftermath of the 2003 Iraq War, other analysts described the international order as an American world empire. In many ways the metaphor of empire is seductive. The American military has a global reach with bases around the world and its regional commanders sometimes act like proconsuls. English is a *lingua franca* like Latin was. The American economy is the largest in the world, and American culture serves as a magnet. But it is a mistake to confuse the politics of primacy with the politics of empire. The United States is certainly not an empire in the way we think of the European overseas empires of the nineteenth and twentieth centuries because the core feature of such imperialism was political control. Though unequal relationships certainly exist between the United States and weaker powers and can be conducive to exploitation, absent formal political control, the term *imperial* not only is inaccurate but can be misleading.

The United States has more power resources than Britain had at its imperial peak, but the United States has less power in the sense of direct control over the behavior that occurs inside other countries than Britain did when it ruled a quarter of the globe. For example, Kenya's schools, taxes, laws, and elections—not to

Iraq War, 2003

mention external relations—were controlled by British officials. The United States has little such control today. In 2003, the United States could not even get Mexico and Chile to vote for a second UN Security Council resolution authorizing the invasion of Iraq. The imperial analysts reply that the term *empire* is merely a metaphor. But the problem with the metaphor is that it implies a control from Washington that fits poorly with the complex ways in which power is distributed today. As we saw in Chapter 6, the United States found it far easier to win the battle in Iraq than to manage the occupation.

In the global information age, power is distributed among countries in a pattern that resembles a complex three-dimensional chess game in which you play vertically as well as horizontally. On the top chessboard of political-military issues, military power is largely unipolar with the United States as the sole superpower, but on the middle board of economic issues, the United States is not a hegemon or an empire, and it must bargain as an equal when Europe acts in a unified way. For example, on antitrust or trade issues, it must meet Europe halfway to reach agreements. And on the bottom chessboard of transnational relations that cross borders outside the control of governments and include actors as diverse as bankers and terrorists, power is chaotically dispersed. To take a few examples in addition to terrorism, private actors in global capital markets constrain the way interest rates can be used to manage the American economy, and the drug trade, HIV/AIDS, migration, and global warming have deep societal roots in more than one country and are outside American government control. It makes no sense to use traditional terms such as *unipolarity, hegemony,* or *American empire* to describe such issues.

Those who portray an empire based on traditional military power are relying on one-dimensional analysis. But in a three-dimensional game, you lose if you focus only on one board and fail to notice the other boards and the vertical connections among them—witness the connections in the war on terrorism between military actions on the top board where the United States removed a tyrant in Iraq, but simultaneously increased the ability of the Al Qaeda network to gain new recruits on the bottom transnational board. Representing the dark side of globalization, these issues are inherently multilateral and require cooperation for their solution. To describe such a world as an American empire fails to capture the real nature of the world the United States faces.

Another issue, often ignored by proponents of the empire model, is whether the American public will tolerate a classical imperial role. America was briefly tempted into real imperialism when it emerged as a world power in 1898, but the interlude of formal empire did not last. Unlike in Britain, imperialism was not a comfortable experience for Americans. Polls have consistently shown little taste for empire. Instead, the public continues to say it favors multilateralism and using the UN. Perhaps that is why Michael Ignatieff, a Canadian advocate of accepting the empire metaphor, qualifies it by referring to the American role in the world as "Empire Lite."

The current distribution of power is one of *multilevel interdependence*. No single hierarchy adequately describes a world politics that is like a three-dimensional chess game. None of this complexity would matter if military power were as fungible as money and could determine the outcomes in all areas. But military prowess is a poor predictor of the outcomes on the economic and transnational playing boards of current world politics. The United States has a more diversified portfolio of power resources than other countries, but the current world order is not an era of American empire in any traditional sense of the word. The world's only superpower cannot afford to go it alone. Globalization is elevating issues on the international agenda that not even the most powerful country can address on its own—witness international financial stability, global climate change, the spread of infectious diseases, and transnational drug, crime, and terrorist networks. The paradox of American power in the twenty-first century is that the strongest military power the world has seen since the days of Rome is unable to provide security to its citizens by acting alone.

The Prison of Old Concepts

The world after the Cold War is *sui generis.* Constructivist theorists are right that we should not overly constrain our understanding by trying to force it into the procrustean bed of traditional metaphors with their mechanical polarities. Power is becoming more multidimensional, structures more complex, and states themselves more permeable. This added complexity means world order must rest on more than the traditional military balance of power alone.

The realist view of world order is necessary but not sufficient to explain today's geopolitical order because it does not take into account the long-term societal changes that have been slowly moving the world away from the Westphalian system. In 1648, after 30 years of tearing each other apart over religion, the European states agreed in the Peace of Westphalia that the ruler, in effect, would determine the religion of a state regardless of popular preferences. Order was based on the sovereignty of states, not the sovereignty of peoples. The mechanical balancing of states treated as empty billiard balls was slowly eroded over the ensuing centuries by the growth of nationalism and democratic participation, but the norms of state sovereignty persisted. Now the rapid growth in transnational communications, migration, and economic interdependence is accelerating the erosion of the classical conception of order and state control, and increasing the gap between norm and reality.

This evolution makes more relevant the liberal conception of a world society of peoples as well as of states, and of order resting on values and institutions as well as military power. Liberal views that were once regarded as hopelessly utopian, such as Immanuel Kant's plea for a peaceful league of democracies, seem less far-fetched now that political scientists report virtually no cases of liberal democracies going to war with each other. In the debates over the effects of German reunification, for example, the predictions of realists who saw Europe going back to the future have fared less well than those of liberals who stressed that the new Germany is democratic and deeply enmeshed with its Western neighbors through the institutions of the European Union. However, as political scientists Edward Mansfield and Jack Snyder point out, young democracies can be more prone to war, and so increased democratization in tumultuous regions, such as the Middle East, should not be expected to yield instant security dividends.

Indeed, liberal conceptions of order are not entirely new and they do not apply to all countries. The Cold War order had norms and institutions, but they played a limited role. During World War II, Roosevelt, Stalin, and Churchill had agreed to a United Nations that assumed a multipolar distribution of power. The UN Security Council would enforce the doctrine of collective security and nonaggression against smaller states while the five great powers were protected by their vetoes.

Even this abbreviated version of Woodrow Wilson's institutional approach to order was hobbled, however, by the unforeseen rise of bipolarity. The superpowers vetoed each other's initiatives, and the organization was reduced to the more modest role of stationing peacekeepers to observe cease-fires rather than repelling aggressors. When the decline of Soviet power led to a new Kremlin policy of cooperation with the United States in applying the UN doctrine of collective security against Iraq in 1990–1991, it was less the arrival of a new world order than the reappearance of an aspect of the liberal institutional order that was supposed to have come into effect in 1945.

But just as the Gulf War resurrected one aspect of the liberal approach to world order, it also exposed an important weakness in the liberal conception. The doctrine of collective security enshrined in the UN Charter is state-centric, applicable when borders are crossed, but not when force is used among peoples within a state. Liberals try to escape this problem by appealing to the principles of democracy and self-determination: Let peoples within states vote on whether they want to be protected behind borders of their own. But, as we have seen, self-determination is not as simple as it sounds. Who decides what self will determine? Less than 10 percent of the states in today's world are ethnically homogeneous. Only half have one ethnic group that accounts for as much as 75 percent of their population. Most of the states of the former Soviet Union have significant minorities, and many have disputed borders. Africa might be considered a continent of roughly a thousand peoples squeezed within and across fifty-some states. In Canada, the French-speaking majority of Quebec demands special status, and some agitate for independence from the rest of Canada. Once such multiethnic, multilingual states are called into question, it is difficult to see where the process ends. In such a world, local autonomy and international surveillance of minority rights hold some promise, but a policy of unqualified support for national self-determination could turn into a principle of enormous world disorder.

The Evolution of a Hybrid World Order

How then is it possible to preserve some order in traditional terms of the distribution of power among sovereign states while also moving toward institutions based on "justice among peoples"? International institutions are gradually evolving in such a post-Westphalian direction. International humanitarian law, and within it the notion of states having a duty to protect individual rights against massive depredations by dictatorial rulers, is gaining increased influence. Already in 1945, Articles 55 and 56 of the UN Charter pledged states to collective responsibility for observance of human rights and fundamental freedoms. Even before the 1991 Security Council resolutions authorizing postwar interventions in Iraq, UN recommendations of sanctions against apartheid in South Africa set a precedent of not being strictly limited by the Charter's statements about sovereignty. In Europe, the 1975 Helsinki Accords codified minority rights, and violations could be referred to the European Conference on Security and Cooperation and the Council of Europe. International law is, therefore, gradually evolving. In 1965, the American Law Institute defined international law as "rules and principles . . . dealing with conduct of states and international organizations." Two decades later, the institute's lawyers added, "as well as some of their relations with persons." Individual and minority rights are increasingly treated as more than just national concerns.

In many, perhaps most, parts of the world, human rights are flouted and violations go unpunished. To mount an armed multilateral intervention to right all such wrongs would be another enormous principle of disorder. But, as we have seen, intervention is a matter of degree, with actions ranging from statements and limited economic measures at the low end of the spectrum to full-fledged invasions at the high end.

Limited interventions and multilateral infringements of sovereignty may gradually increase without suddenly disrupting the distribution of power among states.

On a larger scale, the Security Council may act under Chapter VII of the UN Charter if it determines that internal violence or development of weapons of mass destruction are likely to spill over into a more general threat to the peace in a region. Such definitions are somewhat elastic and may gradually expand over time. In other instances, groups of states may act on a regional basis as Nigeria and others did in the 1990s by sending troops to Liberia and Sierra Leone under the framework of the Economic Community of West African States, or as NATO did in Kosovo in 1999.

Such imperfect principles and institutions will leave much room for domestic violence and injustice among peoples. But the moral horrors will be less than would be the case if policy makers were to try either to right all wrongs by force or, alternatively, to return to the unmodified Westphalian system. Liberals must realize that the evolution of a new world order beyond the Westphalian system is a matter of decades and centuries; realists must recognize that the traditional definitions of power and structure in purely military terms ignore the changes that are occurring in a world of global communications and growing transnational relations.

One thing that is clear is that world government is not just around the corner. There is too much social and political diversity in the world and not a sufficient sense of community to support world government. Reform of the United Nations or the development of new institutions offers new ways for states to work with each other as well as for nonstate actors to facilitate cooperation. In some instances, transnational networks of government officials will foster such cooperation; in other instances mixed coalitions of governments and private actors will do the job. But what does this mean for democracy?

Democracy is government by officials who are accountable and removable by the majority of people in a jurisdiction, albeit with provisions for protections of individuals and minorities. Who are "we the people" in a world where political identity at the global level is so weak? "One state, one vote" is not democratic. Using that formula, as we saw in Chapter 6, a citizen of the Maldive Islands would have a thousand times more voting power than a citizen of China. On the other hand, treating the world as one global constituency implies the existence of a political community in which citizens of 198 states would be willing to be continually outvoted by a billion Chinese and a billion Indians. Minorities acquiesce to a majority when they feel they participate in a larger community. In the absence of such community, the extension of domestic voting procedures to the global level makes little practical or normative sense. A stronger European Parliament may reduce a sense of "democratic deficit" as a European community evolves, but it is doubtful that the analogy makes sense under the conditions that prevail on the global scale. Thus far in world history, democracy has flourished in the context of nation-states.

Accountability, however, is not assured only through voting even in well-functioning democracies. In the United States, for example, the Supreme Court and the Federal Reserve System are responsive to elections only indirectly through a long chain of delegation. Professional norms and standards can help keep the judges and central bankers accountable, but transparency is essential if they are to play this role. In addition to voting, publics communicate and agitate over issues through a variety of means ranging from letters and polls to protests. Interest groups and a free press can play an important role in increasing transparency at the local, national, and transnational levels.

The private sector can also contribute to accountability. Private associations and codes, such as those established by the international chemical industry in the aftermath of the 1984 explosion of a plant in Bhopal, India, can create common standards. The NGO practice of naming and shaming companies that exploit child labor has helped consumers hold accountable transnational firms in the toy and apparel industries. And while people have unequal votes in markets, in the aftermath of the 1997 Asian financial crisis, accountability to markets may have led to more increases in transparency by corrupt governments than any formal agreements did. Open markets can help diminish the undemocratic power of local monopolies and can reduce the power of entrenched and unresponsive government bureaucracies, particularly in countries where parliaments are weak. Moreover, efforts by investors to increase transparency and legal predictability can have beneficial spillover effects on political institutions. Hybrid networks that combine governmental, intergovernmental, and nongovernmental representatives are likely to play a larger role in the future.

There is no single answer to these questions of global governance. We need to think harder about norms and procedures for the governance of globalization. Denial of the problem, misleading domestic analogies, and platitudes about democratic deficits will not do. We need changes in processes that take advantage of the multiple forms of accountability that exist in modern democracies. International institutions are not international government, but they are crucial for international governance in a global information age.

THINKING ABOUT THE FUTURE

What kind of world would you like to live in? You will live in a world that will be anarchic in the terms stated at the beginning of the book, and we must hope not in the Hobbesian sense of a chaotic war of all against all. Order will be provided both by the realists' balance of power among states and by the liberals' evolving international norms and institutions. That order will not always be just. Justice and order are often at odds with each other, even in issues of self-determination. Is it more important to keep borders intact or to pursue humanitarian causes that violate territorial integrity? What do these choices do to principles of order? These debates are not easily reconciled.

But change is occurring. Robert Gilpin argues that international politics has not changed over two millennia, and that Thucydides would have little trouble understanding our world today. If Thucydides were plopped down in the Middle East or East Asia, he would probably recognize the situation quite quickly. But if he were set down in Western Europe, he would probably have a more difficult time understanding the relations between France and Germany. Globally, there has been a technological revolution in the development of nuclear weaponry, an information revolution that reduces the role of geography and territory, an enormous growth in economic interdependence, and an emerging global society in which there is increased consciousness of certain values and human rights that cross national frontiers. Interestingly, similar changes were anticipated by Immanuel Kant in his eighteenth-century liberal view of international politics. Kant predicted that over the long run, humans would evolve beyond war for three reasons: the greater destructiveness of war, the growth of economic interdependence, and the development of what he called republican governments and what we call today liberal democracies.

To understand the current world, we must understand both the realist and liberal views of world politics and be alert to social and cultural changes constructivists emphasize. We need to be able to think about different ideal types at the same time. Neither realism nor complex interdependence exists; both are ideals. The realist sees a world of states using force to pursue security. Reversing that produces complex interdependence, in which nonstate actors, economic instruments, and welfare goals are more important than security. Those two views are at the opposite ends of a conceptual continuum on which we can locate different real-world relationships. All three approaches—realism, liberalism, constructivism—are helpful and necessary to understand international politics in a changing world.

That leads to some final questions. How much will the future resemble the past? Could Europe go back to the future? Will there be another war between great powers? Between civilizations? Will China challenge the United States for hegemonic supremacy in Asia? Will our information age be more democratic and therefore peaceful? Can governments control transnational terrorism? The bipolar world is over, but it is not going to be replaced by a unipolar world empire that the United States controls alone. The world is already economically multipolar, and there will be a diffusion of power as the information revolution progresses, interdependence increases, and transnational actors become more important. The new world will not be neat, and you will live with that.

STUDY QUESTIONS

1. What does Fukuyama mean by the "end of history"? What are the strengths and weaknesses of his concept?
2. Are conflicts more likely to occur between large civilizations or within them? What are the strengths and weaknesses of Huntington's argument?
3. Is there a new world order distinct from that which came to be after World War II? Can we characterize it as multipolar? Bipolar? Unipolar? Does it matter?
4. Is nationalism fading in importance in world politics, or is it stronger than ever? Cite examples. Is empire possible in an era of nationalism?
5. Is the threat of nuclear war a thing of the past? What would happen if terrorists obtained weapons of mass destruction?
6. What are the arguments for and against a diffusion of power away from central governments? Why does it matter? What are the implications for democracy?

7. What kinds of power are important and will be important in coming decades? How will this affect America's role in the world? What does the 1991 Gulf War or the 1999 Kosovo crisis or the 2001 Afghanistan campaign or the 2003 Iraq War imply about the answers to these questions?

8. What does realist theory predict about the future of Europe? Of Asia? What other factors might affect events? What do liberal and constructivist approaches add?

9. What is the difference between global government and global governance? What role do institutions play? What are the implications for democracy?

10. What are arguments for and against portraying the current world order as an American empire?

11. If the Internet strengthens transnational groups, how will that affect world politics?

12. How does security in the twenty-first century differ from security in the previous century?

NOTES

1. Joseph Kahn, "The World's Economies Slide Together into Recession," *The New York Times*, November 25, 2001.

SELECTED READINGS

1. Fukuyama, Francis, "The End of History," *National Interest* no. 16 (Summer 1989), pp. 3–18; Francis Fukuyama, "The Last Man in a Bottle: An Essay on the Tenth Anniversary of the Publication of 'The End of History'" and "Responses to Fukuyama," *National Interest* no. 56 (Summer 1999).

2. Mearsheimer, John, "Back to the Future," *International Security* 15:1 (Summer 1990), pp. 5–56; and Stanley Hoffmann, Robert Keohane, and John Mearsheimer, "Back to the Future: Part II," *International Security* 15:2 (Fall 1990), pp. 191–199.

3. Huntington, Samuel, "The Clash of Civilizations?" *Foreign Affairs* 72:3 (Summer 1993), pp. 22–49.

4. Keohane, Robert O. and J. S. Nye, " Redefining Accountability for Global Governance," in Miles Kahler and David Lake, eds., *Governance in a Global Economy: Political Authority in Transition* (Princeton, NJ: Princeton University Press, 2003), pp. 386–411.

5. Nye, Joseph S., Jr., *The Paradox of American Power: Why the World's Only Superpower Can't Go It Alone* (New York: Oxford University Press, 2002), chap. 5.

6. Dahl, Robert A., "Can International Organizations Be Democratic? A Skeptic's View," in Ian Shapiro and Casiano Hacker-Gordon, eds., *Democracy's Edges* (Cambridge, UK: Cambridge University Press, 1999), pp. 19–36.

FURTHER READINGS

Bacevich, Andrew, *American Empire* (Cambridge, MA: Harvard University Press, 2002).

Barnet, Richard J., and John Cavanagh, *Global Dreams: Imperial Corporations and the New World Order* (New York: Simon & Schuster, 1994).

Brown, Michael, Sean Lynn-Jones, and Steven Miller, eds., *Debating the Democratic Peace* (Cambridge, MA: MIT Press, 1996).

Clark, Grenville, and Louis Sohn, *Introduction to World Peace Through World Law* (Chicago: World Without War, 1973).

Deudny, Daniel, "Geopolitics and Change," in Michael W. Doyle and G. John Ikenberry, eds., *New Thinking in International Relations Theory* (Boulder, CO: Westview, 1997).

Donnelly, Jack, "Genocide and Humanitarian Intervention," *Journal of Human Rights* 1:1 (March 2002), pp. 93–109.

Emmott, Bill, *20:21 Vision: Twentieth Century Lessons for the Twenty-First Century* (New York: Farrar, Straus & Giroux, 2003).

Falk, Richard A., *This Endangered Planet: Prospects and Proposals for Human Survival* (New York: Random, 1971).

Feinstein, Lee, and Anne-Marie Slaughter, "A Duty to Prevent," *Foreign Affairs* (January/February 2004).

Finnemore, Martha, "Constructing Norms of Humanitarian Intervention," in Peter J. Katzenstein, ed., *The Culture of National Security: Norms and Identity in World Politics* (New York: Columbia University Press, 1996).

Gaddis, John L., "Towards the Post–Cold War World," *Foreign Affairs* 70:2 (Spring 1991), pp. 102–122.

Haas, Ernst B., *Beyond the Nation-State: Functionalism and International Organization* (Stanford, CA: Stanford University Press, 1964).

Haass, Richard N., *The Opportunity: America's Moment to Alter History's Course* (New York: Public Affairs, 2005)

Huntington, Samuel P., *The Third Wave: Democratization in the Late Twentieth Century* (Norman: University of Oklahoma Press, 1991).

Ignatieff, Michael, *Empire Lite* (New York: Vintage, 2003).

———, *The Rights Revolution* (Toronto: House of Anansi, 2000).

Kagan, Robert, *Of Paradise and Power: America and Europe in the New World Order* (New York: Vintage, 2003).

Kaplan, Robert, *The Ends of the Earth: A Journey at the Dawn of the 21st Century* (New York: Random, 1996).

Katzenstein, Peter J., *A World of Regions: Asia and Europe in the American Imperium* (Ithaca, NY: Cornell University Press, 2005).

Kennedy, Paul M., *The Rise and Fall of the Great Powers: Economic Change and Military Conflict from 1500 to 2000* (New York: Random, 1987).

Lake, David, and Donald Rothchild, *Ethnic Forces and Global Engagement: The International System and Management of Ethnic Conflict* (Berkeley, CA: University of California, Institute on Global Conflict and Cooperation, 1996).

Mastanduno, Michael, "Preserving the Unipolar Moment: Realist Theories and U.S. Grand Strategy After the Cold War," *International Security* 21:4 (Spring 1997), pp. 49–88.

Mathews, Jessica A., *Preserving the Global Environment: The Challenge of Shared Leadership* (New York: Norton, 1991).

Mitrany, David, *A Working Peace System* (Chicago: Quadrangle, 1966).

Moravcsik, Andrew, *The Choice for Europe: Social Purpose and State Power from Messina to Maastricht* (Ithaca, NY: Cornell University Press, 1998).

———, "The Origins of Human Rights Regimes," *International Organization* 54:2 (Spring 2000), pp. 217–252.

Neustadt, Richard E., and Ernest R. May, *Thinking in Time: The Uses of History for Decisionmakers* (New York: Free Press, 1986).

Russett, Bruce, and James S. Sutterlin, "The U.N. in a New World Order," *Foreign Affairs* 70:2 (Spring 1991), pp. 69–83.

Sagan, Scott D., and Kenneth N. Waltz, *The Spread of Nuclear Weapons: A Debate* (New York: Norton, 1995).

Slaughter, Anne-Marie, *A New World Order* (Princeton, NJ: Princeton University Press, 2004).

Sorensen, Georg, *Changes in Statehood: The Transformation of International Relations* (New York: Palgrave, 2001).

Spiro, Peter J., "New Global Communities: Nongovernmental Organizations in International Decision-Making Institutions," *Washington Quarterly* 18:1 (Winter 1995), pp. 45–56.

Vernon, Raymond, *In the Hurricane's Eye: The Troubled Prospects of Multinational Enterprises* (Cambridge, MA: Harvard University Press, 1998).

Wallace, William, *The Transformation of Western Europe* (London: Royal Institute for International Affairs, Pinter, 1990).

Williams, Phil, "Transnational Criminal Organizations: Strategic Alliances," *Washington Quarterly* 18:1 (Winter 1995), pp. 57–72.

Glossary

Alliances   Formal or informal arrangements made between sovereign states, usually to ensure mutual security.

Appeasement   The act of accommodating the demands of an assertive power in an attempt to prevent conflict. Western Europe's appeasement of Hitler in the late 1930s is the classic example of the dangers of appeasement.

Asymmetry   Situations in which states or agents with unbalanced power capabilities are in opposition to one another. The U.S. war against Al Qaeda is widely regarded as an asymmetrical conflict.

Balance of power   A term commonly used to describe (1) the distribution of power in the international system, (2) a policy of balancing foreign powers to prevent one state from gaining a preponderance of power, or (3) the balances of military power that existed in the multipolar system of Europe in the nineteenth century.

Bipolar   The structure of an international system in which two states or alliances of states dominate world politics. The Cold War division between the United States and the Soviet Union is often referred to as a bipolar system.

Bretton Woods   New Hampshire resort where a 1944 conference established the IMF and World Bank.

Cold War   The standoff between the United States and the Soviet Union that lasted from roughly the end of World War II until the fall of the Berlin Wall in 1989. Though proxy wars were fought on behalf of both sides around the globe, U.S. and Soviet troops did not engage in direct combat, making this a "cold" war rather than a "hot" shooting war.

Collective security   A means of maintaining peace in which a collection of states agree on an institutional framework and legal mechanisms to prevent or suppress aggression. Two examples of collective security actions under the auspices of the United Nations were the Korean War and the Persian Gulf War.

Congress of Vienna   An 1815 agreement that marked the end of the Napoleonic Wars and established the general framework for the European international system in the nineteenth century.

Constructivism   An analytical approach to international relations that emphasizes the importance of ideas, cultures, and social dimensions. John Ruggie, Alexander Wendt, and Peter Katzenstein are considered constructivists.

Containment   A foreign policy designed to contain a potential aggressor. Containment was the cornerstone of American foreign policy toward Soviet communism during the Cold War.

Cosmopolitans   Cosmopolitans value individuals over sovereign states and limit the moral importance of national borders. Charles Beitz is a prominent cosmopolitan theorist.

Counterfactuals   Arguments that run contrary to facts. These are often phrased as "what if" questions and are employed in the analysis of scenarios in international relations to explore causal relationships.

Cuban Missile Crisis   A standoff in October 1962 between the United States and the Soviet Union over the presence of Soviet nuclear missiles in Cuba. The crisis was resolved when the Soviets removed their missiles partly in exchange for a secret agreement that the United States would remove missiles based in Turkey.

Dependency theory A theory of develop- ment, popular in the 1960s and 1970s, that predicted wealthy countries at the "center" of the international system would hold back "peripheral" developing coun- tries. This theory lost credibility when countries like Singapore and South Korea developed rapidly in the 1980s and 1990s.

Deterrence A strategy of discouraging a potential aggressor through threat or fear.

Economic interdependence Situations characterized by reciprocal economic effects among countries or actors in different countries. See *interdependence*.

Fourteen Points Woodrow Wilson's blueprint for a settlement at the end of World War I. Among its most important features was a call for an international institution that would safeguard collective security. See *League of Nations*.

Game Theory A theory of rational action that predicts how actors will react in certain game situations to obtain favorable outcomes. Game theory was popularized in the movie *A Beautiful Mind*.

GATT (General Agreement on Tariffs and Trade) An international agreement on tariffs and trade that began in 1947 and was replaced in 1994 by the WTO (World Trade Organization).

Geopolitics A theory of international politics that considers the location and proximity of a state a key cause of its behavior.

Globalization At its broadest, the term is used to describe worldwide networks of interdependence. It has a number of dimensions, including economic, cultural, military, and political globalization. It is not a new phenomenon—it dates back at least to the Silk Road—but due to the information revolution, its contemporary form is "thicker and quicker" than previous ones.

Hegemony The ability to exercise control within a system of states. The United States is often said to exercise military hegemony today.

IGO (intergovernmental organization) An organization that links one or more sovereign governments. The United Nations and the IMF are examples of IGOs.

IMF (International Monetary Fund) An inter- national institution set up after World War II to lend money, primarily to developing countries, to help stabilize currencies or cover balances of payments. See *Bretton Woods*.

INGO (international nongovernmental organizations) A subset of NGOs that have an international focus. See *NGO*.

Interdependence Situations characterized by reciprocal effects among countries or other actors.

International institutions Institutions created to facilitate international cooperation. The United Nations, World Bank, and International Monetary Fund are all examples of international institutions.

International law A combination of treaties and customs that regulates the conduct of states. International law can also apply to individuals who act in an international context.

Intervention External actions that influence the domestic affairs of a sovereign state. Most often this term is used to refer to forcible interference in another state's domestic affairs.

Jus Ad Bellem A moral code of justifications that must be satisfied for a war to be considered a just war. The elements of this have traditionally included having just cause; being declared by a proper authority; possessing right intention; having a reasonable chance of success; and the ends being proportional to the means used. From the Latin "justice to go to war."

Jus In Bello A moral code of conduct that holds states and individuals responsible for their actions during wartime. From the Latin "justice in war."

Just war doctrine   An intellectual tradition with origins in the Christian church that employs moral guidelines and justifications to sanction the appropriate use of force by states. Just war tradition prohibits killing innocent civilians. St. Augustine and Thomas Aquinas are historical figures in this tradition; Michael Walzer is a well-known modern theorist. See *Jus In Belle* and *Jus Ad Bellem*.

League of Nations   An international organization dedicated to collective security that was founded at the end of World War I. Woodrow Wilson, the league's chief advocate, called for its creation in his Fourteen Points at the end of the war. The league failed due to its inability to prevent the aggressions that led to World War II.

Liberalism   An analytical approach to international relations in which states function as part of a global society that sets the context for their interactions. Classical liberalism has intellectual roots in the writings of Immanuel Kant, Jeremy Bentham, and John Stuart Mill. In the modern era, Woodrow Wilson and Richard Rosecrance are considered liberals.

Multipolar   The structure of an international system in which three or more states or alliances dominate world politics. Many scholars describe nineteenth-century Europe as multipolar.

NAFTA (North American Free Trade Agreement)   A 1994 agreement among the United States, Canada, and Mexico that created a free-trade zone in North America.

National interest   A state's perceptions of its goals in the international system. Realists, liberals, and constructivists all have different perceptions of how states formulate their national interests.

Nationalism   A belief that people belonging to a certain group, whether through shared ethnicity, language, land, culture, or religion, should inhabit a given territory and control a state.

Neoliberalism   An analytical approach to international relations in which the actions of states are constrained by economic interdependence and international institutions. Robert Keohane is considered a neoliberal. See *interdependence* and *international institutions*.

Neorealism   An analytical approach to international relations in which the actions of states are constrained primarily by the structural balance of military power. Kenneth Waltz and John Mearsheimer are well-known neorealists.

NGO (nongovernmental organization)   In the broadest definition, any organization that represents interests other than those of a state or multinational corporation. Most references concern transnational or international groups (sometimes referred to as INGOs). Examples of well-known NGOs include the Catholic Church, Greenpeace, and the International Red Cross.

Nuclear deterrence   A strategy used by both the United States and Soviet Union during the Cold War, in which the possession of nuclear weapons acted as a deterrent to the other side. See *deterrence*.

OPEC (Organization of Petroleum Exporting Countries)   An organization of the world's largest oil-producing states that tries to coordinate policy on oil production and pricing among its members.

Peacekeeping   The deployment of armed troops to prevent conflict or maintain peace in a state. Many peacekeeping operations are conducted under UN auspices, but peacekeeping can also be conducted by a regional organization or a group of countries acting outside the United Nations.

Peace of Westphalia   The 1648 treaty that ended the Thirty Years' War and became the framework for an international system in which the sovereign state was the highest form of authority.

Peloponnesian War   A conflict between Athens and Sparta lasting from 431 B.C. to 404 B.C. that resulted in the defeat of Athens and the end of the Golden Age of Athenian democracy. See *Thucydides*.

Prisoner's Dilemma   A thought exercise in which two prisoners who are separated make independent rational decisions about sharing and withholding information to obtain optimal outcomes for themselves. See *game theory*.

Realism   An analytical approach to international relations in which the primary actors are states and the central problems are war and the use of force. Thucydides, Otto von Bismarck, E. H. Carr, Hans Morgenthau, and Henry Kissinger are all considered realists.

Self-determination   The right of a people to form a state. Woodrow Wilson was a strong advocate for self-determination.

Sensitivity   The amount and rapidity of the effects of dependence. Describes how quickly a change in one part of a system leads to a change in another part.

Skeptics   Skeptics believe that moral categories have no place in discussions of international relations because of the lack of an international community that can sanction rights and duties.

Social liberalism   The belief that person-to-person contacts reduce conflict by promoting understanding.

Soft power   The ability to obtain desired outcomes through attraction rather than coercion or payment.

Sovereignty   The idea that a state has a government that exercises authority over its territory. See *Treaty of Westphalia*.

State moralists   State moralists believe that international morality depends on a society of sovereign states playing by certain rules, even if those rules are not always obeyed.

Symmetry   Situations in which states or agents with relatively balanced power capabilities are in opposition to one another. The nuclear balance between the United States and the Soviet Union is widely regarded as a symmetrical conflict.

Thirty Years' War   A series of European wars fueled by international, religious, and dynastic conflicts that took place from 1618 to 1648. See *Treaty of Westphalia*.

Thucydides   An Athenian commander whose book *History of the Peloponnesian War*, a chronicle of the Peloponnesian War between Athens and Sparta, is one the earliest known works of history and international relations.

Transnational actor   Any nonstate actor or entity that acts across international borders. Transnational actors can range from Osama bin Laden to the Red Cross.

Treaty of Rome   The 1957 treaty that laid the groundwork for European integration, which led first to the creation of a European Common Market and eventually to the European Union and the common euro currency.

Treaty of Utrecht   The 1713 treaty that ended the Wars of Spanish Succession and established the legitimacy of both British and French holdings in North America.

Treaty of Westphalia   The 1648 peace treaty that formally concluded the Thirty Years' War and established state sovereignty as the highest principle in the international system.

Unipolar   The structure of an international system in which one state exercises preponderant power. Some analysts refer to the current military power structure as a unipolar system dominated by the United States.

Vulnerability   The relative cost of changing the structure of a system of interdependence. Can also be thought of as the cost of escaping or changing the rules of the game.

World Bank   An institution set up after World War II to provide loans, technical assistance, and policy advice to developing countries. See *Bretton Woods*.

WTO (World Trade Organization)   An international organization created in 1994 to regulate trade and tariffs among its member states. See *GATT*.

Credits

Photo Credits

Page 1: Alinari/Art Resource, NY. Page 14: With permission of the Royal Ontario Museum © ROM. Page 33: Bettman/CORBIS. Page 44: Reuters/CORBIS. Page 59: Imperial War Museum. Page 71: Imperial War Museum. Page 78: Hulton Archive/Getty Images. Page 87: Bettmann/CORBIS. Page 97: Bettmann/CORBIS. Page 107: Bettmann/CORBIS. Page 115: Bettmann/CORBIS. Page 136: Bettmann/CORBIS. Page 147: Bettmann/CORBIS. Page 157: Kanalstein/UN/DPI. Page 194: Reuters/CORBIS. Page 204: Topham/The Image Works. Page 233: Frank Whitney/Getty Images. Page 255: Ed Eckstein/CORBIS. Page 261: Howard Davie/CORBIS. Page 276: David Leeson/Dallas Morning News.

Box Credits

Page 5, "1910: The Unseen Vampire of War": Excerpted from "From Our December 13 Pages, 75 Years Ago," *International Herald Tribune*, December 13, 1985. Copyright 1985 *International Herald Tribune* and The New York Times Syndicate. Reprinted by permission. Page 132: Excerpted from George Kennan, "The Sources of Soviet Conduct," Foreign Affairs, 25: 4 (July 1947), p. 581. Reprinted by permission of Foreign Affairs, July 1947. Copyright 1947 by the Council on Foreign Relations, Inc. Page 169, "American Intervention in Vietnam": Excerpted from Irving Hower and Michael Walzer, "Were We Wrong About Vietnam?" *The New Republic*, August 18, 1979, p. 18. Reprinted by permission of *The New Republic*. Copyright 1979, The New Republic Inc. Page 211, "Ecological and Economic Interdependence": Excerpted from "North-South Divide is Marring Environmental Talks," The New York Times, March 17, 1992, p. 8. Copyright 1992 by the New York Times Company. Reprinted by permission. Page 214, "Sensitivity Interdependence": Excerpted from "German Shift Felt in Japan," The New York Times, February 26, 1990, p. D1. Copyright 1990 by The New York Times Company. Reprinted by permission.

Map Credits

Page 74: Reprinted with permission from Brian Catchpole, *A Map History of the Modern World* (Oxford Heinemann Publishers Ltd., 1982), p. 13. Page 80: Reprinted with permission from Brian Catchpole, *A Map History of the Modern World* (Oxford Heinemann Publishers Ltd., 1982), p. 15. Page 92: Reprinted with permission from Brian Catchpole, *A Map History of the Modern World* (Oxford Heinemann Publishers Ltd., 1982) p. 27. Page 101: Reprinted with permission from Brian Catchpole, *A Map History of the Modern World* (Oxford Heinemann Publishers Ltd., 1982), p. 69. Page 109: Reprinted with permission from Brian Catchpole, *A Map History of the Modern World* (Oxford Heinemann Publishers Ltd., 1982) p. 73. Page 124: Reprinted with permission from Brian Catchpole, *A Map History of the Modern World* (Oxford Heinemann Publishers Ltd., 1982) p. 83. Page 127: Reprinted with permission from Brian Catchpole, *A Map History of the Modern World* (Oxford Heinemann Publishers Ltd., 1982) p. 123. Page 180: Reprinted with permission from Brian Catchpole, *A Map History of the Modern World* (Oxford Heinemann Publishers Ltd., 1982) p. 197.

Index

Abbas, Mahmoud, 197
Abdullah (Jordan), 190
Accountability, in democracies, 280–281
Acheson, Dean, 107, 126, 174
Ackerloff, George, 253
Actors, 8–9. *See also* States (nations)
  in international political systems, 34
  nonstate, 8–9
  transnational, 241–250
Afghanistan, 163, 195–196
  Soviet invasion of, 26, 27, 134, 148
  Taliban in, 11, 249
Africa, 27, 35
Aggression, justification for, 165–166
Allende, Salvador, 163
Alliances, 69. *See also* specific alliances
  balance of power and, 65
  after Cold War, 272
  nuclear proliferation and, 271
  in Peloponnesian War, 12
  before World War I, 41
Al Qaeda, 189, 207, 239, 248, 272
Alsace-Lorraine, 42, 93
Amnesty International, 9, 244, 246
Anarchic system, 3, 4–8, 9, 15–16, 34, 35, 119
Angell, Norman, 44
Angola, 133, 134, 165, 182
Annan, Kofi, 183
Anti-Comintern Pact, 99
Apartheid, 165, 205, 279
Appeasement, in World War II, 110–111
Arab-Israeli conflicts, 2, 133, 189–192, 226
Arab League, 9
Arab oil embargo, 224, 226, 227–228
Arab world, 180, 187. *See also* Middle East
Arafat, Yasir, 194, 195, 197, 198
Aristotle, 51
Armenians, 9
Asia
  Cold War and, 122, 128
  financial crisis in, 164, 218
Athens. *See also* Prisoner's Dilemma
  in Peloponnesian War, 12–15, 20
Atomic bomb, 96, 123. *See also* Nuclear weapons
Atoms for Peace program, 271
Aum Shinrikyo, 273
Australia, 182
Austria, 39, 99

Austria-Hungary, 75, 79, 93
Authoritarian states, 255–256
Autonomy, intervention and, 164
Axelrod, Robert, 17
Axis Pact, 99

Bacon, Francis, 233
Balance of power. *See also* specific wars
  in Cold War, 116, 129
  after Congress of Vienna, 40
  determinants of, 11
  meanings of, 64–69
  military (1914), 74
  as multipolar systems, 67–69
  as policy, 65
  World War I and, 59–84, 95–96
Balfour Declaration, 189, 190
Balkan region, 72, 75, 80, 168
Bandwagon, 65
Barak, Ehud, 195
Barriers to entry, 250–251
Baruch Plan, 123, 140
Battle of Britain, 96, 101, 102
Beitz, Charles, 26
Belgium, 77, 102
Bentham, Jeremy, 5, 21
Berg, Nicholas, 248
Berlin, 117, 125, 133
Berlin Wall, 44, 134, 136
Bethmann Hollweg, Theobald von, 70
Bhopal, India, explosion, 281
Biafra, 167–168
Bias, in historical interpretation, 19
Bill and Melinda Gates Foundation, 245
bin Laden, Osama, 24, 62, 149, 196, 265, 267, 272
Biological weapons, 149–150
Bipolar structure, 37–38
  as balance of terror, 142–143
  in Cold War, 118, 126, 127, 128
  before World War I, 72
  after World War II, 96–97
Bismarck, Otto von, 33, 35, 40–42, 68–69, 188
Blitzkrieg, 101
Blum, Leon, 103
Boer War, 71
Bollier, David, 240